SAP SCM

APPLICATIONS AND MODELING FOR SUPPLY CHAIN MANAGEMENT (WITH BW PRIMER)

DANIEL C. WOOD

T0368015

JOHN WILEY & SONS, INC.

Copyright © 2007 by John Wiley & Sons, Inc. All rights reserved.

Published by John Wiley & Sons, Inc., Hoboken, New Jersey.
Published simultaneously in Canada.

No part of this publication may be reproduced, stored in a retrieval system, or transmitted in any form or by any means, electronic, mechanical, photocopying, recording, scanning, or otherwise, except as permitted under Section 107 or 108 of the 1976 United States Copyright Act, without either the prior written permission of the Publisher, or authorization through payment of the appropriate per-copy fee to the Copyright Clearance Center, Inc., 222 Rosewood Drive, Danvers, MA 01923, 978-750-8400, fax 978-646-8600, or on the web at www.copyright.com. Requests to the Publisher for permission should be addressed to the Permissions Department, John Wiley & Sons, Inc., 111 River Street, Hoboken, NJ 07030, (201) 748-6011, fax (201) 748-6008.

Limit of Liability/Disclaimer of Warranty: While the publisher and author have used their best efforts in preparing this book, they make no representations or warranties with respect to the accuracy or completeness of the contents of this book and specifically disclaim any implied warranties of merchantability or fitness for a particular purpose. No warranty may be created or extended by sales representatives or written sales materials. The advice and strategies contained herein may not be suitable for your situation. You should consult with a professional where appropriate. Neither the publisher nor author shall be liable for any loss of profit or any other commercial damages, including but not limited to special, incidental, consequential, or other damages.

For general information on our other products and services please contact our Customer Care Department within the U.S. at 877-762-2974, outside the U.S. at 317-572-3993 or fax 317-572-4002.

Wiley also publishes its books in a variety of electronic formats. Some content that appears in print, however, may not be available in electronic format.

For more information about Wiley products, visit our Web site at http://www.wiley.com.

Library of Congress Cataloging-in-Publication Data:

Wood, Daniel C., 1972-
   SAP SCM : applications and modeling for supply chain
management (with BW primer) / Daniel C. Wood.
         p. cm.
   Includes index.
   ISBN: 978-0-471-76991-0 (cloth)
   1. Business logistics–Computer programs. 2. Production
management—Computer programs. 3. APO. I. Title.
   HD38.5.W66 2007
   658.70285′53—dc22
                              2006029337

10 9 8 7 6 5 4 3 2 1

For Gerald

New technologies for supply chain management and flexible manufacturing imply that businesses can perceive imbalances in inventories at a very early state—virtually in real time—and can cut production promptly in response to the developing signs of unintended inventory building.

Alan Greenspan
Former Chairman of the Federal Reserve
Testimony to the U.S. Committee on Banking, Housing and Urban Affairs
February 13, 2001

CONTENTS

PREFACE

Consider boats. Let us imagine that we are a tropical tourist outfit and we have at our disposal a variety of small boats: a canoe, a speed motorboat, a double-sail schooner, and a catamaran. Imagine too that we have a body of boatmen and sailors who are trained and competent to maintain, navigate, sail, and otherwise put our small boats to good use and that they do in fact do just that on a daily basis, employing our small flotilla in some manner of productive economy, but economy that is limited to the scope and capabilities of small vessels, probably extending its reach no further than local seaways. Finally, imagine that we have recently paid for a rather nontrivial upgrade to the fleet, having just purchased several large yachts.

Obvious to everyone will be the fact that the yachts enable us to expand our economy as never before possible when we were limited to the small boat flotilla. The yachts have radar and satellite linkups to avoid bad weather, fuel stores to enable long journeys, and mass to handle tough waters. The yachts are big and can comfortably carry more people—scientists, merchants, diplomats, vacationers—all of whom may add value and opportunity to our oceangoing journeys. The yachts are not an upgrade of quality, such as a sturdier canoe, a speedier speedboat; rather, they are an upgrade of class. Most important, *that* the yachts constitute an upgrade in class, such that both a retraining of our entire staff and an expansion in the scope of our operations is necessary to fully exploit them, is an inescapable reality made obvious by the simple physical presence of the yachts themselves.

In the manner of their physical presence, we must say that boats have something over software. I studied decision and information systems at the university level for some five years in the early 1990s and had the fortune of working as a research assistant with one of my professors, which further exposed me to the state-of-the-art research of the day. At that time academic research in advanced decision methodologies was approaching a nexus with advancements in computer technology that promised to make a new class of products available to organizations and commercial interests with capabilities that had previously been limited to the ivy walls of research journals and the academy. Something was in the oven, but it was still baking.

So, in 1997, when SAP AG released Advanced Planner and Optimizer (APO), I understood that this was something different. In some ways, at the time, SAP had been perceived as behind the curve in decision support systems for supply chain planning. Other companies had already produced highly effective products for forecast and demand management, and SAP was coming from behind. Planned or not, there was something strategic to SAP's timing. Other companies had been, and to this day largely continue to be, content to offer single-problem solutions: a tool for demand management or a tool for shop-floor control. SAP APO was not just one more toolset alternative for forecast and demand. Like all of SAP's products, APO was integrated: integrated with supply planning, procurement and production planning and execution, reporting and advanced data analytics, and, as a decision support system itself, integrated with SAP's transactional data management product, R/3, in such a way that it could be used to largely control R/3 transparently without requiring that the end-user move back and forth between tools.

As it was an integrated, complete planning product, I understood that APO constituted what we were anticipating in the early 1990s: a software product that leveraged off of faster, smarter microchips and operating systems with large memory wells to combine all the best-known methods of the various supply chain planning disciplines into a potent package for total supply chain planning. In APO was found tools for conducting univariate analysis and multiple linear regression as well as lifecycle planning for demand forecast and management; heuristics, priorities, and linear programming for supply network planning; specialized heuristics for the combined needs of procurement execution and production planning; and specialized optimization algorithms for shop floor control. All of this was in one tool.

If previous applications that had been applied for supply chain planning were littoral boats, APO was a veritable blue-water, oceangoing ship. To the trained eye, APO represented a whole new class of supply chain planning software. I was impressed. To my mind, on seeing APO, I understood that this was the "it" that had been in the oven. The problem was that having primed for APO in college, I was ready to be impressed—I was prepared to recognize APO for what APO is: a whole advance in *class* not unlike the upgrade from speedboat to yacht. What I could not be prepared for was that everyone else was not so well primed. What was evident to me was not apparent to everyone else in a position to adopt or effect the adoption of APO.

That mattered. Upgrades of class are not trivial. We would not assign our speedboat crew to a yacht without substantial up-training. Furthermore, we would not limit our new yacht to the shipyards and littorals of a speedboat; we would let it get out and sail! Alas, APO is software, and software is not like a boat or ship. The yacht by its mere physical presence makes both its superiority and superior demands known to all who gaze upon it even if they have no specialized knowledge of ships and boats. Though one software application may display cool graphics and do some quick math, while another comprehends entire global supply chain networks using the same mathematical features previously limited to weather simulators running on supercomputers, both applications present on the same compact diskettes and both applications are reduced to the same 12-by-16-inch monitor when employed by the end-user. How are end-users, executives, and in many cases even developers to know that something more than evolution has occurred?

The failure of organizations to culturally adapt to the change in class represented by APO has at times led to occasion for disappointment. In the time since APO's release, I have watched or heard of organizations whose labors to adopt APO proved frustrated or for naught. The reasons for failures are manifold. Sometimes we have end-users who are insufficiently trained because the difference between APO and their previous legacy software tools was not appreciated by executives and project planners who sought to keep training costs low by limiting training exposure to project teams rather than project customers. In other cases, developers and project managers have advanced knowledge of technical features of APO but insufficient knowledge of the underlying supply chain disciplines or the essential points of integration of those disciplines to successfully bridge the gap between technology and application. We find managers, executives, and whole organizations whose perceptions of the software overcame the facts about the software and who in turn found their way into strategic decisions that torpedoed projects. Such false perceptions hamper the software with expectations it was never meant to rise to (i.e., even yachts cannot fly and even APO with its global model of the supply network cannot think). Those perceptions may also lead to the misapplication of modules either for expeditious reasons (i.e., it is thought to be cheaper to apply one module to two problems rather than two modules to problems appropriate to their competence) or out of literal ignorance.

In the former case, where some exaggerate the ability of APO to plan a network independently of qualitative, human management of planning, we find that two kinds of resistance emerge. The first is from employees who feel threatened and are (rightfully) unwilling to cede final judgment of supply planning over to a computationally smart but qualitatively stupid computer; and the second is from reality: APO, properly applied, enhances the human judgment of buyers, planners, and controllers in the same way a weather simulator enhances the judgment of meteorologists. APO is *not* an artificial intelligence (AI) product that replaces people.

In the latter case we have seen where developers trained in one module such as Demand Planning (DP) or Supply Network Planning (SNP) have made biased recommendations, assuming, for example, that the Production Planning/Detailed Scheduling (PP/DS) module is strictly a shop-floor control product without useful application for subcontractor planning when, in fact, only the DS part of PP/DS is for shop-floor control and the rest is expected, by the product's designers, to take over from SNP wherever the procurement execution horizon starts. Such ill-advised decisions result in the attempt to apply relatively strategic modules like DP and SNP to tactical problems that they were not designed to manage but for which PP/DS is explicitly intended.

The failures of some notwithstanding, APO is still an oceangoing ship and the competition, whether from outside providers or internal, legacy products, remains limited to the lagoon. APO, especially today in 2006, with even more powerful features of the Supply Chain Management (SCM) package in which it comes, packs a powerful punch. I believe that APO can change the economy. Aggregate, macroeconomic efficiency gains in demand and supply planning that result in less of the wrong inventory, more of the right inventory as well as the right product at the right place at the right time, multiplied by thousands of organizations and millions of products, may materially affect the gross national and international economy, increasing efficiency and productivity. The nice thing is that we do not need to reinvent the wheel: Academic researchers have been studying and proving the methods packaged in APO for years, and SAP has already coded the product for us. The challenge is in adoption and the obstacles to adoption appear to be both psychological and practical. Psychologically, we need to get a handle on what we are working with. Practically, we need an easier way to master the learning curve associated with this powerful new tool. SAP SCM succeeds for organizations when teams under-stand the strategies necessary to make it work. What is necessary is a common map that meets the needs of all the stakeholders who come to SCM: developers, project managers, executives, and end-users alike. I hope that this book rises to become that map.

Daniel C. Wood

January 2007

ACKNOWLEDGMENTS

In considering the variety of people who've contributed directly or indirectly to the development of the book, its seems to me that most fall into any of three categories: those who introduced me to the world of SAP and SAP SCM, those who taught me SAP products including SAP SCM, and those who in one way or another helped directly in bringing about this book. Considering the first, I should express thanks to Mark Zinsli, who, back in 1996, long before it ever was really relevant to my job role, allowed me to take courses in SAP R/3 architecture, data models, and ABAP programming. I must further thank Janet Kerby, who deserves credit for bringing me officially into the world of SAP, "under false pretenses," as she artfully puts it. Thanks, too, to Bob St. Louis for the early seeding of this book by exposing me to the state-of-the-art research at a time when APO was probably still just a glimmer in SAP's eye.

As regards those who have at one time or another taught me something of the uses of SAP products, particularly planning products, here I know for sure that I'll go amiss as there are simply too many to remember, let alone mention. Thanks to Peter Kaiser, my very first SAP instructor. Thanks to David Wiley and Gautam Bhattacharya, my very first APO instructors. Thanks also to Bharad Wuppalapati and Steve Blair, who, though never formal instructors, brought me to pace on master production scheduling and materials requirements planning. Hilmer Hintz deserves mention as hands down the best SNP and PP/DS instructor one could ask for, which, as someone who took each class two or three times, I feel well qualified to assess. And among that wide variety of people who never taught a course (at least for me) but who at one time or another engaged with me on one feature or another of SCM that increased my knowledge with bits and pieces that may have found their way into this book, thanks go to Justin Weyand, Chak Tongsak, Jennifer Newman, Rammohan Basineni, Michael Hawkins, Brian Lyles, Tajinder Singh, Chandrasekhar Reddy, Sunil Chebiyam, RJ Ramirez, Bryce Duck, Anupama Velayudhan, and my intro-to-SCM co-instructor, Kamlesh Porwal.

Finally, there are several who provided direct support to critical tasks, decisions, and approvals that led to the production of this book. Thanks first to Steven Miller for the early managerial endorsement, and later to Carl Muppaneni, who inherited me. Exact etymological history is unknown but somewhere between Steven Miller and Steve Blair there lies credit for perhaps one of the most critical pieces of advice found in this text: the "98% solution" in Chapter 4. Thanks many times over to my editor, Sheck Cho, who believed in the project and who exercised mythical patience while obstacles of familial crises followed by byzantine organizational approval processes by no less than three companies and by my infrequent but often-enough writer's block got in the way of expeditious authorial output. Thanks to Greg Valdez, without whose managerial imprimatur this project would never have gone forward; thanks to Robb Gordon, without whose legal shuttling this project would never have gotten off the ground; thanks to Joel Levinson, without whose celestially timed intervention this project would have surely died an ignoble bureaucratic death; and thanks to Andrew Benton of SAP AG, without whose lawyerly approval from SAP this project would be but for naught. Thanks, of course, to Patara Yongvanich of SAP AG for connecting me with the critical and indispensable Ricardo Poli, also of latter company; and last but absolutely not least, thank you several times over to Ricardo (and all your agents and supporters at SAP Labs in Palo Alto) for being an excellent host while I surfed SAP systems for screenshots.

TABLE OF ABBREVIATIONS

APICS   Formerly the American Production and Inventory Control Society, now the Association for Operations Management

APICS	Formerly the American Production and Inventory Control Society, now the Association for Operations Management
APO	Advanced Planner and Optimizer (version 3.1)/Advanced Planning and Optimization (version 4.0+)
ASN	Automated Shipping Notice
ATP	Available to Promise
B2B	Business-to-Business
B2C	Business-to-Customer
BAPI	Business Application Programming Interface
BEx	Business Explorer
BI	Business Intelligence (see BW; historically a general term for advanced analytic reporting technologies—now applied more specifically by SAP AG)
BKM	Best Known Method
BOM	Bill of Materials
BW	Business Information Warehouse (NOTE: At the time of this text's publication, SAP AG was in the process of re-naming BW to BI. For some time, therefore, readers may expect to see both the terms BW and BI used interchangeably for the same product)
CIF	Core Interface
CRM	Customer Relationship Management
CTM	Capable to Match
DCM	Delivery Control Monitor
DEPREQ	Dependent Requirements
DP	Demand Planning
DSS	Decision Support System
EAN	European Article Number
ECC	Enterprise Common Core
ECM	Engineering Change Management
EM	Event Management
EPR	External Procurement Relationships
ERP	Enterprise Resource Planning
FC Req	Forecast Requirements
GATP	Global Available to Promise
GR/GI	Goods Receipt/Goods Issue
ICH	Inventory Collaboration Hub
IM	Inventory Management
IMG	Implementation Guide

INDREQ	Independent Requirements
IT	Information Technology
MDM	Master Data Management
MLR	Multiple Linear Regression
MM	Materials Management
MPS	Master Production Schedule
MRP	Materials Requirements Planning
nMPS	Network Master Production Schedule
OLAP	Online Analytical Processing
OLTP	Online Transaction Processing
PDS	Production Data Structure
PIR	Planned Independent Requirements
PLDORD	Planned Order (R/3)
PlOrd	Planned Order (APO)
PP	Production Planning
PP/DS	Production Planning/Detailed Scheduling
PPM	Production Process Model
PURREQ	Purchase Requisition
R/3	SAP's flagship enterprise resource planning system
RFID	Radio Frequency Identification
RN	RosettaNet
ROI	Return on Investment
RTO	Run Time Object
SA	Scheduling Agreement
SCC	Supply Chain Cockpit
SCE	Supply Chain Engineer
SCM	Supply Chain Management
SEM	Strategic Enterprise Management
SMI	Supplier Managed Inventory
SNP	Supply Network Planning
SOP	Sales and Operations Planning
SQL	Structured Query Language
SRL	Stock Requirements List
SRM	Supplier Relationship Management
TCM	Traditional Chinese Medicine
TLB	Transport Load Builder
TP/VS	Transportation Planning/Vehicle Scheduling
UI	User Interface
UOM	Unit of Measure
UPC	Universal Product Code
VC	Variant Configuration
VMI	Vendor Managed Inventory
XML	Extensible Markup Language
ZBB	Zero-based Budget

1

CULTURAL BACKGROUND: THE BUSINESS AND TECHNICAL CONTEXT FOR SCM

1

How to Use This Book: APO as a Mind Map

As with most SAP applications, the best path through this text is not a straight one. SAP applications in general and SAP APO in particular are simply too multidimensional to be suited to a simple, linear decomposition. Just the same, we have undertaken great pains to make SAP SCM as navigable as humanly possible. SAP APO seeks to replace some work that until recently has been strictly limited to the aegis of the human intellect—yet it ultimately does not replace people as much as it elevates their purpose by providing better computation and leveraging more strongly on the human specialties of reason, interaction, and qualitative judgment. Where SAP APO expands the scope of the system in supply planning is when it computationally takes over as much as possible of what used to be exclusively a human analytical domain; in this respect APO may be said to "map a supply planner's mind," yet there is no simple way to lay out a map to the human mind. The mind, like APO, is nonlinear. In finding the best way through SAP APO we should think of the supply chain models created in it as models of all the objects, relationships, and dynamics that a human master scheduler, buyer, or production planner intellectually masters in order to employ his or her craft.

Our planner, as such, is concerned with certain components of the supply chain: locations of plants, customers, vendors; products, their components, the transportation lanes between them and methods of transport; the means of production. She is likewise concerned with different end-goals in analyzing the information about these supply chains: determining the best, most current picture of demand without respect to supply (demand planning), organizing the entire supply chain to work collaboratively—even collaborating outside organizational walls with suppliers and customers—to optimally meet known demand (supply network planning), and deriving the best schedule to fully utilize the resources of a specific plant (production planning/detailed scheduling).

To grapple with the complex and multidimensional organization of a mind that thinks about the supply chain, analyzes and master plans it, a straight line simply will not do. Instead we will employ the metaphor of a cookbook and divide our treatment into three major functional parts:

1. A *contextual introduction,* such as introduction to the cultural background that gave rise to a particular cooking genre such as Italian or Thai—in this case an introduction of the overall SAP APO architecture and its supply chain context, as well as "tips and tricks" for improving the critical strategic judgments and

decisions of project managers, executives, and project sponsors that have so much impact on APO and SCM projects' success or failure.

2. Ingredient *stocks and bases that form the core of more sophisticated entree dishes*, such as beef or vegetable stock, dressings, batters, and icings—but here with SCM our basis shall be supply chain *master data and transactional data elements* that form the basis of any manner of supply chain model (i.e., locations, products, orders, etc.).

3. *Actual complete entrée recipes,* which simply make reference to bases in the second section without redundantly reprinting them, as they may occur many times over in many different recipes—in our case recipes to deliver with SCM techniques for employing planning modules to work with master data, model supply chains, and forecast or produce operational schedules.

Unlike cooking, however, SAP's SCM product is expansive, crossing boundaries into whole additional disciplines; so in addition to these three sections we must add a fourth to address the major disciplines with a direct impact on supply chain planning:

4. *The SAP BW data basis and analytical adjunct to APO and the SCM ICH application,* the latter of which enables sophisticated planning collaboration with customers and suppliers.

As with a cookbook, the introduction sets the stage for the subject of the text, it explains backgrounds and starting requirements (i.e., kitchen appliances, tools, materials), and sets expectations. From there many cookbooks include a section for making common stock materials that are found as ingredients to recipes for entrees or side dishes, but which are not usually served alone, for example, vegetable stock, gravies, dough, batters, and dressings. The recipes for these stock food components are used repeatedly as parts of other recipes and there is no point in repeating them each time they are used, so they are stated independently in their own section and then referred to whenever they come up later on. The last section of the cookbook may then contain recipes to make the actual entrees, sides, deserts, and dishes that are the business of dinner, which each may or may not refer back to stock recipes as a prerequisite.

Our text closely follows this model. We begin with a basic background in supply chain management that is essential to understanding the use, applications, and power of SAP SCM. Without a solid background in the basics of supply chain management, users run the risk of repeating many of the mistakes made with legacy tools when they deploy the product, using it the same way they used much more primitive tools. One would not purchase a modern rice cooker if one meant only to steam up Uncle Ben's from time to time. One buys the modern rice cooker because there are 6,000 years of multicultural history of rice and thousands of ways to prepare it. Don't get stuck with ordinary, fluffy white rice—learn the basics of supply chain management so that you can deploy the full power of APO!

Second, there are two kinds of data used in APO, as in almost any business-oriented computer system: *master data* and *transactional data*. Master data is the architectural or skeletal data that forms the infrastructure of the system: things like product and location setup. Transaction data is data that is put to use describing actual events, like 100 units of plastic cups that a factory means to build on Tuesday. So much master data in APO is used in every module that there is no use in repeating the steps for setup of locations and products in *both* the SNP and PP/DS modules, for example. The master data section will list instructions for setting up each element of master data.

Like a cookbook, Part Three contains "recipes" for using the actual planning modules of APO to plan and manage the various aspects of the supply chain: demand planning, supply network planning, production planning and detailed scheduling, global available to promise, and transportation planning and vehicle scheduling. Wherever master data elements are called on as prerequisites by these modules, their recipe will be referenced so that readers can go to the appropriate section in Part Two for details of how to set them up.

Finally, in order to empower users, developers, and their respective organizations to employ the full power of APO, we include an additional section that explores two other, major integrated applications found within the SAP SCM platform in versions 4.1 and 5.0: SAP BW and SAP SCM ICH. The Business Information Warehouse (BW) forms both the data basis of SCM, including and especially APO, as well as provides mature, first-class reporting and analytics that are actually integrated with and manifested in Microsoft Excel. SAP SCM ICH, the Inventory Collaboration Hub, comes as a separate application in SAP SCM with APO, but empowers users of SAP R/3 to collaborate directly with external suppliers and customers—either outsourcing materials replenishment to suppliers or including them in the planning process or both. Together, BW and ICH are like height and depth to APO's length: exponentially increasing its power to provide value-return to organizations that adopt it.

ONE BOOK, MANY CURRICULUMS: CUSTOM RECOMMENDATIONS FOR READING ORDER

As indicated earlier, this book will not make for a good straight-line read. Because of its cookbook-like organization, it will not make sense for most users to read this text from cover to cover as most users will not need or interact with all the modules of APO or all the applications of SCM; and even if they did, it still would not make sense to read Part Two in its entirety before reading Parts Three or Four, for example. Readers will need the SCM foundations established in the first section. We always recommend starting there and reading Part One in its entirety. Failure to read this first part may result in an unintentional underutilization of the full power of APO simply by way of ignorance of all the different business and information domain spaces it covers and its depth of integration.

From there, however, *end*-users should skip to Part Three and focus only on the module or modules they expect to use in the course of their work, referring back to chapters in Part Two whenever the planning module "recipe" of their interest instructs them to do so. Even readers who mean to absorb the entire scope of APO's planning modules may wish to skip to Part Three, as this will lead to the most orderly and nonrepetitive coverage of Part Two. For example, if your organization has deployed DP and PP/DS, skip Part Two and read only the DP and PP/DS sections of Part Three. Wherever necessary, those sections will instruct you to go back and read master data sections in Part Two and you will have the option to read only those sections specified, and when you do so it will be in the mental context of how they will be used for the tool you are interested in.

Depending on whether one comes to APO and this text as a first-time learner or seasoned system analyst or consultant, one may go about exploring and reading this book differently. In contrast to end-users, analysts, consultants, and engineers will usually do best to work through the book from cover to cover in a nearly strict 1, 2, 3, 4 order. Executives interested in APO but involved in direct delivery may be interested only in Part One and overviews of modules in Parts Three or Four. Project managers will have a similar scope as executives but should also familiarize themselves to some degree with the use of master data and the CIF in Part Two. Seasoned developers directly involved in construction and deployment may start with Part One, skip to Part Three, and only refer to Part Two in reference. Furthermore, tool experts specializing in DP and/or BW should cover all of Part One but may wish to limit further reading to Chapter 6, on analytical master data, and Chapters 8 or 11, DP and BW. Supply chain planning specialists, however, may start with the same foundation in Part One but cover supply chain master data in Chapter 5 and SNP and PP/DS in Chapters 9 and 10. (See Exhibit 1.1.)

INCLUDED AND EXCLUDED: SCOPE OF THIS TEXT

APO and the wider SAP SCM suite of tools including BW and the Inventory Collaboration Hub that are now included in the SCM package form a truly deep and vast body of software applications—there are more than 4,300 transactions in SCM! It is simply impossible within one volume to do instructional justice to this mighty corpus of tools and it is not our intent to attempt so. In principle, this book is scoped to focus on supply chain planning and its direct support in data management, analytics, and external collaboration (Exhibit 1.2). Specifically we include detailed, modular, and step-by-step "how-to" instructions on the supply-chain *planning* modules of APO, that is, DP, SNP, and PP/DS. Even covering only these three parts of APO it will still not be possible to consider every setting and their effects, but we will seek to comprehensively describe the relevant planning processes of each tool and the range of options available to users. Additionally, since DP is built on the same master-data basis as is BW, a natural bonus of this text will be a miniprimer in the setup and use of the BW tool, which will be by no means comprehensive by itself but which should leave the reader with an appreciation for the business value of the tool, some skills to set it up and conduct minimal reporting, and a sound foundation for further study. Since industry interest has shifted great energies to exploiting return-on-investment opportunities available through increased supply-line efficiency via external collaboration and vendor-managed inventory, and as SAP has greatly expanded the power of SCM ICH in the 5.0 revision, we will also visit this tool and explore its business use, integration with SCM and R/3, and basic configuration.

Much energy has been spent and oil burned hailing the vitality of solvers and optimization in the improvement of supply chain planning and execution, and we will certainly pay our dues here to those important changes in the technical landscape of commerce. Yet, though not often hailed, of minimally equal value to the improvement of supply chain management efficiency, effectiveness, and bottom-line ROI-value in commerce is the quality of two signals that traverse the supply chain: the customer-originated demand

Role-based Curriculum/Common Roles	Recommended Reading Order
Executive/Project Manager	Part I (Chs. 1–4, architecture, strategy)
• Executives	Section: Use of Profiles in APO
• Project Managers	Chapter 11: BW and strategies
	Optional—Chapter 12: ICH
Demand Planning	Part I (Chs. 1–4, architecture, strategy)
• Demand or forecast analyst	Chapter 5: Supply chain master data
• Supply/demand analyst	Chapter 6: Analytical master data
	Chapter 8: (UI section)
	Chapter 9: Demand Planning
	Chapter 11: BW and strategies
Supply Network Planning and External Collaboration	**Novice:**
• Sales/operational planner	Part I (Chs. 1–4, architecture, strategy)
• Master scheduler	Chapter 5: Supply chain master data
• Business analyst	Chapter 8: (UI section)
• Buyer (medium-range)	Chapter 9: Supply Network Planning
	Advanced:▼
	Chapter 7: Core interface
	Chapter 6: Analytical master data
	Chapter 11: BW and strategies
	Chapter 12: ICH and other collaboration
Production Planning/Detailed Scheduling	**Novice:**
• Production planner	Part I (Chs. 1–4, architecture, strategy)
• Production scheduler	Chapter 5: Supply chain master data
• Ground controller	Chapter 8 (whole chapter): Production Planning/
• Buyer (tactical/short-range)	Detailed Scheduling
• Site scheduler (i.e.; factory, warehouse, distribution center, port)	**Advanced:**
	Chapter 7: Core interface
	Chapter 6: Analytical master data
	Chapter 11: BW and strategies
Developer	**General:**
• Business analyst/application consultant	Part I → Part II → Part III
• System analyst	
• Software/SC engineers	
• Other developers	

EXHIBIT 1.1 CURRICULUMS BY BUSINESS ROLE AND EXPERIENCE

▼Advanced users are also counseled to rely on cookbooks wherever possible, selectively dipping into textual explorations only when necessary, thereby avoiding the necessity of digesting all the verbal detail that is required to bring novices up to pace with the tool.

Business Function	SCM Application	Module	In Scope
Supply Chain Planning	APO	Demand Planning	☑
		Supply Network Planning	☑
Supply Chain Planning and Execution		Production Planning/Detailed Scheduling	☑
Supply Chain Planning for Logistics Execution		Transportation Planning/Vehicle Scheduling	☒
Planning Specialization		Global Available to Promise	☒
Supply Chain Execution		Deployment	☒
		Transport Load Builder	☒
Real-time Logistics Tracking	EM	n/a	☒
Supply Chain Planning and Collaboration	ICH n/a	n/a	☑
Supply Chain Data Management and Analytics/Reporting	BW data mart	n/a	☑

EXHIBIT 1.2   SCM PLANNING APPLICATION/MODULE SCOPE

signal and the global inventory signal. The better visibility that suppliers have of changing customer demand data and the better visibility that buyers, planners, and automated planning runs have at all stages of planning—the more time-dollar-cost efficiency will be realized. Collaboration tools such as those provided in SCM and explored in Chapter 12 go to great lengths to make levels of supply chain power available off-the-shelf to small- and medium-sized organizations that were until recently the exclusive domain of such players as UPS and Wal-Mart.

While some discussion of the transactional nature of the CIF interface is essential because almost all installations of SAP APO will acquire master data from SAP R/3 using the CIF, not covered here will be any of the technical basis-level installation, configuration, or management of internal components for liveCache or the CIF, nor for that matter installation of the APO tool itself. Neither will we look at system/server network configuration or optimization.[1] Do not look to this text, for example, for instruction on how to install APO and optimize a server or network platform for its use.

Also not covered are the ancillary SCM tools that have been added to the SCM 4.1 and 5.0 releases: Forecast and Replenishment or Event Management; though in the latter case of Event Management (EM), with a mind to the powerful supply chain advantage of inventory visibility across the supply chain, we nonetheless strongly recommend further investigation outside this text by the reader and any interested organization. The advanced planning techniques of APO, the inventory and demand signal quality advantage of ICH, and the power of the EM tool through its employment of radio frequency identification (RFID) in logistics tracking will together make for a potent blend of twenty-first-century supply chain excellence for SCM-adopting organizations, which have every reason to expect realization of concrete and far-reaching competitive advantages in supply chain execution that would be altogether unaffordable if technology adoption was limited to in-house technical development. Regretfully, space and experience simply do not allow for coverage of EM here.

We will not cover parallel functions of APO in the R/3 tool, such as opening customer orders, management of independent requirements, materials requirements planning (MRP), or inventory any more than they are absolutely essential to understanding their role in APO itself. Other exclusions will be the Global Available to Promise module of APO (GATP), the Transportation Planning and Vehicle Scheduling module (TP/VS), and the Deployment and Transport Load Builder (TLB) submodules. Global Available to Promise, though a powerful planning specialization that can enhance SNP and PP/DS, is nonetheless such a specialization as to be a departure from our key emphasis on planning. The structure of SCM and APO is continuous, stretching from the highest aggregate of planning in the forecasting of the DP module to the lowest level of production order management in the DS submodule, and therefore it does not allow us to dogmatically exclude supply chain execution and control from scope. Sitting at the end of the planning line, the PP/DS module ultimately converts planning to management of day-to-day physical action, and to address PP/DS as we must because of its role in planning, we necessarily address supply chain execution. That said, our intent here is to explore planning, covering other areas only where necessary, so TP/VS, Deployment, and the TLB, each of which are primarily related to supply chain execution, fall outside our scope.

One last note on what is not covered: the Mass Maintenance transaction (MASSD). Found under APO's Master Data node in General Master Data Functions, we feel it necessary to exclude this transaction with special treatment. We usually exclude whole areas without picking on individual transactions, and with greater than 4,300 transactions in SCM to explore we have much reason to do so, but MASSD requires a little explaining for a text that targets the end-user as much as the developer: Why would we exclude a transaction whose existence is explicitly intended to ease the end-users' experience of the tool?

We address this with a few short points: First, mass maintenance is indeed a process that *may* be applied during productive use of the tool and is of limited utility during development and, as the case happens to be, this text is written by a developer. As such, we come to the second point, which is that for data on experiences with this transaction we must rely on the authority of anecdotes from those in the trenches who sometimes are called upon to use it. Anecdotes, unfortunately, are unreliable teachers and should be treated with instructive authority usually only when good research and direct experience supports their suggested conclusions. While we have no research or experience to corroborate the hearsay that sometimes besmirches MASSD, there is a certain air of credibility to the reports about it, and as the consequences are so severe, we choose to err on the side of conservatism and note them here.

This brings us to the third point: the reports. We have heard from many quarters not so much that MASSD is buggy (and we do not claim here that it has any bugs) as that it is *dangerous*. MASSD (Mass Maintenance as the name implies) is a transaction that is applied to make mass changes across whole swaths of master data without being troubled with the necessity of individually investigating each change-case. Of course, it may be a master data manager's *job* to investigate each use case when making mass changes, but we nonetheless face the inescapable fact that angelic beings are in very short supply on the labor market and master data managers are too often of the run-of-the-mill human type. It is nice to have a feature like MASSD when all one wants to do is change a setting from "P" to "S" on 500 products. Nonetheless, it seems to be too easy for some users to include products (or other objects) on their changes lists that they did not notice or intend. Alternatively, it also sometimes occurs that users will make a small, unintended change—or even a small change that was intended but not carefully thought out—but to 500 or 1,000 cases. In a production environment these changes may equate to money, usually money lost and sometimes lots of it—before changes are noticed and corrections made.

So, anecdotes: yes; direct experience or research: no; but strangely credible to the ears of those dirtied by years in the trenches of IT: You better believe it. In fact it is possible to carefully design master data interfaces and business processes to minimize if not eliminate the need for regular mass maintenance, and while we would caution against the oversensitivity of some securities professionals who would "solve" problems such as this via the oft-abused power to forbid, we must nonetheless urge developers to think carefully through data maintenance processes in such a way as to treat use of mass maintenance as an exception process rather than a regular event. As to its use: Like so many of the 4,000 transactions that we cannot cover in one text, nimble SCM/APO users such as the type we wish to create with the following instruction will find it relatively easy to master without explicit step-by-step coverage; and moreover, users should probably not even be in the transaction until they have risen to that appropriate credit of "nimble."

Enough, then, for what we will not cover; let us consider what is included. Generally speaking this text is both inclusive of and limited to whatever facts, techniques, or methods are necessary for a business user to employ SAP APO usefully to conduct supply chain management *planning* on an already-deployed, already-optimized (technically) software platform while expansively applying APO's unique integrative power to add ROI-improving dimensions of data visibility, business intelligence, and data communications that are provided through SCM integration with the R/3 (ECC), BW, and ICH products.

NOTE

1. That is, *system* optimization, which will not be considered. We will, of course, consider linear optimization as APO employs it in the use of developing schedules and plans, as that is one of the central objects of this text.

2

SCM ARCHITECTURE

In its earliest versions, APO was sold as an independent software application built on a data basis of SAP's BW software platform (Business Information Warehouse) and integrated with SAP R/3 via a native Core Interface (CIF). Starting with version 4.0, current versions of APO are now distributed as one application within a much larger software platform of enterprise tools falling under the common label of Supply Chain Management (SCM). At the time of this text's writing, SCM 4.1 is in general distribution and SCM 5.0 is in ramp with the expectation that SCM 5.0 will be in general distribution by the time of publication.

Besides APO, SCM 4.1 and 5.0 contain these other considerable enterprise business applications: Forecast and Replenishment, Inventory Collaboration Hub (ICH), and Event Management (EM). Furthermore, SCM remains built on the BW data basis that APO started with and retains its connection to R/3 via the CIF interface (Exhibit 2.1). R/3 itself, as part of a wider re-platforming project by SAP, is now distributed as the Enterprise Common Core (ECC). We'll discuss R/3, its re-platforming, its relationship to APO, and the role of the CIF in integrating the two applications shortly. There is some word, too, that in future enhancements of SCM, SAP will do away with the CIF in favor of XML, but presently, even in 5.0, the CIF remains fundamental to APO's data integration design and we will treat it here accordingly. Note, though, that where the CIF remains the fundamental native interface between SCM APO and R/3, it has largely been replaced already by XML for SCM ICH. This will be examined more closely later when we examine ICH in detail.

APO's high level of integration with R/3 and its data basis in BW make it necessary to address both in some degree of depth for any serious treatment of the APO product. Covering the entirety of functionality available in SCM will be impossible as the software's features and capabilities simply cover too much ground to adequately address in one volume. Due to size constraints, we will focus our attention on the supply chain planning, scheduling, and analysis features of APO, its integration with BW and R/3, and the ICH product and its functions in planning.

ENTERPRISE LANDSCAPE FOR PLANNING IN SCM

An astute reader may have guessed from our earlier explanation of what is and is not in scope for this text that the SAP SCM product has its fingers in everything. Despite its modular, discretely acronymed presentation, SCM is a fundamentally *continuous* product

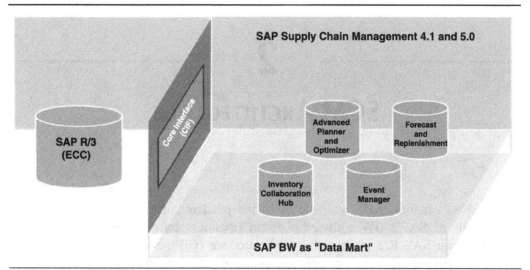

EXHIBIT 2.1   APO ON THE SAP SCM PLATFORM

APO is one of four applications distributed in the SAP SCM platform starting with SCM 4.1. All of these applications reside on top of a data basis created by SAP BW. As such, SAP BW is available as a tool for SCM users, though in more of a "data mart" form, making its data storage and analytics available to APO and APO users. To employ BW's full data *warehousing* capabilities it is necessary to purchase BW as a separate system instance. BW is not the data basis for R/3, so SAP provides a separate native interface between APO and R/3: the CIF. Enabled by the CIF R/3, APO and BW may be used in combination integrating all or most enterprise data to conduct sophisticated analytics.

with one capability integrating and disintegrating into another, rather than distinctly ending at explicit boundaries. The continuous nature of the product and its extreme depth and breadth make even a simple charge such as to address its *planning features alone* somewhat sophisticated and exposed to varieties of interpretation. A supply chain planning decision support system, SCM is deeply integrated into a wider enterprise data management and exchange landscape. Supply chain management demands that we become nimble navigators of the entire enterprise environment in which its planning discipline is practiced, not just at siloed areas of business specialization. To achieve this nimbleness we require a frame of reference, a map of the enterprise supply chain and data pipeline landscape.

While not endeavoring to elucidate the entire body of products and tools available through SCM, Exhibit 2.2 illustrates the scope of these products as it will be presented in this text. Here we are concerned with four areas of the supply chain data pipeline as it criss-crosses through SAP SCM:

1. *Planning.* Core supply chain planning modules
2. *Execution connection.* Integration with enterprise transaction data management and execution
3. *Business intelligence.* Integration with data management, warehousing, and analytics

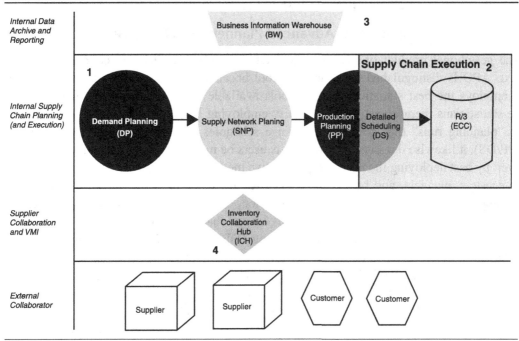

EXHIBIT 2.2   SUPPLY CHAIN DATA PIPELINE LANDSCAPE OF SCM

4. *Collaborative planning.* External integration for collaborative planning and vendor-managed inventory (VMI)

The three core planning modules of APO of interest to us here are Demand Planning (DP), Supply Network Planning (SNP), and Production Planning/Detailed Scheduling (PP/DS) (Exhibit 2.2, area 1). At its most specific, explicit level of planning, PP/DS connects with R/3 and effectively controls actual execution of production builds while simultaneously guiding or informing external procurement activities; so, too, while our primary business interest is planning, we nonetheless address basic integration for execution and control (Exhibit 2.2, area 2). Furthermore, as we will explore in detail later, in order to avoid data maintenance redundancy a substantial native interface exists between R/3 and SCM APO—the CIF, which enables transport of master and transactional data elements between systems without dual data-maintenance.

SCM is built on the data basis provided by the considerable SAP BW product, the Business Information Warehouse, SAP's data warehouse and business intelligence solution. While a separate product from SCM, a *data mart* version of it exists in every SCM deployment and its employment together with any standard SCM project can vastly increase business effectiveness (Exhibit 2.2, area 3). Finally, the ICH is provided in SCM to enable both collaborative planning with external suppliers (and customers) and vendor-managed inventory (Exhibit 2.2, area 4). Note, too, that some collaboration and VMI features are provided within APO without use of ICH. We'll address the differences between the two products in Chapter 12.

SCM APPLICATIONS AND COMPONENTS

Application: Advanced Planner and Optimizer

The gestational product of what has evolved into SCM, APO is the core topic of this text. APO is distinguished as a planning tool because as a forecast or demand planner it employs the best statistical forecast tools available while not requiring that its users be statisticians themselves; while similarly employing heuristics and linear optimization to "planning runs" that generate mid-range schedules (SNP) and short-term schedules (PP/DS), it likewise does not require that its users be mathematicians. In either case, however, by best deploying the superior quantitative methods of a computer system, it elevates forecasters, planners, and buyers alike to better applications of the unique qualities that distinguish humans from computers: negotiation, persuasion, and qualitative judgment.

We've already addressed but may briefly review that APO consists of five major modules and two submodules: Demand Planning (DP), Supply Network Planning (SNP), Production Planning/Detailed Scheduling (PP/DS), Global Available to Promise (GATP), Transportation Planning/Vehicle Scheduling (TP/VS), as well as Deployment and the Transport Load Builder (TLB). Our focus in this text will be the first three. APO comes with the SAP BW product bolted in as a data basis and business intelligence reporting/analytics engine, and in cases of DP deployments will usually rely on a co-deployment of enterprise BW in a separate system for archiving of histories necessary for forecasting. It employs a memory structure known as liveCache, important because (1) it forms a sort of virtual data-layer used by APO but typically populated by R/3, and (2) it controls the nature of stored data in respects that are important to the supply chain business, in particular, distinguishing data as "time-series" or "order" based—a subject we will shortly delve into more deeply. APO employs a Core Interface, the CIF, which is a native, SAP-provided interface between R/3 and APO. Though critical to the use of APO with R/3, note that the CIF is actually managed in R/3, not APO.

The SCM product comes with a specialized product for external collaboration with suppliers and customers that we will also address: the ICH. Collaboration may be for VMI or more detailed levels of planning collaboration. Note, however, that even without deploying ICH, many collaboration features are provided in APO itself.

Component: The Core Interface

Before there was APO there was R/3, and before there was R/3 there was R/2. Both products are best classified as enterprise resource planning (ERP) systems and they were for many years the flagship product offerings of the SAP AG Company. The latter point was so much so, in fact, that in the minds of millions of SAP users today, the term *SAP* is in fact synonymous with *R/3*. The two products, R/2 and R/3, were in delivery the same, but in platform different, in that R/2 was built on a mainframe platform while R/3 employed a client/server, PC network.

R/3 addressed a very wide range of organizational needs from human resources to accounts payable to cost accounting and tax to customer order management and materials management to procurement. The fundamental strength of the R/3 system was in its single-system integration of this wide variety of enterprise system management requirements. While R/3 is not without some analytical and planning features, it is first and foremost a transactional system—concerned with tracking and controlling the actual work of business in all the areas it addresses.

R/3 does contain some critical planning features that are absolutely essential to materials management, including materials requirements planning (MRP) and production planning features that enable production order management. Additionally, R/3 comes with the ability to use a comparatively primitive Flexible Planning module that addresses some of the master production scheduling needs that companies experience, though this module is no longer supported by SAP.

Since first delivering APO to the market, SAP has moved to position R/3 as the enterprise transactional system of record and master data system of origin. That is, transactions resulting in movement, work, and/or recording are managed by R/3, and master data about entities, by their locations, products, routes, and so forth, are all conducted and maintained in R/3. In contrast to this, APO is specialized for planning, scheduling, and analytics—all areas that are at best partially addressed in R/3.

While APO technically can be deployed without R/3 and master data can, therefore, be maintained in APO apart from R/3, this is very rarely the case. Most companies adopting APO have already adopted R/3 and as such are already maintaining master data in R/3 and carrying out enterprise transactions using R/3. Such companies adopt APO in order to improve the quality of enterprise transactions in R/3 by application of its powerful analytics and quantitative, simulative aids to planning. Ordinarily, then, maintenance of master data in APO will be redundant since such data is already maintained in R/3.

Enter here the CIF. APO and R/3 alike are delivered to the customer with a native interface allowing data transfer between the two systems by way of simple configuration rather than cumbersome interface programming. The use of the CIF remains, nonetheless, a bit complicated. Not all master data objects in APO are in R/3. Even among objects in R/3 and APO alike, there are often data elements that are unique to APO that must be maintained once the CIF is completed such as setup matrices, PPM rates, and quota arrangements. Since R/3 is understood as the system of origin for master data, such data can flow only one way on the CIF between the two systems: R/3 → APO. Transactional data, however, is more fluid—wherein orders may be updated by way of planning programs in APO or manually in both systems; therefore, transactional data usually follows a two-way flow between systems.

The ordinary business user of APO does not need to be fluent in configuration and use of the CIF, but minimally should be aware of its existence and the effect it can have on APO processes and their outputs. Furthermore, since use of APO is predicated on simulations and simulations are built on master data, and APO master data, for almost all organizations that use it, will originate in R/3, a reasonably thorough discussion of the CIF will have the dual purpose of familiarizing APO end-users with master data maintenance between the two systems as well as with some of the more technical features of their product.

Application: The BW Data Mart

SAP BW is the Business Information Warehouse, SAP's hallmark data management, analytical, and reporting solution. In general throughout this text, when we refer to *analytics* we will be implying the employment of APO's integration with the BW tool. Many who are already familiar either with various modules of APO or else with BW may be surprised to learn just how integrated the two tools are. They are considerably better integrated than, for example, APO and R/3, the latter upon which the vast majority of APO deployments will rely for most master data.

Indeed, APO relies on BW as its data basis. We have repeatedly used the term *data basis* here in lieu of the more common *database* quite deliberately, as the data basis of APO is considerably more sophisticated and multidimensional than the ordinary database back-end of almost all business information systems. Most business information systems rely on client/server-based user-interface front-ends with SQL-based relational-database back-ends where data is stored and retrieved. The more common SQL/relational back-end of most transactional business information systems is based primarily on the use of two-dimensional tables, storing data in columns and achieving three-dimensional relationships between data by relating more than one table to one another.

APO also has a database back-end, but it is so very much more sophisticated than this. First, in addition to ordinary relational-table-based data storage for transactional processing and retrieval, APO contains a multidimensional, OLAP-based[1] data storage system via BW. That is, instead of storing data in two-dimensional tables, APO, using BW, stores data in many-dimensional data "cubes"—not unlike the popular 1980s Rubik's Cube. Thus, instead of storing away data in a form much like a ledger, and being required to relate ledger-to-ledger by some index whenever data gets complicated, APO can store data in a single cube, easily relating, quantifying, aggregating, and disaggregating like and unlike data elements.

While APO and BW come integrated, one should appreciate that the BW instance within APO is not a full instance thereof. The BW basis of APO will provide the APO user with the following:

- Use of BW's OLAP-based data storage and retrieval
- Use of all of the features and functionality of BW, including dynamic report generation of dynamic reports with either Excel or the Web and publication of reports to the Web

Note that our double-use of the word *dynamic* in the second point was not redundant. BW's report generation features are dynamic in that BW enables end-users to dynamically generate reports as needed, without recourse to programmers. The reports they may generate, for either Excel or the Web, may themselves be dynamic in that they may allow read/write access by users directly to the data they are reporting on in BW. BW's features for OLAP data storage, end-user report generation, use of Excel or the Web, and dynamic reports combine to make it a truly powerful tool that is an awesome enhancement of the already powerful supply-chain tools delivered with APO.

That is what BW integrated with APO is, but what is it *not*? BW, as the name implies, as an individual tool sold separately from APO, is a data warehousing tool. It is not simply intended for advanced analytics; it is intended to be an operational mass data-store for a global enterprise application. An APO box, meanwhile, is specialized for current supply-chain planning, not long-term enterprise data storage. APO's integration with BW gives it access to BW's analytical features, but not to the entire data warehouse archiving and data mining box that an individual deployment of BW, separate from APO, would provide. As such, SAP generally refers to the BW deployment within APO as a *data mart*, in contrast to the data warehouse provided by an individual deployment.

Component: liveCache

Overview

liveCache has the designation of sounding unfortunately technical, but understanding its use in APO is essential to understanding the dynamics of how APO processes infor-mation. We have already said that APO employs BW to gain access to OLAP-based multidimensional data storage, but more important than that is that APO makes use of a variety of data storage technologies and formats. It simply is not limited to either OLTP- or OLAP-based back-ends. liveCache is another dimension of APO data storage.

First, we can learn a little about liveCache just by deconstructing the name. By *live*, something current is implied. A *cache* is a storage unit. *liveCache* then is a storage unit for live, current data. It is a specialized storage unit with some characteristics that every APO user will profit to appreciate.

Time-Series- and Order-Based Data Management

Day-to-day maintenance of liveCache is a sophisticated technical affair, and except for some of the minimum analytics and correctives we will treat it as out of scope for this text.[2]

Regardless of technical, day-to-day administration of APO, everyday APO users from end-users to system analysts should be fluent in the manner in which liveCache segregates data. In that regard, liveCache stores data in either of two ways (Exhibit 2.3):

Time Series Data Storage		Order-based Data Storage	
Time Bucket: Week Data Element: Forecast qty		Order Type: Sales Order Data Element: Customer reqmt	
Week 1	500	Order 1000	500 units Week 1
Week 2	500	Order 1010	500 units Week 2
Week 3	1,000	Order 1020	1,000 units Week 3
Week n	1,500	Order n	1,500 units Week n

EXHIBIT 2.3   TIME-SERIES-VERSUS ORDER-BASED DATA STORAGE

Much data is by necessity stored in order form, but other data types have no orders and are stored according to a time series. To operate a time series, time buckets must be propagated to hold the data quantities. Often data stored in orders will be mapped to time series for display and analysis purposes.

1. In time-series
2. As orders

A time-series data storage entails storing data based on units of time without respect to an order. That is, much business data is not order specific. Various elements of demand data, for example, may have no order basis. Of course customer orders are demand, but it is possible, likely even, that additional demand forecast data will be generated that has no orders. Such data is stored by time series. This is significant to APO users, because time series must often be custom defined. SAP, for example, does not know whether customers will want data stored by month, week, day, hour, or second. Depending on the module and application, needs will vary. Very frequently APO users may be called on to define a time series or else execute a "time series propagation" that will organize data onto a time series.

For example, data may be provided to APO in monthly time buckets, but the user may wish to display the data in weekly time buckets. The time-series propagation will disaggregate monthly data into small weekly clumps, or else it may split the month into weeks, but place all the months' quantitative data onto one week—all depending on the specifications of the user. A time-series propagation may operate the other way as well, aggregating data from hours to days, from days to weeks, or from weeks to months.

Alternatively, much business data is also stored in the form of orders. In other words, the data-storage organizing unit of order-based data is the order, not the time bucket. For example, instead of creating a time bucket of June to hold demand quantities of 100 units of product, customer-order demand may be stored in sales order number 200493, denoting the 100-unit quantity and the June requirements date. SAP parlance very frequently makes reference to "time-series-based liveCache" and "order-based liveCache." All this refers to is whether the data storage in liveCache is organized according to time series as defined by the users or else by order as applied by the system.

Order-Based liveCache and Time-Series-Based Display

An additional complication of order versus time-series data storage is that even though much data may often be stored in liveCache as orders, it may often be more useful to display that data as time series. Again, a time-series propagation may be required to map data stored in orders to the time-based location of the orders. Demand analysts, for example, may not be interested in the fact that demand is from this or that customer order, and master schedulers are unlikely to find it very important that supply is allocated to a particular planned order. In both cases, both users are simply interested in quantities displayed across time, rather than in the orders containing those quantities in the system.

Often, therefore, components or transactions in APO, such as the DP or SNP Planning Book, will display data as a time series even though it is stored in liveCache as order based. Almost always, when this is the case, pegging will be possible. Pegging is the process of identifying the source of a requirement or allocation. That is, if a master scheduler is looking at an allocation of 100 units of supply in a time-series bucket, she may double-click the cell containing the 100 units on the time series and the APO will take her to a detailed display of the order storing the data about those units. If a demand analyst is looking at a requirement of 1,000 units of demand in a similar time-series bucket, he may also double-click the cell containing the quantity and will likewise be taken to a detailed display of the customer order driving that demand.

HINT

To avoid confusion: When instructors, instructional materials, online help, or consultants refer to time-series-based liveCache or order-based liveCache, do not check out. To get your bearings, simply ask yourself whether they are referring to the actual storage of a specific data element in liveCache or whether they are referring to the translation of one type to another for display purposes, such as from order-based storage to time-series-based display.

---

liveCache becomes a fact of life for users of APO first by virtue of allowing customization of time-series propagation, but also due to some necessary headaches that may arise from its architecture (Exhibit 2.4). liveCache will usually receive data from either of two sources simultaneously: any of the APO modules on one hand and R/3 on the other. The CIF interface in fact connects R/3 with APO liveCache and typically maintains a real-time connection. At times, however, since changes may occur on either side of liveCache before requisite cascading updates can take place in all three systems, liveCache at times will be knocked out of alignment with data in either APO or R/3. When this occurs it will

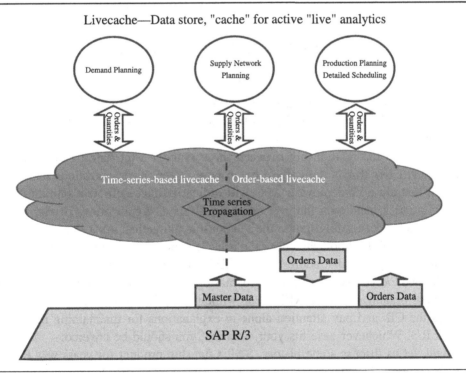

EXHIBIT 2.4   LIVECACHE STORES DATA IN TIME-SERIES- OR ORDER-BASED UNITS (I.E., TIME BUCKETS OR ORDERS)

Time-series propagation maps data between time series and orders for storage and display purposes alike. liveCache also is updated by both APO modules and R/3, and as such occasionally gets out of alignment with one of the two systems.

cause faults and failures in APO procedures, typically in the variety of planning runs. APO administration procedures exist both to detect and correct such liveCache faults and will be addressed briefly.

HINT

If planning run or other procedures in APO just are not working out the way you expect and you are banging your head against your desk wondering why, run a liveCache consistency check and see whether data has been knocked out of alignment with R/3.

Application: Inventory Collaboration Hub

APO comes with collaboration features that enable both VMI and planning collaboration with external parties: customers or suppliers. The ICH is an application in SCM separate from APO that considerably expands an organization's options for external collaboration. APO-based collaboration will be very strictly "planning" collaboration, as APO is a planning decision support tool. To enable genuine VMI where vendors are enabled to automatically replenish stocks, for example, a connection to the transactional data management system, R/3, is necessary. Inventory Collaboration Hub provides this. While sharing master data with APO (i.e., plants, materials, vendors, etc.), ICH connects with R/3 through a separate XML layer allowing external parties visibility and live inventory conditions and the ability to instantiate responses to those conditions.

SIMULATING THE SUPPLY CHAIN

APO and SAP R/3

Users already familiar with R/3 who come to APO will have relatively little challenge understanding SAP's choice to use R/3 as the master-data basis of APO and all the divisions of this-belongs-to-R3, that-belongs-to-APO, that necessarily ensue. Users unfamiliar with R/3 may find the relationship between the two tools a bit baffling at first. Fortunately, in most cases this is unlikely to be an issue. Users at organizations that already use R/3 but that are now deploying APO will ordinarily have sufficient familiarity with R/3 to gain a quick handle on the give-and-take. Users at organizations deploying APO as a standalone tool can safely ignore the relationship altogether. As a rule of thumb, for this text, we make this admonishment to the user: If your organization uses R/3, pay special attention to language that addresses the CIF interface that controls data management between the two tools as your organization's master data will almost surely be maintained in R/3. If your organization uses APO alone without R/3, then totally ignore all language concerning the CIF and pay attention alone to explanations for maintaining master data directly in R/3. Whichever case fits your situation, you should be covered.

That said, let us discuss some history. SAP's flagship product for years was R/3. R/3 is an ERP solution that manages actual transactional control of everything from tax to Human Resources to customer orders to materials requirements planning, purchasing, and inventory. Organizations that use R/3 will have in it their master lists of vendors, internal sites, customers, materials, cost centers, material relationships, production routes, everything that forms the structural basis of the supply chain—what APO views as the supply chain model.

APO, therefore, is delivered with the ability to leverage as much as possible off of previous deployments of R/3. Master data maintained in R/3 should, within reason, not have to be maintained again in APO. To enable minimal remastering of master data, APO comes delivered, off the shelf, with a native interface to R/3 that can be configured to bring almost any combination of master data elements into APO for analytical modeling use.

In addition to master data, however, the CIF may also be used to maintain transactional data. While APO has powerful decision-support capabilities, it ultimately steps into transactional management with the detailed output of planning runs, optimizers, and their solves. Transactional data, essentially the as-is-in-life-now case, is brought into APO via the CIF, analyzed, and may then be further managed, with results going out to update R/3.

Again, though, for nonusers of R/3, we make this strong admonishment: The best way not to be confused about R/3 and its relationship with APO is to ignore it entirely. For your cases all master data will be maintained directly and solely in APO. Potentially you may have legacy ERP systems that are not R/3, which may be interfaced to APO via custom-built interfaces. If that is the case, you will need to familiarize yourself with the specific, unique data exchanges managed by your organization's custom interfaces, which may or may not have the same rule basis as the native CIF.

Master Data

Both R/3 and APO have two primary distinctions of data: master data and transactional data. Master data may be thought of as a data skeleton. It is the *model* of the real world that enables computational analysis and interaction. Products, customers, vendors, internal production routes, external transportation lanes, procurement relationships, factories, and distribution sites—all of these are the master data skeletal model of a company or organization's supply chain.

We like to compare APO to a weather simulator, but all weather simulators simulate the same thing: earth's weather. Every deployment of APO will be different because the details of every organization's supply chain are different. Therefore, much attention is given in this text and in all treatments of APO to master data maintenance. Excellent modeling of supply chain elements, of data relationships, and of priorities, contracts, and costs is the new specialization for the supply chain expert, and APO both puts a microscope on this new specialty and maximally employs it. This is the core distinction the APO makes between planners, schedulers, and buyers of yore versus those of the twenty-first century: Until now, such job roles have been essentially transactional in nature, concerned only with order planning and management. APO elevates all of these roles and asks that they become modelers of the global supply chain environment. The better the model, the better APO's output and the more efficient and effective the supply chain.

Transactional Data

Master data is the skeleton; transactional data represents actual events that occur within the supply chain. Almost all transactional data is either a reservation or an order. A reservation may include as broad a concept as a forecast for production. Orders are actual transactional elements that will cause or otherwise represent action: Customer orders, purchase orders, production orders and their cousins, planned orders, purchase requisitions, and schedule lines all represent and directly control actual work planned, in process, or completed.

Under ordinary circumstances, APO receives a picture of transactional data from R/3 and maps it to its master data model. Using data processing tools from regression analysis to linear optimization as well as human analytical, qualitative inputs, APO generates recommendations for management of transactional data that may either be acted upon, altered, or ignored, usually via systematic, exception processes, by its users. Transactional data may then in turn be returned to R/3 (or any other transactional control system), where it will control execution of work.

APO TOOLS FOR USERS

APO is the metaphorical equivalent of a global weather simulator for SCM and as such, necessarily, much of our attention must be devoted to the sometimes seemingly endless elements of configuration required to employ APO master data to custom-model the complex supply networks whose specifics will vary so much from one organization to another. Nonetheless, ultimately the purpose of so much configuration is to enable a powerful end-user toolset for supply chain planning and analysis. One confusing aspect of APO is that the way that the end-user tools are organized may sometimes mislead users and developers alike to think of a tool as belonging to a specific APO module, when often it is the case that tools presented in one module are available to many others.

For example, the Supply Chain Cockpit (SCC) does not fit this description. The SCC is clearly available apart from any particular module of APO and is implicitly available to APO users, whether those are users of DP, SNP, PP/DS, or whatnot. The Product View transaction presents itself within the navigation tree explicitly in the PP/DS module. While the Product View may be particularly interactive in the functional business of production planning and factory scheduling, it is nonetheless almost always an essential component of DP and SNP solutions, if only sometimes for view-only access to product orders.

Besides its navigation structure, often the manner in which APO is presented in training classes by some instructors can mislead users and developers of APO alike to think of certain tools as being explicit tools of this or that module. This tendency of presentation and its resultant habit of thinking should be resisted by thoughtful APO users, developers, and consultants because it can lead to "in-the-box" thinking where it comes to APO solutions that do not consider all the available power of APO. An organization seeking to deploy PP/DS, for example, should not rule out the possibility that a Planning Book—generally thought of as a feature of DP and SNP—may be a useful component of its PP/DS solution. While adding the optimization configuration necessary to enable SNP might be a considerable scope-increase to a PP/DS project, simply adding access to the Planning Book would be a relatively simple matter that would be easily justified if it empowered superior user interaction. We will make our own effort to resist this pitfall here by looking at the end-user tools provided by APO, but without categorizing them according to the modules in which they present themselves, only noting their location in the navigation tree as a fact, but not a limiting one.

While much work in any APO deployment will be devoted to modeling a specific organization's probably global supply chain, ultimately there are just a handful of actual tools that most users will interact with from day to day. APO's end-user tools fall into two categories: (1) user-interface tools and (2) data processing tools. What follows is a summary of those tools to acquaint readers quickly with each of them and better enable integrated thinking about their features and potential for business solutions. Detailed explanations of how to use the user-interface tools will be presented in Part Two and for the data-processing tools in Part Three.

User-Interface Tools

Conflicting User-Interface Requirements in the Supply Chain Discipline

Our text will address the five user-interface tools that will be most commonly employed by end-users of APO's planning modules, DP, SNP, and PP/DS: the SCC, the Product View, the Planning Book, the Detailed Scheduling Planning Board, and the Production Planning Table. While not perfectly exhaustive of the user-interfaces available to these tools, these five tools will suffice to fulfill the user-interface requirements of the vast majority of APO deployments.

Before comparing and contrasting the five user interfaces, consider the variety of needs that arise in the course of supply chain analysis, planning, and management that must be addressed by any given user interface (UI) and that give rise to the need for more than one UI manifestation. At a high level, the following is a fairly comprehensive list of the interactive requirements for any supply chain tool:

- High-level, executive overview of the supply chain, ideally enabled for visual point-and-click supply-network modeling (described in some quarters as a "dash-board")
- Analysis and planning of supply and demand
- Analysis, planning, and management of capacity
  - Detailed or order-based capacity management
  - High-level or "rough-cut" capacity management
- Times-series view of data
- Order-based view of data
- External collaboration
- Pegging
- Access to mass data processing tools (i.e., statistical engines and optimizers)

We will discuss each of these UI requirements in more detail shortly, but even at a high level it should be immediately apparent that many of these requirements differ from one another in very specific ways, essentially acting to train microscopes on very different supply chain management activities. As such, no single UI will be sufficient to adequately address all of these needs—we can see that specific tensions arise that will be reflected as different specialized interactive screens:

- High-level executive supply-network view versus lower-level, planning or execu-tion-specialized detailed views
- Supply/demand focus versus capacity management focus

- Time-series view of data versus order-based view of data
- Specialized access to mass data processing tools (i.e., demand forecasting tools available to a demand management view, and capacity management tools available to a detailed scheduling view)

While most of these special focus requirements are in natural states of tension, a few at least theoretically may be available to any UI, specifically pegging and external collaboration. In fact, all five APO UIs we will address in this text (and most SAP UIs as a rule) are enabled for pegging. That is, even if a view is time-series based, for example, users may double-click a quantity in a time-bucket cell, say a forecast of 200 units in a December cell, and APO will display the detailed order-information underlying the time-series aggregate data element of 200 units, such as two sales orders for 150 and 50 units, respectively. Even order-based views still enable a manner of pegging. A planned order for 100 units of a finished good may by way of Bill-of-Materials (BOM) explosion give rise to dependent requirements for 100 units of a semifinished good and 200 units of a raw material. When the planned order is double-clicked in the Product View, a navigation tree to these dependent orders will display, allowing the user to drill down into each requirement necessary to fulfill the planned order. While no mechanical restrictions exist to making external collaboration enabled via any UI, this is ordinarily not ideal for most business conditions, so only a few UIs are in fact enabled to directly support external collaboration.

HINT

Are you a business or system analyst, APO consultant, or in any way responsible for configuring APO to the specific requirements of a business or organization? If so, pay special attention to the natural tensions in the varieties of SCM data analysis and planning needs that give rise to the plurality of UIs in APO. When conducting requirements gathering and/or gap analysis, determine which specialized data-view requirements are needed by the business users and match them to the appropriate UI. Do this at the high level described here, not at the low level of actual identification of APO UIs. Ordinary business users are unlikely to be familiar with the strengths and weaknesses of the Product View versus the Planning Book, for example. Even if they have taken an introductory class in APO, such terms are likely to remain technical, vague, and arcane to them. They will, however, be able to easily interact with you and explain their interface needs when you explain to them such concepts as time-series- versus order-based specializations and supply/demand analysis versus capacity management.

Five APO Business User Interfaces

The Supply Chain Cockpit (SCC) (Exhibit 2.5) perhaps most effectively represents itself as a tool for all tools in APO—inhabiting its own place on the APO navigation tree and thus implying its availability to any manner of APO deployment. This is rightly so as the SCC may in many respects be thought of as an executive view of the supply chain, and if not that, certainly as a global, graphical view. The SCC enables both a geographical and a logical view of all the physical relationships between all of the components of an organizational supply chain: sites including factories, vendors, customers, subcontractors, transportation lanes between sites, resources at sites, and products built

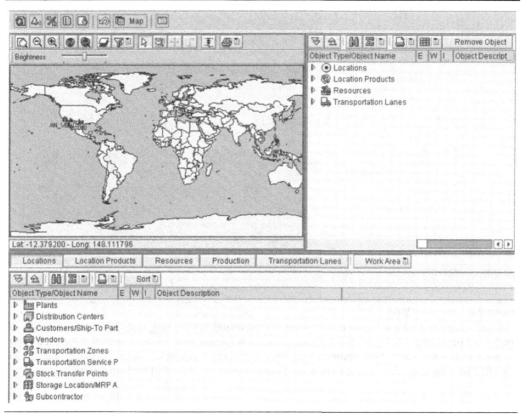

EXHIBIT 2.5 SUPPLY CHAIN COCKPIT

The SCC provides an aerial, geographic, and/or logical view of the entire supply chain master data model maintained in APO. It has applications for executive users of APO, planning users, and developers alike. © SAP AG. Used with permission.

and transported between sites. From this high-level graphical view a user, configurator, developer, or executive can observe either the whole corpus of the supply chain modeled for an organization in APO or else any custom-defined subset thereof, called a "work area." Moreover, from the SCC a user may simply highlight and click any displayed element of the supply chain and will be taken from there to the detailed configuration settings for the item. In almost every APO deployment, no matter the module of APO deployed or the business or hierarchical role of the user, the SCC will almost always have some utility.

The Product View (Exhibit 2.6) is likely to be confused by novice users of APO with the Product Master View, the latter of which is used to maintain product master data or else act as the APO repository for such data as delivered by the CIF from R/3. However much it may sometimes be confused with its master-data counterpart, the Product View is perhaps one of the most transactionally active screens in the entire APO tool. Users familiar with R/3 would do well to think of the Product View as the APO cousin to the R/3 Stock Requirements List, only as a Stock Requirements List on anabolic steroids. Indeed, the functions of the Product View and the R/3 Stock Requirements List are almost identical.

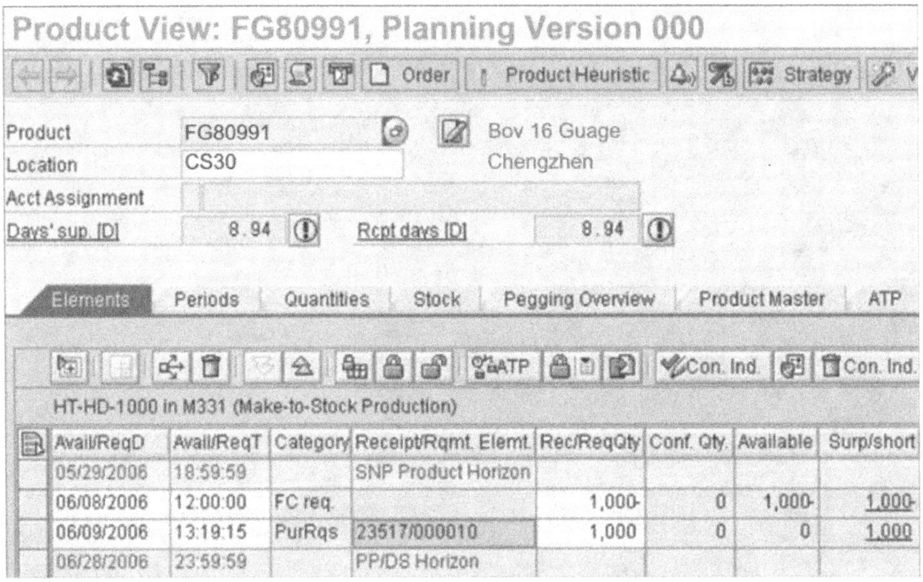

Product View: FG80991, Planning Version 000

| | | | | | | | | □ Order | | Product Heuristic | | | | Strategy | |

Product	FG80991			Bov 16 Guage
Location	CS30			Chengzhen
Acct Assignment			
Days' sup. [D]	8.94	①	Rcpt days [D]	8.94	①

| Elements | Periods | Quantities | Stock | Pegging Overview | Product Master | ATP |

HT-HD-1000 in M331 (Make-to-Stock Production)

	Avail/ReqD	Avail/ReqT	Category	Receipt/Rqmt. Elemt.	Rec/ReqQty	Conf. Qty.	Available	Surp/short
	05/29/2006	18:59:59		SNP Product Horizon				
	06/08/2006	12:00:00	FC req.		1,000-	0	1,000-	1,000-
	06/09/2006	13:19:15	PurRqs	23517/000010	1,000	0	0	1,000
	06/28/2006	23:59:59		PP/DS Horizon				

EXHIBIT 2.6 PRODUCT VIEW

A tabular, single-order-based view that is primarily interested in matching units of demand to units of supply and providing a base for direct, transactional interaction with those orders. The Product View is similar to the R/3 Stock Requirements List, only much more powerful—with access to the PP/DS heuristic Planning Run, the Product Master, and visual views. © SAP AG. Used with permission.

The Product View is an order-based view of supply and demand data for any given product. It is tabular and intended to be used to view and directly maintain and interact with detailed order-data, organized explicitly according to supply and demand, for individual products. As such, using the Product View, a user will be able to see a product's demand elements whether they are forecast elements, sales orders, or pegged requirements from other orders, as well as any supply elements that may be applied to fulfill that demand such as available stocks, purchase orders, production orders or their processing-predecessors, purchase requisitions, and planned orders. Data is organized in the Product View according to the application of supplies to fulfill demands over time and within specific horizons, such as the PP/DS horizon or the SNP horizon, which are explicitly called out.

In addition to these display features, users can employ the Product View to access the Product Master for any product it displays or else to gain access to detailed views of any of the orders presented. These pegged views, for their part, may be used to trace demand chains such as may be the case where APO automatically generates a purchase requisition to fulfill components requirements for a production order that was created to fulfill demand from a sales order.

The Product View is presented in APO in the PP/DS navigation structure. The decision to locate the Product View there is most likely because another feature available inside the Product View is a single-product run of the PP/DS Production Planning heuristic run, and generally, while user-interface views are not explicitly regarded as components of a given module, data-processing tools such as the Planning Run as such are regarded as module-specific solutions. That much is recognized as the likely reasons for its identification with PP/DS, the Product View will almost always be a part of every APO deployment solution in all five modules, even those we are not addressing in this text.

The APO Planning Book (Exhibit 2.7) may first be understood as a time-series-based pivot of the more tabular Product View. That is, where the Product View displays one product for one location in one model and then all of the orders and demands open for that product in tabular form, matching demand element to supply element, in contrast the Planning Book displays data, usually for multiple products, in a time series—as rows, one product on top of a another, with adjacent columns representing forward-going buckets of time—days, weeks, months, and so forth. The Planning Book is for displaying changes in data-states across time and for working with and analyzing products in mass.

The Planning Book can be, and often is, used like the Product View to match supply and demand elements, though where the Product View is an order-based display, showing only one product, all its orders, row-by-row across time, the Planning Book displays many products but none of the orders, column-by-column, across time. The Planning Book does allow pegging; that is, any quantity displayed in a time-bucket may be double-clicked and APO will display the order details underlying it, but the primary utility of the Planning Book is in its time-series-based display, which allows mass viewing, mass analysis, and direct comparison of quantities and trends across time. The Planning Book is used,

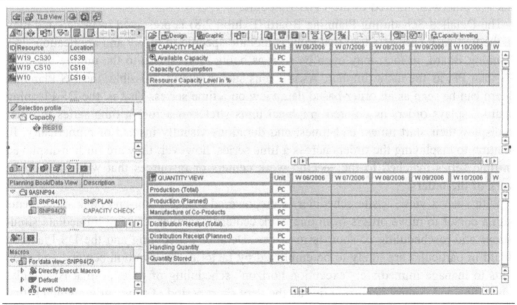

EXHIBIT 2.7 PLANNING BOOK

This is the primary UI for DP and SNP, but may be employed in almost any configuration of APO. The Planning Book is a time-series-based view to data with pegging access to order data underlying it. It may be configured to analyze and work with planning or forecast data or to work with capacity management data—matching medium- and long-term production to work centers and resources. Detailed Planning and SNP data processing tools are made available in the Planning Book. © SAP AG. Used with permission.

furthermore, for capacity planning, where demand and supply quantities are juxtaposed directly against available sources of supply.

Planning Books are presented in both the DP and SNP navigation structures. They may be configured to view specific product groupings, called *books*. Detailed Planning and SNP each have access to one Planning Book that is an "all-books" view—allowing interactive access to any book, or grouping of products, defined for Planning Books. Supply Network Planning presents a Planning Book that is a single book, allowing exactly one book without the capacity to interactively shift from one view to another. The latter version may be useful for companies with strong security concerns. APO user security profiles may be developed that exclude access to the all-books views, and users may be explicitly assigned books that display only data for which they have a need to know.

Otherwise, there is no difference between the all-books Planning Books presented in both DP and SNP. Their presentation on both modules' navigation paths is essentially as a convenience to business units that have one module deployed and not the other.

Planning Books are the primary user interface tool for DP and SNP, and in addition to their data organization features they provide access to the data processing tools of each module, including statistical analyses for DP and three varieties of planning runs for SNP. Again we find that the most likely reason for identifying Planning Books with these two modules is their access to and connection with the data processing tools associated with them. Nonetheless, when facing the variety of business problems posed and creatively thinking up solutions APO may be configured to provide, analysts and developers ought to keep the Planning Book in mind as a potentially useful user interface, even for projects that are otherwise limited to the PP/DS module.

The Detailed Scheduling Planning Board (Exhibit 2.8) is presented in PP/DS and may be the first such case of a tool that truly is module-specific in utility and application. The Planning Board, in fact, may even be seen as being more suited to the unique needs of DS than PP, as the name implies. As much as such a view is possible, the DS Planning Board can be seen as an order-based data view on a time series. That is, the DS Planning Board displays orders as colored graphical units stretched across a time series in order to display their start times, end times, and durations visually instead of numerically. In addition to displaying the orders across a time series, however, they are further displayed on time series matched to the specific work centers or resources that will conduct the work of the orders.

With such a view, a site scheduler is empowered to use point-and-click movements with a cursor to move orders from one work center to another, causing immediate simulations and rescheduling of short-term orders. Detailed scheduling and the DS Planning Board in particular are likely to be employed by factories, distribution centers, and even ports to manage immediate, "execution horizon" scheduling of orders—that is, usually, scheduling and control occurring during the very short period of time during which actual work-in-process is taking place, usually no more than three to five days.

The last UI we will consider in this text is the Product Planning Table (Exhibit 2.9). The Product Planning Table, like the DS Planning Board, is very specifically a tool of PP/DS, though creative developers may find ways of employing it in other modular configurations of APO. Where it concerns the unique world of production planning in the PP/DS module, the Product View covers short- and long-term order management and transactional needs

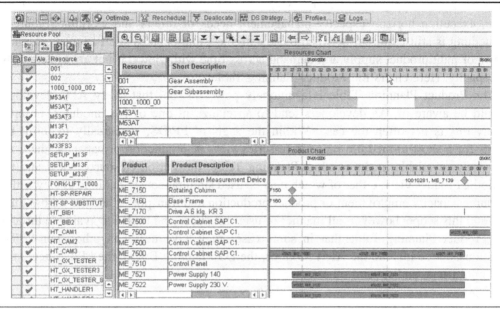

EXHIBIT 2.8   DETAILED SCHEDULING PLANNING BOARD

Specialized for short-term, execution horizon control of working orders and capacity management, the DS Planning Board is a time-series view that places visual representations of orders on resources that will work them, stretched across time. It may be used to assign and reassign specific orders to specific work stations. It has access to the PP/DS optimizer, which enables short-term optimization of capacity resources. © SAP AG. Used with permission.

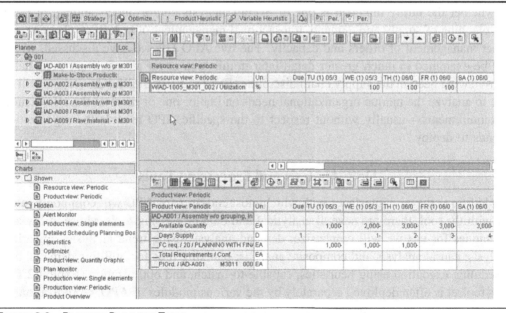

EXHIBIT 2.9   PRODUCT PLANNING TABLE

Ostensibly for a short-to-medium-range time-series view of either supply and demand or capacity in PP/DS, the Product Planning Table is uniquely powerful. It may be employed to display and use any of the views or tools listed under the "Hidden" branch of the "Charts" dialog on the left. © SAP AG. Used with permission.

as it concerns supply and demand while the DS Planning Board covers very short-term, execution horizon capacity management needs of orders and working resources. Something is still required, between these extremes, that enables short-to-medium-range views of multiproduct supply and demand across time with views, if not always controls, to capacity. Here enters the Product Planning Table.

The Product Planning Table is a uniquely powerful tool that every APO developer should be aware of. As developers tend to specialize in one or two modules, unfortunately this is not often the case. Within the aegis of PP/DS, specifically to fulfill the needs for a short-to-medium-range time-series view of production or capacity, there are two views available in the Product Planning Table: the Period Resource View and the Periodic Product View, either of which may be used simultaneously or alone to view either resource capacity employment or product production and transport schedules across time. Beyond this scope, however, all manner of user interfaces and tools are available through the Product Planning Table that in some cases may have utility in other, non-PP/DS solutions. These include the Alert Monitor, the DS Planning Board, the PP/DS heuristics and optimizers, and several others.

Summary of User Interfaces

Data may be stored in APO liveCache in either order-based or time-series units, but often it is more useful to view order-based data as a time series. Data viewing and analysis needs vary greatly from one company to another, from one business unit to another; and even within the same business unit, the same job role may have needs for more than one view of data. Sometimes it should be a geographical, aerial, or logical executive overview. Very often it should be either time series or order based. All of this depends on whether the utility intended is one of overall analysis and/or understanding, analysis and planning of supply and demand, transactional management of orders, or planning and direct management of orders and capacity. The five APO UIs we have discussed, which will be examined in much greater detail later in this text, cover almost every imaginable data-viewing need in the supply chain discipline (Exhibit 2.10). Skillful developers will be able to analyze the unique organizational needs and tailor one or more of the UIs to meet its requirements—usually without respect to the specific APO module the organization intends to deploy.

Data Analysis and Processing Tools

In addition to the user interfaces with which most end-users of APO will commonly interact with the tool, there are several analytical and data processing tools whose utility and techniques for use we will emphasize: demand analysis using trend analysis; univariate analysis; causal analysis and composite analysis; planning runs for fulfilling demand; and scheduling execution using heuristics, capable-to-match, and optimization (Exhibit 2.11). This toolset is often deployed separately by the various modules of APO. Optimization by way of linear programming is available in different manifestations, for example, in SNP, PP/DS, and TP/VS. We will briefly consider these seven tools without respect to their modular deployment. As with user interfaces, this is a useful exercise, as any organization considering APO will do best to consider its tools without respect to the module to which

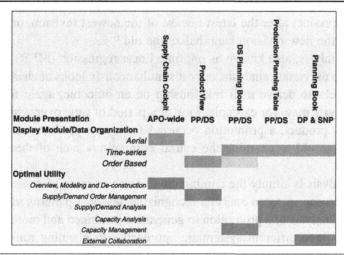

EXHIBIT 2.10   FIVE UIs AND THEIR ANALYSIS OR SCM COMPETENCIES

Module	Data Processing Tools
Demand Planning	• Trend Analysis
	• Univariate Analysis
	• Multivariate Analysis (MLR)
	• Composite Analysis
Supply Network Planning	• Heuristic Planning Run
	• Capable to Match Planning Run
	• Optimization
Production Planning	• Heuristic Planning Run
Detailed Scheduling	• Optimization

EXHIBIT 2.11   APO DATA PROCESSING TOOLS BY MODULE

they belong prior to deciding on which module to use. That will result in the broadest thinking possible about the right modular configuration necessary to meet a business's specific needs.

Trend analysis is ordinarily employed to capture time-series-based projections of marketing, seasonal, or economic cycles that impact demand for a product. Many companies experience seasonal-based spikes and troughs in demand whether due to holidays, the specific needs of the climatic seasons, or even the needs of the financial or tax calendar. Trend analysis is applied to capture and understand these cycles and apply that understanding to best predict demand trajectories based on known past trend data.

Univariate analysis is intended to determine the relationship between specific, individual factors or variables and usually, for SCM cases, to relate that to demand. Normally this entails looking at specific events or drivers and determining the extent of their impact on demand elasticity. How much did demand for a product change, for example, after a specific marketing promotion? How much and how quickly did demand reduce for an old revision of a product after the latest release of the newest revision, or in other words, how quickly did the new revision cannibalize the old?

Multivariate analysis, also known as multiple linear regression (MLR) or "causal analysis," is similar to univariate analysis, only it simultaneously looks at changes in a number of factors and seeks to derive their relationship on an outcome, again for SCM usually on demand. Analysts may, for example, look at a period of time over which a competitor introduced a new product, a promotion occurred for a new product, and the new product cannibalized an old to examine the causal correlations each of these may have on resulting demand.

Composite analysis is simply the combination of one or more aforementioned demand analysis types into one. A trend analysis recognizing seasonal patterns may be combined with a univariate analysis of a promotion to generate a combined and more honed forecast.

APO provides three different systematic approaches to planning runs. Planning runs are any kind of data processing methodology that generates a schedule. Supply Network Planning, for example, generates multifactory build, buy, and ship schedules. Production planning and detailed scheduling are generally tailored for planning runs that generate single-site or site-by-site build, buy, and ship schedules. Transportation Planning/Vehicle Scheduling uses planning run techniques for shipping, receiving, and transport schedules. Materials Requirements Planning, a planning run methodology in R/3 and other ERP systems, is a very common planning run methodology and the heuristic logic of MRP is one of several available in APO.

The word *heuristic* is no more than a technical term for *rule based*. Any rule-based system, therefore, may be said to be heuristic in nature. This is important to know, especially for novices, since heuristics pop up so often throughout APO. The first and most approachable of APO's planning runs is the heuristic run, which is available in both SNP and the Production Planning (PP) portion of PP/DS. A heuristic technique will apply rules to determine which demand among several demand types to meet and then use similar rule structures to determine how to meet it, for example, by applying inventories first, open production orders second, and opening new planned orders third, for unmet demand. The latter planned orders may be evaluated by a planner and converted to production orders that will be used by subsequent planning runs to close demand requirements. Heuristic planning run outcomes will generally result in schedules that will fulfill demand, but since they are unconstrained by capacity they are not always feasible schedules.

Capable-to-match (CTM) uses priorities in addition to rules to control scheduling. Thus, facing constraints, CTM chooses between demands and meets those with the highest priorities. Capable-to-match applies planning runs over and over again until it finds a feasible outcome, and its recommended schedule will be the first feasible case found during processing. Capable-to-match is made available through SNP and is primarily an SNP tool, though in principle it may also be applied as a planning run method for PP/DS.

The optimizer goes beyond rules and priorities and considers very detailed cost settings that may be maintained about a veritable plethora of factors influencing the supply chain. Costs may be associated with the use of one component or another to build a product, one line or another on which to build it, one transportation lane or another on which to source supply or ship the finished good, one vendor or another from which to acquire raw materials, or even one customer or another to which to sell the product. The maintenance of sophisticated cost systems in APO and their consideration by the optimizer allows for generation of an optimal schedule outcome—in other words, the best schedule possible among many, given known constraints. Optimizers are exceedingly sophisticated and are therefore the most demanding in terms of configuration, but they yield the most superior output as well. Both SNP and the DS portion of PP/DS employ native optimizers.

NOTES

1. OLAP (Online Analytical Processing) refers to both (1) the use of multidimensional databases in the back-end to enable more analytical use of data and (2) more sophisticated analytical application of computing than with earlier OLTP (Online Transaction Processing) systems, which rely primarily on two-dimensional relational database back-ends. OLTP systems remain in common use for transaction-processing specializations (i.e., managing sales), while OLAP has become increasingly popular for data analytics (i.e., demand forecasting).

2. For detailed, technical coverage of liveCache, please consider the text *SAP APO System Administration*, Liane Will, SAP Press, 2003.

3

SUPPLY CHAIN LANDSCAPE

It will pay to note that SAP Supply Chain Management Advanced Planning and Optimization is not Microsoft Excel, and while it does in fact contain some spreadsheets, in and of itself it is simply not a spreadsheet product. Respecting the profound power of spreadsheets, SAP has bolted that power onto APO by way of BW (SAP Business Information Warehouse), which enables dynamic reports in Excel based on real-time extracts from APO.

"And why might I care?" the reader should probably be asking. APO's distinction from Microsoft Excel is noted first and foremost because it is possible, even desirable, to have instructional treatments of Excel that are entirely business neutral. That is, Excel can be taught in total isolation from a business context. Spreadsheets are intended to list, cross-list, display, and slice and dice information—*any kind of information that can be reduced to dimensions or quantities*. One can use Excel to draw up project Gantts, to analyze stock market data, to list schedules, or to write cooking recipes. Excel is a veritable "Switzerland" of software applications. So business neutral is Excel that it need not be used for business at all: It is a perfect solution for all manner of scientific and mathematical operations. Excel will do it all; it does not care and is designed not to care about the kind of data a user applies in it. As such, instruction on Excel need not address any particular knowledge domain; in fact, a good instructional treatment of Excel should explore data analysis examples from a multiplicity of domains.

In stark contrast to Excel, APO is a highly specialized piece of software intended for applications in supply chain management; indeed it is the hallmark application of the SAP *SCM* product package. More specifically, APO is designed for applications in supply chain planning, and even more specifically for decision support of the more costly supply chain planning questions. Instruction in APO that ignores its intense and deep supply chain planning context, therefore, is something like instruction in sailing that excludes coverage of basic navigation and nautical weather patterns. One will best understand APO by understanding the landscape of the supply chain planning domain on which it is set. To understand APO, in other words, requires that we understand the business problem it was intended to solve.

SUPPLY CHAIN LANDSCAPE

In the long-run it will not do to learn one or two individual, siloed modules of APO such as Demand Planning (DP) or Production Planning and Detailed Scheduling (PP/DS). To do so would be to make no better use of it than the stovepiped legacy applications that it generally is called upon to replace. The key to understanding APO and its related products connected to or included in the wider SCM platform, including R/3, BW, and Inventory Collaboration Hub (ICH), is to understand the wider supply chain context against which they all were designed to act together as integrated application solutions. Each product and module of the overall package is intended to meet the needs of one or another area or specialized zone of supply chain management, as the discipline has come to be understood through research, experience, and best-known methods in the decades since the 1940s. Therefore, in order to better understand the organization, content, and integration schemes of the SAP SCM package, including APO, we should investigate the supply chain that these tools are designed to plan, support, and control.

SAP's SCM tools are focused on the ongoing planning and execution of the supply chain. Explicitly within the supply chain it is best to think of APO as occupying a very wide middle space between strategic supply chain management (Exhibit 3.1, area 1) and tactical execution (Exhibit 3.1, area 3). Bordering on the outside with strategic SCM is the DP tool, interested as it is primarily in forecasting future demand; on the other side, bordering, indeed dipping into execution and control, are PP/DS as well as other tools out of scope for our text such as Deployment, TLB, and TP/VS (Exhibit 3.1, area 2). Strategic SCM includes such things as plant or site location selection, plant design, and quality control as well as major decisions such as opening and closing new sites or transportation lanes, legal activities surrounding locations, and commercial transport such as with overseas sites and free-trade zones. On the other side, execution and control relates to actual, day-to-day management of goods issues and receipts, customer and production order management, procurement, and interplant/intersite transport.

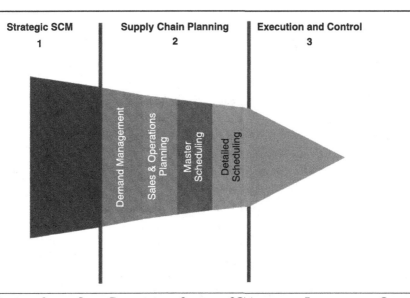

EXHIBIT 3.1 COMPLETE SUPPLY CHAIN DOMAIN FROM STRATEGIC SCM THROUGH EXECUTION AND CONTROL
APO and the other products of SAP SCM mostly address area 2, planning, with some spread into area 3, execution. In the latter case PP/DS, TLB, TP/VS, Deployment, and ICH all play various roles inside the execution horizon.

Integral to this domain-like division of the supply chain are related timelines; indeed, time is a fundamental demarcation of supply chain domain specializations. Strategic SCM is usually concerned with long-range planning, what is usually called the *strategic horizon*, that ranges from about one to five years into the future—essentially the length of time it takes to plan, open, and/or close entire sites or even commercial distribution channels to whole geographies. Supply chain planning completely or partially includes three time horizons. The mid-range horizon is generally treated as anywhere from 3 to 6, or 3 to 9, or 12 months out (i.e., generally based on the economic characteristics of that which is planned). Activities at this level of planning focus on demand forecasting and cross-plant, cross-geography manufacturing, and distribution coordination. As it assumes the outcome of strategic planning and passes into tactical planning, mid-range planning is usually the purest planning area.

Mid-range planning ends—or sometimes slightly overlaps—at a zone called *tactical planning*. The tactical horizon will generally be defined by "lead time," which is the amount of combined time necessary to acquire raw materials and consume those materials in the process of manufacture. Broadly speaking, this is usually from the current date out until about three months, though some notable exceptions arise for very large products such as ships, planes, large military or construction equipment, and so forth, all of which will obviously require a longer tactical horizon (see Exhibit 3.2).

Contained within the tactical horizon is the *execution* horizon, which is generally the length of time necessary to build and package either a single product, in the case of large products, or in the case of smaller durable and nondurable goods, entire product lots. In the majority of cases the tactical horizon will be three to five days, but frequently it may be as long as two weeks. The latter is especially the case where many organizations will seek to put a "lockbox" around a tactical horizon, thereby disallowing planning activities for

SCM Domain	Planning Specialization	Horizon	Range	Execution Scope	SCM Tools
Strategic	N/A	Strategic	One to five years	N/A	N/A
Planning		Planning	9 mo–1 yr	N/A	APO
	Demand	Mid-range	9 mo–1 yr		DP
	Sales & Operation Planning	Mid-range	6 mo–1 yr	N/A	SNP
	Master Scheduling	Tactical	6–12 weeks; longer	Procurement	SNP PP/DS ICH
	Detailed Scheduling	Execution	3 days–2 weeks; longer	Production	PP/DS
Execution and Control	Inventory, Logistics, and Distribution	Execution	3 days–2 weeks; longer	Distribution	N/A

EXHIBIT 3.2 SCM SPECIALIZATION DOMAINS, TIME HORIZONS, AND SAP SCM COUNTERPART TOOLS

several days or a week beyond execution to maintain as smooth a construction, package, and ship process as possible, in effect insulating this period and the manufacturing process from sudden spikes or troughs in demand.

Because of its lockbox structure, the execution horizon typically has a "hard" border with the tactical and mid-range horizons that abut it. In contrast, borders between other time horizons and their respective supply chain disciplines tend to be "soft." Consider demand forecasting, particularly long-range forecasting tapping into calendar zones as far as 10 to 12 months out (or more). From time to time this will run into changes impacted by strategic planning. A business planning opening operations in a new, far-off geography will have to contemplate demand adjustments from the strategic expansion within the planning space—within the space of APO. On the other side, the detailed scheduling (DS) tools of APO PP/DS in fact actually schedule and control production order assignments and executions at individual work centers within the execution horizon. ICH enables suppliers to view inventories and, depending on configuration, respond automatically to inventory troughs within the tactical horizon. Another caveat of the soft boundaries between horizons is that the execution horizon tends to refer to execution of manufacturing and packaging, while the tactical horizon is inclusive of execution of procurement. So while APO and its SCM counterparts remain primarily planning tools, they inevitably are strongly involved in day-to-day management of execution and control tasks.

The middle-space planning supply chain that we are concerned with consists of four major specialized SCM disciplines and several additional contextual data pipelines: (1) demand management, which is demand planning and forecasting in particular, (2) mid-range planning, including sales and operations planning, master scheduling, and capacity planning, (3) tactical planning, including procurement and production planning, scheduling, and integration with execution, and (4) logistics, which includes inventory management, distribution, and execution and control of transportation (Exhibit 3.3, area 1). Closely supporting these four specialized disciplines and spreading out into the larger, integrated data pipelines and feedback loops as well as the external supply chain that connects an organization with its customers and suppliers are (1) demand and supply signals for customers and suppliers (Exhibit 3.3, area 2), (2) order information to and from execution systems (Exhibit 3.3, area 3), and (3) archived data and other advanced, supporting analytics from a data warehouse/business intelligence solution (Exhibit 3.3, area 4). Together, the four SCM disciplines and their contextual data pipelines form a complete business problem ranging from supplier to customer and from data storage, reporting, and structure through physical execution. This wide, strategic problem is addressed together by APO DP, SNP (supply network planning) and PP/DS, SCM ICH, and BW, which in total form the scope of this text.

Putting Together the Big Picture

For a moment compare Exhibit 3.3 with 3.1 and note how the former is a detailed explosion of the middle of the latter, expanding to a more detailed level the pieces of the business picture we wish to address with SAP SCM. Next, compare Exhibit 3.3 with Exhibit 2.2 and note the close overlap of SAP SCM's applications with explicit problems and discipline areas that arise in the planning supply chain. Further compare

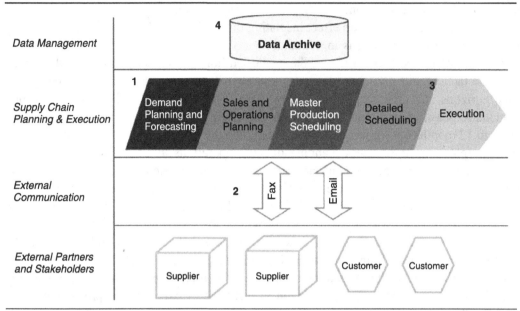

EXHIBIT 3.3   INTERNAL AND EXTERNAL SUPPLY CHAIN DATA LANDSCAPE OF SCM

these exhibits with the time horizons in Exhibit 3.4. Conducting this overlay is not just an academic exercise: SAP SCM, its applications and components, together present *an integrated supply chain solution.* To fully and appropriately exploit their integration, one must avoid the twin traps of becoming lost in an alphabet soup of modules or else becoming siloed in one tool or another. We can succeed here by staying well grounded first in the business supply chain that contextualizes SAP SCM's applications and modules and data pipelines, and second in the manner in which a particular module or application addresses the problems of the respective business area. As such, throughout this text we will repeatedly come back to Exhibit 2.2, using it as a map and anchor to inform us on specifically which part of the supply chain our current module or application addresses and as a guidepost to the modules, applications, and data pipelines that flow into and out of it.

APICS Supply Chain Domain	SCM APO Module
Demand Management	Demand Planning (DP)
Sales and Operations Planning (SOP)	Supply Network Planning (SNP)
Master Scheduling	Supply Network Planning (SNP)
	Production Planning/Detailed Scheduling (**PP**/DS)
Detailed Scheduling	Production Planning/**Detailed Scheduling** (PP/**DS**)
Execution and Control	Outside SCM APO (i.e., in R/3)

EXHIBIT 3.4   MAPPING APICS SUPPLY CHAIN DOMAINS TO APO MODULES

APICS Backdrop of APO Modules

SAP SCM products have always been designed to follow industrial standards and best-known methods. For a product-neutral elucidation of those standards, look to APICS (originally the American Production and Inventory Control Society, it recently renamed itself the Association for Operation Management, while keeping the APICS moniker).[1] As indicated, the supply chain domain specialization areas that concern us in the SAP SCM package include demand, mid-range planning, tactical and execution planning, as well as inventory and distribution management; in the case of this text, we are interested in the first three. The first area of demand management is relatively straightforward with a corresponding module in APO DP. The second area, mid-range planning, provides for a variety of possible solutions using APO.

APICS defines two planning areas for mid-range planning: sales and operations planning (SOP) and master scheduling. SOP is normally applied at a monthly level of detail to determine the overall objectives of an entire organization and then usually at a product family level of specificity; that is, it is a plan for many sites. The outcome of SOP is called a Production Plan.[2] Master scheduling may or may not look at data at a lower level of time-phased detail and may or may not look at products to a lower level of specificity than the product family. The outcome of master scheduling is a master production schedule (MPS), which may take one or more sites into account. The multiplicity of sites in master scheduling is typically concerned with supplying or subcontracting sites directly within the delivery routes for the products or product families addressed by the MPS.[3] Master coordination of parallel product groups and their respective sites is generally conducted at the SOP level. Both SOP and master scheduling must take procurement and outsourced manufacturing supplies and delivery schedules into account, so in each case they cannot be said to be strictly limited to production planning, but are inclusive of procurement, subcontracting, and internal production planning together.

Under APICS's delineations the next level of detail is detailed scheduling and then the actual execution and control of operations.[4] For this final level of detail, mapping to APO products is too relatively straightforward where detailed scheduling is covered by the *DS* tools of the PP/DS module. It is the entire middle zone of SOP and master scheduling where space opens up for interpretation by different organizations using APO. The activities of SOP, being organizational in nature, will almost always require the SNP module. Master scheduling in particular may prove tricky. Some aspects of master scheduling can and often should be done using SNP—in fact, the only way to make use of APO's powerful optimization tools for cross-site and internal-site schedule *generation* is by way of SNP. Nonetheless, PP/DS, in particular the *PP* or "Production Planning" part of PP/DS, provides heuristic planning run tools that operate at a lower level of detail than SNP, while also containing capabilities for cross-site planning, such as supplier and subcontractor planning within production routes. The result is an effective gray zone, where the higher levels of master scheduling will ordinarily and necessarily be conducted in SNP, while lower levels require employment of PP/DS.

PLANNING SUPPLY CHAIN DISCIPLINES
APO DP for APICS Demand Management and Forecast

At the earliest point in the supply chain, demand analysts are ordinarily concerned with constructing *unconstrained* forecasts—that is, forecasts of demand that seek to be the most accurate picture of demand possible without any constraints placed on the demand picture by supply or capacity limitations. Demand management is primarily a semistrategic "intelligence gathering" activity—that is, initially at least, it does not matter how many soldiers a Roman general can call upon to mount a defense against attacking Huns; regardless of the size of his army, just how large is that of Attila's? Similarly, without respect to known and unknown supply and capacity limitations, any organization will wish to know just how much demand exists or is likely to exist for its products or services. Filling this gap is demand planning and management.

Unconstrained demand is sometimes called *raw* demand. Generally there are two information flows that feed into this demand picture: (1) internal forecast, which itself may be qualitative or quantitative in nature or both, and (2) external orders and forecast, that is, actual forecasts or open orders from customers. Each demand source has strengths and weaknesses, and the active process of demand analysis entails leveraging off the strengths of both to minimize weaknesses and derive a best-case forecast.

Customer orders, for example, may initially be thought of as the best forecast; after all, customers are straightaway stating what they need or want. Certainly this seems better than a market-blind, statistical forecast, right? In fact that is not always the case. For one, the further one gets out in time, the more customers themselves are forecasting their own demand, and the forecasts they provide or the forward-looking orders they open will be subject to as much error as any forecast generated in-house, often more as customers often suffer biasing factors that may cause them to inflate forecasts. For example, in the interest of reserving capacity against other customers competing for the same capacity limits, customers may open larger orders now with the anticipation that they will reduce the orders as time approaches execution and their own demand flows tighten up. To boot, some customers are overly optimistic about their own sales prospects and others simply do not forecast very well.

In all such cases, statistical methods may be brought to bear to analyze and "judge" customer forecasts. *Judgments* may entail reductions to customer forecasts applied based on past performance; that is, some customers may be known to forecast more accurately than others. In other cases, experience may show that the closer the forecast to execution, the more accurate the forecast provided by the customer, and a time-phased multiplier may be applied to adjust forecasts lower the further they get out in time in order to reduce modifications as they are brought in closer in time. Finally, known market conditions may act as either a temper on or a driver to customer-provided forecasts. In the last case, for instance, a known market dip may drive an across-the-board judgment to reduce customer-provided forecasts while a steep market spike may trigger a similar across-the-board judgment to increase forecasts—all in advance of the customers' own provision for the increase, which may be delayed by communications frameworks.

Another common facet of demand analysis is aggregate forecasting. Ordinarily, while individual customer forecasts tend to be inaccurate, aggregate forecasts tend to be more accurate. This effect occurs because the net of some customers underestimating forecasts is offset by others who overestimate, leaving a relatively accurate total forecast. The same is true as it relates to the aforementioned judgment tactics. Thus a common forecasting strategy may follow these general steps:

1. Acquire all possible customer forecasts.
2. Aggregate customer forecasts to one geography-level or global-level forecast.
3. Apply a judgment based on known individual customer forecast accuracy to reduce (increase) the forecast proportionally to the amount provided by each customer.
4. Apply a judgment based on known time indicators to reduce (increase) forecasts across time—presumably making the most reductions far out in time and the least in the near term.
5. Apply a judgment based on known market conditions that may act to either increase or decrease the aggregate forecast.

Once customer forecast judgments are applied, additional statistical techniques may be brought to bear in a number of ways to further refine the forecast. Certain variables exclusive of customers may apply pressure on demand one way or another and their net effect can be analyzed statistically. Examples include:

- An upcoming marketing campaign (promotions)
- Cannibalization of an old product line by a new one (decreasing demand for an old product as a newer one ramps up, i.e., sales and discounts to relieve inventory pressure on the old while premiums are applied to maximize profits from the new)
- Introduction of a new product
- Introduction of a new product by a competitor
- Seasonal market shifts

Once a thorough demand analysis of customer and statistical forecast has been conducted, further work may take place that is rightly categorized under the broader aegis of demand management. First, how are customer forecasts themselves handled? Some companies will treat all forecasts as open orders—simply applying "firming" techniques as time closes in on an order due-date. Other companies may choose to represent forward-looking customer forecasts, such as those beyond one or two months, as requirements, allowing actual orders to be opened only once the demand becomes relatively proximate in time.

Often an organization's demand planning process will yield two separate values within the *execution horizon*, that is, the period during which orders become fixed because actual production is taking place to meet current demand. (This period usually will be between the current date and no more than three weeks in the future, but can be longer for highly sophisticated products such as boats and planes.) One value will be open and current orders from customers, which during the execution horizon are probably fixed or close to fixed and unavailable for change except due to special contractual allowances. The other will be the near-term forecast. Among other things, demand management usually entails choosing which value to schedule to, that is, providing answers to questions like this: Which value, current and fixed orders or forecast, should be fed to the master production scheduling process where it will result in purchase and production orders, production and purchasing that costs money, and where it will yield actual finished product ready for ship?

One may be tempted to assume that here, too, build-to-order would presumptively be the rule of the day, but that may not always be so. Short execution horizons may be two or three weeks in length; longer horizons may go on for months. Markets often surprise us and it is often gainful to be prepared for unexpected and highly welcome upsides. Last-minute "do you have any extra of this or that in stock?" orders are known to happen. If market trend and forecast data suggests that demand may be higher than customers are letting on in the short run, it is often beneficial to overbuild. Even if excess product is not sold immediately, it may often be put up for sale or else broken down and used for spare parts or engineering—mitigating mild overbuild costs and making the risk worthwhile.

Additionally, having aggregated demand forecasts to derive an optimal overall forecast and having applied judgments that may have the effect of reducing that overall demand picture, typically it will be necessary to renormalize the aggregate forecast back to individual customers, assigning a lower-judged forecast to the customer than the forecast the customer actually provides. This is a somewhat nuanced contrast to a *constrained* forecast, which is normally the output of supply network planning. A constrained forecast looks at strict supply and capacity limitations that may make it impossible to meet a judged customer forecast and reduces purchase orders and production orders according to what is physically possible. In contrast, a *judged* forecast is more of a way of assigning an analytically derived confidence to a customer forecast in order to limit allocations of limited supply.

For example, consider three customers that provide forecasts for 15,000 units, 20,000 units, and 12,000 units of a product for six months from now. The aggregate forecast for month 6 is 47,000 units. We may know that customers in this geography tend to overforecast 6 months out at an average of 5% each, so we may reduce the aggregate value to 44,650 units, 95% of the original aggregate. Having applied this aggregate judgment, we now have to redistribute the 44,650 that we are choosing to forecast for month 6 back to the three customers. Formulas for such redistributions will vary from case to case but may look at such factors as the customer's consistency, accuracy of forecast, and, of course, any contractual obligations we may have that might restrict or enable such judgments.

The DP module, as such, addresses perhaps the most analytical and least schedule-intensive aspect of the planning supply chain. Supply Network Planning, for example, will result in actual factory build schedules and interfactory ship schedules while Production Planning and Detailed Scheduling generates factory-line-specific build schedules. Demand Planning generates a time-series-based picture of demand, but it is not a schedule in the sense that production or purchasing will align directly to it; instead it is a time-phased forecast that will seed all subsequent scheduling.

As a primarily analytical tool, DP is where the BW data basis of APO is most apparent. Demand Planning users will need to familiarize themselves with the details of how APO stores data elements in "InfoObjects" and "InfoCubes." By way of a common user interface tool, the Planning Book, which is available to other APO applications, DP users may interact with demand data and apply macros for valuation and evaluation. Macros

Tool	DP-Specific	Application
Planning Book	No	User interface for analysis, application of macros, and quantitative analyses
Macro Builder	No	Construction of customized mathematical functions that may be applied by event-trigger or manually in the Planning Book
Data Aggregation	No	Grouping of data to apply aggregate analysis and judgment
Historical Forecast Analysis	Yes	Forecast procedure for deriving and applying trends to forecast data
Univariate Forecast	Yes	Single-variable forecast analysis
Multivariate Forecast	Yes	Multiple-linear regression for causal analysis of forecast
Composite Forecast	Yes	Combination of forecast methods
Lifecycle Planning	Yes	Application of data to derive effects of marketing promotions and cannibalization on product lifecycles

EXHIBIT 3.5   DEMAND PLANNING TOOLS IN APO DP

themselves may be custom built in the macro-builder. Exhibit 3.5 summarizes the tools available through DP to address organizations' forecast and demand analysis needs.

APO SNP for APICS SOP and Master Scheduling

The SNP module may be said to address two areas of the supply chain and it may do so together simultaneously or individually. Industrial standards regard SOP as the process of determining the business goals of an entire organization; usually that is *overall* production goals as they relate to demand. This has until recently been rather broadly defined as addressing broad goals rather than more detailed scheduling output by virtue of the fact that more primitive technology available prior to APO has been of little use to provide detailed multifactory, multiflow scheduling. Instead, organizations have tended to look at aggregate demand outputs of the demand planning cycle, consider known capacity limitations of entire factories, and then apply "goals" to factories to meet their demand. Meanwhile, master scheduling is the process of deriving an MPS for a product or given family of products based on demand as set against capacity and supply limitations at a given site or series of sites on a product or product family's production route. Sales and Operating Planning then usually addresses the operational, organizational plan for a group of factories and/or sites while master scheduling addresses the generation of a single-factory master production schedule.

Supply Network Planning certainly enables scheduling of individual-site master production schedules, but expands the scope of the local MPS to include space that historically has belonged to SOP goal setting. In other words, SNP empowers organizations not only to set generalized, geo-level or global-level *goals*, but to generate specific, global, multifactory *schedules*. The MPS in the SNP universe is no longer just an individual site's scheduled production plan to meet organizational objectives for demand closure, but it is part of a cross-site, cross-geography network MPS (nMPS). To fully understand SNP, therefore, we need to look at the goals and objectives of both SOP and master scheduling. Though broadly speaking it is accurate to say that SNP meets the needs of master scheduling, it is not accurate enough without comprehending that master scheduling techniques are now enabled through SNP to apply to the wider geographical scope of SOP, rather than the more narrow site-specific scope that has been their traditional venue.

Consider then the output of demand planning. First, note that we do not capitalize *demand planning* here to emphasize that, while ideal, it is not necessary to deploy APO DP and SNP simultaneously. Either solution may be deployed first, and while across-the-board deployment of APO to manage as much of the supply chain as possible is ultimately the best strategic plan, nonetheless a paced, sequential deployment, one module at a time, will almost always be the best delivery approach. This means that even organizations adopting APO will usually undergo temporary periods where non-APO tools address supply chain areas such as demand planning that may be best suited ultimately for APO.

Demand management was concerned with deriving the best *unconstrained* forecast—where *best* simply meant the most accurate advanced picture of demand possible given current information. The output of demand planning, therefore, is not necessarily feasible. It may, in fact, be entirely impossible. SOP as APICS sees it and SNP as SAP APO sees it are the co-equal points where constraints are introduced to planning. Supply network planning must concern itself with a number of consequent constraints that restrict our ability to fulfill demand. These typically fall into two categories: (1) capacity and (2) supply. From there constraint analysis and planning may break down into any number of subcategories.

Capacity constraints include maximum factory output of finished goods, but may be variable according to machine and labor availability and elasticity. Sometimes high-capacity machines are available, but unreliable. Sometimes labor is not immediately available, but sufficiently elastic that it can be ramped up substantially if three to six weeks are available to make adjustments. Supply capacity is subject to a number of factors, including the output potential and commitments of suppliers for raw materials, the capacity of the transportation lane and methods to move product from one place to another, as well as inventory shelf capacity and semifinished goods availability.

Supply network planning at an SOP level entails comparing unconstrained demand to *network* capacity constraints—that is, manufacturing dependencies between sites, constraints of overall factory or subcontractor output, and constraints on transportation lanes that move product. In contrast to earlier, more primitive enterprise resource planning (ERP) tools, which had to address each constraint separately, APO ANP combines all network constraints simultaneously to yield a cross-site, cross-geography, build-and-buy-and-ship schedule.

At an MPS level, SNP looks at an individual site or else just sites in a product or product family's production route and is concerned with constraints on raw materials and semifinished good supply availability, aggregate line output, and labor availability across time to yield single-factory output schedules. The APO SNP module may be employed for either or both cases of SOP and master scheduling. In the latter case it can

Tool	SNP-Specific	Application
Planning Book	No	User interface for analysis, application of macros, quantitative analysis, application of scheduling tools, derivation and publication of schedules
Macro Builder	No	Construction of customized mathematical functions that may be applied by event-trigger or manually in the Planning Book
Data Aggregation	No	Grouping of data to apply aggregate analysis and judgment
Heuristic Planning Run	Yes	Quantitative planning technique that applies rules to derive a schedule by accounting for inbound quota arrangements, priorities, and costs—does not account for capacity limits
Capable-to-Match	Yes	Quantitative planning technique that applies priorities to demand and transportation lanes, searches for stocks across a network, and determines whether material can be moved or must be built—it takes capacity into account to derive the first feasible production schedule
Optimization	Yes	Quantitative planning technique that employs linear programming and considers priorities, stocks, capacities, and relative costs to derive an optimal production schedule

EXHIBIT 3.6   TOOLS COMMON TO AN SNP DEPLOYMENT

take scheduling down to a daily level of detail, which may prove useful in constructing tactical schedules.

As with DP, SNP makes use of the Planning Book as a primary user interface and provides for development and application of custom macros that may evaluate and manipulate schedule-relevant data. But where DP is interested in determining the best picture of what will happen, SNP must apply constraints and determine what can or should happen. As such, SNP's toolset differs considerably from DP, with an emphasis on techniques that empower scheduling more than analytics. Exhibit 3.6 summarizes SNP's tools for applying network and site-level constraints to derive cross-site and single-site master production schedules.

Note that it is in the area of SNP applied to SOP and master scheduling that APO makes the most revolutionary changes to the methodology of supply chain planning. Prior to advanced planning systems, SOP and master scheduling could be characterized primarily as goal-setting and calendaring/scheduling activities. APO SNP brings computation power to both that raises their level of applied sophistication by several orders. To enable this computation, however, extensive supply network modeling is necessary. Objects that were, until the time of SNP, mostly help in the mind of production and procurement planners as the basis for largely qualitative goal and scheduling judgments, are now rigorously and systematically modeled in APO in order to bring powerful computation to bear in order to generate detailed, cross-site, cross-geography, forward-looking schedules that never before were possible. Supply Network Planning and its derivative module PP/DS, therefore, extend the specialization of planning to include the systematic computer mapping of a business planner's mind as it is applied to her or his craft.

PP/DS for APICS Master Scheduling and Detailed Scheduling

Demand planning derives a best available unconstrained forecast of future demand. Supply network planning uses the demand forecast as one basis for building a supply network or single-site master production schedule constrained by capacity and supply limitations. But within a site, as we fall inside the execution horizon during which inventory from purchase orders is actively being received and actual product is in the process of being built, day-to-day or hour-to-hour pressures and fluctuations at the level of individual workers, work centers, and storage locations require special, detailed attention. Hour-to-hour or moment-to-moment changes in actual facts on the ground at this level will persistently affect scheduling inputs to the system, and close person–system interaction is essential to attain optimal work execution-to-schedule.

The SNP module refers to the combined maximum capacity of individual resources or work centers within a site to derive a maximum site capacity and attempt to schedule an entire site optimally based on that maximum capacity. But when it comes time to build, if there are two or more work centers on which material can be built, specifically which work center should be used? Supply Network Planning, concerned as it is with optimally scheduling the entire site or supply network with respect to long-term demand pressure and constraining intersite supply flows, does not get down to this level of detail. When we are interested in optimally scheduling entire factories two or more months out in time, it usually is not necessary to know specifically which work center or production line inside each factory will do the work—it is only necessary to know that feasible capacity is available. One way of looking at this is to think of SNP as being tuned to plan for the best long-term, multisite schedule based at least as much on external as internal constraints.

Something is necessary, therefore, to tune more closely to planning the best short-term, single-site schedule based primarily, though not exclusively, on internal constraints. As we observe the special problems of a more detailed level of production scheduling, some more refined issues present themselves to us for resolution. For example, using PP/DS we can apply demand requirements, machine and labor capacity constraints, or supply availability limitations to a several-weeks-long production plan where specific orders generated by SNP are now assigned to work centers for manufacture. But within a much closer horizon, say three days, we may wish to apply limited optimization algorithms to obtain the best schedule possible from available resources and supply. Furthermore, where the system will provide optimization output as good as its input, at the level of hour, minute, and second it is almost impossible to feed computers with perfectly current and accurate information with which to schedule. As such, sometimes the controller on the ground will know that the system has quantitatively computed that only ten orders can be built on a specific work center on a specific day based on "virtual" facts and simulation—but she may nonetheless know that conditions are such that an eleventh can be squeezed in due to actual physical facts on the ground; that is, laborers may be particularly productive on a given day or may have an incentive to work a bit longer than the system is configured to compute their availability.

Observing these special requirements for shop floor scheduling, we can first begin to see why PP/DS is divided into two partial modules. The first aspect of PP/DS, production planning, addresses the overall short-term schedule and the day-to-day management of individual production and procurement orders and their resultant inventory. Production planning takes orders from SNP and assigns them to specific work centers or production lines, keeping production smooth with respect to daily capacity limitations and supply availability. Production planning is also usually thought of as encompassing actual order management—particularly exception management where it comes to highly automated systems like APO.

Typically the system will be configured to manage all or most order scheduling, but will highlight problem areas such as where specific production orders cannot be scheduled on time to meet the demand requirements they are assigned to fulfill or else are unsupported by the system's predictions of available supply. Production planners and procurement specialists alike will focus their energies on the "exception messages" or warnings generated by the production planning scheduling run and work to assure that orders are pulled in when possible or else customers are prepared for possible delays if they are not, and otherwise to assure availability of supply wherever possible.

While production planning is generally thought of as addressing a tactical horizon of two or three weeks, or in some cases as much as several months, detailed scheduling is concerned with immediate execution, what is generally called the execution horizon, and is ordinarily no longer than three to five days. Detailed scheduling applies extremely short-run optimization algorithms to the active build schedule and provides an optimization tool for doing so, but also encompasses the combination of human judgment. In detailed scheduling, system-based optimization is used in tandem with human judgment to carry out such activities as squeezing in orders even if the system does not recommend it either with the production planning scheduling run or with the short-run optimization algorithm.

SUPPLY CHAIN DATA PIPELINES

BW for Data Archiving, Analytics, and Reporting

We wish, of course, not to be redundant and to avoid repeating what we have already observed, and not to jump ahead to what we will later study as it regards BW. We must, nonetheless, appropriately address BW in its critical role in the overall supply chain data pipelines of SAP SCM. In doing so, we note these few, critical aspects of BW.

SAP BW has two major classes of features and is sold in two versions. Its feature classifications are data warehousing/archiving, as the name suggests, as well as advanced reporting and analytics, while its versions are: (1) enterprise and (2) data mart. In its enterprise version, BW is a standalone application that connects with other SAP applications via "data extractors." In its data mart version, BW comes as a bolt-on to other specialized SAP tools such as APO, CRM, and SEM. The fundamental choice involved in deciding whether to employ the data mart bolt-on or the enterprise deployment of BW, for users of SCM and APO, will hinge around data archive needs.

Insofar as BW is intended only for reporting and analytics, such as might be the case with an SNP or PP/DS deployment coupling with BW, then the data mart may suffice. Care should be exercised here in that sometimes this will not prove so and complex reporting and query generation may hamper the system that shares APO and BW. If planning computations are impaired by reporting queries, then a separate enterprise deployment of BW should be considered. For DP applications, which will employ BW's data archiving capacity in great detail, the decision is very clear-cut: Go with the enterprise deployment. In general, the rule to keep in mind is that SAP SCM will sit on a box/server that should be dedicated to planning. If BW can be employed without hindering APO's advanced planning run processing, by all means use the data mart. If planning run processing suffers, however, go with enterprise BW.

ICH and APO for External Collaboration

SAP SCM actually comes with two tools that enable external collaboration with customers and/or suppliers. For one, the application ICH, though presented in SCM, actually links SAP's R/3 product to an external-facing web tool that may be accessed by customers or suppliers. This can be employed for supplier-managed inventory processes whereby transactional inventory availability data in R/3 can be published through ICH to the Web. Alerts may notify the supplier when defined thresholds are met and otherwise the supplier may keep abreast of the inventory situation. The suppliers may then respond to inventory changes with notifications of what level of supply support they have available or, if enabled, they may actually generate supply plans that instantiate orders for fulfillment automatically in R/3.

Alternatively, collaborative planning is available through APO. Like ICH, collaborative planning operates by publishing SCM application data to an externally accessible web-based user interface. The difference is that while ICH provides a sophisticated web interface specialized for responding to transactional conditions in R/3, APO's collaborative features are focused on planning. Thus, the APO collaborative web user interface is based on the Planning Book. Therefore, where we may use ICH for cases of a conversation with a supplier that says "This is my situation: Can you replenish my suppliers?", we use APO collaboration to say "This may be my situation: Should we commit to this or that plan, and if we do, can you support it?"

CIF and XML: The SCM ↔ R/3 (ECC) Data Pipeline

There are two communications layers connecting the R/3 transactional ERP system with SCM: the Core Interface (CIF), and XML. We will go into details of each case later; minimally users and developers should understand that the CIF primarily connects APO with R/3, while XML is used for the ICH and more extensively connects R/3 with the external-facing web-user interface, by way of ICH, which is provided and configured in SCM. Note, however, that master data such as locations and products is shared between APO and ICH. Master data coming over to SCM through the CIF, therefore, is available to and will affect ICH.

INTEGRATED, WALL-TO-OUTSIDE-THE-WALL SUPPLY CHAIN SOLUTION

Adopters of SAP SCM buy into a veritable treasure-trove of supply chain power and that power is provided through two facets of the product: (1) its advanced capabilities and features and (2) its superior integration with the internal transactional supply chain and the external planning and transactional supply chains. Many adopters of APO will appreciate the first; indeed it is exactly SCM's advanced capabilities that move many to adopt it. Too many adopters of SCM are either mentally or strategically unprepared for the second. Not only will this lack of preparation result in a failure to fully exploit the products in SCM, but it may even become a stumbling block as organizations come to the tools prepared for a yacht-like sailing boat, but are presented instead with an enormous cruise liner.

Extraordinary pains have been taken in this text to carefully present and emphasize SCM as an integrated product, integrated as it is among its many modules, among its applications, among other applications critical to enterprise supply chain management, and between external parties. We do not wish the reader to understand SCM narrowly as simply an advanced toolkit for statistical demand forecasting, planning by way of linear optimization, or standard vendor-managed inventory. Our intent is to create adopters, users, and developers of the SCM products who fully appreciate it and exploit it as a complete, wall-to-wall-to-outside-the-wall, integrated supply chain management solution for the twenty-first century.

NOTES

1. www.apics.org.
2. American Production and Inventory Control Society (APICS). *Master Planning of Resources*. December 2001, pp. 1–7.
3. Ibid.
4. Ibid., pp. 1–4.

4

ADVICE TO THE EXECUTIVE CONSIDERING SAP APO AND SCM

Enterprise resource planning (ERP) projects lend themselves to a particular class of strategic decision-making errors. A thoughtful study of those errors will have value both to seasoned executive hands who have already pioneered the ERP hinterlands and to leaders still looking to take the great plunge into twenty-first-century information technology (IT) and supply chain management (SCM). For those who have been there before and who may have already bloodied themselves in difficult or even tumultuous projects, an objective sanity check will go a long way to reconnoitering with past misjudgments and re-navigating a fresh path forward. For those who have not yet started the journey, well, coming from behind, while not usually advisable as a deliberate strategy, is not entirely without advantages.

Stragglers can learn from the missteps of those who have gone before. SAP SCM is a new technology and its application, as the application of the wider practice of "supply chain optimization," has at times been rocky and fraught with misconceptions, mistakes, and poor judgment. Mature executives, project managers, and software engineers all know from painful experience the truth of this scholarly academic consensus: *Poor decision making at early stages dooms projects from the start.* As with most projects in business and engineering, there is an inverse relationship between outcome and its proximity: Decisions made at the most remote time from actual implementation, during a project's exploratory and planning stages, have the most impact on a project's likelihood of success or risk of failure. A good executive makes early decisions such that project heroism on the part of the rank and file, while always appreciated, is rarely necessary for project success.

It is always prior to project initiation or else during project planning that the big "executive" decisions that contribute most to ultimate success or failure are made. Though these are the "big money" decisions, both in that their outcome will have high costs and in that those making them are compensated relative to their great importance, unfortunately these decisions too often are poorly informed.

Consider some examples. Some executives choose not to move forward on advanced ERP systems because current operational planning methods have, until now, worked. Why rock the boat or fix something that is not broken? Others choose to adopt optimization techniques but to build their optimization software in-house. We have an IT staff; this is an IT project, right? Too often when the decision is made to use optimization and go with an outside provider, either pride (we're good enough) or fear (everyone else is already doing it!) inform the executive to charter too aggressive an adoption of a technology that does not just change the techniques of business, but changes the entire framework for business, inevitably setting slow-changing business culture against paradigm-shifting solutions. Finally, while powerful, optimization tools have become ensconced in hype that they do not and cannot entirely live up to, *humans are still required to run and plan business once APO (or any optimization solution) is adopted.* Success with APO entails rethinking the human/system arrangement, not replacing the critical and irreplaceable contributions that humans will continue to make once it is adopted.

SIX SHORT EXECUTIVE LESSONS IN ERP

The executive who thoughtfully bakes these lessons from past ERP experience and plentiful IT and SCM research into his strategic decision making will enjoy two likelihoods: (1) slow but real and substantial positive change (slower perhaps than the 12-month financial reporting cycle), and (2) success. Patience is often treated as a vice in today's competitive, fast-paced business environment, but two factors should give our hares some reason to take sides with the tortoises. First, ERP adoption is not a fad; it is a trend. We do not know exactly where this trend will lead, but we do know this: ERP is the ramp onto the freeway that leads to the future of business as we know it. It is time to get on the freeway. Second, as much as patience may be a vice, success is a virtue that more than overcomes. A successful ERP deployment—especially one of a highly configurable tool like APO—changes the nature of a company, delivers long-term constant return on investment, and positions an organization to dynamically navigate the data-driven, data-populous future. With a mind to success, consider six lessons every executive should account for in their ERP and/or APO adoption strategy.

Lesson 1: Start Using Optimization and Heuristics in Planning

Obviously in a book championing SAP SCM, we offer the strongest accolades and recommendations for the SAP SCM product and particularly for APO. But if you are not already using an ERP system for advanced planning and you have not decided to go with SAP APO, then we must urge you in the strongest possible terms: If not APO, adopt something! Effective, competing products are on the market and if you have not already adopted, you are at best driving on an access road, not yet ramped to the freeway of twenty-first-century supply chain planning where speed and dynamics are changing rapidly; meanwhile you are not even cruising to play.

In his February 13, 2001, testimony to the U.S. Committee on Banking, Housing and Urban Affairs, Alan Greenspan made reference to "new technologies for supply chain management . . ." that "perceive imbalances in inventories at a very early stage . . . and cut production promptly in response to developing signs of unintended inventory building." APO is just such a technology; indeed it is probably the vanguard technology for this new order. Can your business afford not to adopt it?

If your business organization follows a strict, systems-based, APICS-blessed operational planning procedure embracing demand analysis and planning, followed by master production scheduling, followed by materials requirements planning (MRP), then procurement and shop floor control, and completed by inventory management and distribution, then good! You are on the right road for best-known practices in SCM. But if that is all you are doing and you have not yet adopted advanced quantitative techniques for demand analysis, optimization, and heuristics for planning and procurement, then you are operating in the state of the art for 1995.

The IT revolution has changed the way business is done, and the change is not limited to monitors on every desktop and PDAs in every satchel. Even SAP itself has changed, and if you are running your operational planning on 1995 standards, you may not be up to date with everything that has happened in the ensuing ten years at SAP with its newer classes of software (or even with its competitors for that matter). SAP products today are not your granddad's SAP. SAP products like APO, Netweaver, and BW carry little of the old, mainframe-like clunkiness that SAP detractors have been so fond of criticizing. Modern off-the-shelf SAP products rely on visual objects and Internet connectivity and are truly highly configurable.

But that is not why you need to take the decision of adopting APO or similar products seriously. Besides keeping up with the state of IT, the business of the SAP company is to keep up with the state of SCM. A new workforce is brewing: a workforce prepared to use composite forecast analysis in demand planning, a workforce expecting to apply optimization via simulation to plan entire supply networks and to derive manufacturing production and materials delivery schedules. Your competitors will have access to this workforce and the tools they are trained to use. As these tools evolve, your competitors will already stand on their platforms, ready to take simple evolutionary steps into a highly efficient future. Already on the freeway, they will not have to take risky, revolutionary jumps just to get to start. State of the art, 1995, may work for you today, but it will be an intolerable weight to bear in 2015. How long will you let the future pass you by before you get on board?

Lesson 2: Do Not Do It Yourself

What is your business specialization? Manufacturing tires? Distributing materials to home builders? Supplying hospitals? How many PhDs in operations management with specializations in demand forecasting are on your staff to keep up to date with the latest trends, indeed to participate in, evaluate, and lead in the latest research? How many university supply chain programs and think-tank organizations does your company maintain close relations with? Of the computer systems engineers, system analysts, and business analysts on your staff, how many of them are experts on the algorithms used to apply univariate forecasting and multiple-linear regression? For that matter, how many on your staff are familiar with algorithms used to conduct linear optimization programs? Or, if you have mathematicians in your ranks familiar with these tools, are they crossover specialists in SCM and operations planning who are well qualified to decide which variables properly feed these algorithms outside the perfect mathematical abstract, but in the universe of the practical?

Perhaps they can rely on business people in your organization to tell them what those variables are. That will work, of course, but what they still will not know is what variables to include that your business people perhaps are ignoring because they themselves are not up on the latest research and best-known methods. You ignore the current state of research at your company's peril.

If you are even considering ERP, then knowing nothing else about your organization we can be sure it makes ample use of spreadsheets. Yet you outsource spreadsheet design to Microsoft and some of its competitors. You would never dream of assigning your in-house IT staff a spreadsheet development project. What an obvious waste of precious resources!

Face it, you are in the business neither of software engineering nor of supply chain research; SAP, and its competitors, are. Leave the science of forecasting and optimization to the scientists. Outsource advanced software development to companies that specialize in software engineering. For your part, focus on what you *can* do right: Hire staff that can learn your business, competently evaluate off-the-shelf tools, and adapt the complex models employed by those products to models, simulations, and computational planning runs that best enable your business.

You are not convinced, and still think that internal development is the right road? Consider the following two questions: (1) Can your internal IT organization be asked to deliver the following combination of goods: (a) a software package for supply chain planning (like APO) containing all of the most advanced best-known methods for analysis and planning in demand management, supply network planning, as well as production and procurement planning and execution, (b) another software package that enables seamless communication of your demand signal from your customer, through your internal organizations, out to your suppliers (like Inventory Collaboration Hub (ICH)) and of your supply signal from your suppliers back into your planners, buyers, and automated scheduling tools, and (c) still another package, integrated with the above two, that uses radio frequency identification (RFID) to track material at any event-stage in its lifecycle including staging, shelving, de-shelving of raw materials and parts, consumption of parts, production and storage of finished goods, packaging, shipping, transit-points, and deliveries (like Event Management)? (2) If your company or organization had this technology in place running its supply chain, would you expect to experience a competitive advantage with a concrete and noteworthy return-on-investment for your troubles?

SAP SCM is expensive, but so are IT departments. We know this: You are paying for an IT department. Is your IT department developing new technology all on its own when it could be employed to adopt, configure, and deliver a ready-made, off-the-shelf, comprehensive supply chain solution worthy of giants and supply chain success stories like UPS and Wal-Mart? What would you pay for a supply chain system that rivals that of UPS? Maybe it's time to take a look at SAP SCM. Take a look, and find out what is in it for you; do it for your stockholders.

Lesson 3: Succeed through Evolution; Foster Chaos through Revolution

Once the decision is made to go with an ERP system the temptation to go too fast is too often excruciating. ERP systems, especially systems like APO, require cultural changes and culture changes slowly. There is a storied history of ill-fated ERP projects for off-the-shelf software from companies as varied as PeopleSoft, Oracle, JD Edwards, and SAP alike, and for SAP products from R/2 to R/3 to APO and the whole line of new-generation modules. Look at any one of the trouble cases and almost every time there will be a common denominator: too aggressive adoption.

With R/3 there was a built-in temptation to adopt aggressively since the greatest power of the tool was integration: seamless system access from HR through customer order management through planning through manufacturing through procurement through inventory management. SCM, while integrated internally among its many applications and modules and externally with R/3, does not necessitate or even overtly encourage overaggressive adoption. SCM's applications modules are wholly capable of standalone deployment and in almost all cases should be deployed standalone *initially*, with disciplined, deliberate, and cautious follow-up deployments.

There is little science to prove it, but widespread anecdotes from armies of SAP experts and consultants would seem to support that the greatest success will be with initial deployments of either Demand Planning (DP) or Production Planning and Detailed Scheduling (PP/DS). Deploy either, with either one going first, then deploy the other. Do it one-at-a-time, and be successful each time. Target deliberative, professional success, not heroism. Create an SCM success story and follow it up with another one, firmly placing two modules on either side of the most difficult area: Supply Network Planning (SNP). If yours is a multi-arm, multidivision company, deploy at smaller or less complicated divisions first, then grow outward. Make yours a company where all roads do lead to SAP, but acknowledge that many or most parts of the company are still on the road; we will not arrive with a Big Bang. On the contrary, Big Bang projects will probably just foment chaos. While on this inevitable intermediate stage, learn to drive the highways before getting on the freeway. Set realistic expectations and proceed to achieve them.

Lesson 4: Crawl before Walking; Walk before Running

This element of advice applies specifically for SNP deployments and loosely for PP/DS and Transportation Planning/Vehicle Scheduling (TP/VS) deployments, the latter of which is not covered by this text. This, too, is advice that at least should be stated in every SNP class, but simply: Crawl before you walk; walk before you run. Too many organizations will buy SAP SCM and use APO for its powerful optimization features and thereby insist on an immediate charge to the most sophisticated deployments. Supply Network Planning comes with three engines for conducting supply chain planning runs to generate master production schedules and build plans: heuristics, capable-to-match (CTM), and the optimizer. These three tools increase in complexity in that exact order, with the optimizer being a very sophisticated proposition. Furthermore, it is entirely commonplace, and very often totally necessary, to deploy a combination of heuristics/CTM or heuristics/optimizer in a goal-state planning solution.

Do not fool yourself. Optimization is extremely complicated to model, configure, deploy, understand, and use. For many organizations the paradigm shift from highly manual, sequential, and iterative circa-1990s supply chain planning to twenty-first-century supply chain planning with simultaneous planning runs constitutes a leap that is more like that of going from high school to a PhD program. Since the unrelenting march of progress has not provided you or your employees with time to get "undergraduate" degrees, you will have to create the time yourself. Your organization can and will get up and off the ground in APO SNP using heuristics in the short order—think of the heuristics-only phase as an undergraduate education in twenty-first-century supply chain planning. Do that first, and ideally, do *only* that *for awhile*. Give your team—your user community, modelers, analysts, and engineers—time to absorb and get comfortable with APO and system-based planning, then let them go for optimization when they are ready for it and when they have come far enough along psychologically to really appreciate the means and methods they have at their fingertips with APO. Optimization is so powerful that once it is deployed right you will see powerful returns—but the operative word is *right*. Do it right, later; enjoy success, do not pay for mistakes—do not do it wrong now.

Lesson 5: A 98% Solution—Only God Knows the Value of 200 Cost Constraint Variables

The goal of supply chain planning is to plan for the future: Maximize product available to sale while minimizing unsold inventory. There is a difference between planning for the future and knowing the future. APO brokers in planning, not in knowing. There are only three sources one can go to if one wishes to *know* the future: fortunetellers, snake-oil salesmen, and God. With the first, we get what we pay for. With the second, some organizations may be willing to shell out millions to the software provider or consultant who offers a 100% supply-chain solution, but as the proverb goes, "fool me once, shame on you, fool me twice. . . . " As to God: God isn't talking. Indeed, most religious institutions hold that the Almighty quite deliberately puts a veil over our eyes, preventing us from seeing or knowing what the future holds in store. Charlatans and snake-oil salesmen may not respect that veil, but science, oddly enough, does, and APO is a product of science.

APO cannot tell us the future. The goal of applying APO is to have what one manager has called a "98% solution." An organization that has fully deployed APO or APO-like tools does not aim to have inventory available-to-sell 100% of the time while never having expensive overstock. No; we seek to use APO so that 98% of the time we have promised inventory available to our customer while maintaining reasonable and relatively inexpensive inventories. From time-to-time, even with APO, we must set aside science and engage in good-old-fashioned business dealing because we have too little supply to meet current demands or else because we overstocked and need to unload.

Use of a tool such as APO leads to a sort of temptation that, while often very strong in the trenches of any given IT/SCM project, should nonetheless be obviously suspect to any commonsense reckoning. APO allows its users to model hundreds of supply chain rules and costs to derive an optimal outcome. It is sometimes tempting to think of APO as a sort of artificial intelligence, commandeering site and multisite scheduling with its computerized model of the supply chain—but while not wholly inaccurate, this would be to take the analogy too far. The analogy that we prefer is to regard APO as a global weather simulator, only for the supply chain, not for climatic conditions.

This analogy, too, while considerably more accurate than one of artificial intelligence, carries some limitations. Understanding how much of the analogy applies and just where it stops will go a long way to understanding exactly what APO is and is not. Where weather simulators are global in reach and may be specific in application, so, too, is APO global in reach (i.e., DP and SNP) and specific in application (i.e., PP/DS and TP/VS). Where weather simulators are system-based abstract models of external, physical constructs and conditions (the weather), APO is a model, too, of the supply chain. Where weather simulators execute simulative run after run to generate most-likely predictions of weather changes, APO similarly executes statistical runs that seek to predict demand conditions, but goes further to execute planning runs that schedule supply chain activities: buying, moving, and building.

Note, though, that all weather simulators have one model to simulate: the earth. Hence all people involved in weather simulation, all over the earth, are working on the same model. A vast network of interconnected land, sea, and space-based observatories has been set up, all about the corners of the planet, which work to continuously collect and report on changing weather data points: temperatures, barometric pressures, humidity, and so forth. All of these feed into vast computer programs at major weather centers to generate the most up-to-the-minute weather simulations.

Nothing like this is available to any business organization. So while we may note that APO does allow almost any number of rules to be applied and costs to be maintained in the modeling of a business, even this abundance of variables does not approximate the thousands that go into weather modeling. Furthermore, we may reiterate that all weather models model the same thing: earth's climate. SAP has *not* included hundreds of rules and costs in APO so that every business deploying the tool will use every variable it provides. On the contrary: SAP does not even expect any given business to use so much as a plurality of rules and costs available in the tool—to do so is a misuse.

The reason SAP has included so many rules and costs in APO is the difference between APO and a weather simulator: APO may be applied to almost any for-profit, nonprofit, commercial, or government organization. From organization to organization, needs will vary widely and SAP has no way of knowing which rules and costs will be most applicable to any particular deployment instance, so SAP provides as many as possible to make sure they're there for every customer that needs them.

We do not seek to use APO as a replacement for human thinking, or even as a comprehensive abstract model. Instead, APO is an exception-based system. If readers take nothing else away from this text, they must receive this message: *APO is intended to enable exception-based planning.* In a properly run APO project, analysts and consultants will study a business organization's needs and compare them to rules and costs available in APO. From this study they will elicit a small number of rules and costs that will allow the tool to conduct some 75 to 85% of planning automatically and they will configure APO to generate exception messages—alerts—for when conditions arise that are not suited to automatic planning. Those alerts are then monitored by buyers, planners, and supply chain managers who apply qualitative, human judgment and take appropriate action, meanwhile giving the system instructions on how to handle the exceptions and responses.

With this intended use of APO in mind, consider that some organizations have made the nearly inexplicable decision to use hundreds of rules and cost options in their application of APO—and always with results that invite dismay. To use APO this way, among other things, simply goes against common sense. Unless we have 24-hour automated satellites and monitors in place at strategic locations all around our global supply chain, then it would take a small army to keep track of all of these variables and maintain their constant values in APO. Even to take a one-time snapshot would not only be expensive, but most likely impossible. Odds are that God alone knows 200 cost-based data points about a business at any specific point in time. Even if a business analyst set about interviewing all the relevant employees to learn the values of 200 such variables, by the time she finished her survey, some of the values would have changed. With APO as our 98% solution, let us make the following our objective:

The combined DP forecast, SNP global master production schedule, and PP/DS site schedules ought to result in small, inexpensive inventories that, while frequently dipped into to fulfill customer product demands on time—such as when forecasts are off or raw material deliveries are late—are nonetheless rarely depleted to zero. With the above definition of success, how accurate must a demand forecast be: 60, 70, or 80%? How much inventory is small and inexpensive: 10, 15, or 30 days? Answers will vary from one company to another. The more accurate the forecast, the fewer days of inventory are necessary. Our goal is neither to achieve a 100% accurate forecast nor to have such massive inventories as to always have supply available—overstock discard or scrap in effect. Avoiding inventory scrap is not an entirely selfish proposition. Excess industry costs money that is not offset by sales. At best, that cost is passed along to customers; at worst it will drive a company out of business. Customers are hardly well served by a business that maintains such high stocks that it always delivers on time, but runs itself out of business doing so.

Our goal, therefore, is to maximize product available for sale while minimizing unsold stock, knowing full well that from time to time we may have to ask a supplier or factory to expedite an order to provide to a customer on time (which may sometimes be costly), or else apply other techniques when expedite is impossible, like asking the customer to take 10% now and 90% later, or to take a substitution, a discount, or a delay.

Optimization is the notion of coming up with the best plan given constraints; it does not deliver the best *ideal* plan. To apply optimization is to get serious about the fact that ideal is not real; we cannot have our cake and eat it, too. A good heuristic planning run will have as many as 8 business rules and never more than 12. A good optimization run will apply as many as 15 costs, but much more realistically only 5, to achieve the goal of automation for 75 to 85% of cases, applying Alert Monitors to signal to human users that intervention is necessary to plan the rest. Apply APO to achieve business seriousness about making promises you can keep to your customers because constraints are well understood and then building goodwill with those customers by making good on the well-made promises. If that is not good enough for your organization and you will settle for nothing but perfect planning with 100% accurate forecasts and zero or near-zero inventories, neither APO nor this book is for you; you need look no further than the astrological horoscope in the local newspaper.

Lesson 6: Human Glue—Reality Is Art and Craft; Fantasy Is Science Fiction

Repeat these words to yourself, slowly: Optimization solves problems; optimization *does not* solve supply chains. Whatever you have read in journals, heard at conferences, or been told by academics or salespeople alike, you *cannot* optimize a supply chain. Do not let a salesperson tell you this; do not listen to an academic who tells you this; kindly and supportively correct a recent MBA graduate who tells you this. Worry about a consultant who tells you this. You *can* and should apply optimization to plan a quantitatively, qualitatively better supply chain than the one you currently have, but no more than there is a supercomputer simulation of global weather patterns that accurately forecasts the weather is there an ERP software system that will apply math to an abstract model to spit out a solution that optimizes a real-world, physical supply chain. What you already do not believe to be true of the weather, do not believe to be true of the supply chain.

That said, it is not for nothing that every meteorological organization relies heavily on computer-based weather simulations, and the same tools they apply to model and predict the weather are now available to you, via SAP APO, to model, simulate, and effectively plan your business. Those are tools we have already visited: statistical forecast, linear optimization, and heuristics. But understand that the product of those tools is not by itself an optimized supply chain; it is data that will enable analysts, schedulers, and planners to do better supply chain planning. Similarly the product of weather forecasting software is not by itself an accurate forecast, but it is excellent information that a meteorologist uses together with other tools, including his or her own studied reasoning, to derive an accurate forecast.

SAP APO is not artificial intelligence and is not a replacement for people. On the contrary, it does not so much replace people as it both changes and elevates their role in the planning process by providing software that does more of what computers do best—compute—thereby allowing people to do more of what they are unique for—reason. As much as we would like to believe that we have achieved a sort of computational Holy Grail that produces perfect demand forecasts and optimized factory schedules and interfactory/intersite delivery schedules, such a mythical creature remains in the distant future. As with the weather, there are too many variables to model to rely on a computer to get this right. Just as with the weather, we gain the most traction by allowing the computer to do what it does best—compute—and then taking the formulaic output of the computer as a major input to the reasoning applied by an experienced human who uses it to derive a best total conclusion.

As such, with the three primary planning modules of SAP APO, there are three corresponding ways a company can go wrong, making too much of its capabilities, too little of the art, craft, and reasoning capacity of the human intellect, and setting the stage for an inevitable cultural collision wherein APO may appear to be the loser, but the biggest losers are anyone with a stake in the success of the organization:

1. *With Demand Planning.* Failure to allow demand analysts the ability to apply final judgment to the forecast outputs
2. *With Supply Network Planning.* Failure to allow master schedulers or supply network analysts the ability to apply final judgment to intra- and interfactory build plans or master production schedules

3. *With Production Planning/Detailed Scheduling.* Failure to allow production plan-
    ners, production schedulers, and factory schedulers the ability to apply final judg-
    ment to interfactory tactical production schedules

In each of these three cases, the decision to remove final judgment of schedules from the
human role responsible for their output is both common to APO adopters and misguided.
Just as a meteorologist may be able to look out the window and draw a conclusion
that, though overcast, it is not raining as the simulation says it should be, your demand
analysts may be able to look at the output of a statistical run and know, because they
have a telephone and a relationship with your customers, that a large order is on its
way regardless of where the regression line leads. Just as a meteorologist may look at
a simulation that says there should be skin-baking record heat today but tempers that
forecast with input from the almanac on his desk and the live thermometer on his porch
that today just will not be so hot, no matter what the simulations say, your master
schedulers may know that a certain transportation line tends to be very reliable even
though its cost of use may be ungainly high, and getting a certain valuable order for a
certain valuable customer just right is probably worth the payout. Just as a meteorologist
may know, despite the weather simulation forecast that tells us skies should be sunny
and blue, that beachgoers should still flee to higher ground because a nearby earthquake
probably just set off a tsunami, your production schedulers may know that even though
the system says capacity is right for an unusually high order load on a particular line this
week, there is a particular laborer assigned to that line who is just not as high-output as
the average or normalized yields maintained in the computer imply.

Finally and most important, just as no serious twenty-first-century meteorologist would
rely exclusively on thermometer, barometer, almanac, and naked eye to predict tomorrow's
weather, but would put to use the best of computer simulation and satellite observation, similarly no serious business relying on well-managed supply chains for execution should be
doing without the best software available to model its product lifecycles and global and local
supply chains, and employ simulation, statistics, optimization, and heuristics to solve the
specific, quantitative supply chain problems that are most subject to computation.

PROFILE OF AN SAP SCM PROJECT WITH A HIGH LIKELIHOOD
OF SUCCESS

With a mind to where others before us have gone wrong, consider four rules that may
help to steer strategic decision making in a direction of high-success likelihood rather
than risk mitigated only by the heroic efforts of an IT staff and highly compensated
consultants. If we put these four rules together, a consensus profile takes shape for the
successful SAP SCM project:

1. *The company has made an organizational commitment to adopting simulation,
    statistics, optimization, and heuristics.* You would not rely on a newscast that
    insists on predicting the weather using state-of-the-art, circa-1965 technology; why
    on earth would you be willing to run your business on technology and methods
    that became obsolete ten years ago? It isn't enough that your supply chain planners
    have computers on their desks with access to spreadsheets and databases; nor is it

enough that they are certified in APICS or that they can be reached by cell phone and download recent e-mail to their wireless PDAs in real-time. The company, from top down, believes in using state-of-the-art technology, and state-of-the-art technology is technology that uses state-of-the-art methods, in the case of supply chain planning: simulation, statistical forecasts, optimization, and heuristics.

2. *The company has decided to go with an outside provider of software.* The rationale for this is widely publicized, widely understood, and enjoys broad, consensus agreement. No one has a PhD in spreadsheets, yet it is patently obvious that you should outsource coding for spreadsheets to Microsoft or some other able competitor. Thousands have PhDs in SCM, operations management, decision sciences, and decision systems. They are not working in your IT department. Hire people in IT who can run, administer, and configure the software for your company. Hire people in the business who understand and can employ all the software's powerful tools to greatest effect. Specialize in your specialty; leave the research to researchers.

3. *A strategy of gradual, modular deployment is in place.* Quentin Tarrantino's watershed project, *Pulp Fiction*, attributes to a character, Marcellus Wallace, some sharp words about pride and the destitution to which decisions based on pride can lead (words we dare not directly quote lest we offend). The spirit of those words, however, is right on. Let success and the realization of success, not pride, guide you. SAP APO, with its mutually independent modules, lets you take it slow, deploying in a deliberate, system module-by-module, company division-by-division fashion. Enjoy the option: Take it one-at-a-time; tackle low-hanging fruit first—single-division DP, single-site PP/DS, multiple-site PP/DS, and then, and only then, divisional SNP. Surround the toughest target, cut it off, move in for the kill. Before you know it you will have an integrated supply chain operating from forecast through delivery using state-of-the-art planning tools and you will be well placed to quickly deploy the dynamic, evolutionary advances that are continuously being developed by supply chain specialists at companies like SAP.

4. *A detailed vision for doing business with the tool has been created in cooperation with those who will use it.* This vision assigns new roles to software and to business professionals who will continue in new, value-added capacities once the software and business changes are in place. A future where artificially intelligent computers apply strictly quantitative techniques to derive formulaic and absolutely correct decisions and solutions is a fantasy of science fiction, not a real future. We see no future where computational technology is a suitable replacement for art, craft, and the intangible, qualitative contribution of human intellect and judgment. SAP APO does not so much replace humans as it elevates them. We would neither rely exclusively on a computer for weather forecast, nor ignore those vital computational simulations of weather when deriving our own, more qualitatively informed forecasts. SAP APO provides forecast analysts, supply chain planners, master schedulers, and production and factory schedulers all access to the same powerful tools meteorologists now use to simulate and predict the weather, and in so doing elevates them just as meteorologists are so elevated. Do not aim to replace your human staff; aim to teach them to employ these new, powerful tools to their full utility.

2

STOCKS AND BASES: MASTER DATA SCM

5

SUPPLY CHAIN MANAGEMENT MASTER DATA

In this chapter we will examine supply chain management (SCM) master data in particular and work out the steps required to model supply chain networks and factories in SAP APO. All SAP APO projects entail the custom modeling of a business or organization's supply chain, and the supply chain master data expresses the components of that architectural model. Several different modules of SAP APO directly exploit the master data architecture. Supply Network Planning (SNP) employs master data to optimize cross-factory, cross-geography production, purchase, and delivery schedules. Production Planning/Detailed Scheduling (PP/DS) uses much of the same master data but at a more detailed level to specifically optimize individual factory production schedules. Transportation Planning/Vehicle Scheduling (TP/VS) relies on much of the same data to optimize logistics and delivery. For its part, Demand Planning (DP) operates at a more abstract level of forecast analysis than the concrete supply chain components discussed here and generally stays within the realm of the data objects discussed in Chapter 6.

The following examples will create master data for a fictitious supply chain network, with its factories and vendors, that specializes in producing and supplying products for practitioners of Traditional Chinese Medicine, such as herbs, acupuncture needles, vacuum cups, and so forth.

LOCATIONS AND CALENDARS

Locations constitute the foundation of both general and detailed models alike (i.e., SNP versus PP/DS, respectively). They are concerned with both *where* work is done and *between where* the products of work must be moved and delivered. Many location types may be necessary to meet the needs of different supply chain models, each with individualized specializations and particularities. SAP APO comes preconfigured to permit modeling of the following sites, to each of which it applies a specific location type number:

1001 Production plant
1002 Distribution center
1005 Transportation zone
1006 Stock transfer point
1007 MRP area
1010 Customer

1011   Vendor
1020   Transportation service provider
1030   Terminal
1031   Geographic area

Locations may be established directly in SAP APO by way of the location master data transaction, or else if they are plants, vendors, or customers they may be Core Interfaced (CIF'd) from SAP R/3. Most organizations using both R/3 and APO should employ the CIF to establish location master data for plants, vendors, and customers as well as for subset master data such as work centers. Nonetheless, a detailed familiarity with the settings of locations inside APO is essential both to successful employment of the CIF to establish locations as well as to fine-tuning location settings to their successful application by APO modules. Detailed instructions for using the CIF to transfer locations and other data elements from SAP R/3 are provided in Chapter 7.

The location master data transaction lies on the general master data supply chain menu following the path *Master Data → Location → Location* (see Exhibit 5.1). As is common to most SAP interactive transactions, the location transaction has three modes: Create, Display, and Change. In addition to these common modes the transaction also has two features specific to APO: Set Planning Version and Assign Model (see Exhibit 5.2).

When creating a location from scratch in APO, enter the location code in the location field (see Exhibit 5.2, step 1). Many organizations use a plant coding convention with

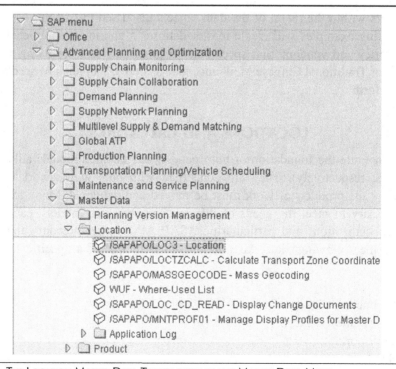

EXHIBIT 5.1 THE LOCATION MASTER DATA TRANSACTION IN THE MASTER DATA MENU
© SAP AG. Used with permission.

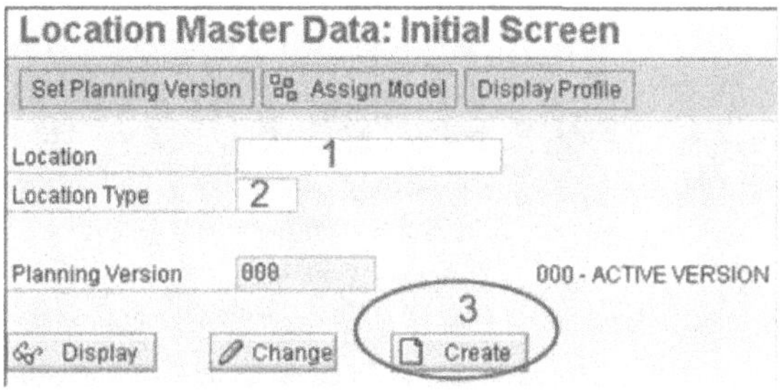

EXHIBIT 5.2 LOCATION MASTER DATA INITIAL SCREEN
© SAP AG. Used with permission.

a four-digit code containing two letters to specify an approximate geography and two numbers to uniquely identify the site. For example, a manufacturing site in China that compiles, builds, packages, and ships medical products for Traditional Chinese Medicine (TCM) may be indicated as CS20: C for China, S for site, and 20 to uniquely identify it from other China sites. To make this location a production plant, enter 1001 in the location type field (see Exhibit 5.2, step 2). Finally, to actually enter screens for creating the location, click the Create button (see Exhibit 5.2, step 3).

Once through the initial screen, a tabular menu of location-specific settings categories displays: General, Address, Calendar, TP/VS, Resources, SNP, and Addit (see Exhibit 5.3). The first tab displayed is the General tab, which itself has six sections: External Location Short Text, Identifier, Geographical Data, Location Priority, Administration, and Partners.

Location

Header and General Tab

The header will display the plant and location type information already entered on the initial screen as well as a description field and a planning version field, which at this point will be empty. Type the detailed plant name in the description field (see Exhibit 5.3, step 1) but do not take action at this time with the Plng version (Planning version) field, which in any case the system assumes to be "000" and disables editing. Later on, once all the settings for the location have been entered and validated, you will assign the location to a planning version.

No direct editing by the user is possible in the External Location Short Text section. If the CIF interface is used to create or update the location, the system will autopopulate these fields itself. The system enters the R/3 plant code in the Ext. Location field, which will ordinarily remain the same name as the APO plant code from the header, and it enters APO in the Bus. Syst. Grp. field (see Exhibit 5.3, step 2). This field controls the logical grouping of systems sharing master data, which are typically R/3 and APO clients. In the Administration section, if the location is created from scratch, the name of the user who logged in to create the location will display in the Created field with the date of creation; otherwise, if the CIF is used, the field is autopopulated with the term "CIFUSER" (see Exhibit 5.3, step 3).

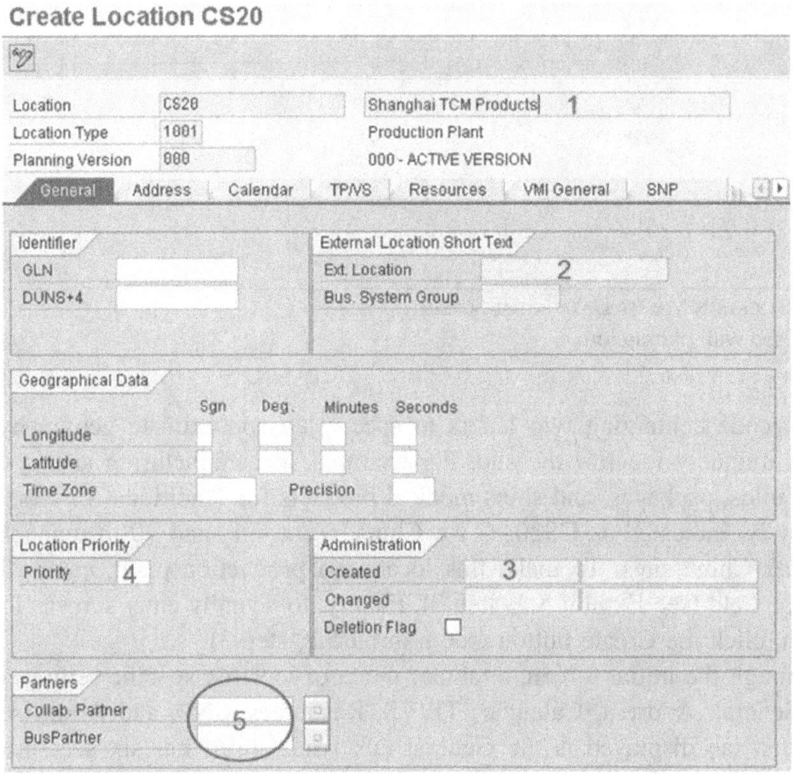

EXHIBIT 5.3 LOCATIONS TRANSACTION GENERAL TAB
Usually external location data on this tab comes in from the CIF or is autopopulated. Geographical data may be maintained to support the supply chain cockpit, but is better maintained from the SCC transaction itself. © SAP AG. Used with permission.

The only essential field in the Geographical Data section is the time zone of the location. The actual latitude/longitude coordinates of the location may also be entered here, and if they are they will display on the map properly in their use for SNP in the Supply Chain Cockpit (SCC). Once supply chain master data objects are created as described here, the SCC, the use of which is described in detail in Chapter 8, can be employed to see and visually work the details of complicated supply chain networks of locations, transportation lanes, and their products (see Exhibit 5.4).

The Location Priority section of the General tab has only one field, Priority (see Exhibit 5.3 step 4). This field may be used by SNP for one of its planning solve methods, Capable to Match (CTM), and by TP/VS. In CTM it is simply a processing priority, where the higher the value the lower the priority. Zero, therefore, is the highest priority. A nonentry in this field is interpreted by the system as a zero. Transportation Planning/Vehicle Scheduling uses this field as a guide to the priority of a cost profile where priorities equate to assignments of penalty costs for late delivery or nondelivery.

Finally, the Partner section of the General tab may be used if you chose to design a collaboration process, whereby several different users conduct specific parts of the supply chain analytical process (Exhibit 5.3, step 5). In such a process, various business

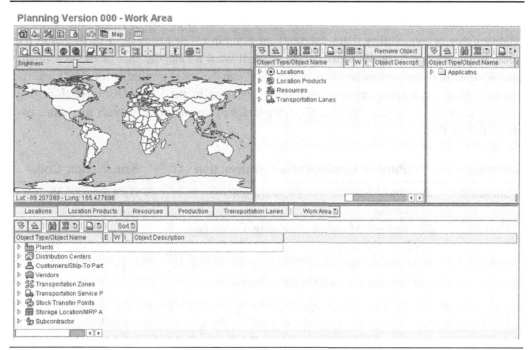

EXHIBIT 5.4 THE SUPPLY CHAIN COCKPIT

Addressed in detail in Chapter 8, the SCC may be used to visually examine locations, transportation lanes, and other objects in a supply network. APO computes approximate longitude/latitude coordinates or else receives them from settings in the location transaction. © SAP AG. Used with permission.

partners may be responsible for conducting sequential steps in an overall process, for example, (1) loading demand to the SNP planning book, (2) running macros to analyze the SNP planning book and create a consensus forecast or a suggested build schedule, and (3) monitoring alerts from the planning runs. A business partner may be a person, organization, department, or any entity responsible for a specific process task or step. An outside company, for example, may be responsible for providing forecast, while an internal planner is responsible for the planning book and planning run, and the purchasing department may be responsible for analyzing planning run outputs that may generate alerts to pull in or increase orders.

Address and Calendar Tabs

The Address tab of the Location transaction is relatively straightforward in terms of its actual inputs, which are all standard addressing information, from the title to whom or to which correspondence or packaging should be addressed to physical and e-mail addresses and various phone numbers. You should populate fields in the Location transaction with consideration given to whether they will be used in various outputs of SAP APO. For example, an SNP or PP/DS planning run may result in planned orders for purchase of materials from an external supplier. When the planned orders are converted to purchase orders, the location data will be referred to by the system to generate mailing and packing slips.

The Calendar tab has just five fields: Production Calendar, Warehouse Calendar, Shipping Calendar, Receiving Calendar, and Display Calendar (PP/DS). Each calendar controls validity dates or availability dates for relevant planning. For example, a factory that has production only 8 × 5, or 40 hours per week, will want a calendar that blocks out downtime so that it is not overscheduled. Calendars can be used similarly for blocking out holidays. While calendars are assigned to the location in the Location transaction, they must be defined elsewhere, though all calendars can be maintained with the same two transaction paths:

Method	Path to Configuration Transaction	Transaction Code
Standard	*Demand Planning → Environment → Current*	S_AP9_75000138
Navigation	*Settings → Maintain Planning Calendar (Time Stream)*	
IMG	*ICH Master Data → Calendar → Maintain Planning Calendar (Time Stream)*	/SAPAPO/CALENDAR

Of course it is wise to have worked out your planning calendars in advance of setting up a location, especially if you are relying on automated methods to set up your location master data. Nonetheless, if you find it necessary, APO makes it possible to define calendars ad hoc while setting up a location by way of the parameters buttons next to each calendar field (see Exhibit 5.5).

Resources Tab

The resources tab ties specific resources (or work centers) to the location. Usually resources may be created, maintained, and assigned to a location from the Resources

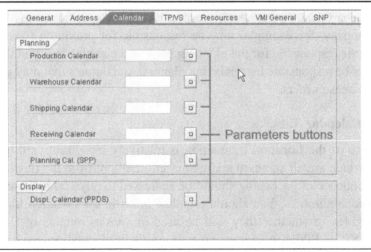

EXHIBIT 5.5   LOCATION TRANSACTION CALENDAR TAB
If calendars were not previously defined, use the parameters button to define them ad hoc. © SAP AG. Used with permission.

transaction and not all resources at a location need be called out here, but certain resources with a controlling nature may require specification. This will be the case if you use SAP APO for TP/VS or PP/DS or else if a storage location is maintained at the site you are defining.

As such, the Resources tab has three sections: TP/VS, Handling Resources, and Storage Resource. For TP/VS, inbound and outbound loading resources may be assigned at receiving and shipping locations. These must be defined in advance of their assignment in the Location transaction. Once the inbound or outbound resource assignment is made, use the Consumption field to control the batch rate for loading and unloading. For example, in a site with ten docks, no more than ten trucks may be loaded and unloaded simultaneously. If you are not using TP/VS, select "None" in this section.

Handling resources are applied by PP/DS as a sort of control resource between actual resource work centers that are planned by the PP/DS planning run that combines goods receipt functions with that of a resource in the inbound case and goods issue functions with the resource in the outbound case. PP/DS will minimally require an inbound handling resource that steers incoming product to a site work center, allowing time and quantity restrictions on goods receipt. At sites with many work centers, an outbound handling resource may be used to logically manage outgoing finished product.

If a site maintains a specific storage location, that location may be represented logically in the system first as a resource defined in the Resource transaction. Its designation as a storage location resource here in the Location transaction will give it storage location properties.

Functional Module Tabs

Remaining tabs are specific to functional area modules that you may or may not employ depending on your specific application of SAP APO: TP/VS, SNP, and vendor-managed inventory (VMI) General. Refer to the Locations cookbook for instructions on their use relative to your organization's application.

Setting the Location Version and Model

We will consider models and versions at length later in this chapter, but for now consider that SAP APO operates by modeling the supply chain, and any combination of master data elements and their attributes, such as plants, customers, vendors, products, and transportation lanes, itself will be a model in APO. Models may have different versions. For instance, model 000, always treated as the "active" model in APO, minimally will have one version, 000, the "active" version. You may choose to simulate differences in your model by creating an alternative version, that is, version 001, in which additional transportation lanes are available or else in which additional restrictions are placed on resource work centers in a factory site.

To be useful a location must be assigned to both a model and a version. If the location is going to be added to the active model and version, this can be done immediately when the location is created or CIF'd over from SAP R/3. If different custom models and versions are used, you may create the location and wait until such time as the models are developed. In either case, assign the location to a model from the initial screen of

EXHIBIT 5.6 ASSIGN LOCATION TO MODEL
© SAP AG. Used with permission.

the Location transaction by pressing the Assign Model button (depicted in Exhibit 5.2). A pop-up window will display a list of the available models. Select the model you wish to assign your location to (see Exhibit 5.6, step 1). Depress the assign model key (see Exhibit 5.6, step 2) and save your changes (see Exhibit 5.6, step 3); you will be returned to the Locations transaction initial screen.

Once your location is assigned to a model, assign it to a version of the model. To do so, click the Set Planning Version button on the initial screen (see Exhibit 5.7, step 1). A pop-up window will display with versions available to this model. For all versions available, click the pull-down and make your selection (see Exhibit 5.7, step 2). Set the version to the model by clicking the Check button (see Exhibit 5.7, step 3).

PRODUCTS

Products, their components, purchase, production, movement, delivery, and sale, are ultimately the point of any supply chain or supply chain modeling and planning exercise. Like locations, products can and usually will be maintained as master data in SAP R/3 and CIF'd over to SAP APO where additional detailed maintenance may be conducted. Instructions for use of the CIF are provided in Chapter 7. Furthermore, once created or in SAP APO manually or extended via CIF, products must be assigned to a model and version. Products may be defined for a single location, individually for multiple locations, or globally for all locations defined in the SAP APO instance. It is important that when viewing or especially when changing products you deliberately select the "Location" or "Global Data" fields on the initial screen. For example, you may wish to change

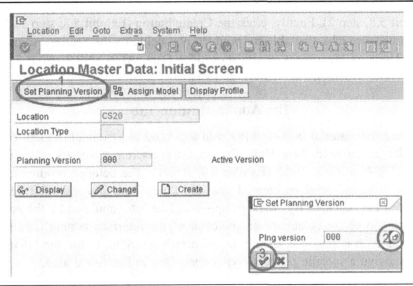

EXHIBIT 5.7 ASSIGN A VERSION TO A MODEL
© SAP AG. Used with permission.

settings specifically at one site but you will change settings at all sites if you fail to press "Location" and specify your site.

The product master data transaction lies on the general master data supply chain menu following the path *Master Data → Product → Product*. It has three modes, Create, Display, and Change, as well as assignments for versions and models and settings to permit definition as a single-location or global product.

In lieu of using the CIF to send SAP R/3 material master data over to SAP APO, create a product in SAP APO by entering the product code in the product field (Exhibit 5.8,

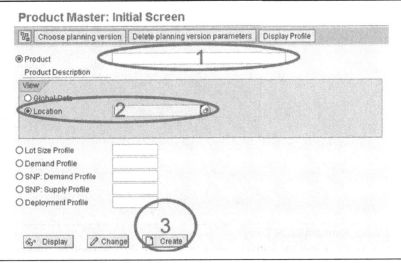

EXHIBIT 5.8 PRODUCT MASTER DATA INITIAL SCREEN
© SAP AG. Used with permission.

step 1), selecting "Location" under "View," and entering the location code in the location field (Exhibit 5.8, step 2). Finally, click the Create button (Exhibit 5.8, step 3). There are 14 data maintenance tabs available for product, not including the header: Administration, Properties, Units of Measure, Classification, Pkg Data, ATP, SNP 1, SNP 2, Demand, Lot Size, PP/DS, Procurement, GR/GI, and Extra.

The Administration Tab

When creating the material in SAP APO, you will need to assign a base unit of measure in the header in the field Base Unit. For ordinary discrete materials this will usually be a piece, "PC," or each, "EA" (Exhibit 5.9, step 1). The detailed product description is a required field and must be entered next to "Prod. Descriptn" (Exhibit 5.9, step 2). Information in the "Created By" data grouping will be autopopulated by the system with either the user id of the creator or an indicator of the interface system (i.e., CIFUSER for CIF). Finally, it is possible, though by no means essential, to use the "Planner" data grouping to assign a specific product owner according to functional area.

Properties and Units of Measure Tabs

All essential fields on the properties tab will be autopopulated by the system, notably the External Product Number (the product code), the Business System Group, Created By data, as well as Gross Weight and Volume. Gross Weight and Volume cannot actually be maintained from the Properties Tab but must instead be maintained directly on the Units of Measure Tab. All other fields are optional according to the needs of the modules and custom configurations you are deploying with SAP APO; for details on their setting options see Exhibit 5.10.

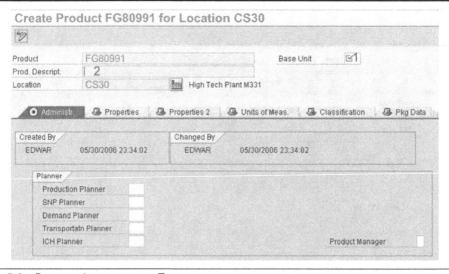

EXHIBIT 5.9 PRODUCT ADMINISTRATION TAB

Some header data comes in from the initial screen and "Created By" data will be autopopulated. Base unit and product description fields in the header are required; other fields are optional. © SAP AG. Used with permission.

Data Group	Field	Use
General Data	Material Group	Product grouping from the SAP R/3 system. This will come over with the CIF if used.
	Transp. Group	Grouping available for products with similar transportation requirements.
	EAN/UPC	European Article Number (Europe)/Universal Product Code (USA).
		Prod. *Hierarchy*. In-store hierarchy, company or organization's unique naming hierarchy.
		EAN/UPC. Indicator of whether EAN/UPC will be applied.
Other	SDP Relevance	Excludes product from DP or SNP computations. This will often be applied, for example, because DP and SNP are usually interested only in end products, though components and raw materials must often be maintained in SAP APO to support requirements of other modules such as PP/DS. Select this to exclude the material (or submaterial, as the case may be) from DP and SNP.
Shelf Life	Plng with Shelf Life	When selected, the system will consider shelf-life requirements and limitations when planning. This field may be populated by the CIF from data maintained in SAP R/3's material master. If selected, maintains the subfields Shelf Life, Maturation Time, Req.Min.Sh.Life, and Req.Max.Sh.Life.

EXHIBIT 5.10 OPTIONAL FIELD SETTINGS IN THE PRODUCT PROPERTIES TAB

Products with sophisticated dimensional definitions can be systematically defined on the Units of Measure (UOM) tab. Simple UOM data from the base unit field populated in the header autopopulates, but you can enter more detailed information about weight, volume, and spatial dimensions.

Classification Tab

The classification tab will normally be used only for PP/DS applications on products with production process models (PPMs). Furthermore, classification can be used only in systems that work collaboratively with an SAP R/3 instance (as opposed to standalone SAP APO or SAP APO with a legacy OLTP system) as material master classification is maintained there. By using classification, you may assign characteristics to products in the SAP R/3 system that allow the grouping of products with similar characteristics. When applied, the system can apply pegging to relate receipt items to appropriate requirements items (i.e., purchased or produced supply to outstanding demand) based on detailed characteristics mapping.

For example, we may create a classification in SAP R/3 called "PRODRM" for production raw materials that delineates characteristics of raw materials that may be used in the production of a product. When this class is assigned to the product in SAP APO in the Class field on this tab, the system will look for raw materials in this class during planning runs to meet demand for this product.

Packaging Data Tab

There are no essential fields on the Packaging Data tab (Pkg Data). You will use these fields only if you wish to maintain the specific packaging requirements data together with a product and have those requirements included in planning. For instance, when fashioning acupuncture needles, we may choose to maintain data about the packages the material will be maintained in. It is important to note that only one package description can be assigned to a given product. It may be necessary, therefore, to maintain more than one version of a product based on its end-state packaging. For instance, our TCM products manufacturer may have 6-inch single-use, plastic hammerhead acupuncture needles that are packaged in boxes of 25, 50, and 100. For each of the three packaging cases a separate product must be defined in APO, which will correspond to three different product code definitions, for instance, 600301 (25 count), 600302 (50 count), and 600303 (100 count).

ATP Tab

Fields in the ATP tab are necessary only when the Global ATP module of SAP APO is deployed. These fields can be maintained to control how limited supply is allocated to sales orders. For example, order priority can be weighted by customer, geography, the "firmness" of a sales order (i.e., the certainty that the customer will not change the order quantity), and other factors.

SNP 1 and 2 Tabs

With one exception that we will discuss later, fields in the SNP 1 and 2 tabs must be maintained only if the SNP module itself is in use, in which case their maintenance is essential. There are three optimizer options in SNP, each of which applies different rules and methodologies to derive an optimal cross-supply-chain global master production schedule: the SNP optimizer, which applies linear programming to determine the best feasible solution; CTM, which applies linear programming to determine the first feasible solution; and heuristics, which apply rules to determine a solution that assumes infinite capacity.

The SNP solution methods work in part by applying costs to certain outcomes, in particular: delayed delivery and nondelivery. Costs applied may differ according to the demand type SNP is planning, of which there are three possible: actual customer demand (i.e., sales orders from customers), forecasted demand (i.e., forecasts based on statistical methods from APO DP), and the corrected demand forecast. All costs assigned on the product master for SNP are relative and may be assigned to the product as it is planned at all locations (Exhibit 5.11, step 1) or as location-specific (Exhibit 5.11, step 2). When entering costs, usually you will enter the highest relative cost as that for nondelivery while a lower relative cost may be assigned for delays (Exhibit 5.11, steps 3 and 4, respectively). Provide a maximum delay to tell the system at what point delay is reinterpreted as nondelivery (Exhibit 5.11, step 5).

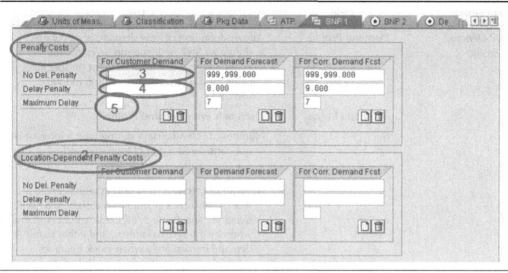

EXHIBIT 5.11 PRODUCTS SNP 1 TAB

Enter relative delay and nondelivery penalty costs according to global settings (1) or as specific location-dependent settings (2). You may similarly split out costs by demand type. Enter a maximum delay quantity to specify for the system when delay becomes nondelivery. © SAP AG. Used with permission.

Even when using the SNP module, fields in the SNP 2 tab will be optional and their actual use may differ widely according to the specific application of SNP, its optimizers, and organizational customization. Note that there is one field on the SNP 2 tab, Priority, that is also a setting for PP/DS. In fact, the equivalent setting in the PP/DS tab does not allow editing, so if Priority is defined for PP/DS, it must be set in SNP 2 even if the SNP module is not deployed. See Exhibit 5.12 for details of the settings available for customization in the SNP 2 tab.

Demand Tab

The Demand tab is used not so much to affect settings in the DP module as to affect how demand is managed in general throughout SAP APO. It might be worth noting that the Demand tab could be just as easily labeled "Demand/Supply," as its settings control the details of the relationship between them. Also notable is the fact that there are so many fields and settings available that three subtabs are required to cover them all. In order to simplify maintenance, a "Demand Profile" field is provided in the header.

Used here, the Demand Profile refers to a collection of standard Demand tab settings that may be applied from product to product. For example, once settings have been applied to a product with common demand settings, they may be saved as a profile and retrieved in the future to apply to all of the Demand tab settings for a newly maintained product. The Demand tab has a footer as well, with a selection for Product Alerts, specifically indicating when the system should generate alerts strictly at the direct level, that is, at the point of final availability, or else network alerts that notify of issues at any time across the pegging structure.

Data Group	Field	Use
SNP Demand Profile	Demand Profile	Allows definition of how demand is calculated during an SNP heuristic run, in particular, enabling the blocking of forecast on specific calendar days from consideration in total demand.
	Forecast Horizn	Used only with Demand Profile.
		Number of calendar days during which forecast is not considered a part of total demand.
	Pull Depl. Hor.	Used only with Demand Profile.
		Number of calendar days during which stock, when it becomes available, is assigned to fulfill demand. Affects the "Pull Deployment Horizon" whereby the system is instructed either to fulfill demand immediately when stock becomes available or else only when stock is due.
	Period Split	Controls how demand is distributed across the horizon when it is released from DP to SNP. <Blank> allows equal splitting including past dates. 1 maintains quantities limited to their proportions if historical dates were included, but only schedules it for dates in the present and future (essentially discounting unmet historical demand), and 2 keeps all demand but splits it out to work days in the present and future.
	VMI Promo.L Time	Used only for customers' locations that are part of a VMI scenario—all other demand elements are computed according to target days supply. This setting specifies an alternative lead time to satisfy demand for the customers in the VMI scenario.
	Fcast Horizon in Past	When set, historical forecast will be considered as part of forecast consumption logic.
SNP Supply Profile	Supply Profile	Corresponding to the Demand Profile, allows definition of how supply is calculated during an SNP heuristic run, specifically blocking when production and stock transfer is possible.
	SNP Prod. Hor.	Use with the Supply Profile or for CTM runs.
		Use to block when SNP can run—for instance, to split the time periods during which SNP versus PPDS is used to plan. (Requires a period type, i.e., days, weeks, months.)
	Extend SNP Prof. Hor.	Period similar to the SNP Production Horizon but allows manual creation of orders.
	SNP Stk Trn.Hor	Similar to SNP Production Horizon but controlling stock transfers.

EXHIBIT 5.12 OPTIONAL FIELD SETTINGS IN THE PRODUCT SNP 2 TAB

Data Group	Field	Use
	Push Depl. Hor.	Period of time during which deployment will consider receipts in the Available-to-Dept. (ATD) Receipt category as receipts available to supply.
	Depl. SS Push H	A horizon that is employed by deployment if a setting of "S" is entered for the Push Distribution Rule, "Push taking the safety stock horizon into account." When used, the system will confirm only issues that can be covered by safety stock if the time between the demand and deploy date is less than the safety stock horizon—essentially allowing fulfillment only within the safety stock horizon.
	Fix Production	May be used with a heuristic run or with the SNP optimizer. With heuristics, when set, planned orders from previous runs falling inside the SNP Production Horizon are not deleted. With the optimizer, planned orders from previous planning runs that are outside the planning horizon are fixed and not deleted.
	Fix Stock Transits	Similar to Fix Production setting, but controls deletion or nondeletion of stock transfers.
SNP Deployment Profile	Deployment Profile	Controls distribution rules, which themselves control how supply is distributed to demand locations.
	Fair Share Rule	Rules for distributing supply should demand exceed it.
	Push Distribution	Rules used for distributing supply when Available-to-Deploy (ATD) is sufficient.
SNP Interactive Order Creation	No fixing	When set, orders created manually in SNP are not automatically fixed.
Other Data	Priority	May be used in PP/DS, CTM, and with SNP capacity leveling.
	Purch. Group	Identifies buyer or group of buyers responsible for the product.
	VMI Purch.Group	VMI exception to the Purchasing Group.
	Cust. Product	Specification of the product code or number that a customer uses to identify this product.
	ATD Receipt	Specify the ATD categories that are increased by receipts of this product.
	ATD Issue	Specify the ATD categories that are decreased by issues of this product.
	SNP Checking Hor.	Use to limit the period during which deployment calculates the ATD quantity. When not used, the entire horizon is considered.

EXHIBIT 5.12 *(continued)*

Data Group	Field	Use
CTM Settings	Demand Selection Horizon	Limits the CTM Demand Selection Horizon to current day + the number of days specified here. Use to customize the selection horizon to products with different lead times.
	Order Creation Frame	Period in advance of the actual demand date during which CTM is allowed to open orders to fulfill the demand.
	Time-based Priority	When checked, CTM will consider time together with product priority in planning (ignore product priority and consider time only by making all priorities equal).

EXHIBIT 5.12   (*continued*)

The three subtabs of the Demand tab are Requirement Strategy, Pegging, and Available Stocks. Requirement Strategy assigns a production strategy to fulfill demand. Pegging controls the assignment of supply to demand elements (i.e., as demand changes, how is supply realigned to it?). Available Stocks defines which supply is available to fulfill demand.

Using a Requirement Strategy

A Requirement Strategy is in fact an MRP concept that refers to the specific method for manufacturing goods. It operates in close concert with a consumption mode that applies manufactured goods to consume or fulfill demand elements such as sales orders. Assign a requirement strategy using the Proposed Strategy field by choosing from the pull-down menu (Exhibit 5.13, steps 1 and 2, respectively). Assign a consumption mode on the field of the same name (Exhibit 5.13, step 3), and depending on whether you use forward or backward consumption, enter days of consumption in the period fields below (Exhibit 5.13, step 4). While quite a few requirement strategies are available in SAP R/3 for actual MRP runs, only four are provided off the shelf in SAP APO. Additional strategies can be custom defined if necessary (see Exhibits 5.14 and 5.15).

Using Pegging

Throughout SAP, whichever applications are concerned, the concept of pegging refers to tracing an object history backward. For example, if we are interested in a production order, the pegging history of the production order will relate all of the demand elements that drive the production order, usually dependent and independent requirements. Requirements, for their part, may in turn also be pegged back to their source as sales orders or forecast elements. Systematic rules governing pegging in SAP APO are applied at a product/plant or product/global level.

Defining Available Stocks

When SAP APO conducts various planning runs to determine a schedule for fulfilling demand, whether using heuristics, CTM, or the SNP optimizer, it will account for stock

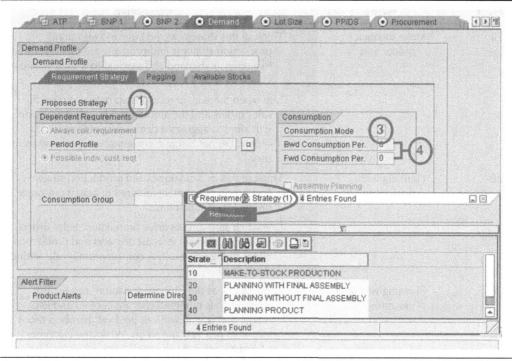

EXHIBIT 5.13 PRODUCT DEMAND TAB, REQUIREMENTS STRATEGY

Assign a manufacturing strategy to fulfill demand and a consumption mode to apply new stocks to close out demand elements such as sales orders. © SAP AG. Used with permission.

that can be assigned to meet demand. Many objects may be considered valid stocks, which to consider so are defined at the product level in available stocks.

Lot Size Tab

One might think that a lot sizing parameter or indicator would be a relatively straightforward matter. It turns out, however, that when determining a standard lot size we run into a number of decisions. How do we match supply lots to demand lots if the lots are of different sizes? What if the lot completes across separate time buckets? How do we relate lot sizes to reorder strategies, where a lot size may take us above or below reorder thresholds?

All of these matters and more are defined on the Lot Size tab which, like the Demand tab, has so many settings that a Lot Size profile is available in the header to assign common lot size settings across the many fields. Minimal lot settings will be for the lot size procedure, of which there are four options: (1) Lot-for-Lot, (2) Fixed Lot Size, (3) By Period, and (4) Reorder Point.

The lot-for-lot procedure is the most simple and will probably be used most often, matching supply lot sizes to demand. In other words, if a sales order is opened for 100, a planned order (or production order or purchase order) will be opened in turn for 100. If the sales order is made for 150, the planned order is opened for 150. Fixed lot size forces the same supply lot size regardless of demand; that is, if the fixed lot size is 20,

Number	Name	Description
10	Make-to-stock production	Think of this strategy as the fast-food restaurant production strategy: End-products are manufactured to aggregate demand and stocked to a shelf where a customer orders the final product only.
		Use when there is no relationship between specific sales orders and the amount produced. Production will align to aggregate demands, not individual orders. Do not assign a consumption mode when in use.
20	Planning with final assembly	Think of this as a catalog-based production strategy: End-products are manufactured to actual customer orders for specific units.
		Use when sales orders drive production. Sales orders consume (replace) forecast demand and production aligns to the net result. A consumption mode setting is required.
30	Planning w/o final assembly	Think of this as the Chinese-restaurant production strategy: Vats of ingredients are cooked and kept ready, that is, chicken vat, beef vat, bamboo shoot vat, snap pea vat, and so on. When the customer places an order the premade parts are assembled at the last minute to create an end-product.
		Use when sales orders drive production and production must dynamically change to the requirements of specific sales orders. Sales orders consume (replace) forecast demand and production aligns to the net result. A consumption mode setting is required.
40	Planning product	Think of this as the online bookstore strategy of production: In most cases a book is simply packaged and shipped, but in some cases it must be gift-wrapped and in others it must be gift-wrapped with a message to the recipient from the sender.
		This strategy is used for cases where the components of an end-product are nearly identical but the actual manifestation of the end-product, even to such a level of detail as the packaging, is the value-added process. As with 20 and 30, sales orders consume (replace) forecast demand and production aligns to the net result. A consumption mode setting is required.

EXHIBIT 5.14   REQUIREMENTS STRATEGIES IN SAP APO

then there will be five planned orders to fulfill one demand order of 100, whereas if it is 25, there will be 4.

Period-based lot sizes define lots according to periods of time, also without respect to demand. Where the quantity must be defined with a fixed lot size, period-based sizing requires that the type and number of periods must be delineated. Reorder point lot sizing is more of a rule set for lot sizing that dynamically creates lots either whenever stocks fall

Number	Name	Description
1	Backward	Sales orders consume only forecast that comes before the demand requirements date, leaving demand beyond the requirements data to forecast.
2	Backward/forward	Sales orders consume both forecast before and after the requirements date, starting with before and continuing into after the requirements date until exhaustion or the end of the forward consumption period, whichever comes first.
3	Forward	Sales orders consume only demand that comes after the requirements date, treating forecast before the requirements date as lost or ignored demand.

EXHIBIT 5.15   CONSUMPTION MODES

below a defined point or else according to an algorithm that assures a minimum available quantity over a specified period of time.

PP/DS and Procurement Tabs

The PP/DS tab is used strictly to define rules and procedures related to how the PP/DS module may be applied to plan for a product at a specific producing or ordering site. There are four general areas that may be defined with PP/DS: (1) the Planning Procedure, (2) Procurement Planning, (3) Order Creation, and (4) Horizons. Additionally, product grouping data may also be applied if used, which will group products with others of similar characteristics.

The planning procedure is the minimal requirement for PP/DS and is an essential setting for that module. Planning procedures determine which rules are applied to the product when planning events occur, such as the creation or change of an in-house or procurement order, the creation of stock or demand, or else master data changes. SAP APO will come with six off-the-shelf planning procedures (Exhibit 5.16), though additional, custom planning procedures can be defined in SAP APO customizing (the IMG), along the IMG path *Advanced Planning and Optimization → Supply Chain Planning → Production Planning and Detailed Scheduling → Maintain Planning Procedures*. When creating new planning procedures in the IMG, add a new line number, highlight it, then double-click "Reaction to Events" to add procedures for various planning events (Exhibit 5.17, steps 1 to 3, respectively, and Exhibit 5.18).

If a product is procured, not made in-house, then additional specifications can be applied under Procurement Planning. Here you can indicate whether the product is acquired as part of a package or otherwise which procurement rule set (heuristic) to use for scheduling requisitions. While an overall heuristic may be defined for the PP/DS planning run, specific product procurement heuristics may be applied at a product-by-product level when they differ individually. Define which task list type, such as a production process model, that SAP APO should use to create orders to by using the Plan Explosion field.

Number	Name	Description and Use
1	Manual with Check	Planning is done manually and an availability check is conducted automatically when a planning event occurs.
2	Manual without Check	Planning is done manually and an availability check is not conducted automatically when a planning event occurs.
3	Cover Dependent Requirements Immediately	No planning is applied for end-products but component parts (dependent requirements) necessary to complete end-products are immediately planned at the time of a planning event.
4	Planning in Planning Run	Planning is conducted only during the PP/DS planning run (see Chapter 9). Nothing occurs immediately from planning events.
5	Multilevel ATP Check	ATP check across all levels of the bills-of-material (BOM) is conducted at the time of a planning event.

EXHIBIT 5.16   COMMON PP/DS PLANNING PROCEDURES

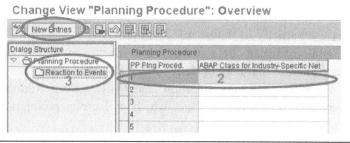

EXHIBIT 5.17   DEFINING A PP/DS PLANNING PROCEDURE IN SAP APO CUSTOMIZING (THE IMG)
© SAP AG. Used with permission.

Finally, PP/DS time horizons must be defined. State the opening horizon, the period during which planned orders must be changed to an executable order (production or purchase), in the Opening Horizon field. With that, assign a conversion rule if the conversion from planned order to executable order is automatic. One may assign a PP/DS Planning Time Fence (also called a "Fixing Horizon") during which it is impossible to change order type. A period during which independent requirements will be deleted if there are no sales orders for them can be defined in the Adjustment Horizon. If there is a period during which forecast should not be considered a part of total demand, define it with the Forecast Horizon.

When used together with SNP, it will be necessary to define an SNP and a PP/DS horizon so that overlaps are controlled. Generally speaking, SNP will be used to plan medium-range demand, such as demand that occurs 2 or 3 months in the future out to 9 or 12 months in the future, while PP/DS is used to plan a tactical horizon, from the present day out until 2 or 3 months. Use the SNP Production Horizon and PP/DS Horizon to define these modules' respective borders and overlaps (Exhibit 5.19).

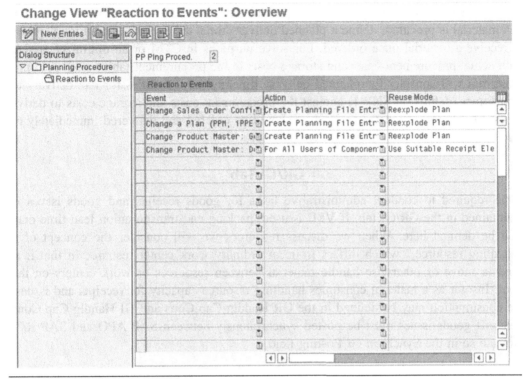

EXHIBIT 5.18 CREATING OR CUSTOMIZING A PLANNING PROCEDURE

Specify the event, then specify the initial action and then the reuse case; for example, indicate the extent of reprocessing. © SAP AG. Used with permission.

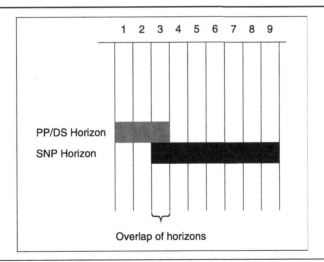

EXHIBIT 5.19 PP/DS AND SNP HORIZONS

The PP/DS horizon is tactical and will usually cover 2–3 months. The SNP horizon is medium-range, covering around 9 months between the 2nd and 3rd month and the 9th or 12th. Horizons may border or overlap.

Most products are either entirely produced in-house, exclusively purchased, or a combination of the two. Define this on the procurement tab in the Procurement Type field. If a material is procured, define a planned delivery time, the expected lead time required to receive a material once ordered. For solve purposes in CTM or an optimizer, assign both actual procurement costs and storage costs in the procurement tab as well. An optimizer run will consider the planned delivery time and any penalties for late delivery to a customer (defined in SNP 1) against the procurement costs and storage costs to derive a best-fit solution of whether a product should be ordered and delivered immediately or else ordered and stored in advance for delivery.

GR/GI Tab

Time required to conduct administrative tasks for goods receipts and goods issues is maintained in the GR/GI tab. If VMI is used, packing and transportation lead time may also be defined here. When we discuss resources we will consider the concept of a "handling resource," which differs from an ordinary work center resource in that it is used to move or otherwise handle material between resources or work centers on the floor. Insofar as a material consumes handling resource capacity for receipts and issues, the consumption may be defined in the GR Handlg Cap Cons and GI Handlg Cap Cons fields. If goods issues must be posted synchronously between SAP APO and SAP R/3, indicate so in the Synchron GI Posting field.

RESOURCES AND WORK CENTERS

Broadly speaking, resources are concerned with where work is conducted, product is made, moved, or acquired, and capacity is consumed. As a rule, resources in SAP APO are analogous to work centers in SAP R/3, and therefore, throughout this text we will use the term *resources* when referring to either resources or work centers. As with locations and products, SAP APO is designed to work closely with SAP R/3 as it relates to resources. In most cases, the CIF will be liberally employed to maintain resources in SAP APO based on work center settings in SAP R/3. We may note, however, that resources have considerably more settings and dimensions in SAP APO than they do in SAP R/3, and in some cases, as with "handling resources," the resources must be exclusively maintained in SAP APO. There are considerably more cases where specific settings must be maintained for resources in SAP APO and not SAP R/3 than their location and product analogs.

Resources are organizational units that represent where in a site or factory operations are conducted. As such they are used to model:

- Machines
- Groups of machines
- People
- Groups of people

Exhibit 5.20 illustrates three general areas controlled by work centers in SAP R/3, only two aspects of which are transferred to SAP APO for processing. Once data is transferred to APO it is broken into two parts:

Area	Description	Data Source/Control
Scheduling	Work center operating times	Transferred to APO from R/3
Capacity Planning	Available capacity at a work center and any formulas controlling it	Transferred to APO from R/3
Costing	Formulas that compute the cost of active operations at a work center	Remain in R/3, no transfer to APO

Exhibit 5.20 Resource Data Categories and System Assignments

1. Available capacity data from the R/3 work center goes into the APO resource.
2. Formulas controlling scheduling and capacity requirements are transferred to the material-specific PPM or PDS.

The resource maintenance transaction is under master data along the path *Master Data → Resource → Resource*. The initial screen is considerably busier than locations and products but a close examination shows that most of the fields provided are simply for filtering. For example, one may wish to display all resources at a location, in which case it will be useful to list only the location, then click the Display or Change buttons. Likewise, one may wish to display all resources assigned to a specific planner or else all of those set to specific models.

Resource Category in SAP APO

A critical early consideration in the establishment of a resource is the resource category, of which there are four. This will determine, among other things, if it is possible to use CIF and SAP R/3 as the ultimate source of the resource. Any given resources must be defined as one of the following: P: Production, T: Transportation, S: Storage Location, or H: Handling Unit. Resources maintained in R/3 and sent to APO via CIF are always of Production category. The other three categories may be assigned to a variety of activities that support specific kinds of supply chain functions.

Transportation resources are used by SNP and CTM and are assigned to the transportation mode in Transportation Lanes (see Resources and Work Centers section in this chapter). Handling resources are required by APO in order to model capacity requirements related to material handling, which may be inbound or outbound. Required times that consume handling capacity may be entered on the transportation lane in the product section.

Storage resources are assigned to locations in order to model material storage capacity requirements. Vehicle resources are used only by TP/VS and represent a "unit load" assigned to a vehicle type, such as a big-rig container or a rail car, each of which possesses a specific capacity.

Resource Activity Varieties

A variety of dimensions may impact the functionality necessary for a given resource. Does a resource conduct single or multiple activities where many activities can be carried out concurrently? Is it used by more than one module of APO? Is measurement of quantities or

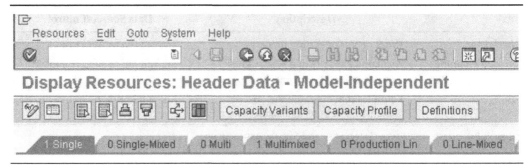

EXHIBIT 5.21   RESOURCE ACTIVITY VARIETY TABS

These tabs indicate how many resources of their type exist under the tab; In this case there is one single-activity resource and no resources of any other type. © SAP AG. Used with permission.

rates a concern? Is it part of a task list or production line? Is the resource for transportation and if so, is it related to SNP or TP/VS? Is it necessary to model activities where capacity should not be taken into account? A tab exists in the resource transaction for each resource variety and each tab displays the number of resources set up under it (Exhibit 5.21). Exhibit 5.22 catalogs to which APO modules and business use-cases the resource variations may be applied.

Setting up Resources

As with products and locations, generally speaking, production resources will be initially created in SAP R/3 and CIF'd over to SAP APO. Nonetheless, all nonproduction resources must be set up directly in SAP APO and even production resources, once they are received, generally will be subject to a considerable level of detailed editing due to the greater level of sophistication of resources in APO versus work centers in R/3. Competency with resource setup in APO, therefore, is essential. For example, here we will consider the case of establishing a handling resource for PP/DS.

General Data Tab

From menu path *Master Data → Resource → Resource*, transaction code /SAPAPO/ RES01/, open the transaction to the initial screen. On the initial screen, simply click the Create button (Exhibit 5.23); the data screen will display. In the Single resource tab, enter the resource name HCS20, "H" for handling and location "CS20" to follow our TCM supply manufacturer's China site (Exhibit 5.24, steps 1 to 3). For time zone enter "UTC + 8" for the Beijing time zone (Exhibit 5.24, step 4).

Three general settings are necessary for defining resource available capacity: Factory Calendar, Activity Variant, and Reference Resource (Exhibit 5.24, step 5). In all cases a factory calendar specifying working and nonworking days and times must be assigned for capacity features to function. The factory calendar can be entered on the resource table with previous general header data, and if the ⟨ENTER⟩ key is depressed, it and all the general header information will be populated to the general header details tab below (Exhibit 5.24, step 6).

Resource Variety	Applicable Module(s)	Use Case(s)
Single Activity	PP/DS	Use when only one activity can be carried out at a time.
Single Mixed	SNP and PP/DS	Only one activity can be carried out at a time and the resource is used by both modules SNP and PP/DS.
Multi-Activity	PP/DS	Use when several activities can be carried out concurrently.
Multi-Mixed	SNP and PP/DS	Several activities can be carried out concurrently and the resource is used by both modules SNP and PP/DS.
Production Line	PP/DS	Use for task-based scheduling where the resource determines working times and rates.
Production Line Mixed	SNP and PP/DS	Same as a production line but used by both modules SNP and PP/DS.
Bucket	SNP	Quantity or rate are important—quantity as it may apply to transportation capacity; rate as it may apply to consumption or production capacity.
Vehicle	TP/VS	Represents vehicle capacity for TP/VS and will reflect time-dependent availability via shift sequence, but not available capacity by time.
Transportation	SNP	Identical to a bucket resource except in the method of scheduling requirements.
Calendar	PP/DS	Only time, not capacity, is utilized for scheduling and there is no setup adjustment time.
Calendar Mixed	SNP and PP/DS	Same as a calendar resource but used by both modules SNP and PP/DS.

EXHIBIT 5.22 RESOURCE VARIETIES, MODULES, AND USE CASES

A capacity activity variant may be assigned according to organizational practice (capacity variants will be discussed shortly). A reference resource may be specified to copy detailed resource capacity assignment information during creation. Additionally, reference resources may be used to cascade capacity changes across all resources that reference them and as such may be useful for maintaining capacity details across multiple work centers (Exhibit 5.24, step 5 for all settings).

Define the resources planning horizon in the Days − and Days + fields under Planning Parameters (Exhibit 5.24, step 7). Bottleneck resources may be displayed separately on the PP/DS planning board and their identification can aid in PP/DS optimization, so calling them out if known here by clicking the Bottleneck Resource check may be useful (Exhibit 5.24, step 8). The Finite Scheduling check and its corollary entry field Finiteness Level are actually a relatively sophisticated feature controlling resource sharing by multiple applications (Exhibit 5.24, step 9). Later we will see where detailed scheduling using the planning board allows a sort of virtual image of the resource with more detailed settings than those maintained in the ordinary resource transaction. When such settings are maintained, it may be the case that two applications share the same resource. Selecting

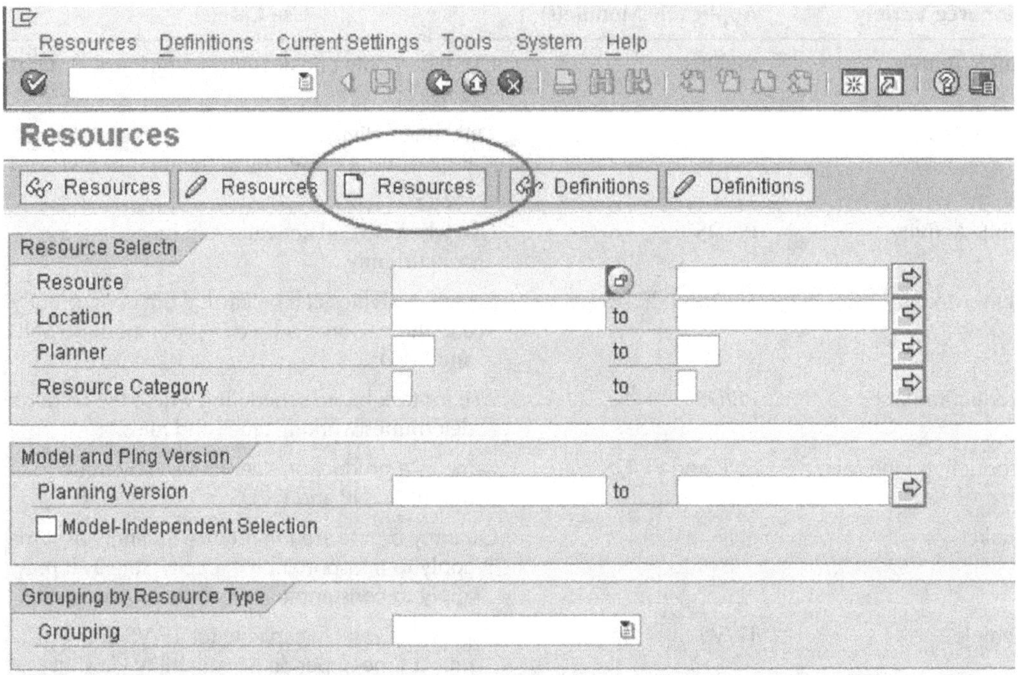

EXHIBIT 5.23   RESOURCE INITIAL SCREEN

If not creating a new resource, all the resources at a specific location can be pulled by filtering by location only. Otherwise, if a specific resource is concerned, it may be pulled exclusively. It may be useful to pull the resource by planning version, either for simulation cases or else when it is uncertain the resource has been assigned to the active planning version. © SAP AG. Used with permission.

Finite Scheduling and assigning a Finiteness level will apply rules for taking current capacity from each application into account. To complete the entry of the General Data tab, click on the Time-Cont. Capacity tab. Though the data has been entered in the table line-item entry at the top of the screen, if you return to the General Data tab it will display.

Time Continuous Capacity Tab

Time continuous capacity is relevant to production and handling resources. Basic capacity settings for production resources will usually be assigned in R/3 and come over via the CIF, though there may be exceptions that we will discuss later, particularly for PP/DS. Default capacities are 24 hours of run time with no breaks and 100% resource utilization. Any of these settings may be adjusted globally or by time bucket. Change them globally in the Available Capacity section of the Time Continuous Capacity tab (Exhibit 5.25, step 1) and make time-bucket-specific changes by clicking the Capacity button (Exhibit 5.25, step 2). Clicking the Capacity button will yield a pop-up with day-by-day capacity settings for each of the capacity dimensions.

The Planning Parameters section holds fields that control time between ordinary operational activities. The setup matrix is a task list with details of the duration and setup

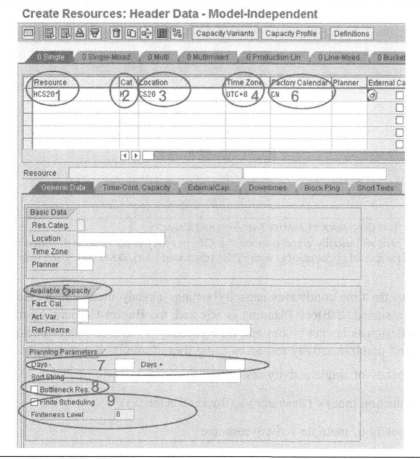

EXHIBIT 5.24 GENERAL DATA TAB ENTRY FOR A RESOURCE
© SAP AG. Used with permission.

costs for sequenced setup activities. Details for configuring setup matrixes are discussed later in this chapter. Time buffers are used by PP/DS as a safety time that accounts for unforeseen delays such as may be caused by material staging for activity. Maximum overlap will limit the length of time the system will tolerate a resource overload before triggering an alert to the planner. The Campaign-Relevant flag may be set to prevent interruption of activities by orders that do not belong to a specific campaign.

PP/DS Bucket Capacity Tab

Use the fields in the Bucket Capacity tab to enable bucket capacities that define quantities, such as that of a warehouse or truck, or else to define production/consumption rate quantities. The Bucket Definition field controls whether bucketing is in use. When bucketing is not used, the Bucket Capacity and Check Plans buttons will be grayed out and the Bucket Schema and Bucket Factor % will be empty.

There are two options for bucket capacity: a bucketing basis from Time Continuous Capacity and from Block Planning. Time Continuous Capacity will import a bucket

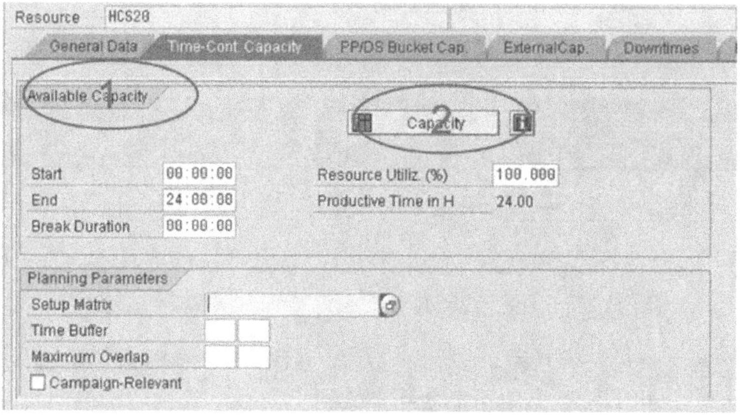

EXHIBIT 5.25   TIME CONTINUOUS CAPACITY TAB: AVAILABLE CAPACITY
Most settings here will usually come over on the CIF, but may need to be maintained for handling resources and for special circumstances with PP/DS (discussed later). © SAP AG. Used with permission.

schema from the time continuous capacity settings already made and a Bucket Factor % must be assigned. If Block Planning is selected, the Bucket Capacity button must be selected to designate bucket blocks and their capacity. PP/DS calculates bucket capacity for single and multiple activity resources using these formulas:

Bucket capacity of single activity resource

= (Production time) * (Resource) * (Bucket Factor %)

Bucket capacity of multiple activity resource

= (Production time) * (Resource) * (Number of capacities) * (Bucket Factor %)

External Capacity Tab

While it is necessary to take pains to describe setup and maintenance of resource master data in SAP APO to assure understanding of the use of the fields and settings in the APO system, we reiterate that in most cases resource master data will be sourced in an SAP R/3 system and sent over via CIF. For such cases, where R/3 is used to maintain details of the time-continuous capacity of single, multi-, line, or calendar resources and any mixed cases, maintain the connection to the R/3 work center in the External Capacity tab. Settings are relatively straightforward. Maintain the Resource as the resource name in SAP APO. The LogSystem (Logical System) will be the logical system name established by your organization's SAP Basis team for the R/3 system containing the work center data. Plant is the plant containing the work center and capacity category is the type of work center in the source system. See Chapter 7 for additional integration setting details for configuring which data is maintained in R/3 versus APO.

Downtimes and Short Texts Tabs

The Downtimes tab is just one more place where system calendaring/scheduling can be conducted. One may of course maintain downtimes via the Time Continuous Capacity tab simply by reducing available capacity hours. It may be desirable, however, to maintain downtimes in the Downtimes tab so as to have a quick, easily accessible screen-record of all downtimes. Downtimes maintained elsewhere will not stand out visually. The Short Texts tab is essentially just for maintaining ad-hoc notes about the resource. The language field does not control anything but just indicates in what language the notes are written.

SNP Bucket Capacity

The SNP Bucket Capacity tab will be available only in SNP-relevant resource tabs, which are generally "mixed" tabs. Fields vary slightly from one resource tab to another, but which fields are available is generally dictated by the Bucket Definition. In principle, SNP Bucket Capacity is similar to PP/DS Bucket Capacity where bucket capacity is used to control quantities and rates in resources. Bucket definition from Time Continuous Capacity will simply inherit time continuous capacity time-bucketing settings while "Maintain" requires the ad-hoc creation of buckets. If Time Continuous Capacity is not referenced for the Bucket Definition, the only alternative is to define it ad hoc, in which case fields will display to support the definition.

The Loss Factor % in SNP follows the same logic as the Bucket Factor % in PP/DS. If your resource has a minimum load under which an alert should be generated, maintain the load in the Minimum Load (%) field. If overloading is permitted, indicate the maximum overload above which an alert should be generated in the Overload (%) field.

If activities may begin only at the start of a time bucket, indicate so by selecting the Schedule on Buckets Prfl checkbox. If activities are allowed to cross over time buckets, for example, starting on one day and continuing across to the next, indicate the permission by selecting the Cross-Period Activity checkbox. Depending on the lot size demand profile you are using, if you are using cross-period planning you may also need to select Period Lot Size to enable cross-period lot size planning wherein smaller lots created across periods are grouped into larger lots to aggregate to the size of demand-based lots.

For example, consider that you are using lot-for-lot planning and there is a customer order for 1,000 units of product. The production lots are assigned to build across period and the rate of production is 500/day. To enable single production lot fulfillment of the customer order lot, that is, a production order of 1,000 units to meet the customer order of 1,000 units, both the Cross-Period Activity and the Period Lot Size boxes must be selected.

The decision to use this combination is not without consequence and a number of configuration prerequisites must be met, including:

- Cross-period lot size planning in the SNP optimizer profile is activated with a time horizon in the Cross-Period Lot Size field.
- The SNP optimizer's selected PPM uses this resource.
- The PPM is allowed to use only one resource for which the *Period Lot Size* indicator has been set and does not use any other resources with fixed resource consumption.
- The PPM duration must be less than or equal to the smallest bucket.

More detail on PPM and related PDS settings will be provided later in this chapter.

Capacity Variants

Generally there will be long-run fluctuations in the availability of capacity at a given resource that may impact budgeting and strategic planning. Variations may be related to changing lengths of workdays, variance in workforce efficiencies such as may be brought about by learning curve, and the alternative use of contractors and regular employees as well as holidays and other planned downtimes, such as for operational maintenance. In SAP R/3 these variations are maintained using intervals and shifts, but that data cannot be transferred to APO via the CIF. APO allows for a considerably greater level of detail of maintenance for these fields than R/3.

To view a resource's capacity variants in simple list form across time, simply press the Capacity Profile button (Exhibit 5.26, step 1). To assign a capacity variant to a resource, simply indicate the variant in the Act Var field in the Available Capacity section of the General Data tab. Otherwise, to maintain distinct models of fluctuations in capacity on the resource across time as independent variants, highlight the resource and click the Capacity Variants button (Exhibit 5.26, step 2). While capacity variants are accessed via individual resources, they are independent of the resources themselves. In other words, one can define complete variants of time-sequenced capacity variations, save them, and then assign those variants to individual resources.

In the Model Independent Variants screen accessed via the Capacity Variants button, the resource will be displayed along with any capacity-variant shift sequences that have been assigned to it (Exhibit 5.27, step 1 and 2). In the exhibit a standard shift definition

EXHIBIT 5.26 VARIANT PROFILE BUTTONS
Use the Capacity Profile button to display long-term capacity variations that have already been maintained. Use the Capacity Variants button to maintain new capacity fluctuations. © SAP AG. Used with permission.

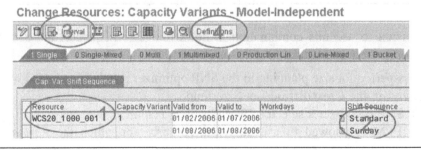

EXHIBIT 5.27 Capacity Variants
Assignment of Shift Sequences and their validity dates. Though Shift Sequences are independent of the resource, the Definitions button on this screen accesses their create/maintain screen. © SAP AG. Used with permission.

is assigned to Monday through Saturday and a special Sunday definition is assigned for a Sunday date. To assign new variants, click the Add Interval button (Exhibit 5.27, step 3) and specify the new variant shift sequence with its validity dates in the pop-up window. Add or edit available shift sequences by clicking the Definitions button (Exhibit 5.27, step 4).

Shift Definitions are applied to all of the following aspects of a shift, each of which is displayed in APO as a tab: (1) Sequence, (2) Shifts, (3) Breaks, (4) Shift Factors, (5) Quantities/Rates, (6) Rate Definitions, and (7) Prod.-Dep. Rates. If you tab through the tabs the shift sequences will be repeated with their aspect-specific fields. In the case of the example, Sunday and Standard are repeated on all seven tabs (Exhibit 5.28).

The Shift Sequence refers to actual shift use-case where the daily sequence of shifts may be defined for an indefinite number of consecutive days as requirements demand. Within the use-case there may be as many as nine shifts on a specific day. Breaks are defined as break patterns in the Break tab. Break patterns are independent objects that may be assigned to multiple shifts and shift sequences and as such should usually be defined in advance of shifts. Use the Shifts tab to assign a shift sequence and a break pattern to a specific date range.

Setup Matrix

Ordinarily resources experience a time lapse and cost associated with sequence-dependent setup activities. These times and costs are modeled in APO in the setup matrix and are necessary for detailed factory scheduling available in PP/DS. The setup matrix must be established independent of the resource and must be assigned to a resource in the Time Continuous Capacity tab in advance of use of the resource by the PP/DS planning run or an SNP optimization run. Setup matrix configuration and display transactions are available following the navigation path *Master Data → Production Planning Master Data → Setup Group/Setup Matrix*. Within this folder there are three germane transactions:

/SAPAPO/CDPSC6	Maintain Setup Groups
/SAPAPO/CDPSC7	Maintain Setup Matrix
/SAPAPO/CDPS_SETUP	Display Setup Matrix

Setup matrixes operate through the interaction of setup groups, which themselves represent a time- or cost-consuming setup activity. Setup groups are location specific but not

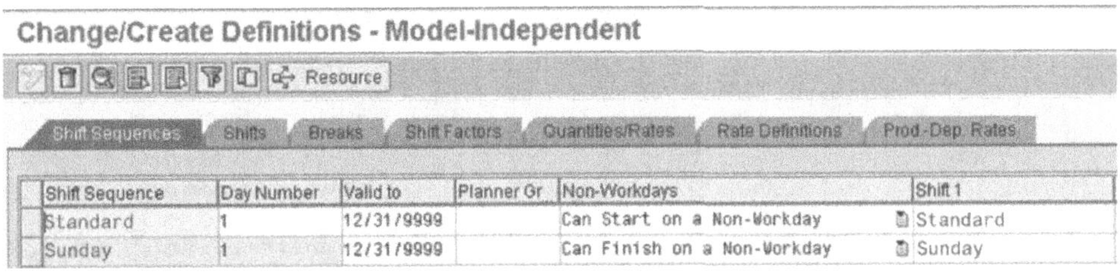

EXHIBIT 5.28 SETTING SHIFT VARIANT FEATURES

Each shift will display in the seven shift-aspect tabs. © SAP AG. Used with permission.

resource specific, and technically may be assigned to multiple resources. This is essentially intuitive since the same machine or line may experience the same setup activity.

Once setup groups are defined, their sequence, times, and costs are configured together on a setup matrix. The matrix is a model that reflects how one activity transitions to another and then assigns its costs in either time, cost, or both. Therefore, to establish a setup matrix, first use the transaction /SAPAPO/CDPSC6 to define the setup groups, again, each activity involved in a setup. To create a new group, click the New Entries button (Exhibit 5.29, step 1), then add the plant location of the resources where the activities take place (Exhibit 5.29, step 2), the setup group name as a simple code (Exhibit 5.29, step 3), and a description of the setup group (Exhibit 5.29, step 4). When finished, save your results.

Next, model the setup groups together on a matrix, defining their transitional relationships with one another. Open transaction /SAPAPO/CDPSC7 and click the New Entries button to define a new setup matrix that will model the setup groups just defined. Enter

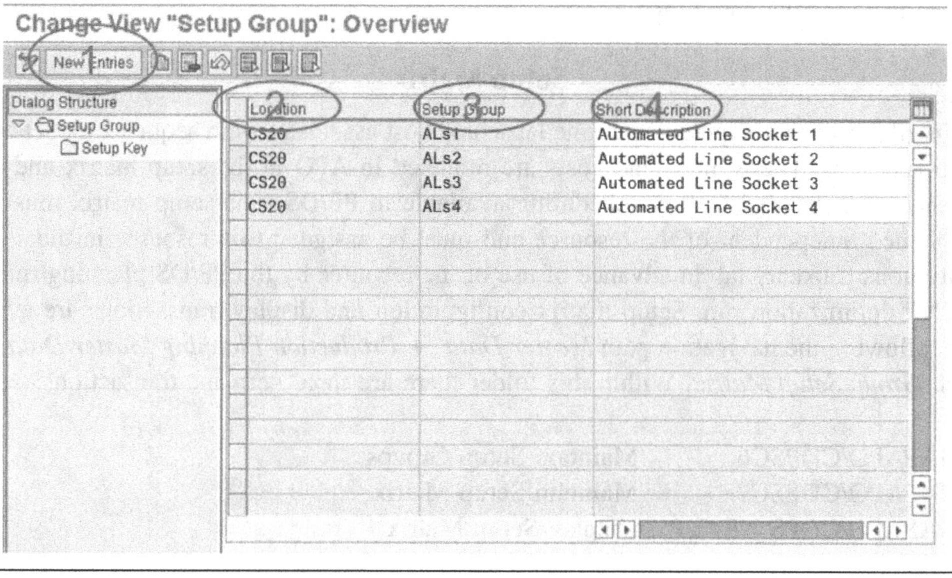

EXHIBIT 5.29 DEFINING SETUP GROUPS
© SAP AG. Used with permission.

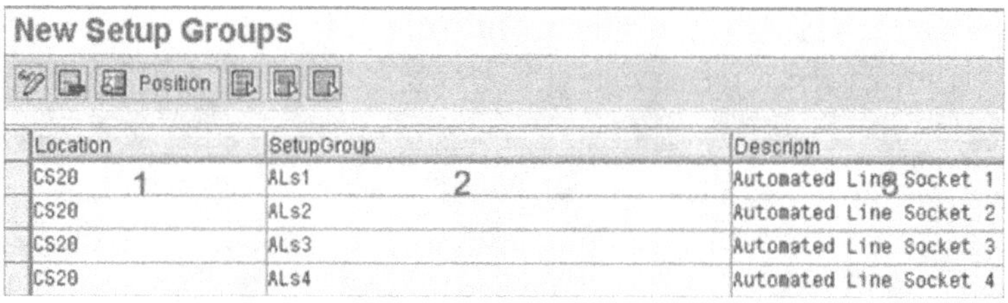

EXHIBIT 5.30 DEFINING THE SETUP MATRIX
© SAP AG. Used with permission.

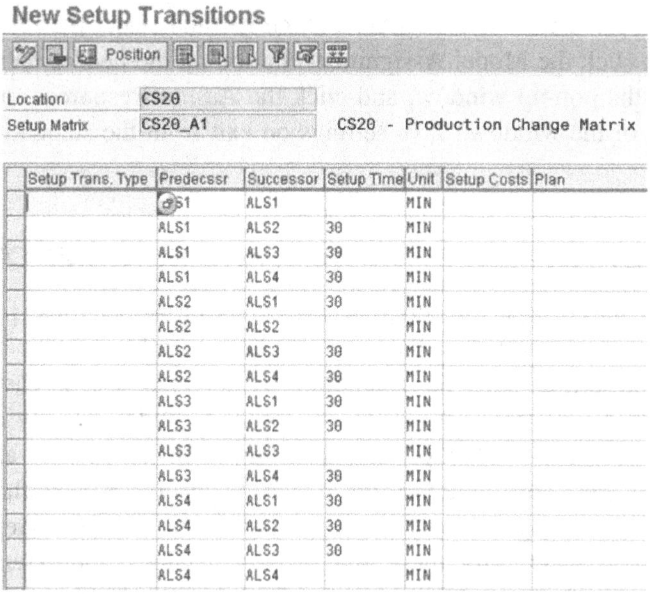

New Setup Transitions

		Position						

Location	CS20	
Setup Matrix	CS20_A1	CS20 - Production Change Matrix

Setup Trans. Type	Predecssr	Successor	Setup Time	Unit	Setup Costs	Plan
	ALS1	ALS1		MIN		
	ALS1	ALS2	30	MIN		
	ALS1	ALS3	30	MIN		
	ALS1	ALS4	30	MIN		
	ALS2	ALS1	30	MIN		
	ALS2	ALS2		MIN		
	ALS2	ALS3	30	MIN		
	ALS2	ALS4	30	MIN		
	ALS3	ALS1	30	MIN		
	ALS3	ALS2	30	MIN		
	ALS3	ALS3		MIN		
	ALS3	ALS4	30	MIN		
	ALS4	ALS1	30	MIN		
	ALS4	ALS2	30	MIN		
	ALS4	ALS3	30	MIN		
	ALS4	ALS4		MIN		

EXHIBIT 5.31 CONFIGURING THE SETUP MATRIX
Each setup group's transition from one to another must be defined. Transition impacts may be as time, cost (relative), or both. © SAP AG. Used with permission.

the location, matrix name, and description, then save results (Exhibit 5.30, steps 1 to 3). Highlight the new setup matrix and click the Choose button.

The actual setup matrix configuration screen will display. Again, click the New Entries button. If this is a standard setup type, the first column may be left blank, otherwise it can be set to "E" for an exception transition. Configure the matrix as in Exhibit 5.31 where every setup group's transition is defined with Predecessor and Successor, a Setup Time, and a Unit of Measure. Alternatively, or in addition to a time cost, a relative cost may also be assigned in the Setup Costs field. When done, save your results. The new setup matrix is now ready for assignment to a PP/DS resource as described in the section on Resource settings for Time Continuous Capacity.

Assigning a Resource to a Model

Once several conditions have been met, resources may be assigned to models where they will be ready for inclusion in processing by planning runs, heuristics, and optimization. A brief review of those conditions includes:

- Resource has been either CIF'd from SAP R/3 or manually created in SAP APO.
- If the resource was CIF'd from SAP R/3, detailed settings unavailable to SAP R/3 have been maintained if relevant.
- If setup matrixes are to be used, they have been both defined and manually assigned to the resource.
- Detailed settings for capacity variants, SNP, and PP/DS have been applied if relevant.

Once all of these conditions are met, assign the resource to a model by opening it in the standard resource transaction /SAPAPO/RES01/and select the resource that needs assignment. Then click the Model Assignments button on the header menu, highlight the desired model in the pop-up window, and click the Assign Resources to the Model button at the bottom of the window. Save settings on exit from the standard resource transaction.

PRODUCTION PROCESS MODELS AND RUN TIME OBJECTS

The supply chain master data objects discussed thus far—locations, products, and resources—all have in common that they are standard, tangible aspects of any organization's supply chain and as such their handling, if not their use, is easily apprehended by most users and developers. The production process model, usually called the PPM, and its related object, the production data structure (PDS), which is also called a run time object (RTO), each constitute the first two APO-specific objects that exist as much for the purpose of modeling a supply chain as they do for what they represent in it. As new concepts to most APO users, these, like models, versions, and external procurement relationships, are too often stumbling blocks to both business and technical users of the tool. These objects are the glue in our supply chain model: necessary to make a model, but not themselves carrying any definitive real-life analog to which one can relate.

While the lack of a perfect analog may be initially confusing to modelers, let us be clear on this point: *There is no reason that this need be so!* All of these new objects are actually quite straightforward—straightforward as glue. With minimal effort they will prove accessible to even novice users. We shall endeavor to provide a careful treatment so that no user becomes "lost in the woods" at this juncture, never to reappear on the other side ready and empowered to apply APO to model and plan complex, real-world supply chains. In order to avoid going astray, let us quickly consider why it is roundabout the PPM that so many would-be APO users lose their way.

APO works its magic by creating virtual models of a supply chain and then running those models through sophisticated mathematical simulations. Many parts of a model are straightforward: location and product, for example. Other parts of a model exist in the universe of the model alone and are necessary to the purpose of modeling, but have no direct analog in the real world. The objects "model" and "version" fit this case. Still other objects do in fact represent real-world objects, but are massaged somewhat to fit the internal logic of the tool. This is the case with PPMs, RTOs, and PDSs (the latter two are in fact the same thing), as well as quota arrangements and external procurement relationships, the latter of which are essentially virtual representations of contractual obligations.

Every supply chain specialist should be familiar with the concepts of BOM and route, the latter of which is also sometimes called a task list. Nonetheless, highly specialized users, such as demand, forecast, or procurement specialists, may have only limited familiarity with these two standard supply chain objects. Such users should look to Chapters 2 and 3 for a brief treatment of these standard objects *before* embarking on a detailed study of the PPM and PDS. Additionally, some users coming to APO from a technical programming or IT background may have very limited familiarity with many supply chain concepts. They, too, should spend time getting acquainted with these two objects before studying the technical details of the PPM and PDS.

Once you are familiar with the uses of both a BOM and route, however, both the PPM and the PDS become relatively straightforward as each object is simply a combination of the two. Where R/3, as system of reference for such master data objects, distinctly separates product from BOM from route, SAP APO maintains product as a separate object identity, but combines the BOM and route objects into one.

One should not come to the PPM or PDS and think of either object as being something new to the notion of supply chain management. Do not let the label get in the way: Both objects simply represent BOMs and routes combined in a single data container. Every time you think of a PPM, concern yourself with the BOM and the route it must represent. The same goes for the PDS. Both the PPM and the PDS are single objects, representing the standard supply chain objects of BOM and route but combining the two in one single object, nothing more.

PPM, RTO, and PDS: Why So Many?

If the PPM and the PDS are both models for the combination of a BOM and route, what is the point of having two separate objects do the same thing? And why, for that matter, are there two names for the RTO and PDS? These are good questions, and addressing them will help us explore the reasons APO uses these newly minted objects to manage old and familiar ones and to explore how businesses may choose to use one or the other depending on their own unique applications of APO.

We may start by saying that the RTO and the PDS are the same thing. While APO's navigation menu describes the object strictly as a PDS, we find that the term *RTO* is widely used in SAP publications synonymously with *PDS*. At this time it is not clear whether there is a strategic intent to this analogous naming or whether it is just a case of unsettled internal naming differences spilling out to the public. For our purposes, we shall exclusively use the term *PDS* when referring to that object.

As it concerns the reason for combining BOMs and routes into one object, we should note that the APO product is not designed to be a transactional system for material maintenance and production. To the contrary, it is explicitly designed as an analytical decision support system whose output will inform and direct material maintenance and production, but which does not control it transactionally. Accordingly, materials, BOM, and production routes are generally master data objects of concern for the transactional system controlling those things in actual production. Companies using SAP will usually rely on R/3 for this.

Since APO is a decision support system that assumes transactional control is being conducted elsewhere, it is neither necessary nor desirable to maintain strict bills of material or routes disembodied from their product. At the highest level two reasons drive this:

1. Not all details of a BOM must be maintained in APO in order for APO to carry out its modeling and decision support functions; hence it would be a waste of APO system resources to manage full-blown transactional BOMs.

2. Separated from their transactional function, routes set apart from the products, and more completely, the BOMs that employ them, have no useful application in APO. Their decision support value is only in their combination, never in their distinction.

A transactional system controlling BOMs must, for example, have sophisticated functionality for engineering change orders, wherein some BOMs are devoted to engineering and test while others are converted to standard production for customer sales. Furthermore, the transactional BOM system will enable component revisions as old components are replaced with newer ones to make more modern versions of finished products. Routes in transactional systems have purposes other than control of production: application of cost to production for financial accounting purposes for example. Such applications have no value to APO.

However, as a decision support tool designed to model and simulate the real-world supply chain as well as possible, APO does have use for specific identification of a BOM *together* with a route, where APO is going to be concerned with all of a product's components that require sophisticated planning and the processes required to make a finished good of those products; ergo we have the PPM and its recent cousin, the PDS.

R/3 and Supply Chain Basis of the PPM

The PPM is used in APO SNP and PP/DS to model and control three aspects of supply chain production: components of a finished good (both raw materials and semifinished goods), scheduling rates, and manufacturing resources. Take a moment to consider each item and why specific data about them is required by APO. First, products are usually sent via CIF from R/3 to APO; however, the product data alone tells APO nothing about the relationships between them. A BOM is necessary to indicate production dependencies between individual finished goods and their raw materials and semifinished goods. The BOM is received into APO and reflected as an element of the PPM. Second, in order to build a product we are concerned with both operational routes, that is, the path from one work center or operation to another that forms a process that yields a finished good and the details governing the pace at which the manufacturing process occurs. This data is maintained in detail in R/3 as a route. Third, very often there is more than one route a product may take from a raw materials state to production. A rudimentary example is that some sites have both manual and automated lines, and others have separate lines for engineering/research and conventional production. These alternative routes to the same product outcome are maintained in SAP R/3 as "production versions." Each of these three aspects of the PPM has an analog in SAP R/3 that we may summarize as follows:

PPM Object or Element	R/3 Object
Components and material relationships (finished good to raw to semifinished good):	BOM
Scheduling rates:	Route
Alternative manufacturing resources:	Production version

We may say then that each PPM represents a specific process for manufacturing that applies to exactly one finished good, one BOM, and one process of production activities and the alternative resources available to it.

Valid, time-phased route alternatives by which a product may be built are maintained in R/3 as "production versions," that is, alternative *versions* of production. By version A, for example, we may assemble a finished good BOM on route 1. By version B, we may assemble the same finished good on route 2. Exhibit 5.32 illustrates these relationships wherein we have a single BOM for a finished good, Product 01, combined with the possible individual routes available to assemble it, routes A, B, and C, in three distinct production versions indicating the three methods, or processes, for assembly. The CIF generates PP/DS PPMs for each production version in R/3 and, if necessary, additional steps are taken in APO to convert the PP/DS PPMs into SNP PPMs.

Using the PPM

We emphasize that in order to interact with PPMs and best exploit their power, in principle it will be essential to understand use of the PPM as if it were entirely maintained in APO apart from R/3 so that users are exposed to all the fields and components of the object whether or not they are normally maintained directly in APO. For that reason we will discuss maintenance of the PPMs in detail apart from maintaining their elements in R/3. Nonetheless, in actual practice, in almost all cases organizations will use the CIF to migrate R/3 data into APO, automatically generating the PPM and populating the majority of its fields. APO users will need to apply their expertise to interact with the PPM and conduct additional detailed maintenance that is unavailable and unnecessary on the R/3 side.

Access the PPM on the APO menu using path *Master Data → Production Process Model → Production Process Model,* or else using transaction /SAPAPO/SCC03. To

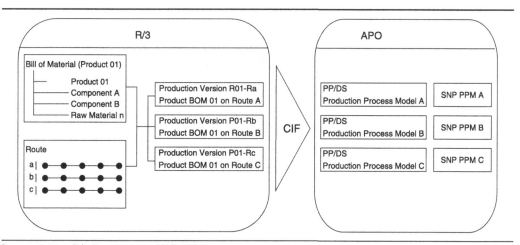

EXHIBIT 5.32 R/3 BASIS OF THE APO PPM
The R/3 BOM and routes are combined relationally in R/3 as the production version and in logical totality in APO as a PPM. Note that alternative BOMs are possible, in addition to the case of alternative routes as depicted in the exhibit; hence additional PPMs are possible in APO to represent alternative BOM combinations.

create, change, or display a plan one must identify the plan number and "Use of a Plan," or plan type, which refers to whether it is used for SNP or PP/DS in APO. If the plan number is not known, its location and product may be used to narrow the list of available PPMs for change and display purposes.

Plan and Plan Number

When CIF'd from SAP R/3, a number will be automatically generated for the PPM and only utilized by the system in PPM maintenance. Users will only see the PPM name (Exhibit 5.34, step 1) that populates the Plan field in the Plan section of the PPM. Plan name generation follows these rules:

Space 1   R/3 task list type that the PPM uses as a source of operations
Spaces 2–9   R/3 task list group number
Spaces 10–11   Counter of the R/3 groups number used to generate this PPM
Spaces 12–15   R/3 production version used to generate the PPM
Spaces 16–   The product and plant when one routing is used in several
                 plan numbers or else if it has more than one product
                 assigned to it

Exhibit 5.33 lists the R/3 task list types and their single-character moniker used in the first space of a PPM name to indicate the R/3 source of operations. The CIF will use the material description as the basis for the PPM description (Exhibit 5.34, step 2), though it acquires the description via the R/3 production version. The usage field indicates which APO module the PPM will be used for while the status field simply indicates whether the PPM is active in APO (Exhibit 5.34, step 3). The CIF will always default the usage field as PP/DS, or "P." One of the PP/DS-to-SNP conversion transactions must be used in concert with the CIF to convert PPMs for use by SNP. Those transactions are also

Character	SAP R/3 Task List Type
0	Standard Network (PS)
2	Master Recipe
3	Rough Cut Profile
A	General Maintenance Task List
E	Equipment Task List
N	Standard Routing
M	Reference Rate Routing
R	Rate Routing
S	Reference Operation Set
T	Task List for Functional Location

EXHIBIT 5.33   R/3 TASK LIST TYPE INDICATORS ON
THE PPM NAME

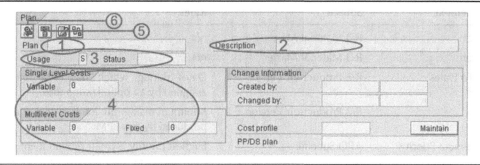

EXHIBIT 5.34   PPM Plan0
© SAP AG. Used with permission.

Cost	Applicable Optimization Engine
Single-Level Variable	SNP Optimizer
Multiple-Level Variable	CTM, PP/DS Planning Run
Multiple-Level Fixed	CTM, SNP Heuristic, PP/DS Planning Run

EXHIBIT 5.35   APPLICATION OF PPM PLAN COSTS IN APO OPTIMIZERS

available under the PPM folder in the Master Data section of the APO navigation menu. The remaining cost fields in the plan section (Exhibit 5.34, step 4) are all APO specific and are not maintained in R/3 or through the CIF. Exhibit 5.35 treats how each cost field is applied by the various optimization engines in APO.

Product Plan Assignment

The product plan assignment stores information for source determination and may be accessed by clicking the Product Plan Assignment button on the Plan section of the initial screen of the PPM (Exhibit 5–34, step 5). Product plan assignment data is used by the various APO optimization tools (SNP optimizer, heuristics, and PP/DS planning run) to determine when to assign a production process to build a product. See Exhibit 5.36 for data maintenance sources for the product plan assignment's data elements and for rules APO applies when determining sources from this data.

Operations

In SAP APO the operation is primarily applied as a container for activities where most production control data is maintained. The operations view is available by default when the initial screen of a PPM is opened, but it can be acquired by clicking the Operations button on the Plan section (Exhibit 5.34, step 6). The Setup Group/Key Field is the primary useful field of the operation and must receive an APO-specific (non-CIF'd) assignment (see Setup Matrix section in this chapter and more detailed coverage in Chapter 8), which will apply setup time and cost specifications to the PPM. Double-click the operation description to access its activities.

Data Element	Source	Rules
Product	R/3 Material Master	n/a
Location	R/3 Material Master	n/a
From/To Dates	R/3 Production Version	Dates during which the PPM may be assigned by an optimization tool
Lot Size	R/3 Production Version	Minimum/maximum lot size that may be produced by this PPM
Procurement Priority	APO Specific	Highest priority is 0—if procurement priority is the same from one PPM to another, PP/DS selects the PPMs with lower costs

EXHIBIT 5.36   PRODUCT PLAN ASSIGNMENT DATA ELEMENT SOURCES AND RULES

Operation Activities

In the APO model, activities contain the detail, steps, and sequences for manufacturing. When transferred from R/3 via CIF, the R/3 operation's setup, process, tear-down, and duration activities are transferred in their order as APO activities. Each activity contains components required for manufacturing and resources necessary for manufacturing, the latter of which are displayed in the activity as alternative "modes." Only R/3 activities that are relevant for scheduling are transferred as APO activities. Exhibit 5.37 lists the data elements of a PPM activity, rules for assigning their values, and the effects of those values in APO models.

Components

A PPM is the combination of a BOM and route. Component parts from a material BOM may be attached to activities so that they are consumed at the activity's particular step in the build process. It is not necessary for every R/3 material and component to be planned in SAP APO; those regarded as APO relevant are so specified in the material master and the CIF will ignore them during transfer. As such, only APO-relevant components on the BOM brought into the PPM will be available as components to the activity.

The PPM describes materials here as "logical components." The point of this designation is that there may be more than one actual, physical, or technical alternative indicated by a specific material depending on point in time. Very often, for example, component parts to a material go through a revision process, or "rev-step," where they may be upgraded as the product is improved or tailored for niche markets. A handheld video game that comes with a battery, for example, may have a more powerful battery from one revision to another, sold as the same final product in either case—a video game—but as an improved revision based on an upgraded component. The battery in this case may be a "logical component," where the battery is always required, but the specific physical component used for the battery varies depending on the date of manufacture.

Every component assigned to the PPM receives an indicator of "I" for input (Exhibit 5.38, step 1), such as raw materials or work-in-process that will be consumed at that point in the build process, or "O" for output (Exhibit 5.38, step 2), such as a semifinished good or stock item that results as a consequence of the activity's process. When the

Data Element	Value Assignment	Rules for Model Control
Activity	The type of activity occurring on the routing, determined automatically if CIF is used; four cases are: P—Production, S—Setup, T—Tear Down, W—Wait Time.	
Activity Type	If CIF is used, determined automatically, matches the activity name as above.	
Description	Automatically matches activity type.	
Scrap %	If CIF is used, will map directly to scrap % field on the SAP R/3 operation.	Production algorithms ordinarily add production units to lots to account for an expected scrap outcome.
Setup Indicator	Automatically set if a setup group and key are established.	Makes the PPM apply the setup matrix to find the sequence-based setup time instead of using setup times transferred via CIF from R/3.
Synchronization Behavior	This setting is not established by the CIF and is native only to APO.	When used, this indicator overrides synchronization behavior of otherwise overlapped activities such as may be the case with multi-activity, multi-mixed resource, forcing schedules by sequence without overlap.
Order Validity	This setting is not established by the CIF and is native only to APO.	Restricts dates during which an order can be scheduled or rescheduled—if set, order can be scheduled only during validity dates; if not, an order can be scheduled on any dates.
Time Dependent	This setting is not established by the CIF and is native only to APO.	When set, indicates that time-dependent planning parameters are maintained in the PPM, allowing time-based parameters for scrap activities, modes, consumption on resources, and components.

EXHIBIT 5.37 PPM ACTIVITY DATA ELEMENTS IN APO MODELS

resulting good is the top-level material on the BOM, the finished good, the primary product indicator is selected (Exhibit 5.38, step 3).

CIF rules for assignment of materials from the R/3 BOM to the PPM are somewhat sophisticated and must be carefully taken into account when business procedures for data maintenance in all systems are defined. Refer to Exhibit 5.39 for CIF rules for component allocation to a PPM. These rules must necessarily be complex since R/3 users have a number of options available to them and the CIF design cannot assume any one such option is in use by any APO PPM user.

In addition to input and output settings, some APO users may choose to apply consumption types for scheduling that will more specifically control when a component is consumed during an activity. If the CIF is used, consumption quantities are assigned

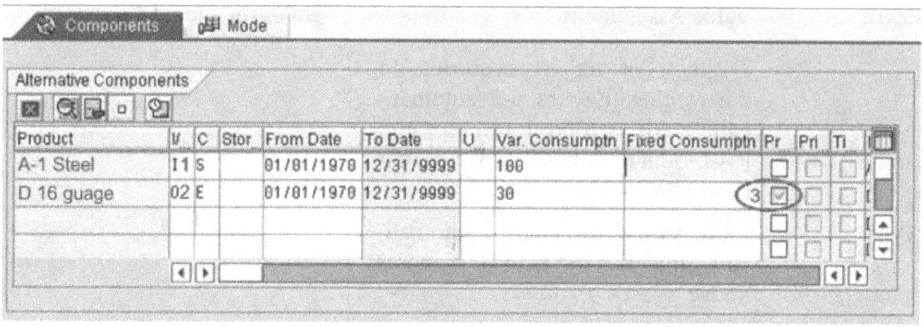

EXHIBIT 5.38 PPM COMPONENTS

Not all components from the R/3 BOM will be available to the PPM, only (1) those that have been manually set up in APO or (2) (when the CIF is used) those in R/3 which have been defined as APO relevant in the material master special material setting field. The final product of a PPM, typically the finished good, is indicated via the Primary Product indicator setting. © SAP AG. Used with permission.

R/3 Route Component Allocation	Operation Activities	Rules for CIF Component Allocation
Applied to PPM	N/A	When route component allocation is used in R/3, the activity assignments from R/3 will transfer with the CIF.
Not Applied to PPM	Produce and Setup exist.	Components are assigned to the setup activity; the finished good is assigned as an output component to the produce activity.
Not Applied to PPM	Setup only exists.	Components and finished good are all assigned to the setup activity.

EXHIBIT 5.39 CIF RULES FOR COMPONENT ALLOCATION TO A PPM

based on the R/3 BOM. When using CTM in SNP, APO users may apply the Prevention of Product Explosion indicator, which will prevent creation of planned orders for the component during PPM explosion on the CTM run. In such cases the system will rely only on available component supplies without creating new ones.

Modes

Modes enable the scheduling of an activity on a resource. The mode on an APO PPM is essentially the equivalent of a work center; where operations are assigned to work centers, therefore, activities are assigned to modes. Each activity has material and capacity requirements determined through the mode by way of the fact that the mode acts as primary determinant of capacity bottlenecks in a production process. APO recognizes two kinds of modes: primary and secondary. There can be only one primary mode but several secondaries. Each mode is recognized as alternative resources available for production of the same activity. When APO's optimization tools execute they consider each mode, its costs and constraints, as an option for production and assign orders to the modes accordingly.

When using the CIF the mode will be generated automatically. The CIF recognizes the work center from an operation with the primary sequence as mode 1, the primary mode. All subsequent modes are assigned sequential numbers and are treated as secondaries. Modes are particularly important for maintaining item-level beat-rate designations and relative priorities. *Beat rate* refers to the pace of production at a work center; for example, a work center may produce one unit every 60 seconds. Each alternative work center or resource on a PPM has a mode and each product/mode combination has a unique beat rate. Maintain the beat rate on every mode with a unit of measure such as second, minute, or hour, and maintain the production value in variable or fixed production. Mode priorities are APO specific and are the most important means by which optimization tools schedule activities onto the modes. Priorities are assigned by letter, with A being the highest and Z being such that material should be scheduled only manually to the mode.

Primary Resources

The top level of the mode tab for activities will display a primary resource line. Work capacity and schedule assignment occur on the primary resource. When CIF is used, the work center with a capacity category of 001 in R/3 will be transferred as the primary resource on the mode along with information for location and unit of measure. Typically formulas are assigned in R/3 to control derivation of schedules based on quantities of work required, in which case the duration is variable and the fixed duration field is blank because APO will rely on R/3 formula data brought by the CIF (Exhibit 5.40, step 1). If formulas are not used, the operational duration is entered in the field instead, which may be automatically by the CIF if CIF is used; otherwise the entry will be manual.

The Break Not Allowed field is APO specific and cannot be maintained via CIF (Exhibit 5.40, step 2). When this field is selected the system will not allow interruptions of processing by breaks in time. For example, if total production time is six hours and only two hours remain in the day before tear-down, the optimization tools will not schedule a new lot for production during the two-hour gap. The other field, Break Without Inter-ruption, is also APO specific (Exhibit 5.40, step 3). When unselected, the optimization tools will allow order scheduling over multiple days without conditions. When selected, add a duration in the field using format HHHHHH:MM, which will apply the longest permissible break between operations.

Secondary Resources

Frequently there is more than one source of a bottleneck or constraint in a production process significant enough to require visibility to the optimization tool, such as time, labor, or equipment. Additional constraints may be established as secondary resources on the mode. Define secondary resources by double-clicking the primary resource in the mode tab of the activity. The primary resource will carry into the resulting screen as the first resource listed, but additional secondary resources may be added to the subsequent lines. Field assignments for secondary resources depend on the activity type the resource

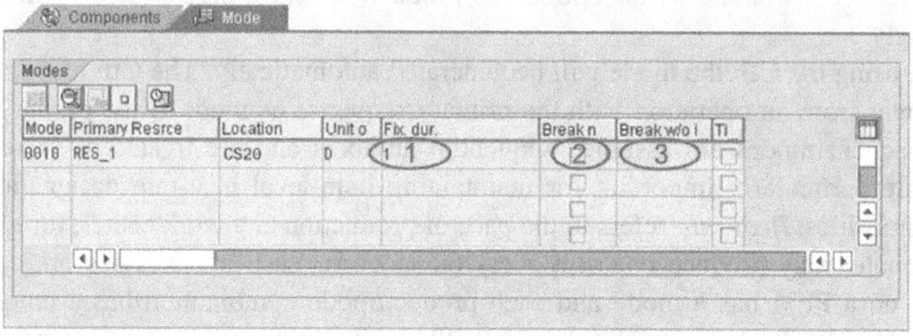

EXHIBIT 5.40 PPM MODES: PRIMARY RESOURCE ASSIGNMENT
© SAP AG. Used with permission.

Resource Type	Consumption	
	Variable Bucket	Fixed Bucket
Single Activity		
Multiple Activity	X	
Bucket		X
Single Mixed Activity		X
Multiple Mixed Activity	X	

EXHIBIT 5.41 SECONDARY RESOURCE CONSUMPTION ASSIGNMENT BY TYPE
© SAP AG. Used with permission.

will be applied to, affecting whether it will employ bucket or variable consumption. Exhibit 5.41 illustrates a simple rule set for consumption assignment by resource type.

PPM Activation

PPMs that are created or edited manually, as would be likely for SNP PPMs, begin as "inactive"; that is, they are unavailable to liveCache. While inactive PPMs may be stored, retrieved, viewed, and edited, they will not be assigned to any models or versions, or applied in any simulations or planning runs. Manually activate an inactive PPM by clicking the Activate button when ready, then saving the PPM (Exhibit 5.42)—activation requires both steps. PPMs generated by the CIF will be automatically activated.

EXHIBIT 5.42 PPM ACTIVATION
For manual activation, simply click the "Activate" button, then save. Once activated and saved, the PPM will be available to liveCache and will begin assigning resources to build a product, plan constraints, and consume components. © SAP AG. Used with permission.

SNP versus PP/DS

The PPM object was designed by SAP to meet the needs of PP/DS first and SNP by extension. This is why when CIF is used the PPM type will come over as PP/DS automatically and must be changed to S, or SNP, using other native APO transactions (Exhibit 5.43). Additionally, where PP/DS is concerned primarily with short-term (usually <1 month) time horizons wherein engineering changes to product lines are not very important to scheduling, SNP is concerned with longer horizons, usually four months to one year, where engineering changes become quite germane to the planning process.

A current product, for example, may have a lifecycle that begins to wane four months out, completely closing six months out. During that time it is cannibalized by a newer revision of the same product. R/3 provides a feature for managing changes to finished goods through BOM structures: Engineering Change Management (ECM). Companies employing considerable engineering changes over the course of a product lifecycle have been limited to PPMs designed primarily for PP/DS, which do not support ECM in R/3. Another feature of R/3 is Variant Configuration (VC), which enhances master data modeling using a master recipe that controls object dependencies. PPMs do not support VC either.

SCM 4.0 and subsequent editions of APO offer companies an alternative object, the Production Data Structure, which is an enhancement of the PPM, enabling variant configuration of object dependencies and ECM for time-based product change management. The benefit of using the PDS over the PPM is that the PDS will enable APO users to employ ECM and VC without restriction in R/3 and in so doing they will be able to import the change management benefits of these capabilities to APO. In other words, by way of adoption of the PDS in lieu of the PPM, a company may employ ECM and/or VC to control changes to object dependencies on components or operations over time and reflect the change control in APO.

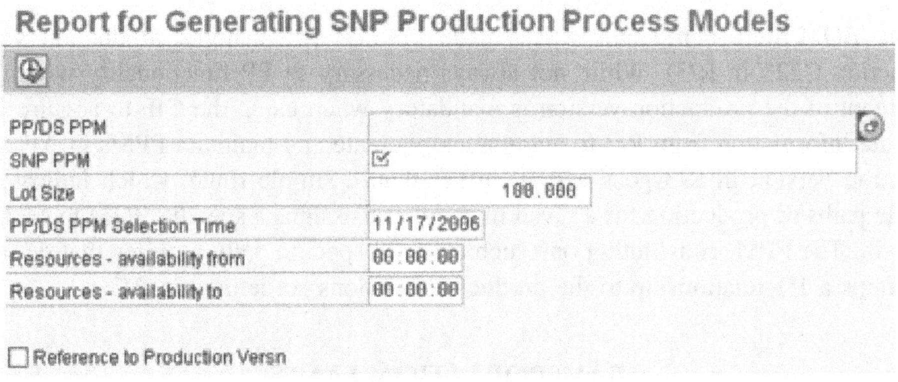

Report for Generating SNP Production Process Models

PP/DS PPM	
SNP PPM	☑
Lot Size	100.000
PP/DS PPM Selection Time	11/17/2006
Resources - availability from	00.00:00
Resources - availability to	00:00:00

☐ Reference to Production Versn

EXHIBIT 5.43 SNP PPM GENERATION WITHOUT LOT SIZE MARGIN
Use to generate an SNP PPM from a PP/DS PPM. Transaction is found on path *Master Data → Production Process Model → SNP PPM Generation without Lot Size Margin* (option also exists for "with"). © SAP AG. Used with permission.

── PDS OR PPM? ──

Companies considering conversion to the PDS from PPMs will generally find these two aspects of the PDS as cause to go about the conversion:

1. The PDS enables change-management capabilities now available in R/3 and inherits them from APO.
2. No conversion of PP/DS to SNP objects is required. The PDS may be directly CIF'd from R/3 to APO as either object type.

Nonetheless, at this time the PDS is not entirely without drawbacks. At the time of this text's writing, versions of APO through SCM 4.1 reflect this limitation of the PDS versus the earlier PPM:

Alternative sequence routes in R/3 yield reflective alternative sequence PPMs; alternative sequence PDSs via CIF propagation in APO are not currently available.

PPM Structure

Apart from the fact that the notion of a PPM may seem a bit new to many users, PPMs also often pose a hindrance by way of their complex structure. Indeed, PPMs do a lot. Once defined and activated they provide the data that allows APO to assign resources to build a product, prioritize those resources, shift build schedules from one resource to another by way of constraints, and consume components during the build process. Their multipurpose nature yields a multilevel structure that can confuse.

Using both a logical hierarchy and the visual analog of the PPM provided by APO within the PPM definition, we can take a top-down view of the PPM that creates a business process narrative for the object. In Exhibit 5.44 we see a PPM plan wherein there is one operation, 0010, employed to build a finished good, FG86991. There is only one activity, 0001, to which work center WC010 is assigned as a resource. The activity has one mode, or process, with which to manufacture the material. Two components are consumed by the activity (note arrows pointed into the mode) and one finished good results (note arrows pointing out of the mode toward the finished good).

CIF Considerations: Use of the Production Version

Specific BOM/route combinations are made in SAP R/3 using a production version (transaction C223 in R/3). While not always necessary to PP functionality within R/3, assignment of the production version is mandatory when using the CIF to acquire BOM and route information from R/3 to automatically create and maintain PPMs in APO. The production version in R/3 goes a step further than a simple route, which indicates the possible paths of production for a given material and assigns a specific BOM to each specific path. The PPM, constituting one such explicit, specific path, requires that definition and retains a 1:1 relationship to the production versions so defined in R/3.

TRANSPORTATION LANES

Transportation lanes are objects that represent the connections in a supply chain network between sources of supply and their destinations. A transportation lane is defined to represent a direct route between two specified locations and the methods of transport

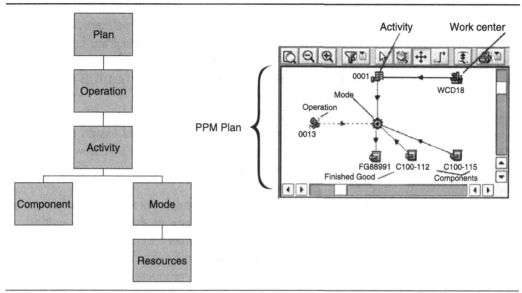

EXHIBIT 5.44 PPM STRUCTURE

Logical view on left: At the top of a PPM is the plan, essentially the header data denoting a manufacturing process. Plans may contain one or more operations, which in turn may contain one or more activities, which will be either setup, produce, or teardown. Activities both consume components and generate goods, which may be the finished good, and they are conducted by one or more modes—or alternative production methods, which themselves rely on resources. Direct navigation through the PPM follows this logic. *Visual view from APO on right*: The entire PPM is displayed as contained in the plan. We see that work center WC010 is assigned to activity 0001, which employs mode 1 to use the work center to build a finished good, FG80991. Two components are planned in APO and consumed by the activity: C100-112 and C100-115. © SAP AG. Used with permission.

employed on that route. They are employed by both SNP and PP/DS, which are covered in this text, but also by other modules of SCM such as deployment, the transport load builder, TP/VS, and Global Available to Promise (GATP). The transportation lane object will contain information about the procurement of product on the lane, the means of transport, which products may be used by that means of transport, the transportation capacity, and costs.

There is no equivalent structure in R/3 to the APO transportation lane, though it is still possible to employ the CIF to create transportation lanes by way of maintenance of a special procurement key on the R/3 material master together with purchasing info records, contracts, or schedule agreements. Such automated maintenance of transportation lanes will be covered in the next section: External Procurement Relationships.

Maintaining Transportation Lanes

Whether or not the CIF and purchasing arrangements are employed to automatically maintain transportation lanes, they may be manually maintained one-by-one or in mass. Transaction /SAPAPO/SCC_TL1, by path *Master Data → Transportation Lane → Transportation Lane*, will open the primary, single-item transportation lane maintenance transaction. On the initial screen a model, start location, and destination location must be specified to uniquely identify the transportation lane to be maintained. Generally the "Display" and "Change" view will be used more often during maintenance, but for example purposes we will assume use of "Create" so as to demonstrate creation of a new transportation lane. To create a new lane, specify an as-yet unused combination of locations between which material is moved and indicate the model that will contain and simulate the lane, then press Create.

The transportation lane transaction will display three panels, the top one being for the assignment of product to the lane. Continue the creation process and assign products by pressing the Create button on this top panel (Exhibit 5.45, step 1). A new panel will display on the right-hand side of the screen with a number of settings for assigning product.

The first thing will be to assign either a specific product, all available products, or else a filtered group of products to the transportation lane in the Products section of the right-hand panel (Exhibit 5.46, step 1). Indicate the dates during which the system should recognize these products as valid for the transportation lane in the Validity section (Exhibit 5.46, step 2). Click the Copy button to save the products to the lane and close (Exhibit 5.46, step 3).

Next, create a means of transport for your lane by clicking the New button on the second panel, which will also open up a right-hand panel to enter the details for the transportation method. In the Validity Period section, enter the means of transport (truck, airplane, train, courier, ship, or car) and the dates during which that means is valid (Exhibit 5.47, step 1). In the Control Parameters section one may indicate whether this will be valid for all products on the lane, if it is valid for SNP or PP/DS (Aggr. Planning indicator), or TP/VS (Detld Planning indicator), and whether to fix duration and distance values or else keep them available to update by automation (Exhibit 5.47, step 2).

The Parameters section will usually be employed when detailed transportation scheduling such as is possible with TP/VS is employed, but there are a number of settings that are nonetheless relevant to SNP (Exhibit 5.47, step 3). A transportation calendar will operate like a factory calendar, for example, in excluding certain days from potential for travel. If durations and distances are not known precisely, you may press the Generate Proposal button to employ the native GIS and gain a proposed value. SNP-relevant costs and cost functions may be assigned on the Transportation Costs and Cost Function fields (Exhibit 5.47, step 4). These will be discussed more in Chapter 8.

When done entering settings, click the Copy button to close the right-hand panel and adopt the means of transport to the lane. Repeat entry of a means of transport for

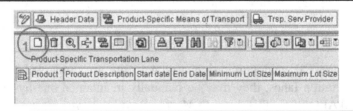

EXHIBIT 5.45   CREATING A TRANSPORTATION LANE
© SAP AG. Used with permission.

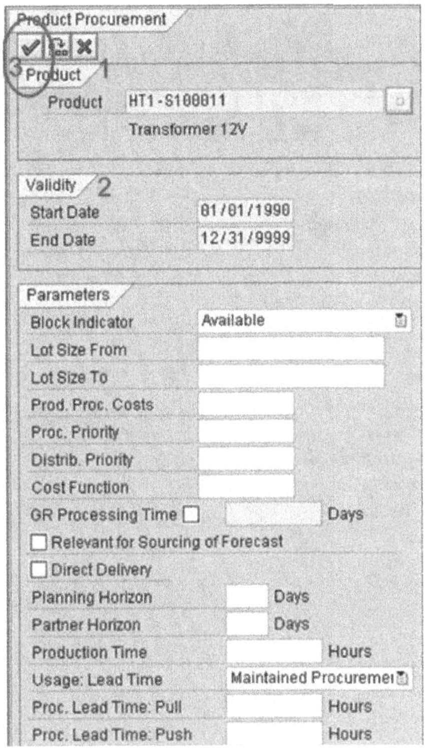

EXHIBIT 5.46 PRODUCT ASSIGNMENT TO A TRANSPORTATION LANE
The only essential maintenance is to indicate which products will be assigned to the lane and the validity period during which the system should recognize those products on the lane for planning purposes. © SAP AG. Used with permission.

each means available to the lane. Save changes before exiting the transportation lane transaction or all changes will be lost.

EXTERNAL PROCUREMENT RELATIONSHIPS

External Procurement Relationships (EPR) is an object in APO that broadly encompasses any procurement contract object governing or in many cases semi-automating purchasing agreements between sites, organizations, and companies. Three purchasing objects in R/3 have analogs in APO as EPRs: scheduling agreements, purchasing info records, and contracts. These three purchasing objects usually have the effect of being blanket purchase orders that automatically go into effect under predefined supply/demand conditions. The existence of an EPR denotes that a transportation lane must exist between the two parties to the EPR. Generally speaking, therefore, if a transportation lane has already been maintained in APO and an EPR is created, APO will link the two. If an EPR is created, or more likely extended to APO by CIF, APO may apply the special procurement key from the R/3 material master to automatically create a transportation lane. For this reason some describe EPRs as "automated transportation lanes."

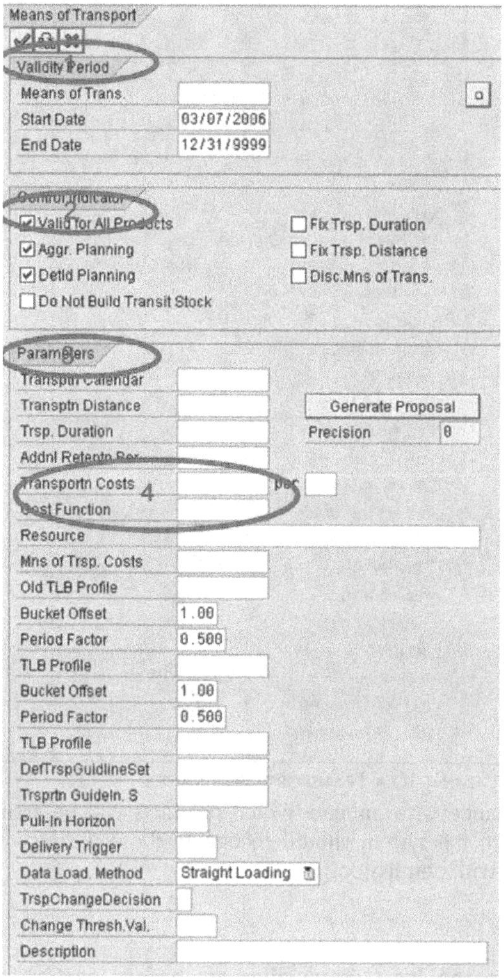

EXHIBIT 5.47 CREATE A MEANS OF TRANSPORT
© SAP AG. Used with permission.

External Procurement Relationships are viewed and maintained in APO using transaction /SAPAPO/PWBSRC1, path *Master Data → Procurement Master Data → Procurement Relationships*. Almost universally, purchasing contract information will be maintained in R/3 and CIF'd over to APO. As such, direct maintenance of EPRs is less important to most APO users than is an understanding of how supply and demand is managed across the two systems when they are used in concert for purchasing by way of EPRs. Generally speaking, there may be three different methods of configuring purchasing object control that will result in three different strategies for relating demand for purchased parts to supply controlled by the purchasing objects and for managing the purchasing objects with either R/3 or APO as the master system. Briefly those three methods are:

1. *Procurement using info records or contracts.* Whenever used between the two systems, info records and contracts are used and reflected in APO but managed in R/3.

2. *Procurement using R/3 scheduling agreements.* Scheduling agreement is used and reflected in APO but managed in R/3.
3. *Procurement using APO scheduling agreements.* Scheduling agreement is used and managed in APO and reflected in R/3.

The three methods vary only in which purchasing object is applied and in the interaction with and governance of the object—that is, whether the object is interacted with in R/3 and reflected in APO, or vice versa.

Refresher: Procurement Basics in SCM

We discussed MRP management of dependent and independent requirements in our earlier treatment of generic supply chain management, but a brief reminder may be in order. Generally speaking, organizations will be interested in forecasting sales of, and master planning of, their finished good product or service that they will provide or sell to customers. Though some exceptions exist where supplies may be highly constrained, components of the finished good, whether they be raw materials or semifinished goods, typically do not require outright forecast or master scheduling. This is because all the components of the finished product may be stored in a material BOM structure. Hence, we know that if we need to assemble a bottle of bottled water, we will need one plastic bottle, one cap, one label, and a specified quantity of purified water, 1 liter for example.

All our water-bottling company needs to forecast and plan for is the final product, the ready-to-sell bottled water. Using the following simple BOM structure we can rely on MRP to derive planning requirements for all the water bottle's components:

1 unit bottled water:
1 plastic bottle
1 pre-glued label
1 cap
1 liter purified water

If we forecast demand of 2,000 units of bottled water and we plan to assemble the bottles at a pace of 500 units per day, we can feed the BOM to MRP, which will generate "dependent requirements" schedules for all the components. The outcome of the MRP run will be to note the following demand elements:

- 2,000 units of bottled water ("independent requirements" provided by master scheduling and forecast)
- 2,000 units of plastic bottles ("dependent requirements" computed by MRP)
- 2,000 pre-glued labels ("dependent requirements" computed by MRP)
- 2,000 caps ("dependent requirements" computed by MRP)
- 2,000 liters purified water ("dependent requirements" computed by MRP)

From our master schedule, spreading assembly over four days, MRP may compute planned orders, destined to become production orders, of 500 units each for the bottled water. Additionally and of particular concern to procurement, it will generate purchase requisitions, destined to become purchase orders, for the plastic bottles, labels, caps, and water itself—assuming of course that none of these components is assembled in-house.

External Procurement Relationships in APO generally govern the following: (1) what kind of purchasing object is used (purchase requisitions and orders versus schedule lines, which are blanket purchase orders drafted according to a "scheduling agreement"), (2) whether only initial generation of the purchasing object is controlled by an APO planning run or else all subsequent scheduling is controlled by the planning run, (3) the degree of manual intervention required to make a purchasing object manual, and (4) in which system, APO or R/3, the purchasing object originates.

EPR with Info Record or Contract

Info records and contracts maintained in R/3 will be transferred to APO via the CIF, where they will create analogous EPRs and transportation lanes (if the latter have not already been maintained). Any demand element such as a sales order will result in dependent material requirements that are either CIF'd over to APO or else generated by one of APO's planning runs. Dependent material requirements in turn cause the APO planning run to generate purchasing requisitions to fulfill them. APO-generated purchasing requisitions are transmitted to R/3 via the CIF and are managed there, where they are (1) converted into purchase orders (whose object is transferred back to APO via CIF), and (2) confirmed (wherein the confirmation updates are also transferred back to APO via CIF), and finally (3) ongoing and final goods receipts are conducted (data changes that are also transferred back to the analogous object in APO via CIF) (Exhibit 5.48).

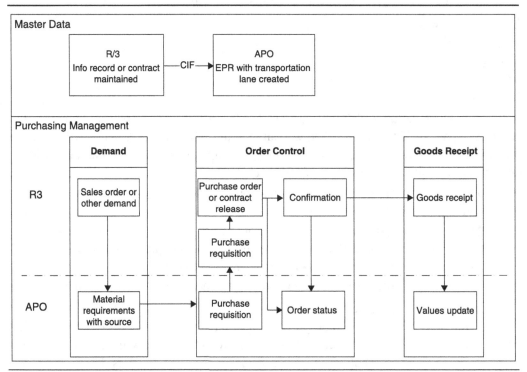

EXHIBIT 5.48   EPR WITH INFO RECORD OR CONTRACT

EPR with R/3 Scheduling Agreements

External Procurement Relationships using R/3 scheduling agreements differs from info records and contracts mostly just in the object chosen for managing the relationship. (See Exhibit 5.49.) The basic governance structure is essentially identical. Scheduling agreements maintained in R/3 are CIF'd over to APO, where they generate analogous EPRs and transportation lanes. Demand, usually sourced in R/3, drives an APO planning run to generate dependent material requirements and external supply as purchase requisitions to fulfill them. The resultant purchase requisitions are sent to R/3 via CIF and converted to delivery lines where their confirmation and acknowledgment is managed. Updates as such are reflected, but not controlled, in APO. Likewise, actual goods receipt is managed in R/3 and subsequently reflected in APO.

EPR with APO Scheduling Agreements

Use of APO scheduling agreements will seem somewhat confusing to a novice user of either R/3 or APO. It may be helpful to keep the goal of this strategy in mind when trying to ascertain it: Use of APO scheduling agreements gives complete control of delivery scheduling to the APO planning run while still using R/3 to manage day-to-day manual updates such as confirmations and receipts.

To use APO scheduling agreements specify that the schedule lines will be created by an external system in the Additional Data tab when maintaining the schedule agreement in R/3. During CIF of the scheduling agreement (SA) over to APO, the SA will be identified

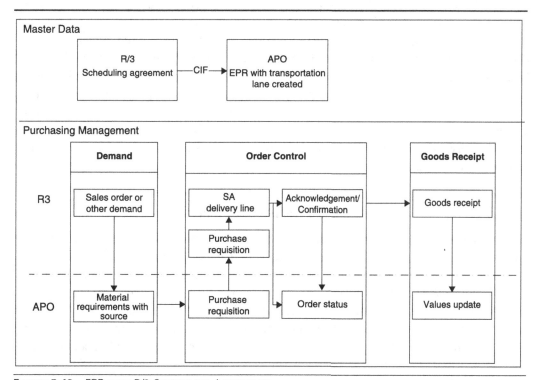

EXHIBIT 5.49   EPR WITH R/3 SCHEDULING AGREEMENTS

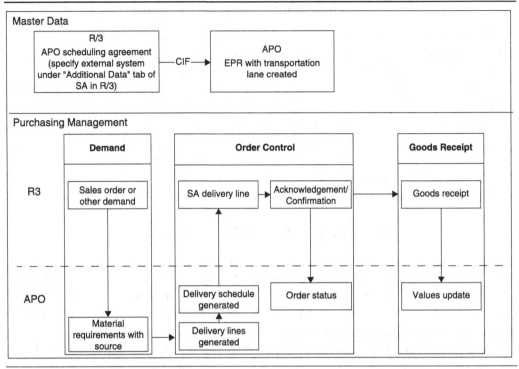

EXHIBIT 5.50   EPR WITH APO SCHEDULING AGREEMENTS

as an APO-controlled object. Initial processing of the APO scheduling agreement will be more of the same of the previous two methods, with demand from R/3 or another external system providing requirements via the CIF to drive an APO planning run, which generates dependent material requirements that in turn require external procurement to fulfill. From here, however, things differ in that APO's planning run generates the schedule lines directly in APO to fulfill the requirements without using the manual purchase-requisition step. Those schedule lines are reflected immediately via CIF in R/3. Actual confirmation and goods receipts continue to be maintained in R/3, and changes to them result in reduced order quantity, cancellation, and stock updates in APO, which are in turn reflected in APO planning runs (Exhibit 5.50).

QUOTA ARRANGEMENTS

The ostensible point of using a product like APO is to determine the optimal method of production and delivery—which is customarily understood to be the lowest-cost method of providing product of sufficient quantity to a customer on time or within reasonable control limits. Very often, however, we are not perfectly free to enact any solution that will result in the absolute lowest short-term cost. Typically, for long-term strategic reasons that are ordinarily justified by a concern for a stable flow of supply, organizations are constrained by contractual relationships with suppliers that mandate specified purchasing schemes. Part of these contracts will be represented in APO via EPR, but the schematic aspect of the contracts—governing how much of a product must be acquired from one supplier or another and at what time or under what circumstances—is governed separately. Furthermore, all of this combines to create short-term constraints on potential scheduling solutions generated by APO.

Resources and production process models tell us much about how a product is built and the costs and time associated with building it, which is, of course, very important information when one is conducting algorithms that seek to derive optimal build schedules. Yet we have already seen that much of the material that goes into production is not built, but bought. This immediately raises an issue of great concern to questions of optimization: Often the same material may be acquired from different sources or suppliers, or else from the same source, but by different means, such as by plane or boat. Different suppliers and methods of supply will entail different costs. Furthermore, very often legal arrangements are derived that require that we favor one supplier over another regardless of cost considerations. Control of supplier choice is maintained in APO via quota arrangements, which assign quotas to the use of one source of supply or another and may work in some cases to override cost considerations by an optimizer if necessary.

Using Quota Arrangements

Quota arrangements are among the rare master data objects that exist in both R/3 and APO, but which nonetheless must be maintained in both places separately and cannot be enabled via CIF. They are defined by location and assigned to a model in APO (Exhibit 5.51, step 1). Within a model they may be version independent, applying to all versions in the model, or version dependent, applying to only one (Exhibit 5.51, step 2). Additionally, quota arrangements may be maintained for both incoming and outgoing product (Exhibit 5.51, step 3). In other words, we may have a quota arrangement that requires that we purchase 80% of a product from supplier A and 20% from supplier B (or else 100,000 from supplier A before purchasing all other units or a percentage thereof

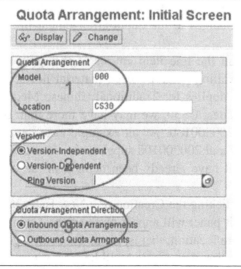

EXHIBIT 5.51 QUOTA ARRANGEMENT INITIAL SCREEN

© SAP AG. Used with permission.

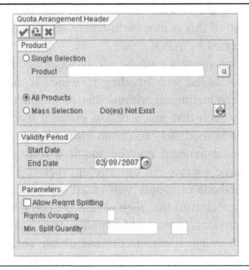

EXHIBIT 5.52   QUOTA ARRANGEMENT EDIT PANEL
© SAP AG. Used with permission.

from supplier B), but additionally we may have a quota arrangement that mandates that we supply customer 1 with 50,000 units before supplying customer 2 at all.

To actively maintain (or even create) a quota arrangement, click the Change button on the initial screen. The inside of the quota arrangement transaction is structured much like that of transportation lanes. As with transportation lanes, to create a new quota arrangement click the Creation of a New Entry in the upper table, which will open an editing panel on the right side of the screen. Otherwise, if just maintaining the quota arrangement, simply double-click the quota arrangement line-item to pull up the same panel. Indicate whether the arrangement is for a specific product, all products at the site, or else a filtered selection thereof. Additionally assign start and end dates for the validity period in which APO should consider the quota arrangement (Exhibit 5.52). Click the checkbox to apply your changes to the quota arrangement line table and close the edit panel.

Next, create or maintain the line item entries of the quota arrangement. These will be the actual entries controlling splits between material flows. Let us use our case of a manufacturer of medical supplies for Traditional Chinese Medicine. If we are trying to supply one of our China sites, CS30, we may have more than one supplier to that size, vendors 200100100 and 200300100. As an example case, assume 200100100 supplies 75% of a product to CS30 and 200300100 supplies the other 25%. The products supplied for this quota arrangement have already been defined in the quota arrangement header above.

Create new entries by clicking the Creation of a New Entry button on the bottom table of the screen; again an edit panel will appear on the right. Ordinarily quota arrangements will be assigned to an entire location; that is, if this quota arrangement has been set up for China Site 30, CS30, each line item entered will be for a separate vendor sourcing CS30. APO permits additional functionality, however, whereby separate quota arrangements may be defined for in-house production within the site.

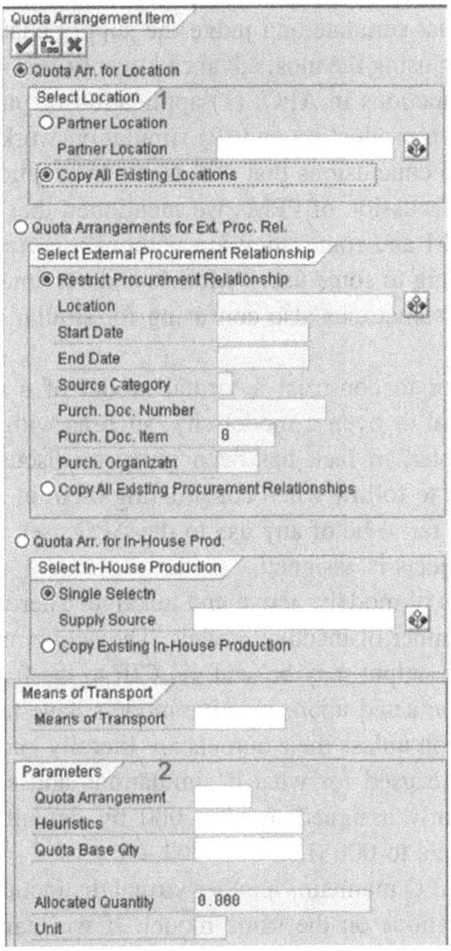

EXHIBIT 5.53 QUOTA ARRANGEMENT LINE-ITEM ENTRY
© SAP AG. Used with permission.

With the more common case of a vendor supplying the site, click "Single Selection" under "Select Location" and enter the vendor source in the Partner Location field, in our case vendor 200100100 (Exhibit 5.53, step 1). Enter the quota percentage for the vendor in the Quota Arrangement field, here 75%. Note that there are some other options. A heuristic or rule-based quota arrangement may be applied, providing for more sophisticated quotas. If a minimum absolute quantity should be acquired from this vendor prior to applying a percentage, enter it in the Quota Base Qty field (Exhibit 5.53, step 2). When finished, click the Copy button to save the quota line item to the quota arrangement and close the edit panel. To manage the remaining 25%, repeat this step, adding a new line item for vendor 200300100 but entering 25% as the quota quantity.

MODELS AND PLANNING VERSIONS

APO is our supply chain weather simulator, and with all the components of the supply chain maintained as master data it will be necessary to start building weather models.

APO models and versions of models are the abstract skeletons against which it works out analytical processes that simulate and judge the supply chain, generating solves that enable full-power planning using the most advanced twenty-first-century methods. Models and versions serve two functions in APO: (1) application of plan-of-record decisions in the "active" model to drive production and (2) simulation work in "inactive" models to analyze data and draw the conclusions that will result in function (1).

When we started our discussion of PPMs we mentioned that as a combination of two supply chain objects, BOM and route, they are without a perfect real-world analog and as such may prove confusing to some users. Models and versions, though not particularly complex in principle, are sometimes also confusing for similar reasons, especially when used together.

With APO we endeavor to construct a virtual model of a real-world supply chain, not unlike a model sailboat or even a model city, such as with the popular video game SimCity. This entire chapter, in fact, has been given to discussing the components of such models and the steps to follow when constructing them in APO. In order for any of the objects described thus far to be of any use to the APO user, a model must be defined into which each of the objects is assigned.

APO contains two types of models: active and inactive. There is only one active model and APO supports any number of inactive models. The active model is primarily distinct from all others because its output may be sent via CIF to the transactional system where its schedules will in fact be acted upon. Inactive models have no such access to the CIF and cannot affect production unless their outputs are literally and deliberately copied into the active model. They are used for what-if simulations and scenario analyses. APO's active model is permanently assigned number 000 by default. Additional models are assigned sequential numbers to 000 (i.e., 001, 002, etc.).

In addition to models, APO maintains another virtual distinction: versions. As the name implies, versions are variations on the same model. If we maintain the model sailboat analogy, we may engage in a thought experiment where there are two separate sailboat models with two separate versions: one is a model of a two-mast boat and the other is a model of a three-mast boat. The two-mast boat has one version crewed by 15 sailors and another with a crew of 20. The three-mast boat has one version crewed with 20 sailors and another crewed with 30. There is a caveat on this example, however: If our model boat floats (i.e., the "active" model), we can only float one boat at a time.

In APO, the active model, 000, has exactly one active version, also called 000. Thus model 000 version 000 together constitute the active production space in which data changes and where planning and optimization runs may affect actual outside production. An organization may employ models and versions by maintaining the active model and active version, 000:000, as closely as possible to the actual, known supply chain. Another version of the active model, 001 (or any other alphanumeric representation), may also model the exact same supply chain but be applied for what-if simulations. Final, approved outcomes of those simulations can be copied from version 001 to 000.

Meanwhile, however, this organization may wish to engage in more strategic simulations where, for example, it is believed that a new factory will open up in a new market six months from now. Compare this case with our boat example, wherein the second model considered the possibility of a whole additional mast. For such a case, an entirely new model may be called for, that is, inactive model 001 with inactive version 001. In a second version of this strategic simulator, inactive model 001, inactive version 002, both a new factory and distribution center, may be modeled and simulated.

By allowing additional models and versions, APO users have access to powerful simulation tools that allow them to analyze current assumptions about supply and demand in future scenarios, where fundamental basics of the supply chain have changed without affecting the decision support capabilities of the production instance. Meanwhile, in the active model where actual known conditions are maintained as close to reality as possible, supply chain analysts may run sophisticated simulations at several levels, not unlike meteorologists, who use similar tools to simulate the weather. The difference is that while meteorologists can apply their simulations only to predict the weather, supply chain analysts may apply their APO simulations in the process of forming plan-of-record actions that guide and control planning and scheduling decisions, whether at the level of the supply network, or an individual factory, or else on specific production lines within a factory.

Managing Models and Versions

Use transaction /SAPAPO/MVM, accessed via path *Master Data → Planning Version Management Model and Version Management*, to maintain models and versions. When accessed, the left-hand navigation screen will display all available models and their versions. Click the arrow next to the model to expand it with all of its versions. Note that the active model and version, 000,000, explicitly states its active status (Exhibit 5.54, step 1). Use the Display, Change, Create, and Copy buttons for administration (Exhibit 5.54, step 2).

For display and change simply highlight the model/version on the navigation panel and click the respective button. When creating or creating by copy, APO will ask whether a model or version is specified. It is usually recommended that rather than create from scratch one is best advised to copy existing native, off-the-shelf model versions and then proceed to customize them as necessary.

Much of the data in the edit panel, including all of the data for the model, is administrative and will not need maintenance, but there are a few important exceptions. One can schedule a deletion from the model-maintenance section. In the planning version section there are a number of settings that are important to both SNP and PP/DS that are addressed in Exhibit 5.55.

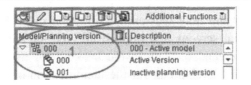

EXHIBIT 5.54 MODEL AND VERSION MANAGEMENT

Models are displayed with their versions; use the buttons to bring up display or edit screens. © SAP AG. Used with permission.

Module	Setting	Configuration Effect
SNP	No Planned Orders without Supply Source	When set, SNP will not generate planned orders for a product unless it has an active PPM defined.
PP/DS	PP/DS Horizon in Days	Length of PP/DS Horizon.
	Determine Priority	Indicates whether the priority field on the location product master is used for order prioritization by PP/DS.
	Take Safety Stock into Account	When selected, PP/DS will account for safety stock values in planning.
	No Order without Source of Supply	When selected, orders will not be generated for demand on products that do not have resources defined for them via active PPM.

EXHIBIT 5.55   Planning Version Settings for SNP and PP/DS

Using Inactive Versions for Simulation

Inactive versions may be applied to support simulation analytics as follows. First, create an inactive version of the active model and version using transaction /SAPAPO/VERCOP, path *Master Data → Planning Version Management*. Indicate the source version from which data will be copied, probably version 000, the active version (Exhibit 5.56, step 1). Then indicate the inactive target version into which the data will be copied (Exhibit 5.56, step 2). Note that this new version must not already exist, and if it does it must be deleted before re-creating with current data; a descriptive text next to its name may be applied at time of creation that may assist in identifying that an inactive, simulative version is in use later when it is called upon by business users for analytics. Indicate that both master and transactional data will be copied, (Exhibit 5.56, step 3), and finally set filter criteria to control which data of the source should be delivered to the target. Filter criteria will of course vary widely according to simulation needs and requirements; but consider that if order and stock data is to be copied, it should be explicitly selected (Exhibit 5.56, step 4), and then further filters such as order types, plant(s), product(s), or products assigned to this or that planner should be specified (Exhibit 5.56, step 5).

Once a new version exists it can be fully utilized in all the ordinary user interface transactions such as those we addressed briefly in Chapter 2, including the Supply Chain Cockpit, the Product View, the Planning Book, Planning Table, and Detailed Scheduling Planning Board. Spend some time reviewing each of these transactions (assuming configuration has been set into place to utilize them; more on User Interface (UI) configuration is available in Chapter 8) and note that each transaction calls for planning versions to be identified on their initial screens and often inside the interactive screens. Analytical processes that may be executed on data in the background in addition to UIs such as statistical or planning runs will also call for the identification of the planning version on their initial screens at run time.

A business process utilizing simulation must ordinarily follow these six steps (Exhibit 5.57):

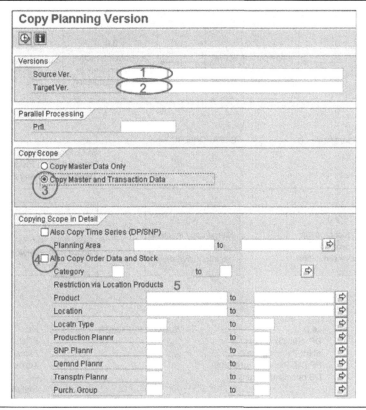

EXHIBIT 5.56   COPY A VERSION
Use this process to create a new (not preexistent) and inactive copy of a version for analytical, simulation purposes. To update an old simulative version, the old copy should be deleted before conducting this step. © SAP AG. Used with permission.

1. [Alternate with step 6] Delete any preexisting simulation model from previous, completed simulation processes.
2. Copy the current active model into the inactive simulation model.
3. Work with the simulation model using ordinary user interfaces, but calling out the inactive model on their initial screens.
4. Similarly run processes on the simulation model (heuristics, optimization, statistics), also by calling out the inactive simulation model on the initial screen of the background runs.
5. Complete analyses in simulation and copy formalized plan-of-record changes back into the active model. Changes in master data may be copied automatically using the version merge transaction; changes in transactional data cannot be automatically copied.
6. Continue work in active model, carrying out changes and executions in production. In anticipation of the next simulation process activity, delete the old inactive model (alternatively this may be the first step, as described above, which may be preferable to keep a record of simulation until it is necessary to remove it).

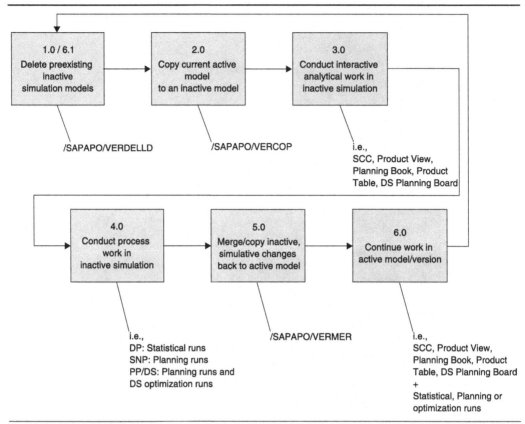

Exhibit 5.57   Process for Planning in Simulation

Deletion of obsolete versions is conducted with transaction /SAPAPO/VERDELLD, which is on the same path as the model maintain and version copy transaction. The version merge transaction for copying inactive version data changes to the active version is accessed via path *Master Data → Application-Specific Master Data → Service Parts Planning (SPP),* then using code *Merge Master Data of Inactive Version with Active Version.* Note that utmost caution should be exercised when conducting a mass update of this kind to the active, production version. Earlier versions of APO did not even allow migration of inactive transactional data to active versions on account of the potential damage that inappropriate use of such a capability can wreak on a production system. Generally a well-engineered, highly disciplined process should be put into place for managing migration of inactive data back into the active model, for example, taking advantage of variants defining explicit product/location cases only and custom configured for each user exercising the merge.

TRANSACTIONAL DATA

Transactional data elements such as orders are technically not a form of master data and one may legitimately question their inclusion in a section on master data. Orders, reservations, and the like, however, are the system-based representation of transactional information that is processed using master data and as such have a direct relationship to master data that should be appreciated by any user. As such, transactional data elements are a sort of segue between the virtual reality of an APO simulation and actual production that APO simulations are employed to direct.

Essentially we may say that whenever there is either a suggested direction or a firmed command that comes out of APO, it will be represented as an order of some type. Furthermore, orders of many kinds from other systems are common inputs to the data-analysis functions of APO, while the finalized, judged outputs of APO are orders that are generally sent to downstream transactional control systems to guide business execution. In this section we will briefly consider the variety of orders available in APO and their use in APO supply chain planning.

First, transactional data is categorized as either stocks, receipts, requirements, or forecast. That is, not all transactional data is order ready or order relevant. Stocks are not so much an order for work as simply on-hand quantities available for immediate use to fulfill demand. Requirements are definitive demand; that is, it is sourced in either an independent order, such as a customer order, or a dependent order, such as a purchase order for raw materials generated by a PP/DS heuristic run off of a finished good that needs the materials for construction. Forecast is demand, but without a definitive requirement to drive it. Receipts are any planned or in-process orders that will generate supplies, or stock, and fulfill demand. Receipts are closest to what we normally think of as orders.

The most common types of transaction data elements are stock, forecast, customer orders (often called sales orders), planned orders, purchase requisitions, production orders, purchase orders, schedule lines, stock transfer requisitions, and subcontractor requirements. Forecast constitutes requirements that are not as yet tied to any specific customer requirement, but represent demand that is expected to materialize. Customer or sales orders are orders opened based on explicit customer demand; that is, a customer asks for 500 units, due in three weeks, and we open an order for the material due to that customer.

Planned orders and purchase requisitions both have a gestational relationship with their parallel objects, production orders, and purchase orders. Planned orders, therefore, are proto-production orders and purchase requisitions are proto-purchase orders. The difference is that the former are the autogenerated output of any systematic scheduling process in APO, such as a heuristic, CTM, or optimizer planning run. Whenever such a run must fill demand that is not already filled by stock or an open production or purchase order, it generates planned orders and purchase requisitions. These may be reviewed in mass by a human planner or buyer.

Ordinarily APO will be configured so that exception messages are generated on any orders that may have problems such as supply or capacity constraints, or too late or too early scheduling. Common business practice is for planners and schedulers to change planned orders and purchase requisitions without exception messages into production orders and purchase orders, in mass. They then go on to work out the specific problems of the orders with exception messages, applying the qualitative judgment and capacities available only to a human being, that is, checking to see if reserve supply is available that isn't in the system or calling up a supplier to call in a favor for an expedited raw materials order.

Order or Reservation	APO Type Code	R/3 Type Code
Stock	Stock (+ many varieties)	Stock (+ many varieties)
Forecast	FC Req	FORREQ
Stock Transfer Reservation	StkTrfRes	StTRes
Sales Order	SalesOrder	SLSORD
Independent Requirement	CusReq	INDREQ
Dependent Requirement	DepDmd	DEPREQ
Planned Order	PlOrd	PLNORD
Purchase Requisition	PurRqs	PURREQ
Production Order	PrdOrd	PRDORD
Purchase Order	PchOrd	PURORD
Schedule Line	SchLne	SCHLNE
Subcontractor Requirement	SubReq	SUBREQ

EXHIBIT 5.58   ORDERS AND RESERVATIONS: TYPES CODES IN APO AND R/3

Schedule lines are effectively purchase orders generated by scheduling agreements, which we've seen are blanket purchase orders. Normally APO (and R/3) is configured to generate schedule lines directly, essentially stepping over the purchase requisition to purchase order process. Subcontractor requirements are opened at the APO model of the vendor or subcontractor to represent upstream demand from an internal site for a product supplied by the vendor. Finally, stock transfer reservations are reservations for specific quantities of material to be moved between sites.

The mapping of transactional data elements from APO to R/3 is not, unfortunately, perfectly exact. The reason for this is that APO tends to exceed R/3 analytically and as such has need for some nuanced differences among its transactional data elements that are unavailable to R/3. Furthermore, we've considered some of the most common transactional data elements, and additional common elements are listed in Exhibit 5.58, but many more are available for highly specific, customized use—more than 100 come available off-the-shelf in SCM 5.0. A complete listing may be found in the APO IMG customizing, accessed by transaction SPRO on the transaction line, then following the path *Advanced Planning and Optimization → Global Available-to-Promise (Global ATP) → General Settings → Maintain Category.*

MASTER DATA RECIPES

Products

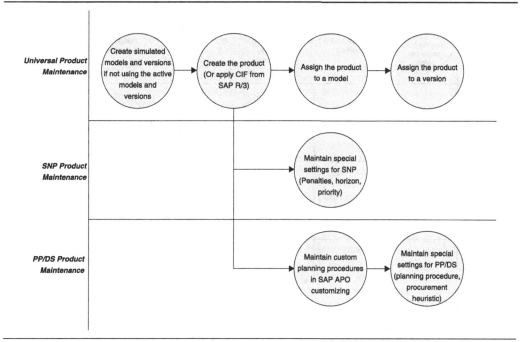

EXHIBIT 5.59 PRODUCT RECIPE

Location Cookbook

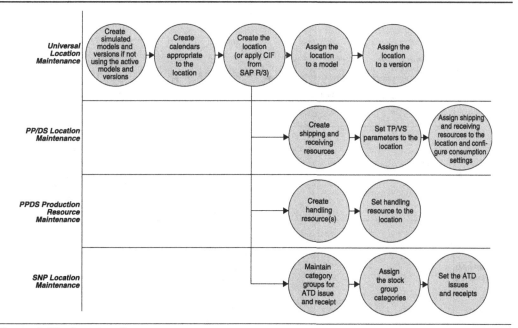

EXHIBIT 5.60 LOCATION RECIPE

Resources

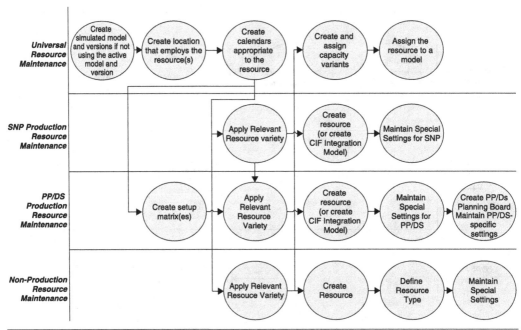

EXHIBIT 5.61   RESOURCE RECIPE

Production Process Model (PPM)

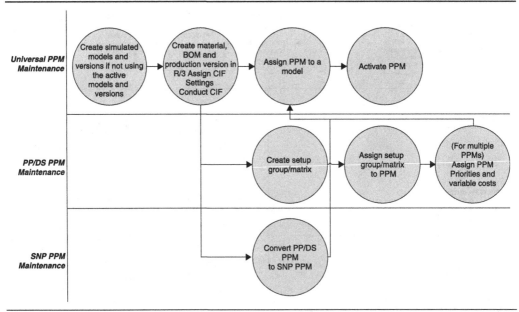

EXHIBIT 5.62   PPM RECIPE

Transportation Lanes

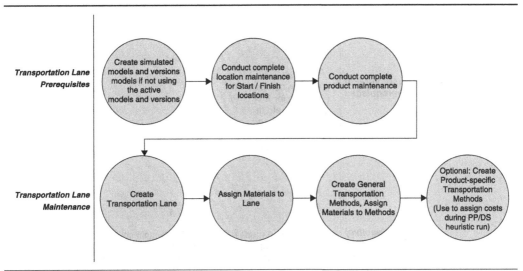

EXHIBIT 5.63 TRANSPORTATION LANE RECIPE

Quota Arrangements

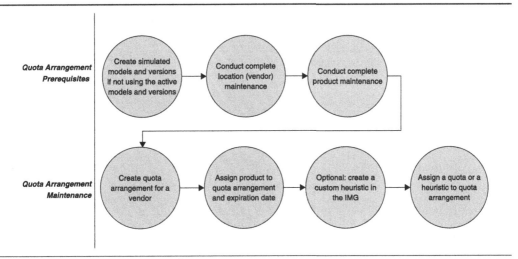

EXHIBIT 5.64 QUOTA ARRANGEMENT RECIPE

Models and Planning Versions

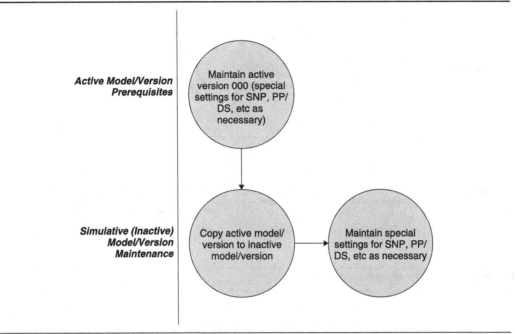

EXHIBIT 5.65   MODEL/VERSION RECIPE

6

ANALYTICAL MASTER DATA: BW PRIMER PART I

Until now we have been primarily concerned with configuring APO to model the actual physical components of the supply chain. Of course this has been essential as APO's value is in simulating the supply chain and running advanced planning runs or solves to coordinate and guide purchasing, production, storage, and delivery. We will see that by using Supply Network Planning (SNP), it is possible to execute any of three different kinds of runs or solves to derive schedules both for individual sites as well as for entire global vendor-factory-customer networks. Using Production Planning and Detailed Scheduling (PP/DS) it is also possible to do some cross-site planning runs, but more important, there are powerful tools for developing short-term factory schedules and highly optimized line-by-line schedules in the very near term.

But APO does more than this. Prior to either supply network planning or production planning, APO provides the Demand Planning (DP) module, which may be used for demand forecast development and analysis. This is a fundamentally analytical activity that relies as much on analytical data objects as it does on physical supply chain objects. Though obscured somewhat behind a "planning area," SNP in fact also makes use of these same planning objects. Moreover, APO is directly integrated with SAP BW, the Business Information Warehouse, which provides advanced reporting capabilities for all of the APO modules, even those not covered in this text, by way of an online analytical processing (OLAP) database. For all of these specific data objects exist and must be maintained in APO above and beyond the more tangible supply chain objects.

SCM VERSUS "ANALYTICAL" MASTER DATA

When contrasted with "analytical" master data, the supply chain management (SCM) master data explored in detail in Chapter 5 may be primarily thought of as "concrete." Though obviously *data* in nature, the entire point of the SCM master data exercise is to model actual physical objects—locations, plants, customers, vendors, products, production processes, and so forth—and model them as virtual analogs in order to effect their simulation and planning. Analytical master data differs in nature as it is more concerned with organizing information in such a way as to maximize its analytical utility. A few reasonable parallels to analytical master data might be found in the organizational scheme of a dictionary or phone book, in a file-folder on a computer, or especially in the Dewey Decimal System used to organize books in libraries. Analytical master data, in effect, allows us to *index* physical master and transactional data in such a way as to maximize our ability to analyze.

A short word on computer history of database and data storage may be in order. When computers first entered the scientific and commercial scene, disk storage space was at a premium. Many will recall that not long ago magnetic-disk tape was a common, respectable, and legitimate computer-data storage device. For decades, then, computer science oriented itself around the memory-space-as-premium constraint and when researchers and programmers labored to find ways of storing information in computers, they aimed first and foremost to develop *data structures* that most efficiently accommodated for limitations in physical storage space. This focus gave rise to the still-common and highly useful *relational* database systems empowered by Structured Query Language (SQL), and which are available on the market from such providers as Microsoft and Oracle. Relational databases and SQL continue to be the best data structure solutions for transaction-intensive systems, known generally as online transaction processing (OLTP), and are used in everything from logistical delivery systems to retail systems to human resources and payroll to credit cards to bank accounts.

Online transaction processing, while optimal for efficient data storage, has some weaknesses where it concerns analytics. Naturally, when analyzing we are mostly interested in rapid queries that slice and dice information in order to probe or *mine* it. Online transaction processing efficiently stores data in the least redundant form possible on two-dimensional tables with standard columns and rows in order to preserve memory. Though efficient for purposes of space, this is not ideal for analytics because more physical space must be traversed to find all data elements whenever data processing occurs. For example, whenever three dimensions are necessary to compare two unlike data elements stored on different tables (e.g., students and their grades), a "JOIN" operation is required. That operation may link the student table with the grade table to form a useful analytical combination, but conducting the join costs time and system processing resources. The more the data, the longer it takes to complete the query and display the outcome of the join.

As technology advanced, however, disk and "upper memory" space (where memory is available by way of the electrons flowing through a silicon chip without even the necessity of disk storage and retrieval) increased geometrically as cost plummeted while the time necessary to traverse the space dropped almost as fast as the cost. This new landscape of cheap and plentiful memory set the stage for new directions in data structures that could be optimized for different purposes.

To state the reversal most clearly: It turns out that the enemy of limited disk space—data redundancy, which researchers spent decades looking for ways to eliminate—is the best friend of rapid data analysis. So long as data-repetition is conducted systematically, the more often data is repeated in its organizational structures, the more quickly it can be absorbed into an analytical model, making it possible to conduct faster queries of much greater slices of data quantity. This reversal of data organization led to what is now described as *multidimensional* databases and data models optimized for OLAP. Online *analytical* processing does away with the avoidance of redundancy and consciously groups tabular data into *data cubes*: three-dimensional datasets that are physically linked to one another, typically a "UNION" rather than a "JOIN." The time required for systems to conduct joins for queries and analyze three (or more) dimensional data drops rapidly with structures oriented this way.

While elements of both OLTP and OLAP are to be found in both R/3 (ECC) and SCM 4.1 (where OLTP is still important for many APO functions), we may still broadly say that R/3 is a transaction-intensive tool that primarily employs OLTP while APO is an analytically intensive decision support system that makes frequent though judicious use of OLAP. The combination of the two tools may be the largest and most seamless fully integrated OLTP/OLAP product anywhere on the market today—fully employing all the applied power of each data orientation strictly according to their respective specializations.

STAR SCHEMA

Decades of research in relational, OLTP data structures, dedicated to finding the least redundant, most space-efficient means of organizing information, yielded a process called *normalization* that entailed splitting data apart into related but nonrepeating elements and mapping each to tables that could be linked when necessary by join statements. Online analytical processing turns this space-is-premium/time-is-plentiful logic on its head, deliberately causing data repetition in order to minimize processing time while maximally exploiting cheap memory space. Online analytical processing data redundancy, nonetheless, is not achieved willy-nilly. As with relational OLTP, there is a deliberate data-modeling methodology necessary to successful construction of multidimensional OLAP databases. BW's modeling methodology is the "Star Schema." While it is not our intention to make advanced data modelers of our readers, some rudimentary familiarity with this method of data organization is advisable to anyone wishing to employ or interact with BW.

In a data model employing the Star Schema, a central "fact table" is surrounded by "dimension tables" in a relationship metaphorical to that of a star, with the facts as the star's center and the dimensions as the points of the star (Exhibit 6.1). With BW, key figures and their numerical data are stored in the central fact table while characteristics are stored as the varieties of dimensions of a key figure, each one with its own dimension table along the points of the star. For example, Factory Production Plan might be a key figure denoting weekly and monthly production quantities for a factory site. There are a number of "dimensions" common to a Factory Production Plan—characteristic attributes such as Location master data, Product master data, and Time. One can visualize these relationships first as a familiar spreadsheet. Characteristics form the structure of the spreadsheet: factory as column one, product as column two. Time overlays the top of the report stretching out on the first row, starting with column three and across the defined time horizon. The report is populated with "key figures"—the time-bucketed quantities of the Factory Production Plan.

With characteristics thus understood as the columns of a report, creating analytical structure, and key figures as the quantitative data, creating an information-rich body, consider how this data might be stored according to the concept of the Star Schema. "Facts," individual or cell-by-cell data about key figures, such as demand or production quantities, are stored in the fact table in the center of the star and each columnar dimension gets its own table at any of the points of the star (Exhibit 6.1, View 1). In the

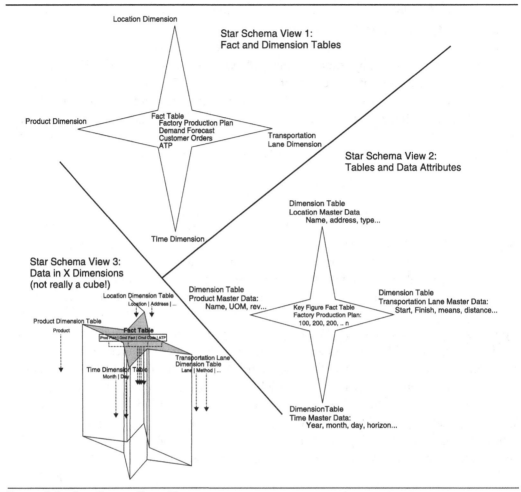

EXHIBIT 6.1 STAR SCHEMA: THREE VIEWS

Several different views of the Star Schema are provided to illustrate through different angles the many aspects of multidimensional data storage. In View 1 we see that "dimension" tables (location, product, time, etc.) are related to "fact" tables (forecast quantities, production plan quantities) in a similar manner as are spokes of a star to its center. In View 2 we see a similar view, only with examples of the data elements that might be stored in each dimension. In the third view, we illustrate directly that this is in fact a three-dimensional star, with data in each table listing downward. By way of View 3 we can see that where it concerns data analysis, in contrast to space, which has just three dimensions of height, width, and depth, many more dimensions are possible—there can be as many dimensions as there are structural characteristics of data.

example used, there are four points, four dimensions: product, location, transportation lane, and time. The star concept helps to emphasize that the key figures at the star's center are what the entire data structure is about while each point on the star is a dimensional characteristic, a variety of the key figure, for example, with the time dimension: December, January, February, and so forth represent time buckets in which the key figure facts—the production plan—are stored (Exhibit 6.1, View 2). We must really think of the star in three dimensions (Exhibit 6.1, View 3) to appreciate that each zone, fact, or dimension, is itself physically a table.

By thinking of the Star Schema as a three-dimensional star, two very important notions should be received that are often underappreciated by novice users of OLAP/ multidimensional systems. First, dimensions of data are not limited to three, such as dimensions of physical space, which has only height, width, and depth. Dimensions, broadly understood, are ranges of possibilities along specific factors of measurement and there is no universal limit on the number of descriptive dimensions available for any given set of facts. Thus, in our example, we see four dimensions, but we could have 3, 5, or 10; it just depends on the precise data needs of the analytics we are preparing.

The second lesson of our three-dimensional star is a bit of an oddity where it comes to OLAP training. It seems that universally, wherever OLAP is explained, the Star Schema is inevitably introduced to illustrate how data elements are structured in a multidimensional system. This is good, and accurate. Oddly, almost as universally, once the Star Schema concept is introduced and explained, almost all treatments go on to describe their individual data structures as "cubes." We believe this is to emphasize the greater-than-two-dimensional nature of multidimensional systems, such as to emphasize the difference with the two-dimensional "tables" of relational database. For example, we are not using two-dimensional tables here; we are using greater-than-three-dimensional "cubes."

Yet this is not exactly the case. First, cubes are only three-dimensional and multidimensional databases are n-dimensional, where the numerical value of n is whatever the data-user needs n to be. Second, in terms of how data is actually physically structured in multidimensional databases, it does not so much look like a star as it definitively resembles a three-dimensional star—that of the Star Schema.

Unfortunately, we find that BW follows this same path, giving the name "InfoCubes" to what are in fact three-dimensional stars with n spikes. A much better choice might have been "InfoStars," or just "Stars," but alas, "InfoCube" is what we are given to work with, and we will.

BW, APO, AND ANALYTICAL DATA OBJECTS

SAP BW is sold as a separate product from SAP SCM, the package that contains APO. This separate BW instance is what we will henceforth refer to as "enterprise BW." Later we will discuss the differences and similarities between BW and its smaller "data mart" instance in APO, but for now let us be content with this: The BW data mart instance deployed together with SCM is the *analytical data basis* of the APO product. So tightly integrated are BW and APO, in fact, that it is impossible to study the SNP module and especially the DP module without mastering many of the fundamental data objects of BW. Though our interest here is in laying the master data foundations for developing and working with DP and SNP, it is these BW data objects—designed as they are to enable advanced data analysis and data warehousing—that are the analytical master data elements that we will explore in this chapter.

Furthermore, while diligence requires that we point out and acknowledge the existence of a "bigger, stronger" instance of BW separate from APO, enterprise BW, that instance is not the subject of our text. While we will get to addressing the strengths and weaknesses of the two instances as it relates to forming deployment strategies for using one or the other with APO deployments, we will strictly consider the APO BW "data mart" when addressing technical steps for configuration.[1]

We have seen that analytical master data is concerned with the organization of physical master and transactional data in order to suit explicitly analytical purposes—such as in the way the Dewey Decimal System organizes subject/topic areas in order to enable easy navigation of the massive book, journal, and data content of a library by the library's users. For its part, BW organizes analytical master data into the following groups:

Data Staging Objects	DataSource
	Extractors
	InfoSource
	InfoPackages
Data Organization Objects	InfoArea
Warehouse Management Objects	InfoCubes
	InfoObjects
	Key Figures
	Characteristics

At first blush this list may appear simultaneously daunting, arcane, and even distracting. The latter is so with the repeated use of prefixes like *Data* and *Info* on so many objects. To the first-time learner we suggest the following technique to eliminate this distraction: Until some degree of comfort is achieved with the various analytical data objects, simply ignore words like *data* and *info* whenever they occur as a prefix. The only exception may be with "DataSources" and "InfoSources," which may be understood as mirror-image extractors with the former object extracting data from an external source and the latter managing communication structures and transfer rules that are employed to convert the now-internalized data to BW's three-dimensional data cubes.

Once comfortable with DataSources and InfoSources as mirror images of external and internalized data, when one starts ignoring *Info* in front of every other object, almost immediately tasks seem simplified and it becomes much easier to understand some of the arcane qualities of the analytical objects—for now we have two "sources" that are mirror images, areas, cubes, packages, and objects. The *info* distraction removed, take a moment and survey these and notice how a topology begins to take form.

Consider that BW is for analysis and archival—*it is not a business system in and of itself.* That is, BW may report on HR; another system is required to do HR. BW reports on financials; other systems are necessary to conduct financials. With APO, BW reports on planning and forecast, stores related data, and even provides useful data objects for statistical analysis, but APO is necessary for actual forecast and planning. Wherever BW will be employed in either its analytical or warehousing capacity, data must be extracted from some source system where it naturally originates. For this several tools are provided by SAP: replication, a communication structure, and transfer rules. Replication creates a safe dataset separate from any source system; a communication structure moves replicated data between its source and BW; the transfer rule governs the contents of the data movement. Data in a source system that BW is interested in is a "DataSource" (which may require creation of a view).

Objects that are generically termed *data elements* in most non-SCM systems are characterized in SCM as either key figures or characteristics. Key figures are transaction-oriented packages of data representing quantities that often change, such as inventory, demand forecast, customer orders, production plan, ATP, and so forth, and each or any of these elements as time buckets. Characteristics are the skeletal foundation of any data element such as location, product, customer, and vendor, as well as time characteristics such as calendar or fiscal year, and so on. Where many database systems do not discriminate between these object types, BW and SAP SCM do. Characteristics and key figures are grouped broadly together in each tool and described generically as "InfoObjects." An "InfoObject Catalog" therefore is an organized grouping of characteristics and key figures. Note that besides the external distinction between each, both characteristics and key figures are potentially hierarchical or aggregated. That is, characteristics may exist as atomic elements (i.e., products and locations) or as hierarchies (i.e., product hierarchy rolling into product families; location hierarchy with plants rolling into a corporate entity). Likewise, key figures may similarly exist as atomic elements (i.e., demand forecast or inventory-on-hand) or as aggregates (i.e., demand forecast monthly and quarterly totals; inventory-on-hand by storage location, entire plant, or geography).

When mapping from external systems, then, the data elements from an external Data-Source must be mapped into InfoObjects—key figures and characteristics—for BW and APO. At this level of transfer, data continues to be physically organized in much the same form as in its source OLTP system: typically in two-dimensional tables. The mapping process creates mirror-image flows between systems external to BW (including APO in this sense) and internal to BW where the external system DataSource goes through a transfer structure that has a matching pair inside the BW system to which it populates an "InfoSource." The InfoSource is a final, locally stored (internal to BW) staging zone for data that will be loaded into a cube (Exhibit 6.2).

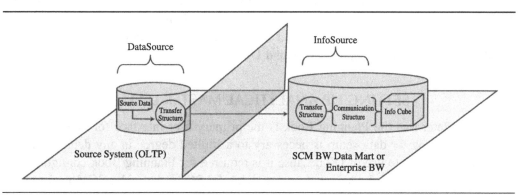

EXHIBIT 6.2 TOPOLOGY OF ANALYTICAL MASTER DATA

Analytical data will always need to be replicated from a source system. Source data is moved into a transfer structure forming the "DataSource." This is mirrored or "replicated" in the "BW data mart" of APO (or in BW enterprise, as the case may be). There the transfer structure mirror and communication structure, or InfoPackage, form the "InfoSource" that loads the three-dimensional, OLAP "InfoCube," enabling OLAP-based data analysis, which is put to work in DP and elsewhere as part of BW. *Note that even though APO and its BW data mart share the same system, APO itself may be the "source system" in this example, providing tabular data to BW for analysis.*

Until now, data has been two-dimensionally structured in tabular form, as is the standard of OLTP. At this final stage, "update rules" or "InfoPackages" are applied that load two-dimensional tabular data into a three-dimensional "InfoCube," the multidimensional OLAP structure described earlier; that is, they package the tabular data and update it to the cube. Here data is subject to sophisticated analytical processing available in both BW and the DP module of APO. More than one InfoCube may be used, so an organizational scheme is provided that groups separate but related InfoCubes—such as all those related to inventory management, for example—into "InfoAreas." An InfoArea then may simply be thought of as a *folder* that contains individual but related InfoObjects and InfoCubes.

BW IN THE SCM DATA MART

Note that whereas throughout this text we have referred to the specific application, APO, in lieu of the wider package of applications in which it is delivered, SAP SCM, in this chapter we have opted differently. We do this first because analytical master data presents itself by way of the BW data mart that is integrated into the wider SCM solution, and in delving into analytical master data we are in effect stepping outside the strict limits of APO. Second, we do this because as a basis of the wider SCM tool, not just APO, the BW data mart delivered with SCM should *not* be thought of as explicitly limited to the APO application in SCM.

One will find that many texts and courses on APO, particularly on SNP and especially on DP, make detailed reference to the analytical master data objects we are addressing here and even explain them in great detail but without noting that these are in fact BW objects existing in SCM as shared components between the SCM BW data mart and APO. Perhaps this is done to tend carefully to neophyte users who may be confused by tools with so many layers and dimensions, but we believe this is a mistake. Just as depth offers vast layers of precision and complexity to length and width, BW adds a whole dimension of application power to APO that is ignored only at extraordinary opportunity cost to the organization doing the ignoring. Besides, integrated as BW is with APO, especially with DP, to learn DP without understanding it as a powerful application of BW technology would surely be to incompletely understand DP.

SETTING UP ANALYTICAL MASTER DATA

We will see later that the Planning Book is the primary user interface for both SNP and DP. Analytical master data setup is necessary to a limited degree in any deployment of SNP and is essential to use of DP because it is required for Planning Book configuration. Apart from Planning Book use, whatever module of APO or the wider SCM package an organization may choose to use, the need for analytical master data will be a function of how much analytical features of the BW data mart are exploited—a powerful potential that we will explore more later. In other words, while analytical master data is generally irrelevant to the business conduct delivered by a PP/DS implementation, for example, where the APO features are deployed to empower both tactical purchasing and execution of production so that analytics are not generally important, a sophisticated deployment may nonetheless employ analytical master data in order to allow PP/DS users to interact with APO by way of Excel or the Web, rather than the native APO transactions. We will see later that there are potent reasons for considering this approach to deployment, regardless of the APO tool involved.

Creating a DataSource, an InfoArea, and InfoObjects

When APO stores supply chain master or transactional data about, for example, locations, products or inventory, planned orders, purchase orders, production orders, and so on, it stores that data in its own tables and data structures that share a system with BW but that are not expressly a part of BW. Hence we describe APO as "integrated with" BW; they are not the same and should not be thought of as being the same. Thousands of tables exist in APO that are not part of BW.

These tables may be viewed using transaction SE11, ABAP Dictionary, which is found along the SCM path *Tools → ABAP Workbench → Development*. Despite the integration of BW and APO, APO tables and data structures are treated as external to BW and must undergo a replication process to BW in order to enable use of BW functions, either apart from or as a part of APO modules (such as development of a query in the former case or application of data to a forecast model in DP in the latter). By treating APO separately and replicating its data in BW, we create a safe environment for data analysis that also happens to parallel the path to BW of any other external data source.

DataSources retrieve data for BW, whether from entirely external systems such as R/3, or other legacy OLTP sources, or else by way of integration from APO. They are maintained in BW in the SBIW transaction, Data Transfer to the SAP Business Information Warehouse. To be available to BW, a DataSource must be created—creation entails denotation of a specific DataSource and indication of its target source from which data will be extracted and replicated—using this we duplicate the DataSource for use inside BW. As an example we will maintain a DataSource for transactional data from PP/DS. Execute SBIW and create a transactional DataSource by following the path *Generic DataSources → Maintain Generic DataSources*, then click the radio button for Transactional data and enter the name of the DataSource to be created (Exhibit 6.3, step 1) and click the Create button (Exhibit 6.3, step 2).

In the resulting DataSource creation screen, indicate the application source of the data in the Applic. Component field by clicking the pull-down. For our example, pulling data from APO PP/DS drill down BW DataSources to BW DataSources, 0SCM, 0APO, 0PP/DS, and double-click "0PP/DS." Provide a short, medium, and long description, then note that the data may be extracted from an APO table or view, by way of a saved query from SAP tables or a function module such as would be created with macros (see Working in the Planning Book IV: Macro section in Chapter 8). Click the button on the right corresponding to the source to free the fields at the bottom, in this case Extraction from View, then select a table or view in the Table/View field. Save settings and note that the new DataSource may be assigned to a package as a grouping or simply saved as a local object by clicking the Local Object button.

With a DataSource now established and saved, replicate it in BW. Open the BW Administrator Workbench, transaction RSA1, or open it by following path *Demand Planning → Environment → Data Warehousing Workbench*. Saved DataSource systems

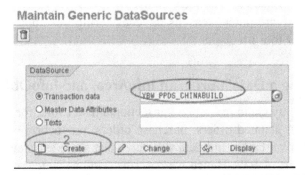

EXHIBIT 6.3 CREATE A TRANSACTIONAL DATA SOURCE

Parallel processes exist for creating a master data or textual data source as well as for change and display of existing data sources. © SAP AG. Used with permission.

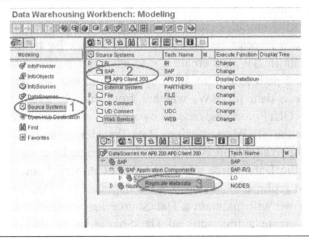

EXHIBIT 6.4 BW WORKBENCH SOURCE SYSTEMS
© SAP AG. Used with permission.

will be found in the Modeling panel under "Source Systems" (Exhibit 6.4, step 1). In Source Systems in the navigation panel on the right, double-click the client system containing APO to find the DataSource just created (Exhibit 6.4, step 2). On the right under DataSources drill down the BW DataSources tree node-path to the PP/DS node and look for the DataSource (Exhibit 6.4, step 3). Right-click the DataSource and select "Replicate Metadata." The replicated DataSource is now available as a sort of data mirror in BW from which you can extract data to populate an InfoCube and otherwise safely work.

In order to work with DataSources as a mirror of external data and maintain InfoObjects (characteristics and key figures) as well as InfoSources that will transfer data into an InfoCube, an InfoArea is necessary. The InfoArea is effectively a folder in which to hold and group related data. Create InfoAreas in the Administrator Workbench by clicking the Modeling panel on the left, then clicking "InfoObjects." In the resulting right-hand InfoObjects panel, be sure to be scrolled to the top and click the top node, "InfoObjects," then right-click and click "Create InfoArea." Keeping in mind the nature of this object as basically a folder, provide a name and description.

When saved, the folder will populate to the InfoObject tree in the panel—scroll down to the new InfoArea. Here, create new characteristics and key figures. Characteristics and key figures in InfoAreas must be organized into "InfoObject Catalogs"; that is, a separate catalog object is necessary to group and organize the characteristics and key figures that belong to the InfoArea. Highlight the new InfoArea (Exhibit 6.5, step 1), right-click it, and select "Create InfoObject Catalog" (Exhibit 6.5, step 2). Provide the new InfoObject Catalog with a name and description, assign a type, either characteristic or key figure, then activate it. Normally there will need to be InfoObject Catalogs for both characteristics and key figures, so this process will probably be exercised twice, one to create each InfoCatalog type.

The InfoArea is now our folder for grouping related InfoObjects, and at least two InfoCatalogs exist, one for InfoObject characteristics and another for InfoObject key figures. Use these catalogs to model external data structures such as flat files, tables, or hierarchies. To create an InfoObject (characteristic or key figure) in an InfoCatalog, click the catalog (Exhibit 6.6, step 1), right-click, and select "Create InfoObject" (Exhibit 6.6, step 2), much as with creating the catalog itself. BW provides the option either to create an independent InfoObject or to use a previously existing object from the APO/BW data dictionary as a template. To create a new one without reference, simply enter its name in the Char or KeyFig field.

Several tabs are presented for creating characteristics: "General," "Business Explorer," and "Hierarchy," and others depending on the characteristic type. For example, a resource

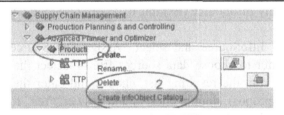

EXHIBIT 6.5   INFOAREA: CREATE AN INFOOBJECT CATALOG TO STORE CHARACTERISTICS AND KEY FIGURES
© SAP AG. Used with permission.

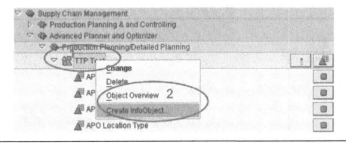

EXHIBIT 6.6   CREATE INFOOBJECT FROM AN INFOAREA
© SAP AG. Used with permission.

characteristic will have "Master Data Texts," "Attributes," and "Compounding." Similarly three tabs are presented for creating key figures: "Type/unit," "Aggregation," and "Additional Properties." In each case the fields presented are database element definition fields, the most important of which will be Data Type (i.e., Character, Number, Date, Quantity, etc.) and, if a character type, Length. "Hierarchy" for characteristics and "Aggregation" for key figures can be used to define hierarchical relationships and aggregate summations where necessary. The "Business Explorer" tab of characteristics is concerned with attributes related to the use of the characteristic as an object available for filtering in queries through the BW Business Explorer (BEx Explorer), which we will address later. Whether characteristics or key figures, be sure to activate data with the wand icon before exiting.

Creating an InfoSource

The DataSource is replicated from external systems, and manipulated and structured for use in BW in the InfoArea and its InfoObjects. These objects remain essentially two-dimensional in nature, however, and must be transferred into the InfoCube to become OLAP/three-dimension enabled. The communication structure, transfer structure, and transfer rules are maintained in an InfoSource that delivers the contents of the DataSource to the InfoCube.

Select "InfoSource" in the Modeling panel of the Administrator Workbench and be sure to be scrolled to the top. Create a new InfoSource by clicking the top "InfoSource" node and right-clicking "Create Application Component." Provide a name and description, then click continue and find the newly created and saved application component in the tree on the right-hand panel. Right-click the component and select "Create InfoSource." Indicate whether this will be a transactional-and-master-data InfoSource (Exhibit 6.7, step 1, first tab) or a master-data-only InfoSource (Exhibit 6.7, step 2, second tab). Select the continue checkbox.

Right-click the new InfoSource and select "Assign DataSource." The initial dialog window is simply a filter to choose data sources from—select the system in which the DataSource is saved. From the resulting list, choose and enter the DataSource recently created (or otherwise apropos), double-click it, and answer "Yes" to the "Save" question dialog window that results.

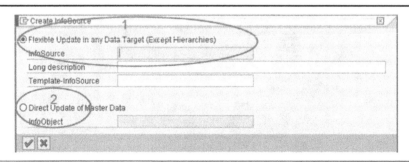

EXHIBIT 6.7 CREATE INFOSOURCE
© SAP AG. Used with permission.

EXHIBIT 6.8 INFOSOURCE DIALOG WINDOW
© SAP AG. Used with permission.

The resulting screen will have two tabs: Transfer Rules and DataSource/Trans. Structure. Transfer rules may be "PSA" or "IDoc," where PSA moves data directly into BW into a "Persistent Staging Area" and IDoc packs the data into IDocs, then saves it persistently to BW and as a view through the IDoc Store (Exhibit 6.8, step 1). Click the button to "propose transfer rules." This will migrate DataSource fields on the right to the InfoSource on the left (Exhibit 6.8, step 2). Activate changes and exit. You are now ready to create an InfoCube.

Creating an InfoCube

Earlier we noted that InfoCubes, the ultimate data structure of the BW OLAP system multidimensional database, are more stars than cubes. While there is no need to revisit this argument, we will remind the reader of the point here before moving on to describe the process for creating one. Manage InfoCubes under "InfoProvider" in the Modeling panel. Find your InfoArea, right-click it, and select "Create InfoCube." Provide a name and description in the dialog window (Exhibit 6.9, step 1). Notice that cubes may be defined as a "BasicCube" or "Virtual Cube." Start with a basic cube (Exhibit 6.9, step 2). Virtual Cubes come into play when data is not available in the local instance of BW and must be queried off external SAP systems or by way of a BAPI (Business Application

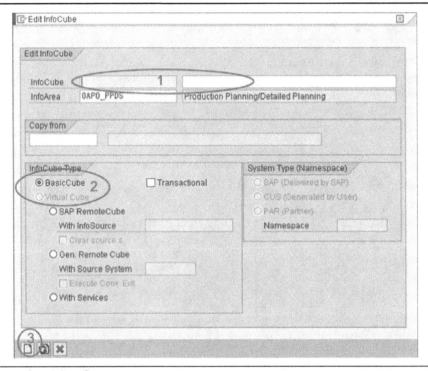

EXHIBIT 6.9 CREATE INFOCUBE
© SAP AG. Used with permission.

Programming Interface). Cubes that are used in association with the SAP product SEM (Strategic Enterprise Management) will require the Transactional checkbox checked. With these settings, click the Create button (Exhibit 6.9, step 3).

An Edit screen will open where the basic characteristics, time characteristics, and key figures of the new InfoCube can be maintained. Each characteristics tab has three or four views: (1) transfer view (default), (2) detail view, (3) dimension view and for the characteristics tab alone, and (4) navigation attributes. The key figures tab has views for transfer, detail view, and units. Create dimensions in the cube by moving characteristics in the transfer view from the left tab to the right, then click the Dimensions button and click the Create dimension button in the resulting dialog window. Enter a description for the dimension and click the Assign tab. Check every checkbox, highlight the new dimension, and click Assign.

In the Time characteristics tab transfer a time-bucket characteristic from the right- to left-hand panel (i.e., 0CALDAY, 0CALMONTH, etc.). Add key figures, thus creating the "fact table" in the Key Figure tab. Transfer the data elements that will become rows of reports here. With the key figures assigned, activate the InfoCube and exit. Right-click the new InfoCube and select "Create Update Rules." Enter the name of the InfoSource created earlier to populate the cube. Click the next screen icon, highlight, assign an update rule, then activate it. The cube is now created with an InfoSource assigned; all that remains is to enable an object for running a process to load the InfoCube from the InfoSource.

Creating an InfoPackage

DataSources extract data from source systems. InfoSources mirror DataSources on BW and replicate data into BW in an untransformed, tabular structure. InfoCubes create a Star Schema enabling OLAP-style data mining, querying, and overall analytics—but it remains to populate the InfoCube from a loaded InfoSource. This is done by InfoPackages.

To create an InfoPackage that will load tabular data into the InfoCube Star Schema, open "InfoSources" under the Modeling panel on the left side of the BW Administrator Workbench. Select the application component from the right-hand navigation panel that contains the InfoSource with data to load and expand it to find the InfoSource. Right-click the Data Source System that displays beneath the InfoSource, then select "Create InfoPackage." Provide the InfoPackage with a name and select the original DataSource, then save. In the resulting screen, open the Schedule tab, choose the option "Start Data Load Immediately," and execute. To validate the ongoing or completed data load, click the Monitoring button.

NOTE

1. For a complete treatment of enterprise BW, see *Mastering the SAP Business Information Warehouse*, Kevin McDonald, Andreas Wilmsmeier, David C. Dixon and W.H. Inmon (Wiley, 2006).

7

CORE INTERFACE

In Chapter 5 we took great pains to illuminate the intricacies of supply chain master data in APO, which is necessary to form the skeletal foundation of any supply chain model. Nonetheless, most organizations that will adopt APO will already be using SAP's R/3 product for enterprise resource planning (ERP) and the majority of the supply chain master data employed by APO is already maintained in R/3; therefore to maintain it in APO would be needlessly redundant. To minimize this problem, SAP provides the native Core Interface (CIF) that links these two powerful tools. Even for the (likely rare) cases where APO is deployed in absence of R/3, a similar master-data core arrangement will likely prove both necessary and desirable.

APO is most of all a decision support system. It is true that the PP/DS module has capabilities and features that are so close to purchasing and production control as to straddle the line from decision support to transactional management, but this is a relatively small part of the larger corpus of APO functionality. APO's sister product, SAP R/3, meanwhile, is expressly designed for enterprise transaction management. APO is usually expected to be deployed, therefore, in support of the supply chain transactional functions of R/3, but it can nonetheless be deployed in lieu of R/3 as a decision support system (DSS) for either a legacy transactional ERP system or a transactional ERP system from another provider. In any case, as a DSS, APO will probably never be deployed apart from the preexistence of some kind of transactional ERP tool. In other words, there are exactly three possible configurations of APO in deployment together with a transactional ERP system, with the first being by far the most common:

1. APO as supply chain DSS; SAP R/3 as supply chain transactional ERP
2. APO as supply chain DSS; legacy system as supply chain transactional ERP
3. APO as supply chain DSS; product from company competing with SAP as supply chain transactional ERP

From the point of view of any educational treatment of APO, whether as a classroom delivery or textual reference, the first case is the only case we can address directly and explicitly because it is the only case that has standard features—any case involving an in-house legacy or competing product for transactional ERP will vary such as to make direct treatment speculative. We will, nonetheless, at least address a few of the basic questions that organizations will have to answer if they fall into either case two or three; then we'll move on to look at the first case and the role of the CIF in enabling that architecture.

WHEN R/3 IS NOT THE TRANSACTIONAL DATA MANAGEMENT SYSTEM

First, if R/3 is not the transactional data management system used together with APO, organizations must determine whether master data will be maintained in APO entirely, partially, or not at all. When R/3 is used with APO, master data, already having been maintained in R/3, continues to be maintained there almost exclusively and is then sent to APO by interface, considerably reducing the work of data maintenance. Nonetheless, even with R/3 some unique master data elements must be maintained in APO, so split solutions here should not be ruled out. The cost of arrangement that does not employ R/3, of course, will be the necessity to construct a custom interface to port master data from the transaction management system where data originates to APO. In such cases, organizations will need to decide the trajectory of master data flows (i.e., whether master data changes in APO can cause changes in the transactional system). When following the R/3 model, this should be disallowed. Of course, if R/3 is not a constraint, it may go the other way, too: Master data may be maintained in APO as a source, and then ported elsewhere.

Next the question of transactional data should be addressed. While master data flows will generally need to be unidirectional in order to avoid architectural chaos, transactional data will probably have to be two-way, otherwise the utility of APO as a DSS will be lost. Generally speaking, transactional data will originate outside APO in the transaction system (a necessary point but one that does not seem to be saying much), be ported to APO by interface, analyzed, and judged, then returned to the transactional system where it will be enacted upon in production or commerce. While the transactional component of such an interface itself must be two-way, another corollary decision will be whether to permit changes in the transactional system to data that has been analyzed in APO. In some cases, it may be necessary to build a lockbox of some kind around APO-modified data to distinguish it from data that has not yet been analyzed or worked in APO. Whether to do this will vary of course by business process, but there will generally be good rationale for conducting specific activities in specific data processing locations or systems.

USING R/3 WITH APO

The question of how to manage the relationship between APO and the transactional data management system for supply chain management will be considerably more controlled for the majority of organizations that already have R/3 in deployment and that are adding the supply chain management (SCM) package and APO application. First, though a separate application from R/3, APO is designed to work in direct cooperation with R/3. The central hinge around which this cooperation is built is the CIF, which is frequently and redundantly referred to as the "CIF Interface."

The CIF is a native, SAP-provided, configurable interface between R/3 and APO. Any APO deployment built in connection with R/3 will rely on the CIF as a fundamental construct of master data management. There are several important characteristics of the CIF that APO users and developers should be familiar with:

- It is primarily configured in R/3, not APO.
- It may be used for transactional and/or master data.

- It can be used only for supply chain master data (see Chapter 5) and cannot be used for analytical master data (such as described in Chapter 6).
- Master data transfer is one-way only: R/3 → APO.
- Not all master data is covered by the CIF; some master data must be maintained in APO.
- Transactional data transfer is two-way: Changes to orders in APO will be reflected by the CIF into R/3 where order data will be overwritten.
- It will not prevent manipulation of APO-planned transactional data once that data returns to R/3.
- It works by way of "integration models," which are custom-conExhibitd constructs of data elements that are included in an interface exchange between systems.
- Integration models will be configured only to contain objects that are relevant to analysis, planning, and/or management with APO. Especially where it concerns products, this will *not* be all R/3 objects—business rules are needed to control which R/3 objects are subject to work in APO.

Pursuant to the first point, with some small, low-level exceptions in the IMG (R/3 and APO's technical configuration center), the CIF is configured in R/3; this will be the only chapter that addresses use of R/3 screens and transactions rather than APO. Note, too, that in the interest of staying current, our R/3 screens are taken from a recent Enterprise Common Core (ECC) release of the product.

BASIC INTEGRATION MODEL CONFIGURATION
Overview of CIF Integration for R/3 and APO

Underlying master data requirements vary according to both the APO module applied and the specific application any organization will make of that module. Generally speaking, however, minimally the following supply chain master data objects must be set up in APO to enable demand planning (DP), supply network planning (SNP), and/or production planning/detailed scheduling (PP/DS): locations, resources, products, production process models, and transportation lanes. Therefore customized APO designs must accommodate that the majority of master data maintenance for all of these or related objects will originate in R/3 and then be sent over to APO via the CIF. Throughout this text, when we address the cases of individual modules, we labor to point out where specialized master data maintenance is necessary that cannot be conducted in R/3—it is generally more appropriate to enumerate these cases in the modules where they occur. Suffice for now to note that while the basics originate in R/3 (i.e., a specific plant with an address and capacity bearing work centers), a great deal of specifics related to master data objects must be maintained in APO (i.e., that the plant has "handling" resources in addition to the capacity bearing work centers or that specific costs unavailable to R/3 are associated with use production of a given product).

Furthermore, master data maintenance between R/3 and APO with the CIF is explicitly one-way. First, for example, a location manually conExhibitd in APO cannot be CIF'd back to R/3, while any such locations in R/3 can be CIF'd to APO and ordinarily would be in lieu of their manual establishment there. Second, where data elements such as resource relationships, capacity variants, and costs are maintained as additional master data subelements in APO, these, too, cannot be returned to R/3 as R/3 does not even have an analog to receive them into.

Unlike master data, transactional data is two-way in the CIF. That is: stocks and inventory of all kinds, planned independent requirements (raw demand), dependent requirements (the Materials Requirements Planning Bill of Materials (MRP BOM) exploded, "processed" and upstream demand), as well as orders of any kind (planned, purchase, sales, production, etc.) can be sent both from R/3 to APO and from APO to R/3. The exact configuration for transactional data exchange between the two systems will vary greatly according to deployment. Let us briefly consider very general cases of R/3 interacting individually with DP, SNP, and then PP/DS (Exhibit 7.1).

In the case of DP, DP will rely on R/3 master and transactional data to conduct demand analysis and planning, but in most cases DP's downstream client is not R/3, but the SNP module. It will be relatively uncommon, though not unheard of, to send DP-processed transactional data straight back to R/3 as normally it will go through SNP first. The case will not be unheard of, however. One theoretical deployment of APO with R/3 that exclusively uses DP would be for an organization that uses DP as designed to conduct forecasting and demand planning, but which does not yet use SNP or PP/DS and is not using a legacy system for any kind of materials planning, but which instead is using R/3's older "Flexible Planning" technology, with MRP downstream from there. In this case, very likely stocks, production orders, and sales order

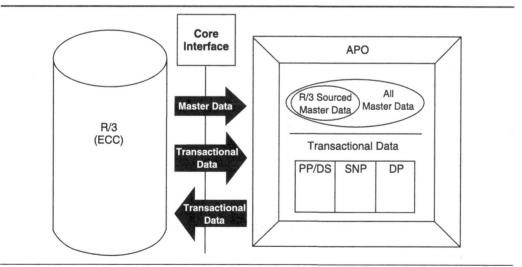

Exhibit 7.1 CIF Data Trajectory

Supply chain master data originates in R/3 though some settings are necessary in APO that are not available in R/3, particularly settings related to maintenance of costs or heuristic algorithms for planning and optimization runs. There are also cases where some kinds of resources must be maintained in APO as they have no analog in R/3. Transactional data movement is bidirectional. Organizations will need to determine whether data planned and modified in APO can or should be further modified on return to R/3. If not, the CIF cannot prevent editing once data lands in R/3 and other techniques to lock the data will be required.

demand would be CIF'd from R/3 to APO DP, and analyzed in DP; then a judged forecast might be returned to R/3, master scheduled in Flexible Planning, and then transferred to MRP.

As that example entails employment of an outdated R/3 tool, we hope that it is relatively rare. It is far more likely that organizations will deploy some combination of DP and SNP with R/3, wherein the first link in the chain would remain the case as before, with R/3 providing stocks, production orders, and sales order demand as such to APO DP, and APO DP in turn generating a forecast or demand plan and then releasing it to APO SNP. Using capacity analysis together with heuristics, optimization, or some combination thereof to balance demand and supply, SNP may then be applied to generate a cross-site, cross-geography operational planning schedule for production, transportation, and procurement. Once a medium-range multisite operational build/buy/transport plan is generated, it will be either sent back to R/3 or sent to PP/DS. In either case, more detailed, tactical production planning will be conducted to schedule and directly manage the short-term build/buy horizon, and MRP may be applied in R/3 on some nonconstrained parts.

A last scenario, involving R/3 and PP/DS, straddles the previous one. Either SNP or R/3 will supply PP/DS with a short-term production signal. This signal begins as the somewhat generalized form of a medium-range plan, which need not schedule orders down to any level of detail more granular than a day and in many cases will not be more granular than a week. PP/DS, in contrast, plans data at a level of detail as acute as a second and rarely less so than a day. Having received its signal either via CIF from R/3 or via release from SNP, PP/DS executes a heuristic planning run and requisite alerts that drive short-term, detailed order planning. Capacity analysis, at the level of individual work centers, laborers, hours, and days is conducted, specialized optimization algorithms may be used to perfect the work schedule, and definitive execution tactical and execution build plans are generated. The detailed master production schedule is finally returned to R/3 via CIF as planned orders, production orders, purchase requisitions, purchase orders, and schedule line items, where their effective conduct is transactionally managed, consuming raw materials and semifinished good inventories and generating and shipping finished goods. A continuous feedback loop must be in place through the CIF with R/3 returning updated inventory and order completion information back to APO to keep PP/DS as up to date to-the-second as possible.

Basic Integration Models in R/3

A CIF *integration model* is a configured construct of master or transactional data objects—data elements like locations (master data) or stock or orders (transactional data)—that are identified by the user for the CIF to include in its data transfers between R/3 and APO. Integration models are wholly configured in R/3 (ECC)—*do not try to find the CIF integration model transactions we will discuss here in APO*. The paths and transactions we will address apply strictly in the R/3 system, where they can be found at *Logistics → Central Functions → Supply Chain Planning Interface → Core Interface Advanced Planner and Optimizer*.

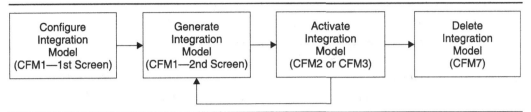

EXHIBIT 7.2 BASIC CIF INTEGRATION MODEL PROCESS

Models are (1) configured, where objects and filters are included and excluded in the model definition, (2) generated, where the objects and filters are applied to acquire a snapshot of data elements in R/3 at the time of generation, and (3) activated, where data from the integration model is moved into APO. Only one model may be active at a time and objects cannot be dynamically added or removed from a model during activation. To increase or decrease the number of data elements in a model, and thus available to APO, models must be deactivated, then regenerated, and subsequently reactivated to capture new or deleted objects in R/3. After deactivation, (4) old models should normally be deleted to prevent an accumulation of obsolete models.

Integration models must be configured, generated, activated, and even deleted according to a prescribed and relatively linear process (Exhibit 7.2):

- *Configuration.* Integration model is defined using transaction CFM1, Create Integration Model, where it is named; the objects included are specified and any filters limiting which data elements to use are applied.
- *Generation.* A sort of "step 1" of CFM1, Create Integration Model, this action queries R/3's database for the specified objects according to any filters saved in the integration model configuration step and saves those objects as an inactive integration model.
- *Activation.* Only one integration model for each data element in R/3 may be active at any time, though many may exist with different configurations of objects and filters. Activation specifies which integration model the CIF will employ currently—it necessitates deactivation of any previous models that affect the same data objects. Two transactions are provided for integration model activation: CFM2 and CFM3. The only difference between the two is that the latter, CFM3, is enabled for execution in batch, which in actual production is normally the way CIF will be managed.
- *Deletion.* Integration models are *not* dynamic. That is, if there is, for example, an integration model for "products" that has a filter limiting it to products at plant A, then only products at plant A in R/3 at the time of model generation will be found in the model. If any products are added to plant A in R/3 after model activation, they will remain invisible to APO. To avoid activation of incomplete integration models, old models should be deleted and new ones created on a regular basis to keep APO most current with R/3. Transaction CFM7 is provided to enable model deletions.

CIF usage to enable R/3-APO data exchange typically requires a few additional procedural components as well. Recall from Chapter 5 that Production Process Models and Production Data Structures are the combination in APO of the BOM and route in R/3 based on the R/3 production version. Production Process Models (PPM) and Production

Data Structures (PDS) exchange between R/3 and APO entails use of SAP "IDocs" or "intermediate documents," which are containers that package data exchanged between two logical systems. A prerequisite to use of IDocs is the creation of "change pointers." IDoc change pointers enable R/3 to keep APO up to speed with master data changes in the content of BOMs, for example, which may affect APO PPMs. PPM change pointers are created and instantiated with R/3 transaction CFP3, Sending Changes to Production Process Models, and deleted with CFP4, Delete Change Pointers. Production Process Models change pointers should be initially created at the time PPM integration models are activated. When the model is deactivated they should be deleted and then created again on model reactivation. Managing this will require careful batch configuration.

R/3 Transactions for CIF and Integration Model Maintenance

Initial configuration of CIF integration models is conducted in the SAP R/3 system using transaction CFM1, Create Integration Model along path *Logistics → Central Functions → Supply Chain Planning Interface → Core Interface Advanced Planner and Optimizer*. The transaction has four major parts: header, "Material Dependent Objects," "Material Independent Objects," and "General Selection Options for Materials" (Exhibit 7.3, steps 1–3, respectively). All integration models are uniquely identified by the combination of the three characteristics in their header: Model Name, Logical System, and APO Application. The Model Name is literally the name to associate with a particular group of object settings, the Logical System is the identification of the APO target system the integration model will control data transfer between, and the APO Application essentially provides a subset to the integration model; think model "applied" in case of<application A>or<application B>. APO help defines the CIF's APO Application as "an evaluation criterion within the source system for which a data package is created in the integration model." A project may, for instance, have more than one filter applied on a CIF for materials—perhaps one filter for one plant's materials and another for a different plant. There may be one integration model but two applications thereof saved, each possessing the individual filter case.

Two object selection and filtration sections of the integration model screen operate in tandem: "Material Dependent Objects" and "General Selection Options for Materials." In contrast, the section "Material Independent Objects" stands on its own. The latter section, which usually must be scrolled down to, as it is so low on the screen, contains objects such as ATP Customizing, Customers, Shipping Points, Vendors, and Work Centers for which material-based filtration is inapplicable. Note that to establish "resources" in APO, their R/3 equivalent, "work centers" must be CIF'd.

The section General Selection Options for Materials allows filters that will be applied to all objects selected for CIF migration in the Material Dependent Objects section. Individual objects in both the Material Dependent Objects and Material Independent Objects sections can be filtered by selecting the multiselection drop-down arrow to the right of the objects listed (Exhibit 7.3, step 5). If no such button exists for any given object, it means either that the lone object can be filtered only through the general selections section or that no filtration is even applicable and, by selecting the object, all objects of

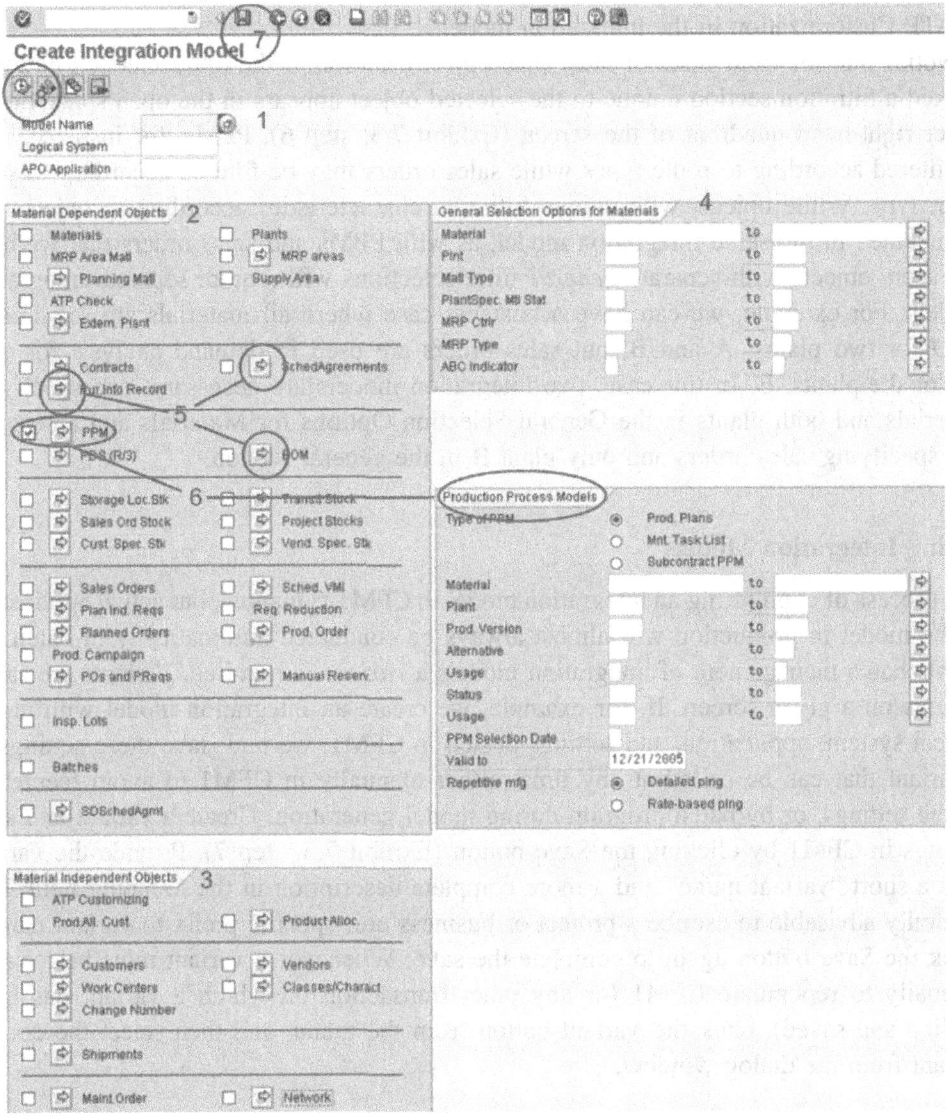

EXHIBIT 7.3   CFM1—CREATE INTEGRATION MODEL
Use this R/3 transaction to choose data objects and apply filters that will populate a new integration model. Broad application filters may be applied in the section, "General Selection Options for Materials" (step 4), and where applicable, narrow, single-item filters may be applied by clicking the right-arrow multiselection buttons to the right of data elements (step 5). For regular ad-hoc use or batch processing, save settings as a variant (step 7). © SAP AG. Used with permission.

that type in R/3 will be included in the integration model to APO. In the former case, note that no multiselection drop-down exists for Materials but materials can be filtered using the section General Selection Options for Materials. One might do so by selecting Materials to be included in the model, then including a filter in the adjacent general selections section, perhaps filtering for all products at a plant, of a given material type or even for specific, individual materials. In the latter case, ATP Customization, under

Material Independent Objects, cannot be filtered—selection of this object will include all of ATP Customization in the integration model.

Notice that for valid cases of individual object filtration, if the multiselection button is clicked a filtration section unique to the selected object appears in the open space on the lower right-hand quadrant of the screen (Exhibit 7.3, step 6). PPMs, for instance, may be filtered according to route types while sales orders may be filtered according to sales order type. While objects with unique filtration characteristics according to object may be included in the same integration model, as with PPMs and sales orders that we have just seen, objects with separate *general* filter selections will require separate integration models. For example, we can have a business case where all materials are required in APO for two plants, A and B, but sales orders are used in demand analysis for only one of the plants, B. In this case, two integration models are necessary: one specifying materials and both plants in the General Selection Options for Materials and a separate one specifying sales orders and only plant B in the general section.

Saving Integration Models

The process of configuring an integration model in CFM1 is manual, but actual application of the model in production will almost always be conducted automatically in batch. To enable batch management of integration models a *variant* is required. Variants are saved settings on a given screen. If, for example, we create an integration model with name, logical system, application, and settings posted in CFM1, we may save these settings as a variant that can be called at any time, either manually in CFM1 to avoid reentering all the settings, or by batch program during model generation. Create a variant and save settings in CFM1 by clicking the Save button (Exhibit 7.3, step 7). Provide the variant with a short "variant name" and a more complete description in the Meaning field. It is generally advisable to ascribe a project or business-unit-specific prefix to variant names. Click the Save button again to complete the save. Whenever a variant must be recalled manually to repopulate CFM1 (or any other transaction on which a variant has been applied and saved), click the Variant button from the menu, and then select the correct variant from the dialog window.

Generating a Model

The selection settings on the initial screen of CFM1 will act as a query that goes out and grabs all the selected and filtered data elements and then places them in a virtual integration model. This filter for data elements and population of a model occurs when the integration model is executed by clicking the Execute button on the initial screen (Exhibit 7.3, step 8). The resulting screen will display the integration model's identification characteristics (name, logical system, etc.) (Exhibit 7.4, step 1), a list of each of the objects selected for inclusion (Exhibit 7.4, step 2), as well as the number of data elements resulting for inclusion based on any applied filter (Exhibit 7.4, step 3). At this point, the executed but unsaved integration model is strictly "virtual." The precise contents of the model—that is, exactly which data elements were selected when the filters were applied—can be seen by double-clicking any listed object. Following the

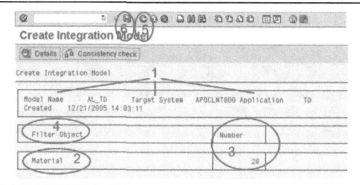

EXHIBIT 7.4   CREATE INTEGRATION MODEL: MODEL GENERATION SCREEN
The model is identified by model name, logical system, and application in the header. Contents are listed under "Filter Object" and details may be viewed by double-clicking the data object (i.e., Materials) or by single-clicking the object and clicking the Details button. © SAP AG. Used with permission.

example in Exhibit 7.4, one would view all the materials selected for a materials integration model, for example, by double-clicking the Material element listed in the "Filter Object" column (Exhibit 7.4, step 4). All the filtered materials that will be included in the model will display. If results are unexpected, return to the initial screen of CFM1 using the white arrow in the green bubble and adjust the filter (Exhibit 7.4, step 5). Otherwise, if the correct data elements are present, "generate" the model by clicking the Save button (Exhibit 7.4, step 6). Note that while the Save button on the initial screen saves a variant of selection and filter settings, the same button generates the actual resulting integration model on the results screen. Once generated, the integration model ceases to be virtual and exists in memory, where it can be applied to control data transfer between R/3 and APO. This will not occur, however, until the generated model is "activated."

Activating a Model

More than one generated model may exist at a time, but only one model covering the same data elements may be "active." Active models alone actually work to include and control data transfer between R/3 and APO. Two transactions, CFM2 and CFM3, are available for model activation. They are identical except that CFM3 is specialized for use by batch programs. Often CFM2 will be used in development to work with ad-hoc integration models until they are finalized; then CFM3 is applied for ordinary execution by batch in production environments.

In either transaction, enter the Model, Logical System, and Application combination that uniquely identifies a model generated with CFM1, then click the Execute button. The resulting screen will display a list of both active and inactive generated integration models. Active models are distinguished by having a green check mark next to them; inactive models are unselected (Exhibit 7.5, step 1). Any previously active model must be deactivated in advance of activating a new model: Mark a model for deactivation by (1) placing the cursor/focus on an active model, and then (2) clicking the Active/Inactive button (Exhibit 7.5, step 2); a red "X" will display next to the model (Exhibit 7.5, step 3).

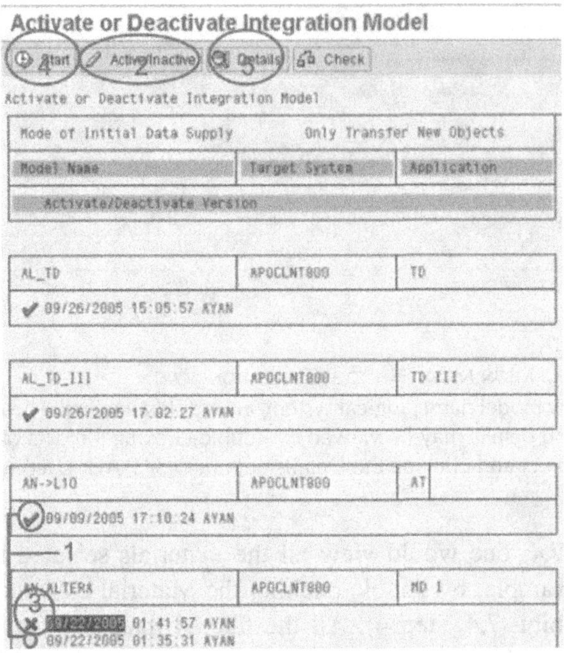

EXHIBIT 7.5 RESULTS SCREEN FOR CIF INTEGRATION MODEL ACTIVATION

Active models or models marked for activation have a green check, models marked for deactivation have a red "X," and inactive models are not marked. Double-click a model or single-click, and then press Details to see its contents. Once all markings are conducted with the Active/Inactive button, click Start to effect changes. © SAP AG. Used with permission.

Next select a model to activate by following the same steps: Place the cursor/focus on the new model and click the Active/Inactive button. When integration models to be deactivated and activated have been selected, carry out the activation and deactivation by clicking the Start button (Exhibit 7.5, step 4). The newly activated model is loaded in APO liveCache and takes over control of data transfer.

Note that as with the results screen of CFM1, the activation screen of CFM2 and CFM3 allows display of model details, that is, the data element contents of listed integration models. Simply double-click any model, or else single-click the model and click the Details button (Exhibit 7.5, step 5). Model contents may then be examined for appropriateness. As with CFM1, back out using the button with a white arrow in a bubble. To assist with ad-hoc reruns or to enable batch management of CIF activation, save CFM2 or CFM3 settings as a variant.

Sometimes business needs will call for preservation of deactivated models for a time, but ultimately deactivated models must be deleted as they become obsolete and simply take up memory while providing no value. Use CFM7 to deactivate models by entering the name, logical system, and application, then selecting the obsolete model, marking it for deletion, and saving. Deletion settings can and probably will need to be saved as a variant as they, too, will be managed by batch processing.

Recall that in addition to activation it is necessary to "Send Changes" for Production Process Models that use IDocs to package data transferred between R/3 and APO. On activation of a PPM integration model, execute CFP3, Send Changes. Select for relevant materials, plant, and production version and indicate whether PPMs are generated from R/3 routes that are built for DP or Rate-based Planning. Here, as with model generation, activation, and deactivation, a variant is likely to be advisable on the initial screen to ease ad-hoc execution and enable batch execution. During execution of change pointers a clock appears on the screen-bottom; but unlike generation and activation, execution is immediate with the results screen displaying outcome, not options, for conclusion of the step.

As with integration models, change pointers should similarly be deleted as they become obsolete. Here, too, while this will be an ad-hoc process in development it is typically set up as a batch process in production. Use transaction CFP4, Delete Change Pointers. Filter either for obsolete change pointers or processed change pointers and provide a date-range. Additional filtration may be entered to specify materials, plants, or production versions. It is naturally advisable for the deletion filter to follow the same settings as the "Send Changes" filter. Click the Execute button to conduct the deletion.

CIF Process in Review

The CIF empowers organizations that use R/3 for transactional ERP data management to maintain most of their supply chain master data once without need for duplication of data-entry in R/3, and then transfer it to APO in real-time. In most applications of APO some additional master data maintenance is still required on the APO side—we will address these on a case-by-case basis as we address individual modules—but by any measure the majority of data maintenance can be conducted once, in R/3, then CIF'd to APO by way of actively maintained integration models.

Core Interface integration models are conExhibitd in R/3. Integration models are not just the settings for what data will be exchanged between R/3 and APO; once generated they become actual lists of specific data elements referenced by the CIF interface to keep updated between systems. As such, only one integration model for the same data element can be active at a time. Note that by *data element* we mean the actual, atomic data element, not the class of data elements. For example, while there may be two active integration models for materials, both models must cover separate materials, such as materials belonging to separate sites or business divisions.

Data elements in integration models are populated into APO liveCache (Exhibit 7.6). The quantity of data elements in an integration model is static. That is, the elements are queried and populated into the model at the time of generation and no elements may be added or deleted from the integration model at any time thereafter. Only the "contents" of data elements may change, that is, the unit quantity of a customer or planned order, the shipping address on a site, or the planning strategy assigned to material. To account for added or deleted elements in an integration model, obsolete models must be deactivated (and eventually deleted) while new models are generated and activated.

The deactivation, regeneration, and activation of integration models together with the potential for deletions or changes in APO that are not properly reflected in R/3 will at times result in some inconsistency in liveCache. Successful CIF maintenance, therefore,

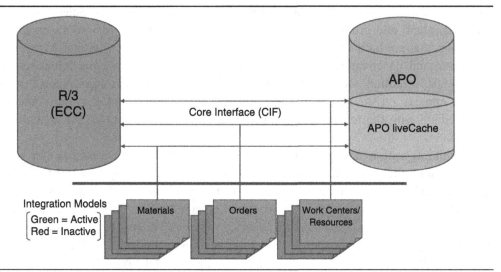

EXHIBIT 7.6 OVERVIEW OF THE CIF AND INTEGRATION MODELS

requires vigilant attention given to liveCache consistency and processes to correct inconsistencies. While most CIF maintenance is conducted in R/3, liveCache maintenance must be conducted in APO.

liveCache Consistency

Every organization using CIF will periodically run into consistency issues in liveCache. These issues will typically manifest in either of two ways: (1) execution of ordinary

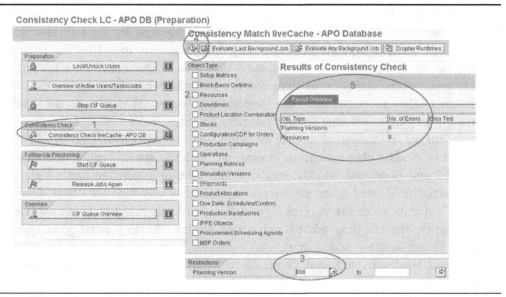

EXHIBIT 7.7 LIVECACHE CONSISTENCY CHECK

Indicate objects to check, planning version, then execute. Any found inconsistencies should be addressed by a system administrator. © SAP AG. Used with permission.

activities in APO such as planning or optimization runs that results in errors that explicitly note that liveCache problems are their cause in dialog windows, or (2) inexplicable system behavior that does not reveal itself conveniently via error messages. In the latter case, users and developers must endeavor to remember that liveCache consistency may at times be the culprit and conduct a consistency check to rule it out. Failing to do so when liveCache is in fact at issue may result in hours spent in vain checking and rechecking master data, configuration, and inputs.

liveCache consistency should be periodically checked and basic inconsistencies may be safely corrected. To do so, in APO drill down the navigation tree to *APO Administration → liveCache/LCA Routines → Tools* and open "liveCache Consistency Check," transaction /SAPAPO/OM17. Once there, click the middle button, Consistency Check liveCache—APO DB (Exhibit 7.7, step 1). In the resulting screen, indicate which objects to conduct the consistency check upon as well as the planning version, which will always

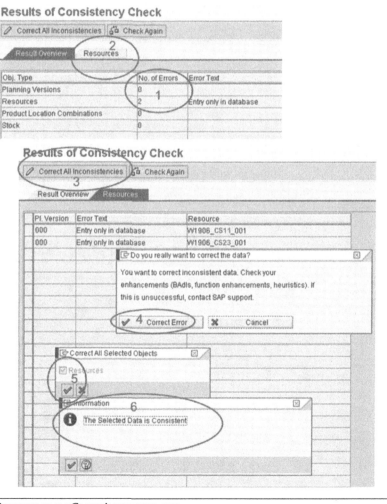

EXHIBIT 7.8 CORRECTING LIVECACHE INCONSISTENCIES
© SAP AG. Used with permission.

be 000 in the case of CIF-relevant consistency checks (Exhibit 7.7, steps 2 and 3). Click the Execute button to carry out the check (Exhibit 7.7, step 4). If data is consistent, a dialog window says so. Once acknowledged, the results window will display a table listing the objects checked and the number of liveCache errors found for each object (Exhibit 7.7, step 5). Zero indicates no errors—consistency between APO and R/3.

Any value found besides zero should be investigated and corrected (Exhibit 7.8, step 1). When errors are found, additional tabs will display in the results screen labeled by the object containing errors (Exhibit 7.8, step 2); click the new tab to view the found errors. Most errors can be easily corrected by clicking the Correct All Inconsistencies button (Exhibit 7.8, step 3). A dialog window results from this, indicating possible originators of inconsistencies that should be checked to avoid future inconsistencies; click the Correct Error button (Exhibit 7.8, step 4). A further dialog window will result, listing the possible objects to correct. Click the checkbox next to each object requiring correction and click the green check (Exhibit 7.8, step 5). APO then executes the correction and displays a dialog indicating outcome (Exhibit 7.8, step 6).

3

ENTREES: APO PLANNING MODULES

8

APO User Interfaces and the PP/DS Module

Note

This text should be used both as an instructional tool for first-time learners and as a reference tool for developers and experienced users. Unfortunately, the needs of these two reader communities are often divergent, and that is particularly the case in the sections addressing actual employment of APO modules. For every module addressed in this text—demand planning (DP), supply network planning (SNP), and production planning and detailed scheduling (PP/DS)—we ask that you carefully consider your own learning in choosing a reading sequence between sections on "Configuring" and "Using." In some cases we have elected to place "Configuring" first in the sequence because, of course, in actual application it will be necessary to configure each module prior to their use. While this is appropriate to experienced application, *it may not be the best way to learn the module for the first time.*

We often find that for purposes of learning it is wise to consider one of the "seven habits of successful people" and "start with the end in mind." Configuration details will seem very abstract, particularly for people thus far unfamiliar with SAP tools and software, and it will be hard to establish an early mental link between configuration settings and their final use. Therefore, if you are new to APO, consider reading the section on "Using" first, then come back and read the configuration sections. These more technical sections will make much more sense once you have an appreciation for what you are seeking to put together with configuration settings.

In Part One we introduced supply chain management in general and APO in particular. In Part Two we addressed the vast corpus of modeling that now becomes a core component of planners' and buyers' twenty-first-century job roles, enabling them to model global supply chains as a meteorologist models the weather in a weather simulator. In Part Three we introduce the tools available for direct day-to-day use in APO, the methods for configuring them, and techniques of putting APO into use in the daily course of business.

If we were to organize this section strictly according to the sequence of the supply chain, moving from most general, DP, to most specific, PP/DS, this chapter on PP/DS would come last, as would also be the case were we to organize the section simply according to its topology within APO. To place PP/DS last, however, poses some headaches for the instructional writer, because several user interfaces available in PP/DS are absolutely necessary to all other APO modules. The Product View, for example, is a PP/DS view *essential* to all APO deployments, regardless of whether PP/DS is used. The Supply Chain Cockpit and the Alert Monitor, while not explicitly a part of PP/DS, are nonetheless almost always used in PP/DS deployments as well as those of other modules. Finally, some designers may find use for specific PP/DS views in non-PP/DS deployments, such as the Detailed Scheduling (DS) Planning Board or the Product Planning Table.

In fact there is only one user interface (UI) that is extremely unlikely to be found profitable in exclusive PP/DS deployments: the Planning Book—and even that cannot be entirely ruled out of possibility. In some cases, the time-series PP/DS views provided by the Planning Table and DS Planning Board just may not suffice; and as we will see, the Planning Book is an extraordinarily powerful UI that is so very configurable that able and creative developers facing peculiar organizational business needs may indeed find it best suited for some PP/DS deployments. Hence, where almost all UIs are either core to PP/DS or else used in PP/DS, at most just one is unlikely to find a home in PP/DS. For that reason, we are addressing configuration and general interaction with all major APO UIs in this chapter together with the overall PP/DS module, its configuration and use.

GENERAL APO USER INTERFACES
Supply Chain Cockpit

The Supply Chain Cockpit (SCC) provides the most global view of the supply chain available in APO. When we describe APO as an attempt to "map the supply chain manager's mind," we are thinking of the SCC. Where most other APO UIs may be seen as varying from side-to-side, juxtaposing varieties of time-series-based views on one end to order-based data views on the other, the SCC is a top-down, executive view that is best described overall as aerial, but which may be applied in either geographic or logical views. Where other UIs focus on displaying large quantities or specific elements of transactional data against individual master data components such as a product at a site or a product at a working resource, the SCC is intended to graphically illustrate the entire variety of master data elements that make up the supply chain and their relationships with one another as well as any number of subsets of those elements that the user may need to examine. From the vantage point of the SCC, we may see the entire supply chain as it is modeled in APO, or any corner thereof, and be informed thus of the model or models available to APO's variety of planning runs that will run supply chain simulations and compute schedule and execution solutions.

Unlike many views, the SCC is neither enabled for transactional manipulation, nor is it even a portal to transactional manipulation. It is, however, a global view of almost all supply-chain master data with portals to any displayed master data element to enable their updates and configuration. The SCC may itself be configured to the needs of individual users, including only customers, sites, and vendors, for example, that are germane to this or that user's job functions.

The SCC is accessed via the transaction path *Supply Chain Monitoring → Supply Chain Cockpit*, transaction /SAPAPO/SCC02. It sits on its own location on the APO navigation tree apart from any modules and at the top of the tree—indicating its global availability as a tool for any APO deployment. From the initial screen (Exhibit 8.1) the

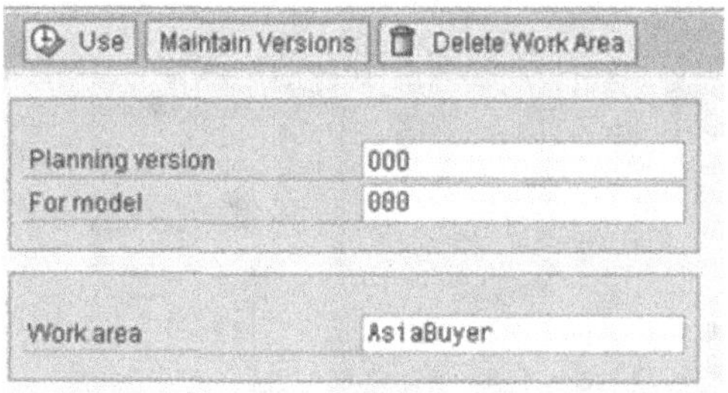

EXHIBIT 8.1 SUPPLY CHAIN COCKPIT INITIAL SCREEN

It is not necessary to indicate a work area on the initial screen. The field may be left blank if viewing the entire model/version or else if setting up a work area for the first time. © SAP AG. Used with permission.

user is prompted for a model and version to observe through the cockpit, as well as a work area. Work areas in the context of the SCC are specific SCC cases saved according to the needs of individual users. A work area may be defined, for example, for the entire supply chain, inclusive of all sites, transportation lanes, and products stored in the model. Other work areas may be set up and saved that include only master data relevant to particular roles. An Asia Buyer, in the case of our TCM supplier example, may only be interested in vendors, factories, and distribution sites, their requisite products and transportation lanes, in Asia. Other master data would be left out of the visual model in order to keep it from being cluttered. It is important to note that exclusion of master data elements from the visual model displayed in the SCC does not exclude them from the model or version.

The most notable feature of the SCC that immediately presents itself on entry is the world map. Any site and its transportation lanes in the model/version selected can be added to the map and saved as part of the work area. Click the expand and reduce icons above the map to focus on specific geographies or to gain a global view. To move across close, detailed map views, position the mouse cursor on either of the map's four sides. Click when an arrow displays pointing in the direction you wish to toggle across the map.

To add sites to the work area, click on the location object type in the lower panel under the location tab and right-click, then select "Add objects to work area" (Exhibit 8.2, step 1). A dialog-window pertinent to the object type, in this case locations, will display; click in the cell under the column title "Internal char. value" and a pull-down circle will display. Click the pull-down circle to pull up a match-code dialog window and either click the check to display all locations or use the Location Type field to filter by type such as plant or vendor (Exhibit 8.2, step 2). The site selected from the list will display in the column (Exhibit 8.2, step 3). Click the green check on the dialog window to exit. The site should now display on your SCC map.

HINT

If your site does not display on the map initially, don't fret. Save your settings to a work area, and then close and reenter the SCC. There you will find your sites on the SCC map.

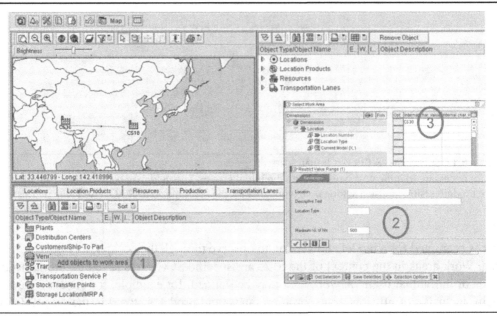

EXHIBIT 8.2 SUPPLY CHAIN COCKPIT

Sites are displayed by default against a geographic map according to their latitude/longitude settings. Transportation lanes between sites also display. Add and delete SCM master data elements to the SCC work area by clicking on any of the master data tabs for location, location products, resources, production, and transportation lanes. View alerts that have been set for the site by double-clicking the site icon. View transportation lane master data configuration by double-clicking the transportation lane line-icon between sites. View location or related master data, such as location's products, by clicking the location icon and then single-right-clicking to pull up a menu of options. © SAP AG. Used with permission.

The SCC in effect provides three different views to the supply chain model—to APO's map of the supply chain manager's mind: (1) a geographical map view, (2) a logical map view, and (3) a hierarchical view. The geographical map cannot be missed. If geography is unimportant to a particular utility or else distracting, click the "Settings" option on the menu and click "Logical View." APO will prompt for a name for the logical view. Provide one but note that the name is not used unless it is saved either on exit from the SCC or return back to the geographical view. The logical view will only display supply chain elements and their relationships; it will remove any geographic displays that may hide or obscure the data elements. Finally, the hierarchical view is available in the lower panel where data elements are listed by tabs wherein the various object types within data elements (i.e., vendor, plant, etc. are locations) are displayed.

Locations in the hierarchical view are relatively straightforward. Note the APO does not simply present Products, but presents "Location Products." APO does this because products in and of themselves, without a location parent, are not meaningful to the system. Just think generic Sarah as opposed to Sarah, a student at Roosevelt High School—the latter is specific and usable, the former too vague to work with. Resources are available by their four types, and in Production either production process models (PPMs) or production data structures (PDSs) may be used, according to whichever has been modeled for the organization. Transportation lanes, like location, is relatively straightforward.

A rule of thumb for the SCC is click, then right-click. Sites on the SCC map, when right-clicked, will yield a menu of options availing to the users their location master data, assigned products' master data, or even their version-specific assigned products' master data. Additionally the menu may be used to pull up the Alert Monitor and any alerts that have been assigned to the site as well as the primary UI screens for all the APO modules with a pivot or filter based on the selected site. Sites or data elements may similarly be deleted from the work area and map via the right-click submenu. All of these nodes and connections are also available when the data elements are selected and right-clicked from the hierarchical navigation panel in the location, location products, resources, production, and transportation lanes view.

Overall, work area management may also be conducted more directly by way of the Work Area button. Click the Work Area button to add single objects of any type from the model/version to the work area, to remove individual items, to empty the work area of all items, to save changes, or to save changes as a new work area.

HINT

If you cannot find your data elements on the geographic view, try the logical view under the "Settings" menu item to be sure they've been assigned to your work area.

Supply Chain Cockpit Cookbook

The SCC is intended to be a flexible, high-level view of any necessary angle of a supply chain model, up to the entire model. As such, a strict linear cookbook will succeed at suggesting only one of many potential ways users may set up and interface with the SCC. A simple cookbook will still be useful for the occasional first-time SCC work area setup (Exhibit 8.3).

Product View

The Product View is a PP/DS UI that will be employed in deployments of any module of APO. APO users familiar with R/3 may be advised to think of the Product View as an R/3 Stock Requirements List (SRL) on steroids. While serving the same basic purpose as the SRL, the Product View has a variety of additional components in APO that make it considerably more powerful than its R/3 counterpart.

In terms of basic presentation, the Product View is a tabular view of single-product, order-based supply and demand data. The Product View is employed to gain direct views to the exact data elements driving demand for product at a site and the exact supply elements in play there to fulfill the demand. Where time-series-based views of data tend to be useful for trend analysis, long-term scheduling, production smoothing, and capacity balancing, the order-based view provided by the Product View is intended to provide the maximum interactive access to the orders in actual production. In other words, if one wishes to work with overall quantities across time without respect to the specific order types represented by the quantities and to look at products in mass, the Product View is *not* the place to go. If, however, one is working within a tactical or execution horizon and must interact directly with order quantities, start and finish dates, and other physical

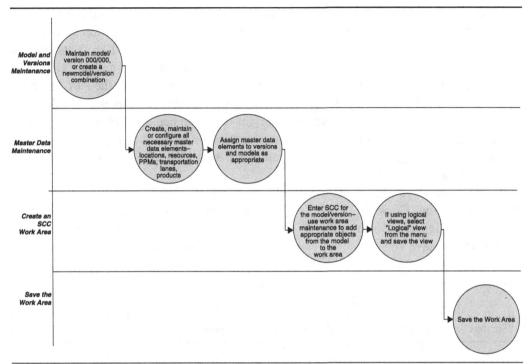

EXHIBIT 8.3 COOKBOOK FOR THE SUPPLY CHAIN COCKPIT
Note that master data configuration is an essential prerequisite to use of the SCC.

dependencies whose execution in business is directly controlled by orders, or else if one simply needs to know specific order information on any product's situation, the Product View is the window to the supply chain from which to work.

The Product View is accessed via path *Production Planning → Interactive Production Planning → Product View*, transaction /SAPAPO/RRP3. From the initial screen a planning version, product, and location are necessary to identify a unique product case. Inside the Product View transaction there are six interactive areas to work with: (1) the standard SAP SCM menu bar, (2) the Product View PP/DS menu bar, (3) the header, (4) the tabs, (5) the tab detail screens, and (6) the tab menu bar.

The SAP SCM menu bar is relatively standard from one screen to another and as a matter of course we do not usually address much of its contents. In the case of the Product View, however, an exception to that rule is necessary. In addition to the standard SAP SCM menu headings of Edit, Goto, System, and Help, the user should take special note of these three headings in the Product View: Interactive Planning, Settings, and DS Planning Board.

There are a number of reasons why the Product View is presented as part of PP/DS in spite of its availability to, and use by, all other modules of APO. First, where other modules such as DS, SNP, and Global Available to Promise (GATP) are likely to work with a longer-term future planning scope and at the level of aggregate quantities without necessary reference to orders, PP/DS is specialized for the tactical and execution horizons—usually no more than three months out in the former case and only three to five days out in the latter. In this space quantities are less often generalized guesses and more often immediate orders due to customers on a specific date or else due to fulfill customer orders. For PP/DS, therefore, orders matter—in fact orders are what it is all about.

Second, detailed order management being a natural function of PP/DS, the tools of PP/DS are particularly important to an order-based view such as the Product View. We immediately encounter this in the SAP menu bar where, first, under Interactive Planning, we may change the Product View from a simple "display-only" view likely to be valuable to any modular application, to a "change" view enabling interactive work with orders (Exhibit 8.4). When converting to change mode a dialog window will display asking for a propagation range, which defines the time period available for change. Typically the off-the-shelf standard range, "SAPALL" will suffice, which may be taken from the pull-down box in the dialog box field. Click the green check to apply the range and free the Product View for change mode.

After being shifted to change mode, another menu item under Interactive Planning becomes available: heuristics. The heuristics item opens to a lengthy submenu of PP/DS heuristics that may be applied in the Product View to automatically plan and schedule single products—matching and rematching available and new supplies to whatever demand picture is being maintained. This is in contrast to the wide-scope use of heuristics elsewhere in PP/DS where their applications in the planning run apply to entire groups of products, whole sites, or series of sites. Heuristics are discussed in more detail in the section on Using PP/DS.

The Settings heading under the SAP menu is common on SAP SCM screens, but there are a number of nonstandard settings available in the Product View, such as Production Planning Strategy, Heuristics, Propagation Range, and so forth. These are portals to the profiles for maintaining PP/DS tools settings that may be brought to bear in the Product

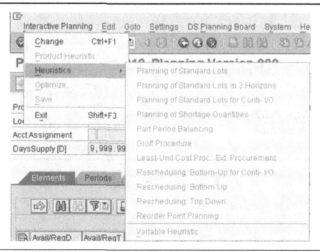

EXHIBIT 8.4 PRODUCT VIEW SAP MENU: INTERACTIVE PLANNING
Click Change to enable Change mode and open up orders for editing and to enable PP/DS tools such as heuristics. Use the Heuristics submenu to apply PP/DS planning run heuristics on a single-item-only basis to the product open in the Product View. © SAP AG. Used with permission.

View. Finally, the DS Planning Board heading is a portal to the other primary PP/DS UI. Between the Product View's order-based Elements tab, time-series-based Periods tab, and the DS Planning Board, which marries orders to a times-series view of working resource capacity and allows visual, interactive order and resource management for detailed scheduling, a PP/DS user has almost all the tools necessary for her job at her fingertips.

The Product View PP/DS menu bar is the visual, button-based menu bar just above the header (Exhibit 8.5, step 1). A number of buttons are available here, but initially the most important are the Pencil button, which sets the Product View on change mode, and the Refresh button immediately to its right, which enables users to move from one product to another in this screen without having to back out (Exhibit 8.5, step 2). Using the pencil icon to switch to change mode is no different from using the Interactive Planning menu item—both will require selection of a propagation range. To change the Product View to another product without returning to the initial screen, change the product in the Product field on the header (Exhibit 8.5, step 3) and then simply click the Refresh button to update the Product View with the new product's details.

Other details of the header are entirely standard, but notice that when the Product View is in Change Mode some additional buttons appear on the PP/DS menu bar, particularly the Order and Product Heuristic buttons (Exhibit 8.6). The Order button opens a dialog window that allows creation of new orders for the product at the site (Exhibit 8.7). To create an order for receipts, enter a positive quantity in the Rec./Reqmts Qty field in the dialog window, which APO will record to the Product View as a planned order (PlOrd) if the material is configured for building or a purchase requisition (PurRqs) if the material is configured for buying and its external procurement relationships are maintained and applied to the relevant transportation lane. To enter demand, enter a negative quantity by adding a negative sign to the quantity in the Rec./Reqmts Qty field and APO will record

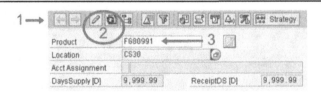

EXHIBIT 8.5   PRODUCT VIEW PP/DS MENU AND HEADER IN DISPLAY MODE
© SAP AG. Used with permission.

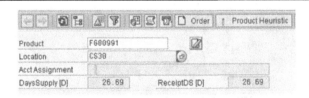

EXHIBIT 8.6   PRODUCT VIEW PP/DS MENU AND HEADER IN CHANGE MODE
Note availability of order creation and single-product heuristic execution. © SAP AG. Used with permission.

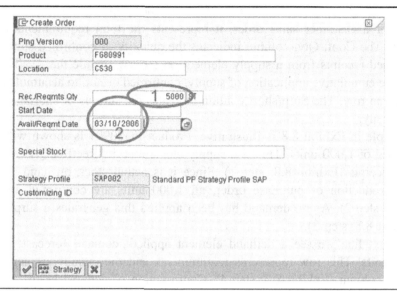

EXHIBIT 8.7 ORDER CREATION DIALOG
Enter a positive quantity to create a receipt order (planned order or purchase requisition) and a negative quantity to create a forecast/demand order (FCReq). © SAP AG. Used with permission.

it to the Product View as a demand element, a forecast requirement (FCReq). Typically the Start Date fields for date and time should be left blank, but an Avail/Reqmt Date will be required. Click the green check when finished and APO will apply the forecast or planned order to the Element tab table in the lower panel.

With orders available to process, use the Product Heuristic button to apply a PP/DS heuristic planning run algorithm to the single product in the Product View without replanning an entire group of products, site, or series of sites, as might happen if the ordinary planning run were executed. While helpful for simple product replanning or system tests, there are some limitations to carrying out heuristic planning this way. We will see later on that a full-fledged planning run allows application of any number of heuristic rules, while execution from the Product Heuristic applies only one, simple, make-to-stock rule that can be configured ad hoc in the resultant dialog window for lot-size control, calendar, quantity determination, scheduling, and management of stock.

The Product View has seven tabs, the first six of which we will address: (1) Elements, (2) Periods, (3) Quantities, (4) Stock, (5) Pegging Overview, (6) Product Master, and (7) ATP. On entry to the Product View, APO defaults to the Elements tab; this is appropriate as this is almost always the most useful window of the transaction. The Elements tab is most like the Product View's R/3 counterpart, the Stock Requirements List. It is a table of supply and demand elements, which places stock elements on its top rows (if they exist) and the proceeds with each subsequent row to list each order/element of supply and demand as they progress further out in time. Supply elements are ordinarily grouped row-by-row with the demand elements they are intended to fulfill.

The Rec/RecQty column may be initially confusing to novice users. If the element on the row is a *receipt* element such as stock, a purchase or a production order, this represents the total receipt quantity of the element. If it is a demand *requirements* quantity such as forecast or a customer sales order, it represents the total requirements quantity of the element. The Conf. Qty. column indicates the quantity of confirmed supply (i.e., the total confirmed receipts from a supply element on the row) while the Available column represents the cumulative application of supply, confirmed or not, to accumulated demand up to the given row. The Surp/short column indicates the surplus or shortage of all rows or that row only.

The example in Exhibit 8.8 is illustrative. Product FG80991 is shown with a starting stock on hand of 1,000 units. This is a supply element so its Rec/RecQty of 1,000 units represents receipts (Exhibit 8.8, step 1). Since it is actual stock on hand, not a work-in-process production or purchase order, all 1,000 units are confirmed and available (Exhibit 8.8, step 2). As no demand has been applied this generates a surplus of 1,000 units (Exhibit 8.8, step 3).

On the next line we see a demand element applied: demand forecast, or FC reqs, for 10,000 units. This row represents requirements and the quantity is negative in the Rec/RecQty column (Exhibit 8.8, step 4). Confirmation of demand is not applicable so the Confirmed column is 0. Since all 1,000 units of the previously unrestricted stock on the line above must be applied, the cumulative available quantity after 10,000 units of demand are applied is negative 9,000 (Exhibit 8.8, step 5). The supply/demand net for this individual line is negative 9,000 units as well (Exhibit 8.8, step 6).

With original supply and demand elements in place as such, generally a user may apply a heuristic planning run at this point to fulfill the demand. For build parts the planning run generates planned orders, which are gestational production orders. The planned order quantity necessary to close demand requirements in this case is 9,000 and

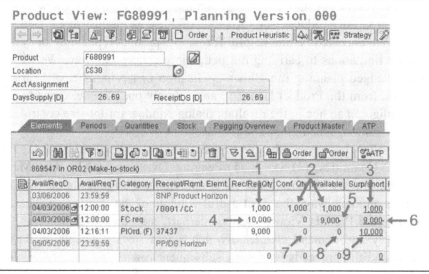

EXHIBIT 8.8 PRODUCT VIEW ELEMENT TAB

Supply (receipts) elements are applied in tabular form to fulfill demand (requirements) elements with an ultimate planning goal of netting out to zero—no excess supply, no unmet demand. © SAP AG. Used with permission.

this can be seen on the next line. Unlike stock, at the time of order generation, none of the supply is confirmed (Exhibit 8.8, step 7). Its application by the planning run to close the known demand results in no availability of supply for future demand without further orders—netting supply and demand to zero (Exhibit 8.8, step 8). The Surplus/shortage for the given line alone is 9,000 units (Exhibit 8.8, step 9).

The Product View Elements tab has a large number of additional columns that will find use in specific business deployment needs and by advanced APO users, but one other column should be addressed. The Planning Run in PP/DS, as in SNP and as in SAP R/3, does not generate purchase orders or production orders. Instead it generates "purchase requisitions" and "planned orders" that are gestational orders—essentially "suggested" orders from the system that in aggregate form a suggested build/buy schedule—that must be approved by a human user and applied respectively on approval as purchase orders and production orders. Since these are schedule-order suggestions, not absolute orders for execution, the system treats them as *unfirmed*. That is, if demand requirements change by the next time a planning run is executed, the system edits or completely eliminates unfirmed purchase requisitions and planned orders to make room for a better, more precise schedule. Where planning runs treat purchase and production orders as *firmed* supply—just like stock, whose basic data cannot be altered due to demand fluctuations—unfirmed supply in the form of purchase requisitions and planned orders is treated with maximum flexibility.

A half-way point exists, however, between unfirmed gestational orders and firmed purchase and production orders, which is "firmed" purchase requisitions and planned orders. These orders have not yet been converted by a user to purchase and production orders, but have been flagged as "firmed" by the user to disallow the system from altering their basic data while nonetheless maintaining their gestational status. Orders can be firmed both within transactions detailing the orders and from within the Product View; in the latter case this is done simply by highlighting their lines in the Elements tab and clicking the Order button on the tab-menu—the button with a closed lock image on it. Unfirm them by highlighting and clicking the Undo Firming button—the button with the open lock image on it. When firmed, "PP-Firmed" flag will show a check. Another important button on the tab-menu is the Delete button, represented with a trash-can icon, which is necessary to delete orders of any kind and which is only available in change-mode.

Wherever we have referred to the Product View up to this point we have always noted its specialization as an order-based view of data. That is not to say a time-series-based view may not occasionally be useful. The Product View provides a single-product, time-series view of data in the Periods tab (Exhibit 8.9). Any specialized time-series analysis or interaction with data will almost always require configuration and provision of a more sophisticated time-series view such as may be provided by the Planning Book or the Production Planning Table; but especially in the case of PP/DS deployments where neither of these other transactions are available, the Periods tab will do as a simple and universally accessible time-series view to orders data.

The other tabs of concern to us are the Quantities, Stock, and Pegging Overview tabs. The Quantity tab provides a time-series, graphical view to available quantity as it is expressed against cumulative requirements and receipts. Ordinarily demand and supply,

Product View: 869547, Planning Version 000

Product	F680991
Location	CS30
Acct Assignment	
DaysSupply [D]	26.69	ReceiptDS [D]	26.69

Elements | Periods | Quantities | Stock | Pegging Overview | Product Master | ATP

Product view: Periodic	Un.	Due	FR (1) 03/1	SU (1) 03/1	FR (1) 03/2	SU (1) 03/2	FR (1) 03/3
869547 / 32BIT MPU BX80547P(							
__Available Quantity	ST		1,100		3,500		2,100
__Days' Supply	D	11.500	8.500	6.500	8.458	6.458	1.458
__FC req. / Orig.	ST			1,100-		3,500-	
__Total Requirements / Conf.	ST						
__PlOrd. / 00000000000086954	ST		1,100		3,500		2,100

EXHIBIT 8.9 PRODUCT VIEW PERIODS TAB

The Periods tab allows a time-series view of data from within the Product View. © SAP AG. Used with permission.

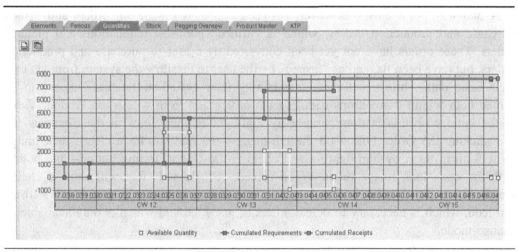

EXHIBIT 8.10 PRODUCT VIEW QUANTITIES TAB

Cumulative requirements and receipts are depicted graphically across a time series as they relate to available quantity. While demand and supply is expected to fluctuate, good planning will result in a relatively straight Available Quantity line. © SAP AG. Used with permission.

that is, requirements and receipts, will fluctuate from time bucket-to-bucket, but well-planned supply chains will result in a consistently available quantity at or very slightly above zero—or in cases where excess supply targets are intended, at the target level (Exhibit 8.10). The Stocks tab may be applied by users to find all stocks, of all kinds, for the product at all sites. The Product Master is a convenience that allows display of the product's master data configuration from within the Product View.

Alert Monitor

As with the SCC, the Alert Monitor is a transaction that is generally available to all APO module deployments. Unlike the Product View, it is not a part of PP/DS, in fact it is totally nonspecific to all APO modules. Nonetheless it has powerful applications in that module, in many cases more direct applications than those of the SCC. The Alert Monitor is found along the navigation path *Supply Chain Monitoring → Alert Monitor → Alert Monitor*, or with transaction /SAPAPO/AMON1.

Throughout APO a paradigm shift is applied to the practice of supply chain management: Human planning is transformed from active, universal product planning to active, universal supply chain modeling with limited direct planning—that is, automated planning overall except for *exception-based* active, human-user planning. In other words, the new supply chain manager uses APO to model the supply chain and automatically plan the majority of it. Human engagement with supply chain planning is focused on working the qualitative, sophisticated exceptions (i.e., outlying conditions not well suited to automation that require human intervention to resolve). Central to this model of planning is the Alert Monitor, and as such it will have considerable applications in all of the modules we will consider.

A good supply chain model in APO will result in the clockwork, automatic scheduling of most products and their components, but even the best model will often result in less-than-ideal outcomes. In other words, it is nature, not the software, that does not allow us to have our cake and eat it, too. APO *helps* us to make the best choice between having and eating given constraints, priorities, and costs by applying quantitative punch that is simply impossible to any human mind; but there are limits to quantitative analysis. The best outcome of quantitative analysis may not be the best balance of having and eating actually possible. The qualitative contributions of a human—such as by brokering deals or calling in favors with suppliers or the shop floor—may contribute to make a better solution than the strictly quantitative one generated by APO.

APO users apply the Alert Monitor to assign tolerances to automated outcomes from planning runs, and when those tolerances are exceeded, for instance, by sudden, unanticipated spikes in demand, APO will generate alerts that notify the planner of the necessity to investigate and potentially intervene. Humans, at this stage, can add considerable value. With a large, unanticipated new customer order on the short horizon, a human planner can call up suppliers, work out win-win last-minute expedite arrangements, motivate the factory to work longer shifts, and generally pull out the stops, all in order to make the unusual happen so long as its worthwhile. If that is not possible, the planner may still be able to assuage the situation by contacting the customer and determining whether alternative paths to fulfillment exist, either taking the order a little late, or a smaller amount on time and a larger amount later, or else by checking if another product may be brought to bear to fulfill the demand. The Alert Monitor is the trip wire that lets us know when the system's work has finished and human work must begin.

Configuring Alerts

The initial screen of the Alert Monitor differs from that of most APO transactions in that it is much more active, particularly once Alerts have been programmed. Note immediately

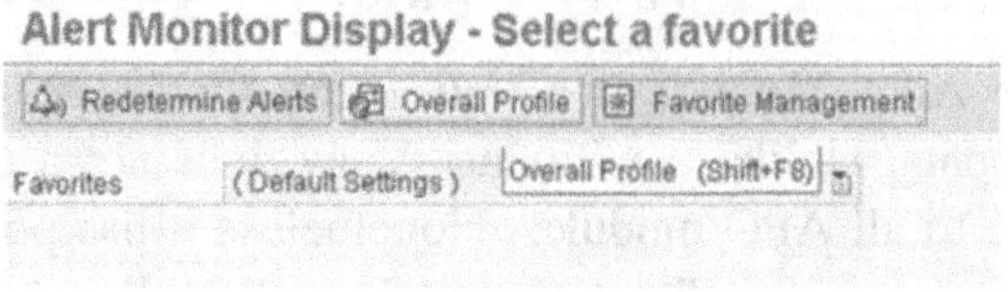

EXHIBIT 8.11 ALERT MONITOR INITIAL SCREEN
There are three options: (1) to generate new Alert Profiles, click "Overall Profile," (2) to assign Alert Profiles to the Favorites pull-down, click "Favorites Management," (3) to execute an alert check on the selected profile, use the pull-down menu to select alert profiles that have been assigned as favorites, select a Favorite Alert Profile from the list, and click "Redetermine Alerts." © SAP AG. Used with permission.

that instead of the more common "Display," "Create," and "Change" options, the Alert Monitor poses these three selection options: (1) Create new Alert Profiles, (2) assign Alert Profiles to the user's Favorites List, and (3) execute Alert Checks on selected favorite Alert Profiles (Exhibit 8.11).

Different Alert profiles will be necessary for different job roles and often for different individuals within job roles. Master schedulers, for example, will not usually be interested in alerts with strictly short-term significance, while such alerts may be of great import to factory schedulers or production planners. Buyers will be interested in alerts related to purchasing and inventory but will likely not be interested in alerts related to shop floor or dock performance. They may be interested in short-term demand changes but are unlikely to be greatly concerned with such changes when they occur far out on the time horizon. Any number of Alert Profiles may be custom generated in APO to satisfy the variety of needs that arise.

Creating New Alert Profiles

To generate a new profile, click the Overall Profile button. Within the Overall Profile screen, new alert profiles may be defined and old ones may be maintained. The screen has a section for the name and description of the profile (Exhibit 8.12, step 1), its time horizon (Exhibit 8.12, step 2), and the actual conditions of the alert, "Application-Specific Alert Profile" (Exhibit 8.12, step 3). The latter panel actually sets up module-specific subprofiles within the Overall Profile. Thus, an overall profile may contain alerts that cover DP, SNP, and/or PP/DS (or others), but within that profile will be individual module-specific subprofiles. The time horizon may be defined as either relative, pivoting off of the current date and moving forward (i.e., today + 3 months), or else absolute, specifying explicit from and to dates. The name of the overall profile and its time-horizon apply to all subprofiles.

Alerts themselves are organized by application or module. Note that there is not a perfect 1:1 relationship between the APO modules and the given tabs in the Alert Monitor, at least in terms of naming. The "VS" tab controls alerts relevant to transportation planning/vehicle scheduling (TP/VS), the Vendor Managed Inventory (VMI) tab controls alerts relevant to vendor-managed inventory, and Supply and Demand Planning (SDP) controls the balance of what may be considered SNP alerts. Supply network planning users may find themselves toggling between Transport Load Builder (TLB), VMI, Supply and Demand Planning (SDP), and Vehicle Scheduling (VS) to find the full variety of alerts they require.

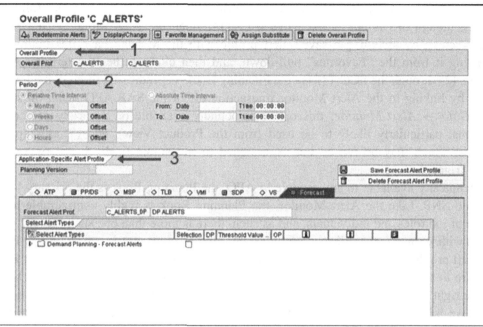

EXHIBIT 8.12 BASIC ALERT SETUP
© SAP AG. Used with permission.

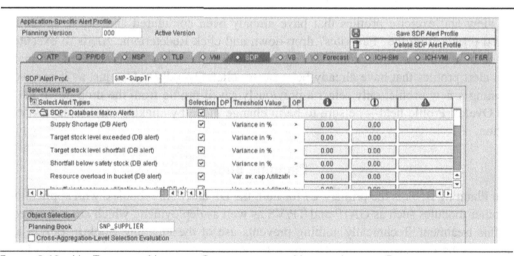

EXHIBIT 8.13 USE THRESHOLD VALUES TO CONFIGURATION OF VARIABLE ALERTS BY PRIORITY.
Assign the Alert Profile to a planning book if applicable. © SAP AG. Used with permission.

Alerts default to version 000 of model 000. If a specific version is required, it should be explicitly noted. When the module-tab is selected, click the navigation arrow on the text, "Select Alert Types" on the left of the lower dialog panel to expand a list of all available alerts. Click the "Selection" flag in to enable an alert. Many alerts are *dynamic*, that is, allowing or requiring that the users specify explicit tolerances (e.g., if a target stock level is exceeded by 5%, the alert kicks in) (Exhibit 8.13).

Once profiles are configured, alerts are ordinarily viewed by any of the following means, though this is not an exclusive list: (1) through the Alert Monitor itself in the initial screen by assigning a saved alert profile with the Manage Favorites button and selecting it from the "Favorites" pull-down, and then clicking the Redetermine Alerts button, (2) through the SCC, (3) via the Planning Book, (4) indirectly through the Product View by linking to the Alert Monitor transaction off of the SAP APO menu on screen top (*Goto → Alert Monitor*; this option is actually available on a variety of screens, it is just particularly likely to be used from the Product View), and (5) as output of macros, which may be run ad hoc or assigned to run automatically based on explicit event triggers.

Technically available to any module in APO, the Planning Book is the primary UI for DP and SNP. Like the Alert Monitor, the Planning Book is highly configurable to the needs of job roles and individuals, and as such, there is more than one such "Book," each saved with its own name. When configuring the Alert Monitor, if using the Planning Book, the alert profile may be assigned to a previously configured Planning Book (Exhibit 8.13). Be sure to save an application-specific alert profile or its changes: Click the Save button on the right of the dialog panel above the module tabs; save the overall profile by clicking the Save button at the top of the screen. Once saved, the profile will be available from the initial screen under Manage Favorites from where it can be assigned to the initial screen Favorites list.

Manage Favorites and Run Alert Checks

To view and exercise profiles that have already been configured and saved, select the saved profile from the "Favorites" drop-down and click Redetermine Alerts to execute a check of conditions throughout APO against the criteria of the Alerts selected. To maintain alert profiles that have already been saved, click Overall Profiles just as if one were creating a new profile, only select a previously saved profile from the drop-down list of the Overall Profile field—be sure to be in change mode by clicking the Display/Change button.

Planning Book

The Planning Book is the primary UI for both the DP and SNP modules, with applications in other modules such as GATP and TP/VS as well as deployment, which are not covered in this treatment. Technically nothing prevents use of the Planning Book in PP/DS and data may be used and manipulated via a Planning Book on otherwise exclusive PP/DS applications, but no tools unique to PP/DS are available via the Planning Book. Normally most analysts will find that the Planning Book is not ideal for PP/DS solutions on account of the absence of any PP/DS tools as well as the fact that other PP/DS-specific UIs are available in the DS Planning Board and the Production Planning Table. Data analysis and processing tools specific to DP and SNP, such as statistical analysis and SNP planning runs, respectively, are made available through the Planning Book UI. All in all then, while we cover all UIs in our PP/DS section because several PP/DS UIs are broadly available to all APO modules—especially the Product View—it does not run well the other way and in most cases the Planning Book will not be germane to PP/DS.

Regardless of its application to PP/DS, however, the Planning Book is the fundamental UI for both DP and SNP and is the most diverse, robust, and configurable UI offered in APO. There are three nodes on the APO navigation tree that access the Planning Book: one via DP and the other two via SNP. Via DP, the Planning Book is accessed along path *Demand Planning → Planning → Interactive Demand Planning*, using transaction /SAPAPO/SDP94. The first node in SNP is the "single-book" view accessed along path *Supply Network Planning → Planning → Interactive Supply Network Planning*, which is transaction /SAPAPO/SNP94. The second node is the "all-books" view, which follows the same nodal pathway and is just below the first transaction; it is also the same transaction as one in the DP view: /SAPAPO/SDP94. The "single" and "all" books views of the Planning Book refers to the fact that while the entire transaction is called the "Planning Book," falsely implying that there is just one book, in fact any number of configurations of *books* are available to any APO deployment. Each individual configuration instance of the Planning Book is itself considered a "book." For clarification and consistency, wherever we discuss the Planning Book in this text we will use the full term and uppercase, *Planning Book*, to refer to either the transaction or the overarching concept, while using the lowercase *book* or *planning book* to refer to a single, configurative instance. For the former, we see that there are two cases: the single-book and all-book transactions. In the latter, there may be as many books defined and configured in APO for an organization as necessary.

The single-book view in SNP may therefore be applied as a sort of security control on projects where security is sensitive. If certain users—especially external users who may be involved in collaborative planning projects—need access to the Planning Book, security profiles may be enabled that disallow their access to any version of the transaction except for the single-book view. The individual users may then be assigned to specific Planning Book configurations by way of the "Assign User to Planning Book" transaction, /SAPAPO/SDPPLBK, along path *Supply Network Planning → Environment → Current Settings*.

The two different multiple-book views of the Planning Book are identical to each other in both their DP and SNP instances. In any APO deployment case where flexibility of views is important this version of the transaction will be critical; generally speaking, we encourage its use over that of the single-book view. Since the Planning Book serves a variety of purposes that are applied through different and often mutually exclusive configurations, this will most likely be the preferred normal approach. Obviously the Planning Book is suited for both demand analysis and supply planning, so whether the statistical and forecast tools of DP or the planning run tools of SNP are available to a given Planning Book instance is subject to the underlying configuration of the book in use, *not* to the navigation path used to access the transaction.

The Planning Book provides a time-series-based, medium- to long-term view of planning data. Pegging is almost always available, which allows view to the orders behind order-based data elements whenever necessary—that is, wherever the order quantities have been aggregated or disaggregated to suit a time-series display. Time-bucketed quantities may be viewed and changed manually across the horizon, statistical and planning data processing tools may be applied on single or multiple products and single or multiple sites, production requirements—either as demand or scheduled production—may be viewed against available capacity resources, and individual bucketed quantities may be double-clicked and pegged to their underlying data objects, ordinarily orders. By way of these techniques, the Planning Book is applied for demand analysis, SNP, and capacity leveling on an individual- or multiproduct basis and on an individual- or multisite basis.

Overview of Planning Book Architecture

There are four underlying architectural components of a Planning Book: (1) the Planning Object Structure, (2) the Planning Area, (3) the unique-configuration *instance* of a Planning Book (what we will only call a "book" in this treatment for purposes of distinguishing it from the wider controlling "Planning Book" transaction), and (4) the Data View. Planning Object Structures and Planning Areas are both created and maintained through the transaction Administration of Demand Planning and Supply Network Planning, code /SAPAPO/MSDP_ADMIN, on path *Demand Planning → Environment*. The book and data views are created and maintained through the transaction Define Planning Book, code /SAPAPO/SDP8B, on either path *Demand Planning → Environment → Current Settings* or *Supply Network Planning → Environment → Current Settings*. The latter transaction is identical regardless of the path used to access it.

Planning Book data is composed of "Characteristics" and "Key Figures." Characteristics are typically organizational, structurally identifying data elements that are not going to be changed by the business conduct within any book. Locations, products, resources, and transportation lanes are common characteristic values assigned to books. Key figures are data elements that are usually more transactional in nature and that carry analytical or planning value and purpose. Stock on Hand, Safety Stock, Reorder Point, Target Day's Supply, Day's Supply, Total Receipts, Total Demand, Forecast, and VMI Demand are common key values used in books. Where characteristics create the characterizing data structure that we view through and navigate with a book, key figures provide data elements that are actually analyzed and/or modified.

The Planning Object Structure is the underlying database structure that organizes and stores characteristic data that is employed in a book. Some, though not necessarily all, of the characteristics assigned to an object may be navigational in nature—some attention must be paid to navigational characteristics as they will be available on the Planning Book "shuffler" that is used to select and filter data elements for use in a book. Navigational characteristics and the shuffler will be examined in the section: Working with the Planning Book—Navigation Panel.

This is the formative, step-by-step basis of a Planning Book: First, Planning Object Structures are assigned to Planning Areas and provide the underlying characteristic foundation. Second, from this foundation, key figures are assigned to the Planning Area. Third, a book is configured by combining the Planning Object Structure and Planning Area—the book is formed from the characteristic structural foundation of the Planning Object Structure and key figures with which to work from the Planning Area. Fourth, since all key figures available in a Planning Area are not necessary to the roles of every user, specific key figures that are actually viewed under one circumstance or another are defined by the creation and assignment of data views.

Defining Time Horizon and Time Buckets

In addition to all this, a time horizon and its time buckets must be defined to use the Planning Book via the Planning Area. Recall that the time horizon is defined for the Planning Area through Periodicities that are initialized as a time series on the Planning Area to create physical storage space in the database. This is inherited by books and their data views when the Planning Area is assigned during book configuration. Periodicities for Planning Areas are configured on a Storage Bucket Profile, containing time horizons with the transaction Periodicities for Planning Area, code /SAPAPO/TR32, accessed via path *Supply Network Planning → Environment → Current Settings*. Periodicities specify time bucket units (days, weeks, etc.) and horizon scope (start and end date).

This provides a time-bucket scope and data storage, but additional detail is necessary for display. Specify time-bucket details with the transaction Maintain Time Bucket Profile for DP and SNP, accessed via the same path as the Periodicities for Planning Area transaction and found on the node just above that transaction on transaction code /SAPAPO/TR30. Understand that while Periodicities defines the creation of time-based storage units in the database, controlling their horizon scope and unit storage type, the Time Bucket Profile controls their actual display on a planning book Data View, which may be less than the entire horizon scope and may include aggregations of the time bucket. For example, a Periodicity on a Planning Area may define a 12-month horizon with daily storage buckets while a Time Bucket Profile assigned to a planning book may further clarify that in a specific Data View only six months are visible and they are aggregated into weekly displays. Again, the Periodicities are assigned to the Planning Area while the Time Bucket Profile is assigned to control the Data View of a planning book.

Usually, Always, and Never

Three rules must be burned into the heart and mind of every APO user or developer who is ever tasked with configuring the Planning Book. While certain doom does not lurk ominously for those who violate these rules, ceaseless and totally unnecessary headaches do. It is the latter point that we emphasize: *totally unnecessary*. One can violate these rules and still successfully use APO, but only at great long-term risk. Since it costs no more work to follow these rules than to ignore them, we can see no point in ever violating them and every reason to adhere to them religiously.

First comes the weakest rule: *usually*. In both development and production: *Usually* use custom-built books with custom data views and Planning Areas. The one architectural element this rule will not often apply to is the Planning Object Structure, which will rarely require any customization. However, if for any reason Planning Object Structures are found to require some customizing changes, then absolutely copy the object and customize the copy: Do not customize the SAP-provided object. This rule holds across the board for other objects as well. A number of planning books come off the shelf with APO and may by all means be used to initially get acquainted with the toolset—SAP training classes do as much. But in the long run, for both development and production purposes, it is best to have your own custom books defined so that no one accidentally makes changes to anything that comes off the shelf. Initially it may be believed that customization will be unnecessary, but if that belief is found wanting, one will be best prepared if one is working off a copy rather than an off-the-shelf view, area, or book. The best way to avoid accidents is to make them impossible; defining custom planning books with custom data views and planning areas is a simple practice that will provide this accident security.

This brings us to the second rule: *always*. Always *copy* from preexisting data views, planning books, Planning Areas, and Planning Object Structures when custom-creating your own. Yes, it is technically possible to create these from scratch, but there is so little reason to do so and entirely sufficient reasons to eschew the practice. For one, it is wholly unnecessary; and for another, it is entirely too likely to lead to problems. Developers will encounter the fewest problems across the board by applying this simple process when configuring the planning book: When setting up data views, planning books, and Planning Areas (or Planning Object Structures), (1) find the off-the-shelf, preconfigured objects that most closely match the organization's needs, (2) copy them as custom objects, and then (3) add or delete key figures (or characteristics if copying a Planning Object Structure) as necessary to perfect the custom configuration. Again, yes, it is *possible* to simply create any of these from scratch, but it is not any easier than copying and it is a path so fraught with problems that it is simply not worth going there. Do not repeat others' mistakes. This isn't worth learning from experience; just copy.

Finally, *never*: Never delete or edit an off-the-shelf Planning Book object *of any kind*. That is, never edit or delete any of the off-the-shelf, SAP-provided data views, planning books, Planning Areas, or Planning Object Structures. Follow all three rules, there is no reason not to; but woe to him who violates this last rule. Every off-the-shelf object is a resource from which any number of copies can be made and modified to fit unique organizational needs as they arise. Delete any, modify any, and you have uselessly and profitlessly eliminated or diminished a very hard-to-replace resource. There is no reason to do this, there is no profit in it; but as an opportunity cost the quantitative cost of making this regrettable mistake can never be fully quantified, though it will be felt over and over again.

Configuring the Planning Book

Selection of a Planning Object Structure will ordinarily be the first step in Planning Book configuration. Use the transaction Administration of Demand Planning and Supply Network Planning, which defaults to the Planning Area view. A pull-down button in the upper left under the screen title "S&DP Administration" indicates the view with the name Planning Areas. When clicked it offers two choices: Planning Areas and Planning Object Structures; select the latter to do maintenance (Exhibit 8.14). Either of two off-the-shelf Planning Object Structures will form the characteristic foundation for almost all DP and SNP planning books: 9ADPBAS for DP and 9ASNPBAS for SNP. There will be occasional defections where other Planning Object Structures will make a better-suited data basis for a configuration, but for such cases developers will need to carefully explore the characteristics available in each Planning Object Structure to ascertain those that are best suited to their unique organizational use case. In almost all ordinary DP and SNP cases, 9ADPBAS and 9ASNPBAS will suffice.

To view the details of a Planning Object Structure, right-click the object and select "Detail." Administrative properties of the structure (who created it, when, it's internal object type, etc.) are displayed with the characteristics assigned to it. Hierarchical

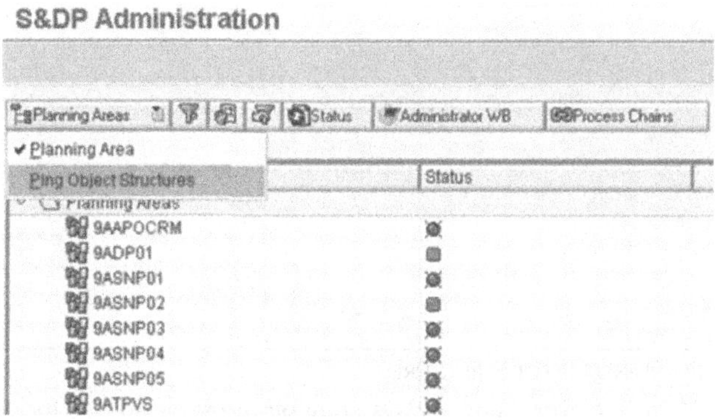

S&DP Administration

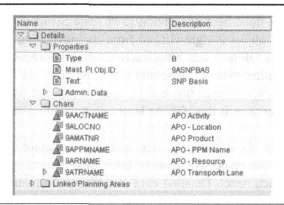

EXHIBIT 8.14 S&DP ADMINISTRATION
Select whether to maintain Planning Areas or Planning Object Structures; note that the Status column indicates whether a Planning Area (or Planning Object Structure) is activated by way of color. © SAP AG. Used with permission.

EXHIBIT 8.15 PLANNING OBJECT STRUCTURE DETAILS
Hierarchical characteristics have an arrow to the left. Planning Areas that have this object assigned to them may be listed by expanding "Linked Planning Areas." © SAP AG. Used with permission.

characteristics are displayed with an arrow to the left that, when clicked, displays the component characteristics of the hierarchy. All Planning Areas to which a Planning Object Structure is assigned are displayed under "Linked Planning Areas." The latter node will be important when making changes to a Planning Object Structure—which, we reemphasize, is something that should be done only on custom-created objects (Exhibit 8.15).

To create a new Planning Object Structure, right-click an existing one that will serve as its starting basis and select "Copy." Give the new structure a name and description, and then click to create it (Exhibit 8.16). To add or remove characteristics from the *new* structure, right-click the Planning Object Structure on the navigation path and select "Change," and then add characteristics by selecting them in the right-hand panel and clicking the left arrow to move them to the left-hand panel. Remove them from the structure by carrying out the opposite steps. Planning Object Structures for use by SNP must have "SNP Possible" checked; by checking this field you will automatically enable

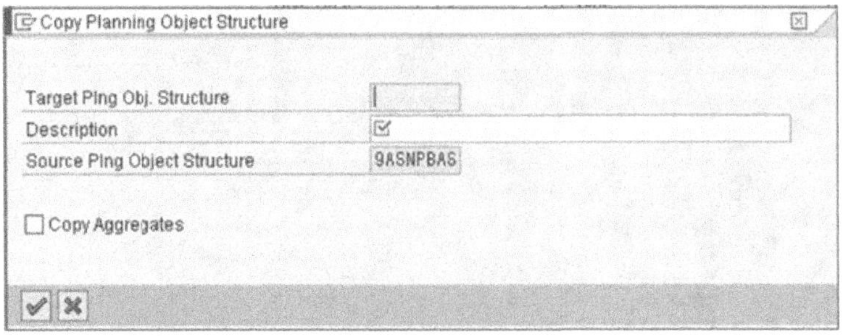

EXHIBIT 8.16 COPY A PLANNING OBJECT STRUCTURE
Remember "Usually, Always, Never," and always copy off-the-shelf objects for customization. *Never* edit or delete an off-the-shelf structure. Generally speaking, Planning Object Structures *can* be assigned to Planning Areas and books without the necessity of copying and forming new ones, but if some reason is found that makes it necessary to edit a preexisting one, always make the changes in a copy and work from that. © SAP AG. Used with permission.

a "Standard SNP Planning Level" that enables planning with SNP on the Planning Object Structure. Since this is done here, the option to "Create Standard SNP Planning Level" when the *newly saved* object is right-clicked from the navigation path may be ignored. Those objects for use in DP may use "Characteristic-Based Forecasting" or "Relevant for DP BOM," though neither option is essential to DP employment. Click the Navigation Attributes button to view attributes that can be used to sort and filter the Planning Book from among those entered in it thus far. At least one navigation attribute is essential for any working book.

To analyze and learn about characteristics' qualities, highlight the characteristic from either panel and click the respective Display InfoObject button on the bottom; there is one such button for each panel. Detailed data dictionary information about every object is available and objects may be activated or deactivated from here. When done editing the Planning Object Structure, click the Activate button. You may also activate and deactivate entire Planning Object Structures by right-clicking them on the navigation path and selecting the appropriate action. Notice that on the navigation path a green box is displayed under the Status column for activated Planning Object Structures and a red circle is displayed for those that have not been activated. Delete custom objects as necessary by the same methods—but again, we cannot emphasize this point enough: *Never* delete an off-the-shelf Planning Object Structure.

Once a Planning Object Structure is selected, created (if necessary), assigned to SNP (if necessary), configured with the right characteristics (if necessary), and activated, assign the object to a Planning Area. Either click the toggle button to go back to Planning Areas from the Planning Object Structures screen or else reenter the transaction for S&DP Administration (Administration of Demand Planning and Supply Network Planning). As with Planning Object Structures, there are several standard, off-the-shelf Planning Areas that will almost always suffice as the basis of custom Planning Areas, specifically, for DP: 9ADP01 and for SNP: 9ASNP01.05. Use the right-click "Details" option as with Planning Object Structures to view Planning Area details; 9ASNP02 is a good first-time example. Notice that a standard bucket profile, 9ASNP, has been assigned to create a time horizon and the minimum-bucket basis of the horizon. This is one bucket profile maintained in transaction Periodicities for Planning Area.

Planning Area 9ASNP02 has Planning Object Structure 9ASNPBAS assigned, causing it to inherit the latter's characteristics. Characteristic and key figure assignments may be viewed by expanding the arrow to the left of "Master Pl.Obj.Str." Data element aggregations, administrative data, and configured planning books to which the Planning Area has been assigned are also visible.

Maintenance of new Planning Areas closely follows the process for maintaining new Planning Object Structures. While we have not counseled the absolute necessity of making copies of every Planning Object Structure employed simply because it is less likely that any editing of such objects will ever be required (they can usually be left fully intact for any project's applications), we do, however, counsel making copies of standard Planning Areas exactly because they are far more likely to require editing. Right-click an existing, off-the-shelf object (or a previously copied custom area so long as the custom area has proven itself reliable) and select "Copy." Give the new Planning Area a name (note that underscores are allowed in the name but hyphens are not) and click the check to establish the area. Custom configure the new area by right-clicking it on the navigation path and selecting "Change." A tab-based screen will appear with options for Info, Aggregate, Key Figures, Key Figure Aggregation, and Key Figure Assignment.

Storage bucket profile (periodicities again), unit of measure, and currency data (the latter only if relevant) are all maintained on the Info tab. Add or remove key figures on the Key Figures tab. Assign or deassign aggregations of key figures on the Aggregates tab and assign key figures to Aggregations on the Key Figure Assignment tab. Enter the computation type for key figure aggregations on the Key Figure Aggregation tab. Initialize new Planning Areas by right-clicking them on the navigation path and selecting "Initialize Planning Version." The same Status-indicating green/red square/circle feature is available on Planning Versions as with Planning Object Structures. If it proves necessary to delete a custom Planning Version, also right-click it from the navigation path and select "Delete." Expect a warning that all dependent objects—planning books, data views, and so on—will also be deleted. Once again, *never* delete an off-the-shelf, SAP provided Planning Area.

Finally, with Planning Areas, while the Periodicities will define the length of the time horizon and what size of time buckets (day, week, etc.) are *logically* available to a book, the simple definition of Periodicities does not actually create physical memory for the time buckets in the APO database. Recall that data may be order-based or time-series based and that this characteristic of data may refer separately to *both* its physical storage and display, depending on context. The Planning Book defaults to display all data, regardless of its physical origin in an order or any other data element, as a time series. Therefore, cells or buckets must be created in memory to store and retrieve the time-series basis of the data when it is not otherwise stored that way. For example, a product may have build quantities stored in an order and there may be five orders for that product assigned to a given week. If the Planning Book's Periodicities are set at weekly time buckets, those five order-based quantities must be aggregated into one single time-series time bucket: a week. The last step to enabling a Planning Area, therefore, is to initialize the time-series objects, an action that creates time buckets for all of the key figures based on the assigned horizon and bucket definitions in Periodicities. This is done by right-clicking the Planning Area on the navigation path and selecting "Create Time Series Objects."

With a Planning Object Structure chosen as the characteristic foundation and assigned to a Planning Area that has been edited to include all necessary key figures, a planning book with corresponding Data Views may now be built. Planning books may be created or maintained on path *Supply Network Planning → Environment → Current Settings → Define Planning Book*, transaction code /SAPAPO/SDP8B. The resulting transaction is a planning book "wizard" that assists users and developers in the process of creating or maintaining both planning books and Data Views. It is not readily apparent from the initial view of the screen, but planning books and Data Views are created simultaneously and both are done from the Planning Book radio button option. The Data View radio button option is for viewing the results of configuration conducted in the former. Very little actual configuration can be done in the latter, though it is highly useful as a physical view to construction activities that may otherwise seem quite abstract.

The SCM design for copying planning books and their Data Views is not entirely intuitive and requires some careful elucidation. To copy an off-the-shelf, SAP-provided planning book, enter the planning book name that you will be assigning the new planning book (i.e., MyProject_9ASNP94, in the "Planning Book" field), but choose the Data View radio button (Exhibit 8.17). Next, enter the name you wish to assign to the Data View in the Data View field and select the "With Ref." checkbox. Notice that a new, grayed-out "Planning Book" field displays below the original one (Exhibit 8.18). Now choose from an existing Data View, probably one from an off-the-shelf, SAP-provided planning book you wish to copy, which you can enter as a filter-string from the match-code pop-up window. For example, if we are copying from 9ASNP94, we will have options to copy SNP94(1) and SNP94(2) (Exhibit 8.19). Notice that when the standard Data View has been selected, its standard planning book parent autopopulates to the grayed-out "Planning Book" field. Now, to finish the process of creation, click the Create button. Initial selection of the Create button does not cause entry into the wizard. To enter the

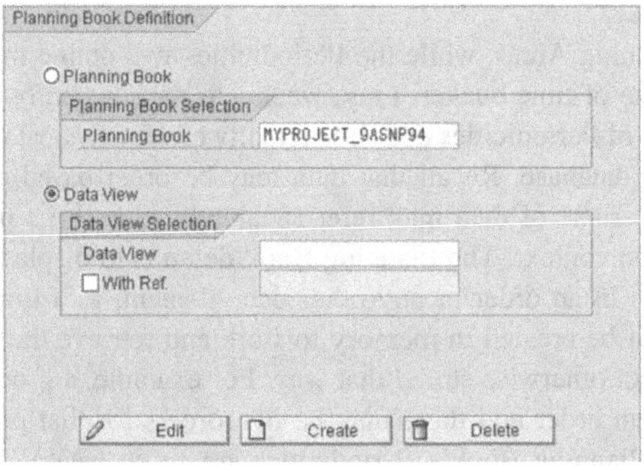

EXHIBIT 8.17   COPY A STANDARD PLANNING BOOK (I)

Enter the name of the new planning book and select the radio button for Data View. © SAP AG. Used with permission.

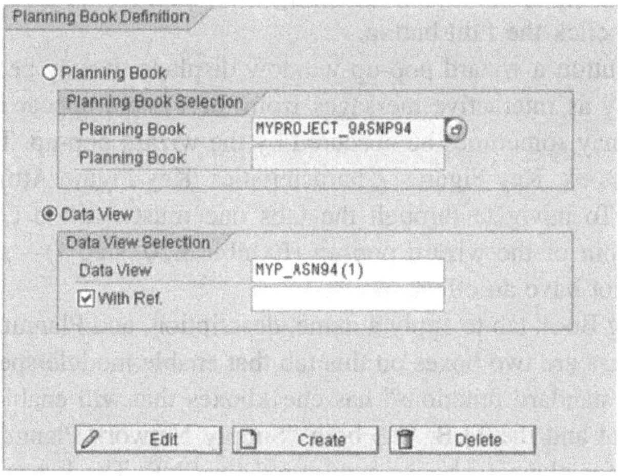

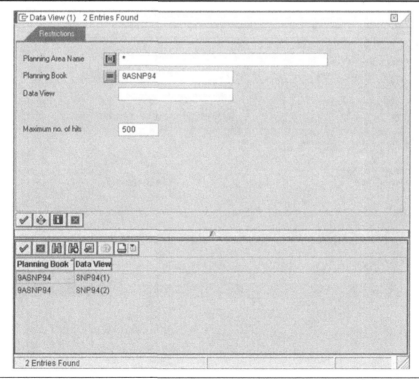

EXHIBIT 8.18 COPY A STANDARD PLANNING BOOK (II)

Enter the name of the Data View to be created, then click the "With Ref" checkbox. Notice that a new, grayed-out Planning Book field displays in the box "Planning Book Selection." © SAP AG. Used with permission.

EXHIBIT 8.19 COPY A STANDARD PLANNING BOOK (III)

Choose a Data View from among the varieties of standard views available. One may restrict options based on a standard planning book known to contain relevant data views. © SAP AG. Used with permission.

wizard and make changes, choose the Planning Book radio button on the newly created planning book and click the Edit button.

From the Edit button a wizard pop-up window displays. It may be necessary to raise the window slightly as interactive messages from the system appear in the lowest SAP panel/row, which may sometimes be obscured by the wizard pop-up. The pop-up has six screens: Planning Book, Key Figures, Characteristics, Key Figure Attributes, Data View, and Key Figures. To navigate through the tabs one must use the Continue and Back buttons at the bottom of the wizard pop-up (Exhibit 8.20, step 1)—simply clicking on the tab titles will not have an effect.

Use the Planning Book tab to apply a name, description, and Planning Area to the new planning book. There are two boxes on this tab that enable module-specific features. The first box, "Include standard functions" has checkboxes that will enable features relevant to SNP, deployment and the TLB. Use both "Supply Network Planning" and "Capacity Planning" options for planning books configured for SNP. The lower box, "Navigate to views" is strictly for enabling Demand Planning options.

The Key Figures tab allows assignment of key figures from the Planning Area onto the planning book—not all key figures in the planning area need be assigned to the book. The same is the case with the Characteristics tab. Database and display attributes of key figures may be viewed or edited in the Key Figure Attributes tab. To do so, select the

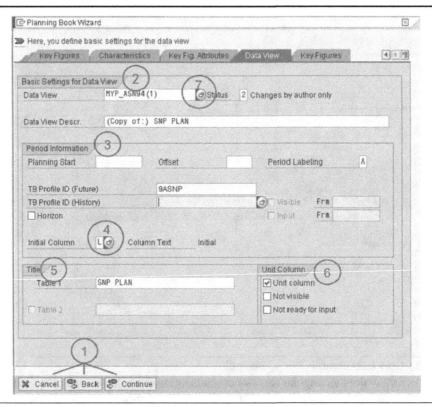

EXHIBIT 8.20 CONEXHIBIT DATA VIEWS IN THE PLANNING BOOK WIZARD
© SAP AG. Used with permission.

key figure from the "Key figure" field at the top of the tab and details will update in all lower fields. We must advise extreme caution where it comes to editing Key figures here. Generally this will be most useful for learning key figure details that may be applied in determining their inclusion on a planning book and their use within it, but making changes is not ordinarily advisable. The most important details will usually be the "Key figure accuracy," which indicates decimal precision, and the "Key fig. functn," which indicates its purpose (i.e., what kind of data element it is: an order or aggregate quantity element and a supply or demand element).

The Data Views tab allows Data Views to be both created and assigned to the planning book. Enter the name, status, description, and time-bucket profile for the Data View in the section "Basic Settings for Data View" (Exhibit 8.20, step 2). One can define a time subset time-horizon for the Data View within the parameters allowed by the time bucket profile assigned in the "Period Information" section (Exhibit 8.20, step 3). The time bucket profile here is defined in the Maintain Time Bucket Profile transaction (/SAPAPO/TR30) and operates as a display conditional on the Periodicities inherited by the Planning Area assigned in the Planning Book Tab. There are three critical structural choices about a Data View that must be made on the Data View tab:

1. *Whether to apply an initial column.* This may be useful if there is applicable "initial" data such as stock balance on hand (Exhibit 8.20, step 4).
2. *Whether to use one or two tables in the data view.* This is set under the "Title" section. Broadly speaking, it is common for simple production and purchase planning views to have one table, and while two are usually required for capacity planning, for example, one table will simply show production values while another will show production versus resource constraints (Exhibit 8.20, step 5).
3. *Use of a "Unit Column."* Set this for inclusion of an aggregate, quantitative summary column if one is required (Exhibit 8.20, step 6).

The last Key Figures tab allows assignment of key figures from the limited list of those assigned to this planning book in the earlier Key Figures tab to a more limited list of those available to the current selected Data View in the Data View tab. Once a planning book is ready, new Data Views may be added to it following the same copy process as we started with, only now indicating the new Planning Book when entering a Planning Book from an initial screen. Old Data Views already assigned may be accessed without reference on the initial screen by selecting them from the pull-down menu on the Data View tab (Exhibit 8.20, step 7).

The process of configuring a planning book will often be iterative with many stops at the Planning Area, adding or removing key Exhibits, and with many fits and starts within the Planning Book wizard getting all the definitions straight. During this process it will be helpful to go to the Data View from the Define Planning Book transaction on a regular basis to view a planning book in construction. This physical process, going back and forth between planning book definition and Data View, will ultimately be the most instructive toward building books effectively and efficiently as it will concretely illustrate for users and developers the relationship between wizard settings and the actual physical layout of the book. It is easy to work between the wizard and the Data View by clicking the Planning Book button within a Data View to go back to configuration (Exhibit 8.21,

Physical Data View for SAP Standard Planning Book Data View SNP94(1)
Specialized configuration for Master Production Scheduling of the Supply Network

Planning Book: [Design] SNP INTERACTIVE PLANNING / SNP PLAN

Planning Book | Icons | Transport Request

SNP PLAN	Unit	INITIAL	03/22/2006	03/23/2006	03/24/2006	03/25/2006	03/26/2006	03/27/2006	03/28/2006	03/29/2006
Total Demand	ST									
Total Receipts	ST									
Stock On Hand	ST									
Supply Shortage	ST									
Safety Stock	ST									
Reorder Point	ST									
Target Days' Supply	D									
Target Stock Level	ST									
Days' Supply	D									
ATD Receipts	ST									
ATD Issues	ST									

Physical Data View for SAP Standard Planning Book Data View SNP94(2)
Specialized configuraiton for Capacity Planning

Planning Book: [Design] SNP INTERACTIVE PLANNING / CAPACITY CHECK

Planning Book | Icons | Transport Request

CAPACITY PLAN	Unit	03/22/2006	03/23/2006	03/24/2006	03/25/2006	03/26/2006	03/27/2006	03/28/2006	03/29/2006
Capacity	ST								
Capacity Consumption	ST								
Resource Capacity Level in %	%								

QUANTITY VIEW	Unit	03/22/2006	03/23/2006	03/24/2006	03/25/2006	03/26/2006	03/27/2006	03/28/2006	03/29/2006
Production (Total)	ST								
Production (Planned)	ST								
Manufacture of Co-Products	ST								
DistrReceipt (Total)	ST								
Distribution Receipt (Planned)	ST								
Handling Quantity	ST								
Storage Quantity	ST								

EXHIBIT 8.21 PHYSICAL DATA VIEWS
Toggle back to the Planning Book wizard for the Data View by clicking the Planning Book button. From there, return by clicking Cancel. Notice that in these two standard planning books their table settings from the planning book wizard Data View tab have resulted in two entirely different kinds of layouts: one with one panel and the other with two. © SAP AG. Used with permission.

step 1) and once there clicking the Cancel button to close and return to the Data View. For self-instruction purposes, we recommend that learners spend time contrasting the settings and resultant physical Data View display for two views of 9ASNP94: SNP94(1) and SNP94(2), the first of which is specialized for master production scheduling and the second of which is specialized for capacity planning. In Exhibit 8.21 we have a contrast of the two Data Views where we see the first has one panel and a number of key figure fields specialized for master production scheduling of the supply network and the second has two panels with different fields specialized for analyzing and planning capacity constraints.

Working in the Planning Book I: Navigation Panel

We've addressed that APO provides two versions of the Planning Book transaction: single-book view and all-books view. Beyond that, there are two identical all-books Planning Book transaction nodes: one found under DP and the other found under SNP. In either case their duplication is strictly for the convenience of the user as there is no difference between the two instances. Do not be misled by the fact that under DP it is called "Interactive Demand Planning," and under SNP, "Interactive Supply Network Planning." Again, it is the same transaction.

When using the Planning Book itself and not the Data View displayed on the planning book wizard, up to four additional boxes display on a left-hand panel next to the larger, right-side Data View panel(s), from top to bottom: the shuffler, the Selection Profile, the Planning Book/Data View, and Macros. Their order of presentation on the screen follows their likely order of common employment by a user, where the top three boxes are related to each other and present in order of descending use, and the very bottom, Macros, is unrelated to the other three and its frequency of use will vary widely by user and user role. Thus, most users will use the shuffler to navigate most often, apply the selection profile to filter objects available in the shuffler less often, and switch between planning books and data views least of all. How often one uses macros or not relative to these other three tasks will scope all over the map. We note this about order of presentation because for purposes of instruction it is necessary to start toward the end, with the Planning Book/Data View, and work upward.

The Planning Book/Data View box is obviously used to move between the planning books and Data Views that we have so far configured. These will update which planning book and which of its Data Views to display on the Data View display panel on the right (Exhibit 8.22, step 1 for the box and step 2 for the display panel). The Selection Profile (Exhibit 8.22, step 3) provides a means to apply user-defined filters on objects available to the shuffler to populate the display panel with. These filters are actually created within the shuffler itself, and we will address that shortly, but to add a filter to the Selection Profile double-click in the title bar with the pencil icon. A pop-up window will display with two panels: Maintain Profiles and Reference. Maintain Profiles has the user-id of the current user and a folder for that user (and any additional folders that may be manually created here), and the Reference panel has a list of all saved filters, which are called "Selection IDs." To add a Selection ID to the user-id or any user-defined folders, single-click it on the right and hold down the mouse-button, then carry it over to the folder under Maintain Profiles on the left and drop it directly on top of the folder by letting go of the mouse button. Save the settings with the disk button and exit with the check button. Added Selection IDs will then display in the Selection Profile box.

The top box, the shuffler, will be the most commonly used of the three addressed so far as this box is actually used to carry out filter-queries and populate data onto the display panel (Exhibit 8.22, step 4). Saved filters as selection IDs, when double-clicked in the Selection Profile, will immediately update themselves onto the shuffler as a list of selected items from the filter. Any individually displayed item may be double-clicked on the shuffler to display its details in the display panel.

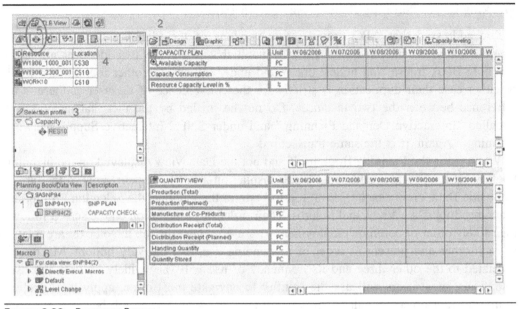

EXHIBIT 8.22   PLANNING BOOK

There are two main panels with five boxes between them. On the left from top-to-bottom are the shuffler, the Selection Profile, the Planning Book/Data View, and Macros—all of which control applications of data or processing to the right-hand data display panel. © SAP AG. Used with permission.

To create new filters, click the Selection Window button on the shuffler (Exhibit 8.22, step 5). An Object Selection pop-up window will display (Exhibit 8.23). Achieve the fastest understanding of the organization of this window by reading it left-to-right, top-to-bottom. A label indicates "Show," and then a field allows the user to choose what kind of object to show, while the following line reads, "that meet the following conditions" (Exhibit 8.23, step 1). Fields thereafter follow on which filters can be defined (Exhibit 8.23, step 2). Typically for planning, for example, we will need to filter by planning version, location, and product. A common filter may read:

Show	[APO Location Product] that meet the following conditions
APO Planning Version	000
APO Product	FG89089
APO Location	CS10

When filtering for product groups, simply click the right-facing arrow to the right of the filter fields and list out the filter parameters in the resulting window (Exhibit 8.23, step 3). If you wish to save the filter as a Selection ID for future use in the Selection Profile box, click the save icon (a disk image) and give the filter a name, then save it (Exhibit 8.24). When a filter has been applied, either ad hoc using the Object Selection dialog or else by way of a Selection ID double-clicked on the Selection Profile, the filter's resulting item list displays in the shuffler box window.

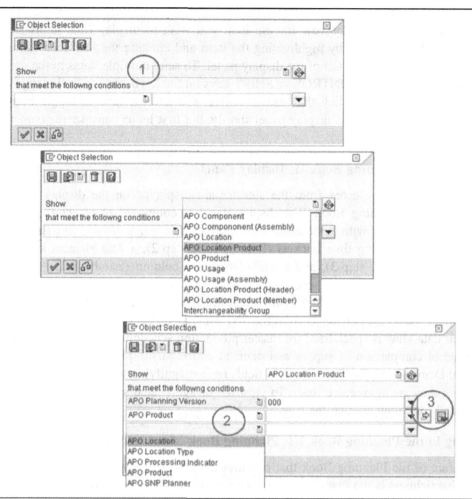

EXHIBIT 8.23 APO SHUFFLER: BUILDING AN AD-HOC FILTER OR "SELECTION"
© SAP AG. Used with permission.

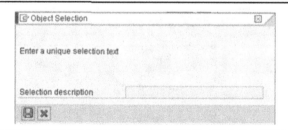

EXHIBIT 8.24 SAVE A FILTER AS A SELECTION ID

When saved, the filter becomes retrievable through the Selection Profile box, but only after it has been assigned by double-clicking the title bar on the Selection Profile box. © SAP AG. Used with permission.

Populate data for a single selected item in the shuffler box window to the display panel by double-clicking the row for the item you wish to display (line items shown in Exhibit 8.22, step 4) or by highlighting the item and clicking the load icon (an open folder image) on the upper left of the display panel. To send multiple items to the display window, hold down the CONTROL or SHIFT keys on the keyboard while clicking items in the shuffler, and then click the load icon. We will address how to toggle between multiple items loaded on the display panel shortly, but first let us consider the content of the display panel itself.

Working in the Planning Book II: Display Panel

Quantities for items selected from the shuffler are displayed on the display panel on the right of the Planning Book. The display panel is composed of an icon menu line (Exhibit 8.25, step 1) with various options for data mining, analysis, and processing, a time-series line listing time buckets (Exhibit 8.25, step 2), a data element key figure column (Exhibit 8.25, step 3), and a unit-of-measure column (Exhibit 8.25, step 4); it may have an initial column if one is configured on the Data View, and lastly a data-display grid that shows actual key figure quantities (Exhibit 8.25, step 5). The sample in Exhibit 8.25 shows data elements from the SNP94(1) Data View of 9ASNP94 where that particular data view is specialized for master production scheduling, which is particularly interested in comparison of supply and demand and requisite planning of supply. Both the Total Demand and the Total Receipts fields have magnifying glass icons next to them, indicating they are aggregated rows. To view the disaggregated source key figures for an aggregated row, double-click the row.

Working in the Planning Book III: Planning Book Menu and the Display Header

One feature of the Planning Book that overlays the rest with a whole new dimension of interactive richness is the Planning Book menu, which is an icon-based menu on the pane that sits atop both the navigation and display panels (Exhibit 8.26). There are six options on this menu, three of which we will address (the other three's use is either obvious or the subject of functionality we are not addressing in this text). The first icon is the Switch

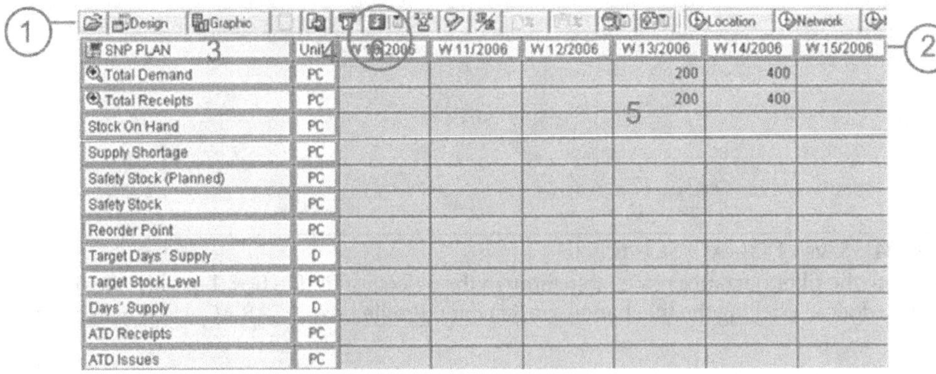

EXHIBIT 8.25 PLANNING BOOK DISPLAY PANEL
© SAP AG. Used with permission.

EXHIBIT 8.26 PLANNING BOOK MENU
© SAP AG. Used with permission.

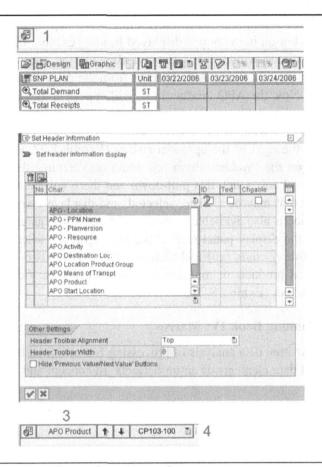

EXHIBIT 8.27 PLANNING BOOK DISPLAY PANEL HEADER SETTINGS
© SAP AG. Used with permission.

Selection On/Off button, which allows users to remove the entire left-hand navigation panel from view if they have made their filter selections, applied their macros, and now need to work exclusively in the display panel (Exhibit 8.26, step 1). Applying this has the advantage of displaying more time buckets on a single screen without scrolling. The second button, identified with a pencil, is the Change Mode button (Exhibit 8.26, step 2). Clicking this button both un-grays protected fields that are available for direct data update and enables data processing buttons from SNP or DP menus. The fifth button on the menu, with a hat image, is the Header On/Off button (Exhibit 8.26, step 3). Clicking this button will create a header over the display panel which itself has a number of features and details (Exhibit 8.27).

Use the header button for the display panel whenever using multiple products. The first time the header button is clicked, a header box will be added above the display panel with just one button in it: Header Information Settings (Exhibit 8.27, step 1). Click this button to list and add custom header items. For example, let us say we have saved a Selection ID that finds all products from location CS10 in version 000 and let's further say that we have highlighted more than one of these products from the shuffler and clicked the "load" icon above the display panel. All items are in fact now in the display panel, but can be viewed only one at a time. To enable toggling between items, click the Header On/Off button from the Planning Book menu (Exhibit 8.26, step 3), then click the Header Information Settings button in the newly displayed header (Exhibit 8.27, step 1). The Set Header Information dialog window will display, allowing the entry of products on the header (Exhibit 8.27, step 2). Select APO Product from the drop-down list; then click the green Adopt button. Now the APO Product label will appear in the header along with up and down arrows (Exhibit 8.27, step 3). Click the up and down arrows to toggle between products that have been loaded to the display panel. The displayed product will be listed in its own button to the right of the up/down arrows (Exhibit 8.27, step 4).

A pull-down list on the Product button has additional features that contribute to the power of the planning book. Click this pull-down and there will be a list of all products available for display that may be clicked, selected, and displayed without going through the arrows. A total line is also available to display the sum total quantities of all products in the selections on the display panel grid. If the total option is selected, two additional options come available: Details (all) and Details (filter). These two options provide for displaying all selected products or multiple-selected in the Data View at one time as a wide-ranging spreadsheet (Exhibit 8.28).

Working in the Planning Book IV: Macros

Macros are custom-written data analysis or processing formulas and functions that can be applied to individual data elements or entire datasets. In concept and application, macros

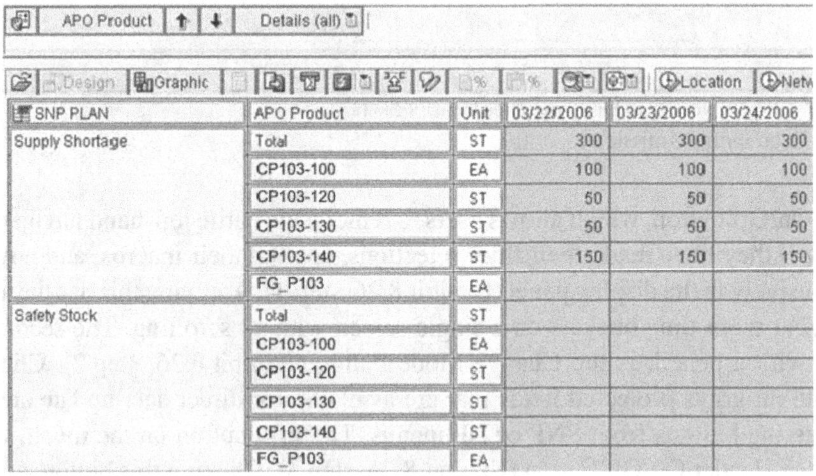

SNP PLAN	APO Product	Unit	03/22/2006	03/23/2006	03/24/2006
Supply Shortage	Total	ST	300	300	300
	CP103-100	EA	100	100	100
	CP103-120	ST	50	50	50
	CP103-130	ST	50	50	50
	CP103-140	ST	150	150	150
	FG_P103	EA			
Safety Stock	Total	ST			
	CP103-100	EA			
	CP103-120	ST			
	CP103-130	ST			
	CP103-140	ST			
	FG_P103	EA			

EXHIBIT 8.28 PLANNING BOOK DISPLAY PANEL WITH DETAILS (ALL) OPTION FROM THE HEADER

Each key figure is displayed with a sublist of all loaded data items and their quantities on that key figure.
© SAP AG. Used with permission.

in APO are identical to those used in Microsoft Excel and other popular spreadsheet or desktop database programs like Access or Paradox. Macros written for application in APO can be applied for DP or SNP either in the Planning Book to analyze or process data or via an Alert Monitor (such as may be the case where a custom formula is written to test data elements for a threshold of some kind and whenever that threshold is reached, an alert is generated).

Since macros are primarily applied as tools in the conduct of demand or supply planning, the macro design transaction, called the Macro Workbench, like the Planning Book, is found as a separate though identical node along the navigation path of both modules in the APO navigation tree. In DP the macro transaction is found along path *Demand Planning → Environment → Current Settings*, as transaction Macro Workbench with transaction code /SAPAPO/ADVM. In SNP it is found along path *Supply Network Planning → Environment → Current Settings*, with the same name and code.

Our treatment of macros in this text will focus on interacting with macros and applying them as a feature. We will not go into detail on the mechanics of writing macros. Simple macros, like simple mathematical functions, are accessible to anyone. But also like math or computer programming, an entire text could be written on macro design. While we will not go into such detail, we hope the reader will note this: *Macros add enormous customizing power to APO*—as much power as is possessed in the combined creativity and expertise of the user or developer. In general, APO raises the expertise demanded of users, but macros are one area where the quality of an organization's people will really matter. Macros constitute one way sophisticated APO users can apply APO to achieve competitive advantage over other companies that may use the same tool; the same way sophisticated users of Microsoft Excel or Access may apply their expertise in those office software packages to give their employers a competitive advantage, they can similarly apply personal expertise with APO macros to gain a leg up.

LEARNING MACROS

The best way to raise oneself to an intermediate or advanced level of macro expertise is at the fingertips of any APO user: Simply spend time in APO going through the examples in the SAP-provided, off-the-shelf macros. Apply those macros to sample datasets in a planning book in a safe test or sandbox environment. Copy the macros, modify them, and play around with them. Give yourself 20 hours to do this for a week, do it again for 20 hours after two or three weeks to let learnings sink in, and if possible do it once more in another two or three weeks. If 20 hours per week is too much, try 15 or 12. Macros, like math and computer programming, are learned better through practice than through reading or even class lecture; but give yourself the time and luxury of practice and reflection and in a very short time you (or the employees you assign the learning task) will be a macro expert capable of multiplying the power of the tool. *That's a lot of power.* APO is not cheap; it is worth giving employees the time to make themselves competitive APO experts. The return they give in providing advanced, customized APO functionality will be easily worth the investment of their time in learning.

On opening the Macro Workbench the user is presented with a list of "macro books." Macro books are simply groupings of like macros, typically by purpose. Each macro book may contain any number of individual macros. In Exhibit 8.29, we see examples of some

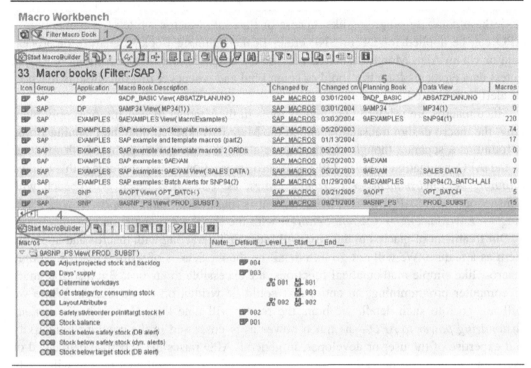

EXHIBIT 8.29   MACRO WORKBENCH

Macro "books" contain lists of macros typically grouped by application and general purpose, but assigned to specific planning books. Notice that macro books are assigned to planning books at the Data View level of detail (step 5). Macro books are created for planning books and their Data Views at the time of Data View creation. To find macro books for custom planning books, simply sort the macro book list on the Workbench by clicking the Planning Book column and pressing the "Sort in ascend. order" icon (step 6); then search by Planning Book name. Be sure that you haven't set a filter that will exclude your Planning Book! © SAP AG. Used with permission.

books that have 0, several with 5 to 17, and one with 220. Which macro books present themselves on the Workbench can be filtered though the dialog window that is instantiated when clicking the button Filter Macro Book (Exhibit 8.29, step 1). The Workbench has a fairly standard icon menu that among other things permits opening of a lower panel with a list of macros stored in a book by highlighting the book of interest and clicking the Display Macros button (Exhibit 8.29, step 2). The macro list on any book may also be acquired by right-clicking the book and selecting the option to "Display macros."

Macros are actually designed, built, and modified in the MacroBuilder. The MacroBuilder can be accessed by selecting a macro book from the book list and clicking "Start MacroBuilder" in the menu of the upper panel (Exhibit 8.29, step 3), double-clicking the macro book name or else clicking anywhere in the lower panel listing individual macros, and clicking "Start MacroBuilder" off that panel's menu (Exhibit 8.29, step 4). When opened, the MacroBuilder will display a working screen with a panel in the lower left-hand corner called the "Depot" that lists all the individual macros in the opened book.

The MacroBuilder consists of a menu and six panels: Elements, Depot, Planning table, Macro workspace, Events, and Clipboard. The Elements panel contains macro commands

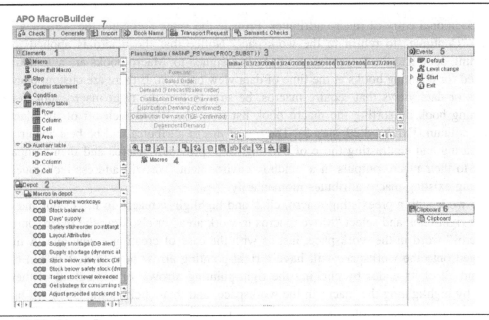

EXHIBIT 8.30   MACROBUILDER
© SAP AG. Used with permission.

and instructions and is used to actually create, write, and edit macros (Exhibit 8.30, step 1). The Depot, as we have seen, contains all the macros that have been stored in the currently open macro book (Exhibit 8.30, step 2). The Planning Table is primarily a visual aide so that the macro writer can have in mind the spreadsheet layout of the macro book he's writing macros for (Exhibit 8.30, step 3). The workspace is where macros are actually interacted with and edited (Exhibit 8.30, step 4). Events allows assignment of a macro to automatic execution on the occurrence of predefined events (Exhibit 8.30, step 5). The clipboard contains copied macros or macro commands that may be used to move working commands from one macro to another without complete rewrites (Exhibit 8.30, step 6).

With macros, one will start either with the writing of a new macro or with the editing of an old one. Very often the best way to write a new macro will be to start by copying an SAP-provided macro and making changes. Since we are primarily interested in teaching interaction with the Workbench and enabling the user's learning process with macros, we will address these four things in our treatment of the subject: (1) use of Elements and the workspace to create and add commands to a macro, (2) use of the Depot to access and edit macros, (3) creation of a new macro by copying an old, and (4) assignment of macros to events. Note that since the various panels on the MacroBuilder that are used for these four techniques are closely interrelated and interdependent, it will be impossible to present the four areas in exactly that order, so instead we will address all four objectives in a composite treatment.

Entirely new macros may be generated in either of these two ways: (1) Click on the node "Macro" in Elements, hold down the right mouse button and drag the element over to the word "Macros" in the workspace, then release the mouse button, or (2) right-click on the word "Macros" in the workspace, then select options *Create New Macro → Add macro*. Either way a dialog window will appear requesting a name for the new macro and additional entry of macro attributes. Provide the name and enter the attributes, then click "Continue" to return to the workspace. Notice that the macro is applied to the planning book that the current macro book is assigned to. Macro books are automatically created for planning books at the time of data view creation. If there are custom planning books or data views that require macros, be sure to find the right macro book for the planning book by sorting the macro book list from the Workbench off of the planning book column (Exhibit 8.29, step 5). The use of macro attributes will be best acquired by comparing and contrasting those of existing, SAP-provided macros and then comparing them to their macro outputs in a sandbox environment. We will address techniques for viewing existing macro attributes momentarily.

To work with a preexisting macro, click and highlight a macro in the Depot and then either right-click and select "Move macros to work area" or else drag the macro onto the "Macros" word in the workspace, just as with the case of creating a new one. A macro dragged onto the workspace will have a right-pointing arrow next to it. You can either expand all of its nodes by clicking the right-pointing arrows, or expand all of them at once by highlighting the macro in the workspace, and then clicking the Open All button from the workspace menu (Exhibit 8.31, step 1). Assign a macro to an event by picking it up off the workspace and dragging it and dropping it on the appropriate event in the Events panel. Macros must be moved onto events from the workspace; they cannot be moved directly from the Depot.

Experiment with macros by observing their instructions in the workspace and then executing them from the Planning Book. Active macros (those with a green box next to their name) will be visible in the macros box on the Planning Book (Exhibit 8.22, step 6). If they have been assigned to an event, they will display in the Planning Book macro box under the appropriate event. If they are active but are not assigned to an event, they display under the node "Directly Execut. Macros" and are run by expanding that node and double-clicking the appropriate macro. At the time of macro creation APO prompts for macro "attributes." Examine the attributes of existing macros by putting them in the workspace and clicking the Attributes button (Exhibit 8.31, step 2).

When working with macros, either to write a new one or read or edit an existing one, move macro "elements" from the Elements panel onto the workspace using drag/drop. When dropping, note that APO will promote for "INSERT/APPEND." INSERT will

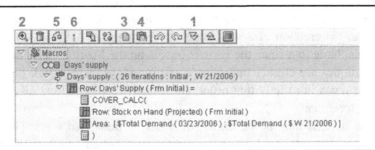

EXHIBIT 8.31 MACROBUILDER WORKSPACE PANEL
© SAP AG. Used with permission.

Element	Description and Use in Macro Building
Step	A single operation of a macro, such as computation of workdays in a time horizon, determination of values relevant to alerts, or the display of an alert on recognition of its condition—a macro may have one or more such step operations.
Control Statement	If/then statements, that is: IF/ELSE/ENDIF, CASE/WHEN/ENDCASE
Operator/Function	A mathematical operation, that is: Row [Forecast] > 0
Condition	Container to combine data elements (i.e., row/column) and formulas (operator/function) that together express a condition that may be the subject of a control statement, that is: Control Statement of "IF" **Condition** of: Operator/function for Row (Forecast) > 0
Alert/Status	Controls alerts that are used in the Alert Monitor—includes creation and deletion of alerts.
Process Message	Message sent to the APO screen—usually as the result of some conditional data processing executed by the macro.
Action Box	Container for a series of substeps that may be necessary to carry out a complex operation.
Document	Generation of a message document, that is, e-mail, to be sent to a user or user role under defined conditions.

EXHIBIT 8.32   MACRO ELEMENTS

enter the element prior to the element it is being dropped on; APPEND posts it after that element. Excluding tables, there are nine macro elements one may work with whose basic functions are described in Exhibit 8.32. There are two "tables" available for macro work on Elements: the Planning table and the Auxiliary table. The Planning table refers to the actual table in the planning book and elements of it: row, column, cell, and area; these refer to specific key Exhibits and characteristics upon which the functions of a macro may be conducted. Use this for macros that analyze and/or update data from the Planning Book table's grid. The Auxiliary table is intended for computations that require the dimensions of the table and its data elements, but which may not result in an update going back onto the cells of the table.

There are a variety of cases where macro copying becomes germane. For one, since a macro book is created at the time of Data View creation with new planning books, so long as the user follows our advice to always create new planning books by copying SAP-provided books, then the macro book for the SAP-provided planning book will also be copied, automatically bringing over a list of potentially relevant macros. Macros may also be copied from one macro book to another while inside a macro book by clicking the Import button (Exhibit 8.30, step 7).

Within a macro book, in the MacroBuilder, copy a macro for editing by moving it off of the Depot, onto the workspace, then clicking the Copy to Clipboard button (Exhibit 8.31, step 3). Remove the original macro back to the Depot (or leave it there; it does not really matter as long as they are not confused with one another), then click the Insert from Clipboard button to put the copied macro back into the workspace (Exhibit 8.31, step 4). Immediately change the name of the newly copied macro by clicking Attributes and changing its "Descriptive Text." From here, use the copied macro as a basis for a new one, adding, editing, and removing elements as necessary. Move the macro back into the Depot when done and, if necessary, assign it to an event.

Macros have three statuses: inactive, checked (or compiled), and generated. The statuses are designated by the three boxes to the right of each macro in the Depot panel, where inactive corresponds to red, checked to yellow, and generated to green. All macros will start as inactive; for example, if a series of copied macros are in the Depot due to having been copied at the time of Data View creation, they will all start off as red, or inactive. During macro setup periodically check for internal consistency and errors by clicking the Check button (Exhibit 8.31, step 5). At completion or else to test an outcome, if it compiles without errors and both it and the Planning Book are ready for combined use, activate it by clicking the Generate button (Exhibit 8.31, step 6).

Working with the Planning Book V: Alert Monitor

Alert profiles that have been set up in the Alert Monitor may be activated directly in the Planning Book. First, they may be assigned to specific planning books at the time of Alert Profile creation or any time as a matter of maintenance. They may also be written into macros that are assigned to planning books. One other way to apply alert profiles in a planning book is directly by way of the planning book itself. Within an open planning book, off the SAP APO menu at screen top, select *Settings → Alert Profile*. A dialog window will display allowing user-specific assignment of relevant alert profiles to the planning book. Once assigned, activate the alert profile by clicking the Display/Refresh Alerts button (Exhibit 8.25, step 6). Alerts will immediately be redetermined and results will display to a new panel at the bottom of the planning book screen where they may be examined, exported, or forwarded.

PP/DS CONTEXT

PP/DS manages (1) production planning during the procurement execution period in preparation for production execution as well as (2) procurement execution and (3) production execution (Exhibit 8.33).

Production Planning and Detailed Scheduling occur in close collusion at the final tips of the supply chain planning cycle wherein planning and scheduling finally gives way to detailed execution of the physical tasks of commerce and business. Production Planning is inclusive of the entire procurement tactical horizon while Detailed Scheduling affects only the production execution horizon. Prior to PP/DS an overall, cross-site, cross-geography "rough cut" schedule is generated in SNP (or otherwise by a legacy SOP or

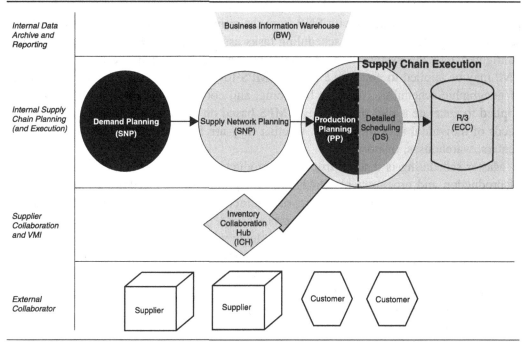

EXHIBIT 8.33 PP/DS IN THE SUPPLY CHAIN CONTEXT

master scheduling product) on the mid-range horizon, going out as far as 12 months. The characteristics that distinguish SNP from PP/DS include that (1) PP/DS begins scheduling within "lead time," which is ordinarily the time required to plan, order, and receive raw materials while SNP operates outside this zone, (2) SNP will be organizational in scope, while PP/DS generally adheres to supply lines whenever it expands into cross-plant scheduling, (3) since SNP schedules out in time and is used to coordinate physical resources to align to constantly changing demand signals, it operates with the most flexibility using planned orders and purchase requisitions to freely and frequently change schedules; but PP/DS operates within lead time and has less flexibility to alter schedules in response to sudden demand or supply changes—the closer orders get to execution the less tolerant they can be of change until when they enter the execution horizon controlled by DS and changes are all but entirely ruled out, and (4) SNP can operate on aggregate quantities spread over weeks or months in a time series; PP/DS is concerned with discrete quantities over weeks, days, or even hours and minutes and must manage them on an order basis.

The PP aspect of PP/DS is applied across the tactical horizon to yield a master production schedule, or MPS, which generally includes both a build or production schedule and a buy or procurement schedule. In this respect there is potential for some crossover of function between SNP and PP/DS where either are capable of addressing master scheduling business requirements. The exact delineation will vary somewhat from one organization to another depending on such factors as the relationships between divisions and their sites and on the complexity of the supply line routes that feed final production.

In other words, standard master scheduling tasks as defined by APICS may be assigned to processes that are conducted with SNP from the point of view of overall network master scheduling. In contrast, master scheduling tasks assigned to PP/DS will be designed and configured into the system from the *point of view* of individual site planning.[1] Thus, SNP may be applied to generate a network MPS for an entire geography, with the needs of geographic scheduling, resource balancing, and coordination in mind. PP/DS may be applied to generate a site- or route-level MPS based on fulfilling the planning/scheduling needs of individual sites themselves, whether they are for example factories, distribution centers, warehouses, or ports.

Master scheduling is distinct from strict production scheduling because it is inclusive of production and procurement scheduling. For procurement schedules PP is applied to solidify actual working purchase orders or contract schedule lines (such as with a blanket purchase order) to invoke the buying process and procure goods. In other words, in SNP, original but flexible procurement schedules will have been proposed with a mind to optimally supplying the entire production network. With PP acting on the tactical horizon in lead time, these procurement proposals must be settled, firmed, and sent to an execution system such as R/3 where they can be enacted as purchase orders or active schedule lines in the case of scheduling agreements.

For PP production build schedules the planned order proposals from SNP are firmed and/or converted to production orders and similarly sent to the transactional execution tool (i.e., R/3) as well as DS as a production schedule baseline. Since these orders are not started until the execution horizon opens, it is generally unnecessary to firm them during the master scheduling process as early as procurement orders. A "firmed" or "fixed" planned order may remain so throughout its lifecycle during the tactical horizon, prior to entry into the execution horizon, in order to strike a balance between the need to minimize supply lines changes while maintaining capacity balancing flexibility. For example, a planned order is not rigidly tied to a specific work center, so while firming will prevent changes to key characteristics such as quantities and dates, it continues to allow periodic work-center reassignment either manually or by the DS optimizer until its entry into the execution horizon, at which time it should be dispositioned. A production order in open status, not yet released, is similarly capacity-change flexible yet supply-change restrained. Either state, therefore, firmed planned order or open but unreleased production order, suits the supply-change conservative requirements of tactical planning.

As time passes out of the tactical horizon and into the execution horizon, DS kicks in to further refine the production schedule to yield a detailed execution schedule at the level of individual work centers and hourly starts/stops (even up to minutely) that is adhered to for the purpose of manufacturing production or other relevant site-level productive activities. Detailed Scheduling is applied to generate an optimized execution horizon build schedule that takes into account labor, machines and alternative work centers, setup time, material availability, and so on. Unlike the SNP optimizer, the DS optimizer does not propose new orders to fill supply gaps and as such does not seek to balance demand with supply. It strictly takes orders as received from PP, balances capacity by distributing them across available work centers, and generates the most optimal short-term work schedule for their execution.

PP/DS MASTER DATA AND CIF

Introduction: Master Data Prerequisites and CIF Requirements

Configuring PP/DS requires the following three or four object setup activities: (1) supply chain master data setup, (2) CIF setup (if R/3 is used), (3) the setup matrix, and (4) PP/DS profiles. Refer to Chapter 5 for detailed supply chain master data setup instructions and to Chapter 7 for CIF setup instructions. Minimal standard master data for PP/DS includes:

- Locations (internal and supplier in almost all cases; customers in many cases)
- Products
- Production resources
- Production process models
- Transportation lanes
- External procurement relationships (and quota arrangements)

In most cases all of these will be set up as original master data in R/3 and CIF'd over to APO. Locations in APO will correspond to R/3 plants, vendors, and customers, APO products to R/3 materials, and APO resources to R/3 work centers; APO production process models will be formed from R/3 BOMs and routes via production versions; APO transportation lanes will be deduced from company/vendor relationships in R/3, APO EPRs from R/3 contracts, info records schedule agreements, and APO quota arrangements from R/3 quota arrangements. Organizations not using R/3 will maintain all of this master data directly in APO without use of the CIF.

Specialized Master Data Requirements

PP/DS is concerned with actual production, shop floor scheduling, execution, and control. Recall, too, that the APO PPM, or production process model, is a model of the bill of materials and route of production necessary to build a good. Where SNP is interested in longer-term production and does not consider detail at a lower level than that of a day, PP/DS—which directly informs manufacturing execution—is capable of modeling production to the level of detail of the *second*. Several additional objects and configuration elements are required to manage this heightened concern with detail: (1) a handling resource, (2) the assignment of a handling resource to a location, (3) a setup matrix, and (4) the assignment of the setup matrix to the production process model.

Handling Resource

The handling resource has no analog in R/3 and must be manually set up in APO as a Single (first tab in the Resources transaction), in contrast to production resources that are CIF'd from R/3 or manually set up, which are Single-Mixed for PP/DS. It is used by PP/DS to represent the movement of material from one activity to another. Use the ordinary resource transaction and refer to general instructions in Chapter 5 for resource setup when establishing the handling resource, only follow these specifications:

- Set it up as a Single (first tab).
- Consider adding an "H" as a prefix to its name to make it clear on sight to users that this is a handling resource without productive capacity.

- Establish it with category "H."
- In its PP/DS Bucket Capacity, the handling resource will have a bucket definition of "No PP/DS Available Bucket Capacity."
- It will be unnecessary to construct any detailed capacity profile for the handling resource. Simply give it a broad start/end of 24 hours, no breaks, and 100% resource utilization on its Time Continuous Capacity definition.
- Even though a resource is assigned to a location on definition in the Resource transaction General Data tab, it must also be assigned to a Location with a specification of whether it is inbound or outbound; once the handling resource is assigned to the model and saved, in the Location transaction on the Resource tab in the Handling resources section, assign the handling resource to the "Resource inbound" field. Save this change.

Setup Matrix

Another specific requirement of PP/DS is the creation of a Setup Matrix. At the DS level of manufacturing acuity it is necessary to note time requirements for moving materials from one process to another. Such processes and their time requirements are maintained in PP/DS as Setup Matrices. Setup Matrices must both be configured and assigned to production process models. There are two Setup Matrix transactions, both of which are necessary for Setup Matrix configuration: Maintain Setup Groups (code /SAPAPO/CDPSC6), and Maintain Setup Matrix (code /SAPAPO/CDPSC7). A display-only transaction is also available by code /SAPAPO/CDPS_SETUP. The path to the Setup Matrix transaction is *Master Data → Application-Specific Master Data → Production Planning → Setup Group/Setup Matrix*.

It may be easier to think of Setup Groups as "setup items" as the fundamental point of this object is to denote a specific point of time-consuming activity. If in the process of manufacture we have any two activities where cost is experienced as elapsed time or otherwise from the transfer of one activity to another, then each activity should be defined as a Setup Group. The time cost of transfer activity between groups is maintained on the Setup Matrix.

Maintaining a Setup Group in the Maintain Setup Group transaction is simple and straightforward. Click the New Entries button and enter each activity as a single-row Setup Group in the table indicating its location, name, and description (Exhibit 8.34, step 1). Save these entries.

Once activities with time costs for transfer are maintained as Setup Groups, the actual values of transfer from one activity to another should be maintained in a Setup Matrix. More than one Setup Matrix may be defined for the same site and Setup Groups. From the initial screen of the Maintain Setup Matrix transaction, one is prompted for either a site or both a site and a specific Setup Matrix. If a Setup Matrix is already known to exist that needs maintaining, enter it with the site name and APO will go straight to the "Change Setup Transitions" screen. If one is not known or else you are creating a new one, simply enter the name of the site at which there will be a Setup Matrix. In that case, instead of going straight to the Change Setup Transitions screen, APO will display another table on a screen called "Change Setup Matrix" where a new Setup Matrix can be defined

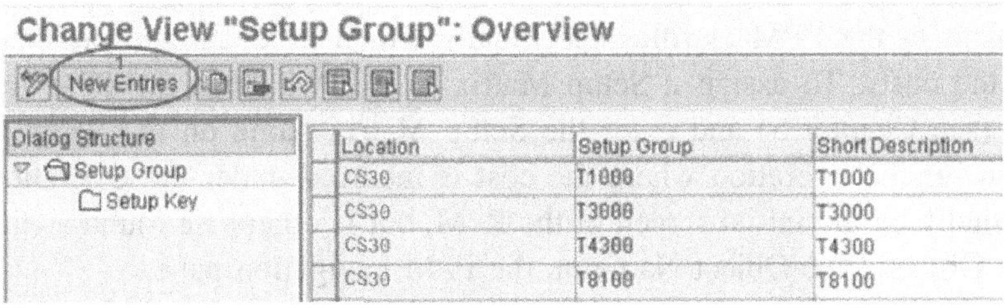

Change View "Setup Group": Overview

New Entries

Dialog Structure	Location	Setup Group	Short Description
▽ 🗀 Setup Group	CS30	T1000	T1000
🗀 Setup Key	CS30	T3000	T3000
	CS30	T4300	T4300
	CS30	T8100	T8100

EXHIBIT 8.34 SETUP GROUP
Each activity with a time cost should be maintained. © SAP AG. Used with permission.

New Setup Transitions

Position

Location   CS30
Setup Matrix   CS30_SM01

S	Predecssr	Successor	Setup Time	U
	T1000	T1000		S
	T1000	T3000	15	S
	T1000	T4300	15	S
	T1000	T8100	15	S
	T3000	T3000		S
	T3000	T1000	15	S
	T3000	T4300	15	S
	T3000	T8100	15	S
	T8100	T8100		S
	T8100	T1000	15	S
	T8100	T3000	15	S

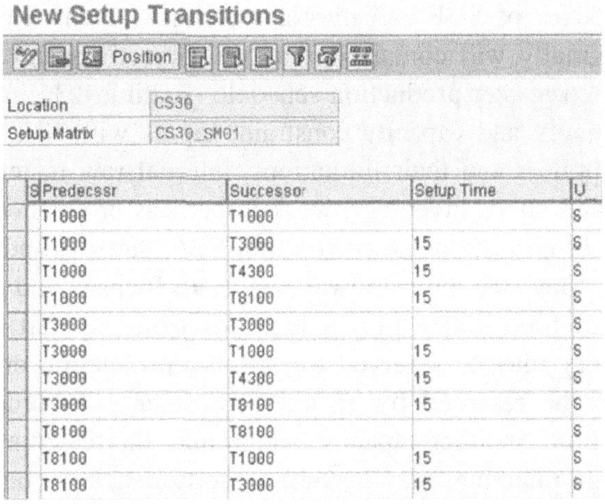

EXHIBIT 8.35 SETUP MATRIX
© SAP AG. Used with permission.

and created and where others at the site indicated on the initial screen will be displayed. To create a new one, simply click the New Entries button and enter the name of the Setup Matrix and an optional description. On save, APO will return to the Change Setup Matrix screen. From here double-click the Setup Matrix that requires further definition or maintenance; if it is an entirely new setup, the "New Setup Transitions" screen will come up and if it is maintenance the "Change Setup Transitions" screen will appear. Both screens are virtually identical in function.

On this screen each Setup Group should be established as either a predecessor or a successor in a here-to-there relationship. Setup time is defined with a quantity and unit of measure. This is a matrix, so if we have four activities 1, 2, 3, and 4, then there will probably be predecessor/successor cases maintained of 1:1, 1:2, 1:3, 1:4, as well as 2:1, 2:2, 2:3, 2:4, and so forth. Self-reflective activity transitions, that is, 1:1, will simply be maintained with zero time cost (Exhibit 8.35). Maintain each actual physical relationship, save changes, and exit.

Once Setup Matrices are maintained they must be assigned on PP/DS PPMs. The existence of a Setup Matrix alone is not sufficient to inform PP/DS of time costs as it relates to the production of any particular material during planning or optimization runs; the assignment to the PPM clarifies specifically which products and production events will entail the costs. To assign a Setup Matrix to a PPM, open the PPM maintenance transaction (see Chapter 5) and enter the Setup Matrix name on the Setup Group/Key field column for the operation where the cost is incurred under the Operations section. This will usually be the initial screen of the PPM, but is otherwise found as the top-most node of the Object Type/Object Name on the PPM navigation pane.

USING PP/DS

The PP/DS context and process mirrors that of SNP in many respects, only carrying all aspects down to a more narrow scope or lower level of detail. SNP or a legacy system serving the purposes of SOP and master scheduling feeds a mid-ranged schedule into PP/DS that minimally will contain operational objectives and may include all the detail of a sophisticated master production schedule (Exhibit 8.36, step 1). PP/DS shares many of the same supply and capacity constraint inputs with SNP at this level: external (and internal) suppliers and their limitations, internal raw materials or semifinished goods supplies, finished goods inventory, work-in-process production, factory work centers' capacities, and in-transit inventory (Exhibit 8.36, steps 2 and 3). While the data inputs are analogous, they will almost always be more focused and detailed with PP/DS due to the urgency of time. Since PP/DS horizons generally fall inside of lead time, raw materials inventory may be reserved for specific production orders while finished-goods inventory may be reserved for specific customer sales orders, restricting their wider supply application. Supplier capacity, which may be treated as theoretically wide-open during mid-range planning, may become opportunistically constrained during lead time, with one's own outstanding purchase orders against a given supplier constraining the supplier's ability to make additional capacity or supply available. However, work-in-process and in-transit inventories are each on the brink of becoming applicable supply.

Supply Network Planning and its disciplines of SOP and network master scheduling must be concerned with finding the best schedule to meet demand expectations. PP/DS has less liberty to be so focused on achieving the best possible world; it must assume that SNP has already done much of the work of supply/demand optimization at the supply network level. Once demand is fed to PP/DS as an SOP or MPS from SNP, the needs of cross-geography, cross-site coordination have already been built into the schedule proposals through higher-level decision models. This includes having taken into account the maximum aggregate capacities of factories, transportation lanes, and distribution sites as well as the maximum reliable supply available from vendors or subcontractors.

Besides operating on the assumption that much factory or network level optimization and capacity leveling has already been yielded through SNP, PP/DS is further limited in making responsive changes due to the rising cost of change as planning yields to execution during its tactical time horizon. In other words, when used for master scheduling and supply/demand fulfillment, PP/DS not only must take into account demand changes when rescheduling, but must carefully consider the disruption any changes may wreak on a supply chain that is not just being modeled and simulated, but is actually dynamically

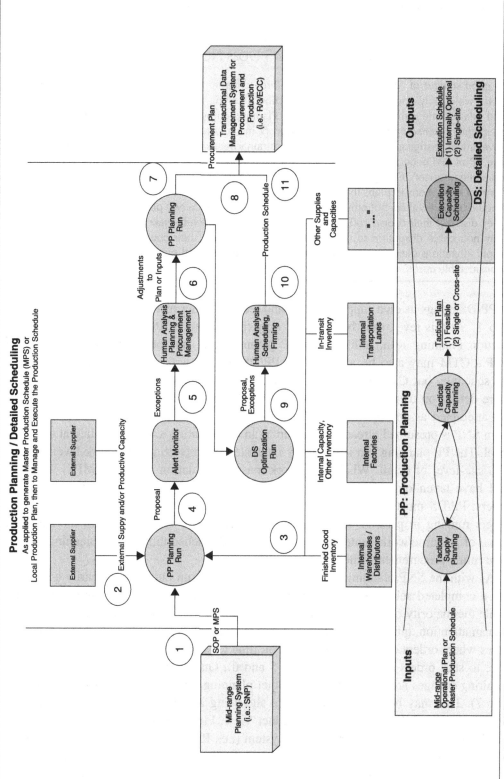

EXHIBIT 8.36 PP/DS PROCESS IN CONTEXT

manifesting itself through purchase settlements, shipments, deliveries, issues, productions, and distributions.

TIME IS MONEY AND PP/DS DOES NOT HAVE MUCH TIME

A good student of APO may wonder why three different planning run engines are available in SNP, while only one is available to production planning in PP/DS. The answer is found in the old adage, time = money. Supply Network Planning enjoys the benefit of time: *It can afford* to frequently reschedule the entire supply network in order to achieve optimal results at a network level under changing supply and capacity constraints because time for SNP is plentiful. Conversely, the PP of PP/DS occurs in the procurement execution horizon and DS occurs in the production execution horizon. Changes cannot be made during these horizons without creating a cost in the form of disruptions to plans that are in actual execution; if absolutely necessary, changes can and should be undertaken, but only with great care. It is not unlike two planes on a collision course. If they discover their course 100 miles apart, each pilot can gently make course corrections without any noticeable disruption to the travelers. If they discover their course just one mile apart, the rapid alterations necessary on either side, while necessary, will nonetheless cause the passengers considerable upset.

PP/DS brings its own supply and demand feeds together in a planning run (Exhibit 8.36, step 4). At this level, strictly speaking, only the PP part of PP/DS is in effect. The Production Planning Run, unlike the SNP planning run, has only one engine: heuristics. SNP's CTM may also be applied to a PP/DS plan providing additional intelligence to the schedule, but CTM is nonetheless carried out outside the PP/DS Planning Run. For more details on using CTM, see Chapter 10. At the PP level additional optimization is not attempted as any operational plan or network Master Production Schedule (nMPS) from SNP is presumed already optimized to an organization's level of policy at a network level. The PP planning run is primarily interested in converting a network-level schedule to a site-level of detail. Where a network master production schedule (MPS) from SNP will have taken only the aggregate capacities of a site into account when generating orders, PP/DS must assign orders to specific resources at specific times—often having orders running in parallel, simultaneously on alternative resources. With the additional detail of resource/work-center level production order-scheduling the PP planning run will then refine procurement schedules.

As with the SNP planning run, the PP/DS planning run output is primarily a proposal, not a completed schedule. Alert conditions may be defined with the Alert Monitor and while the majority of planning will result from application of the planning run schedules, human attention, qualitative analytics, judgment, and personal skills will be required as in cases where orders cannot be completed on time to ship or supply cannot be procured on time to start orders (Exhibit 8.36, steps 5 and 6). Once human analytics, judgment, and resulting changes are applied to plan another planning run may be executed (Exhibit 8.36, step 7). This may be either on the entire site using a full-blown run or individually by product using a heuristic run in the Product View. Firmed build and buy schedules from PP/DS are returned to the transactional system (i.e., R/3) where they are actively worked. Procurement orders (purchase orders or schedule lines) will normally begin execution in R/3 immediately or in the very short term (Exhibit 8.36, step 8). Production work may wait in queue for several weeks until the execution horizon is reached.

On reaching the execution horizon, the DS aspect of PP/DS kicks in. There are two primary objectives to DS: (1) optimization of the execution-horizon build schedule across alternative resources and (2) final assignment of production orders for production. The first goal is achieved through application of a highly focused optimizer (Exhibit 8.36, step 9). The DS optimizer differs from the SNP optimizer in that it does not take demand into account and it cannot propose or create new supplies (i.e. new planned orders). The DS optimizer is strictly limited to working with production orders that are already in existence and to those within its short defined horizon, which will normally be five days or less. This optimizer considers orders that come up for start during its horizon, compares them against work center resources available during that period, and runs a configurable algorithm to assign orders optimally to resources. The optimizer displays its proposals on a graphical Detailed Scheduling Planning Board. Orders may be moved around manually on the board by planners and ground controllers using simple point-drag-click motions and planners may choose to do so with orders that are not yet fixed (Exhibit 8.36, step 10). Order movement on the DS Planning Board is disallowed once production orders are released and production has started.

The finalized schedule arrived upon between the output of the DS optimizer and ground controller's detailed refinements to that output using the Planning Board will return to the transactional system for execution (Exhibit 8.36, step 11). Detailed scheduling of orders on the Planning Board is the closest that APO gets to execution and control, and since changes other than confirmations, deliveries, and scrap are not allowed, DS becomes the *de facto* shop-floor control center. The client transactional control systems such as R/3 are in fact entirely constrained by detailed scheduling commitments made in PP/DS at this level. Transactional control effectively returns to the transactional system only when goods from orders are completed and arrive into inventory, at which point inventory management and distribution systems take over outside of APO.

Heuristics

PP/DS Planning Run

Utterly nonintuitive and reminiscent of something out of higher-order math and physics, the word *heuristic* must seem terribly intimidating to those not familiar with it. This is unfortunate, because very little more is required in defining a heuristic other than to call it a rule. What little more can be said is that it is not just any rule like a law or guideline, but a structured rule or set of related rules that when conducted together carry out a process. Usually, we might add, heuristic processes have a point. Moreover, slightly beyond a rule one might also think of a heuristic as a command to the system, declaring how one wishes the system to carry out scheduling activities.

Scheduling activities for the most part are carried out through "planning runs." APO applies planning runs in a variety of places to generate mass schedule proposals. Here we are interested in planning runs of the SNP and PP/DS modules, though similar processes are available in TP/VS. Planning runs generate schedule proposals that organize known sources of supply such as on-hand inventories, in-transit inventories, and work-in-process against known demand, all within capacity constraints such as bottlenecks created by a limited number of work centers or supply channels.

A simple and probably common heuristic example in planning might play out as follows, wherein three heuristics are applied in sequence to incrementally build a complete plan:

Heuristic 1	SAP MRP	Commands system to open up new planned orders and purchase requisitions to fulfill unmet demand. Orders are backward scheduled: The start date is computed by subtracting lead times from the due date. All orders are assigned to a default work center without respect to the work center's capacity limitations.
Heuristic 2	Find Capacity Shortages	Commands the system to detect where demands have exceeded capacities on the default work center.
Heuristic 3	Reschedule	Excess demands are rescheduled to specified alternative work centers, reducing or eliminating work center capacity overloads. Where sufficient capacity cannot be found, demand is either left unmet or else work centers are overloaded but alerts are generated to spur human intervention.

Product View

PP/DS employs a heuristic planning *run*, or rule-based planning run, which like all such planning runs in APO is for mass scheduling. While the heuristic planning run is a native capability of the PP/DS module, a single-product heuristic can be executed in the Product View and technically this product heuristic may be applied regardless of the APO module in deployment. As it is a simple heuristic applied to a single product, the Product View product heuristic makes for a useful tool to introduce the concept of heuristic planning and scheduling.

There are two product heuristics available in the Product View: (1) the aptly named product heuristic and (2) the variable heuristic. The first is intended as a quick-and-ready heuristic to be run on-the-spot whenever a changed situation requires replanning, such as when new demand has been manually keyed in or old demand has been manually deleted. The variable heuristic is intended to provide a wider degree of latitude where both (1) a variety and (2) a multitude of heuristics may be applied all to one product within the Product View. This may be the case for when a product requires special attention, or it can prove useful for development or debugging. In this respect the variable heuristic in the Product View can be applied as a sort of heuristic trial zone where single-product heuristics similar to their multiple-product counterparts that are used for the planning run can be applied to a specific product's plan and their results immediately studied.

Configuration and use of the product heuristic is relatively straightforward. In the Product Master on the PP/DS tab there is a field called Product Heuristic. Apply a product's standard, "quick" product heuristic here. To execute the heuristic, open the Product View. The view must be set to change mode by clicking the Pencil button from the button menu, otherwise the Product Heuristic button will not display and the option will be grayed out in the SAP menu. Once released for change mode, the Product Heuristic button displays on the button menu and is straightforwardly labeled "Product Heuristic." On clicking the button APO will prompt for a propagation range, which will normally be SAP_ALL unless a different, custom range has been defined (see PP/DS Profiles section in this chapter for configuring the PP/DS propagation range profile). Be sure when executing the heuristic that changes have been made to the product's situation in display on the Product View or there will be no changes to view. The point of applying a heuristic is to apply a rule for fulfilling open demand with new supplies, dropping planned supplies when demand disappears, or both. To view a heuristic in action, simply add some demand or delete a supply element, then click the button to run the heuristic.

For mass planning purposes and some individual planning purposes single-heuristic applications such as the product heuristic will not suffice. Alternatively, in the process of learning the applications of the multiplicities of heuristics that come off the shelf from SAP with APO, one may wish to have a "variable" heuristic that allows easy toggling between alternative heuristics without going back and forth between the Product View and the Product Master. Either goal can be achieved with the variable heuristic, whose button lies just to the right of the Product Heuristic button. When applying the variable heuristic, PP/DS will prompt for a selection from among all available single-product heuristics. Once applied, one can select another heuristic and apply it as well, allowing for planning with a combination of heuristics.

PP/DS Planning Run

Individual product heuristics in the Product View are available regardless of the APO module(s) in deployment, but the PP/DS planning run is the hallmark capability of the PP/DS module. This planning run will generate schedule proposals for an entire site, a proposed MPS. It can even make proposals for complete supply lines including suppliers and subcontractors supporting a site (i.e., going beyond the generation of purchase orders to suppliers). The PP/DS planning run can generate subcontractor orders at the subcontractor sites as well as *purchase requisitions at the subcontractor* that will provide raw materials supply to support the subcontractor orders.

As with the variable heuristic, more than one heuristic can be applied to generate a schedule using the planning run, though with the planning run all heuristics are configured to operate together automatically, rather than one-by-one manually. As we've cautioned earlier, normally no more than five to eight heuristics should be applied in a given planning run. Any more not only is excessive and hampers processing, but will almost assuredly run into a *law-of-diminishing-returns* wherein very little planning superiority is achieved as consequence, though complexity and time for execution is greatly increased.

The planning run can technically be executed ad hoc or in batch, though we expect that most organizations will opt not to allow so cavalier a power to end-users. In most cases, ad-hoc execution will probably be reserved for developers, who must trial run the engine over and over again with alternative configurations to derive the most stable settings for production. Experimental application of heuristics to an entire site by way of the planning run by end-users, for example, can have disastrous potential if conducted in the active model and version. Remember, in PP/DS we are as close to execution as one gets with APO—purchase requisitions coming out of a PP/DS planning run may be converted to purchase orders and be immediately transmitted to suppliers. As such, developers will use the ad-hoc runs to determine the most applicable combinations of heuristics to an organization's unique supply chain situation and stabilize them. During actual production, the PP/DS planning run will probably be executed exclusively in batch mode, leaving only the product and variable heuristics available to end-users for everyday, day-to-day, ad-hoc execution.

Alerts, Analysis, Planning, and Procurement in PP

However comprehensive the planning run's combination of heuristics, its output will necessarily be a proposal until it is reviewed by a human planner. Even the best configured planning run may yield conditions that still require human intervention and fine tuning. Demand may exceed all available capacities and prioritization of orders may be necessary. Raw materials supplies may be unavailable to support planned production or else demand may be so low that capacities are left unused, leaving open the possibility that future planned production may be brought in.

Despite the hype, there is no such thing as "optimizing a supply chain." The best planning is not the result of a perfectly designed AI device; it is the combination of the most advanced quantitative analytics with the qualitative reasoning and skilled intervention of experienced, *human* buyers, planners, and ground controllers. We seek to apply APO and its planning runs to model supply networks and generate the best schedules that can be derived from computational analytics alone. This becomes the starting point for the refinements of still human-based planning. The intersection of the various planning runs with human intervention is the alert monitor. During development and indeed throughout the productive deployment of APO, users can derive threshold conditions that should result in notifications to one or another human actor: internal buyers, planners, ground controllers, and their external counterparts.

CONFIGURING PP/DS

Use of Profiles in APO Module Configuration

Thus far in this text we have concerned ourselves greatly with master data and user-interface configuration. Suffice it to say that SAP SCM is a highly configurable system and we are hardly finished with our treatment of the variety of ways in which it can be configured. Master data configuration yields a model of a supply network on which the work of supply chain planning may be conducted. User interface configuration makes flexible graphical user interfaces available to enable appropriate human interaction with the toolset. But APO provides capabilities beyond models and user interfaces that indeed are the reason so many organizations find it value-added, capabilities we have so far alluded to frequently: In PP/DS and SNP there are heuristic and optimization-based planning runs; in DP there are statistical tools for demand and forecast analysis.

All of these tools are configured by way of profiles. Profiles are simply charters of settings that are concerned with specific aspects or dimensions of the modules' capabilities. Time profiles, for example, define, control, and limit time scope while propagation ranges similarly define, control, and limit the physical scope of application, such as which sites or products are included in a planning run. Optimization or cost profiles, in turn, control the algorithms and variables applied during such runs. It all amounts to a lot of configuration and makes for much to master, but there is a silver lining to it. Some note SAP's competitors' advertising and the way these competitors like to single out the use of the ABAP programming language in SAP products, which they pose as undesirable against standard programming languages like Java. We urge skepticism in the evaluation of such advertising. When considering the merits of these claims, consider for a moment just how much coding in ABAP has been addressed in this rather thorough treatment of so many SCM modules: none.

If a competitor indicates that their product is desirable on account of its use of Java or its "open source" basis, odds are a lot of Java *coding* is required. With respect to SAP's products, at least where it concerns SCM, we are dealing with a highly, indeed massively configurable tool. Except in cases of dealing with custom data extractors involving integration with an outside BW client or other legacy systems as well as other relatively rare events, coding almost always gives way to configuration for SCM adopters. "It is not your grand-dad's SAP," they say. Competitors peddling their own product on the merits of relative programming accessibility are selling a car that is easy to work on when customers are looking for one that's easy to drive.

A Map to LA: Not a Travel Guide to the Exits and Stops

Note that as configurable as SCM is, there are actually thousands of settings available in its many profiles, far too many to permit detailed treatment of every field and all their options, combinations, and permutations in this or any single text. There are almost 4,400 transactions in SCM, to say nothing of the number of fields in all these transactions, to say nothing again of all the settings in all the fields and say nothing still of the cumulative effects of all the combinations and permutations of the millions of possible resultant settings. A text attempting coverage at such a level would not so much be an instructional manual as a multivolume, encyclopedic desktop technical reference. Readers, unfortunately, must not look here for detailed information on every profile setting.

Such information is available from the help function and online from help.sap.com. The first of the two may be accessed by first placing the cursor in the field of interest, then right-clicking and selecting "Help." While this extensive help is available inside the tool and off the Web, what neither source offers is a detailed *map* through the profiles that lays out (1) which profiles to use, (2) for which resulting business functionality, and (3) in what order to configure those profiles, all to the end of getting APO's modules to an initial, minimum state of configuration where they work. Our objective, therefore, is not to generate a reference tome to all these thousands of settings or millions of combinations, but to provide the map that lays out the sequence and method of applying settings. We will provide the map to LA, but there are a number of stops and exits along the way that we cannot describe at length. Use the map—it will create sense and structure out of online help that is in short supply anywhere else. As to the varieties and effects of settings alternatives on the way through the profile configuration sequences, the reader is left to spend time alone with the tools and their help functions.

Fret not. If one keeps getting lost on detours and exits, one will never find the way to California no matter how detailed the travel guide is that expounds on the activities and sites of each exit. Use our text to learn to get from here to there and *then* work on the minor variants in between by way of online help and experimentation. We urge the reader to save time by using this guide to explore profiles and populate their initial settings according to our instructions in order to learn the sequence of the way through APO configuration. Then, with some level of familiarity and mastery achieved, use the online help to examine the multitude of configuration alternatives.

PP/DS Profiles

Generally speaking it will be necessary to conduct master data setup in advance of profile configuration because profiles' filters are based on master data settings or the existence of transactional data that itself is predicated on master data. Profiles concerned with scope, for example, will require locations, resources, or products upon which they may filter. With the sole exception of the heuristic profile, which is accessed through the IMG (implementation guide), all PP/DS profiles are found for maintenance along the path *Production Planning → Environment → Current Settings*. PP/DS profiles are available for configuration by ordinary users through the APO navigation tree but are also part of lower-level IMG configuration. Customizing IDs may be required as a final step whenever making changes to profiles. Naturally, security profiles will likely be applied to disallow or limit end-user access to configuration profiles in production environments.

One may note, too, that some PP/DS profiles are useful for both the PP and DS aspects of PP/DS (e.g., propagation range), and others are useful for DS only (e.g., optimization and heuristic profiles), while the strategy profile has what can be called "mixed" applications in either area (Exhibit 8.37)—that is, it is used by both, but in a slightly different way by each; thus it is not expressly shared like a propagation range. We will first address profiles necessary for overall PP/DS configuration and we will address DS-specific profile requirements later in this chapter when we look at their use and application in the Detailed Scheduling Planning Board.

Profile	PP/DS	DS Only	Mixed Use
Propagation Range	X		
Work Area	X		
Time	X		
Strategy			X
Planning Board		X	
Heuristic		X	
Optimization		X	
Overall		X	

EXHIBIT 8.37　APPLICATION OF CONFIGURATION PROFILES IN PP/DS

Propagation Ranges

Propagation Ranges simply control which resources and products will be planned in the PP/DS heuristic planning run, either in a background run or else on a simple heuristic run such as in the Product View. In the former case the range delineates the whole range accessible to the run, while additional subfilters in a run-definition may further limit application. In the latter case, since a product heuristic in the Product View is, by definition, limited to a specific product, the propagation range simply controls which resources are available to the heuristic during run. The Propagation Range transaction is /SAPAPO/CDPSC8 and is relatively straightforward. While the screen presents options for "Resource" and "Product" selection, be aware that one can assign an entire location, with all its resources and products, to the Planning Run by assigning the location through the Resource Selection button.

Define custom entries in this transaction by clicking the New Entries button (Exhibit 8.38, step 1), assigning a Propagation Range code and description, select the "From Workarea" checkbox column (Exhibit 8.38, step 2), and then save the new range code. Highlight the new range code and click the Resource Selection button (Exhibit 8.38, step 3). Move the Location field from the right panel to the left (Exhibit 8.38, step 4), then click the "Continue" check. Enter the name of the location containing the resources that should be included in the Planning Run in the resulting dialog window (Exhibit 8.38, step 5) and click the "Continue" check. Save these settings.

Work Areas

Propagation ranges control the range of application of the PP/DS heuristic planning run, which under ordinary circumstances will be executed against the broadest scope of a

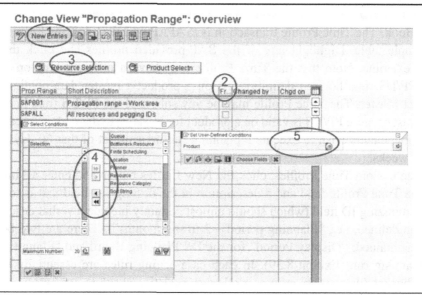

EXHIBIT 8.38 PROPAGATION RANGE
© SAP AG. Used with permission.

PP/DS deployment, but the DS Planning Board may have a more refined scope limited by specific resources, orders, or products as it is used to directly manage individual orders during the manufacturing execution horizon on a day-to-day basis. The scope of the DS Planning Board as such is maintained in the Work Areas profile, transaction code /SAPAPO/CDPSC3. Maintenance of Work Areas is loosely similar to Propagation Ranges only its settings vis-à-vis resources, orders, and products is controlled via a navigation tree rather than buttons.

Notice the configurations for two of the SAP-provided Work Area profiles: SAP001, "All Resources," and SAPALL, "All Products." Highlight the first and then double-click "Resource View" from the navigation tree on the left: All resources are chosen. Click the other navigation tree options for Order View and Product View—there are no settings for these other two. Now try the same for SAPALL. In this case all products are selected, but nothing for resources or orders.

Custom Work Area profiles specifying unique ranges are set up by clicking the New Entries button and adding the Work Area profile code, a description, then selecting from the Resource, Order, and/or Product column to indicate that only selected objects as defined from this profile are to be displayed in the DS Planning Board. Save the new profile, then highlight it and double-click the filter element in the navigation tree as appropriate, such as resources if it is resources that are used to limit display. Click the Set button and in the resulting dialog window click the Choose Fields button to select a filter. If choosing all resources at a location, for example, select location and move it from the right panel to the left. Finally, enter the filter criteria, such as the location code, and click the "Continue" check. Save the changes.

Time Profile

Time Profiles are used by both the planning run and the DS Planning Board and literally control the time horizon of each in a manner similar in many respects to Periodicities in the Planning Book. The Time Profile transaction is /SAPAPO/CDPSC4. Time Profiles present with a simple table. Highlight any of the SAP-provided profiles and click the Details button to examine. Note that the Time Profile may have a different horizon definition than the PP/DS time horizon definition set on a product's master data configuration in the Product Master. The Time Profile may be any subset of the PP/DS time horizon. For example, just because PP/DS is valid on a product for 60 days, under certain circumstances one may nonetheless wish to execute a planning run on a subset of that 60 days, perhaps the first 3 weeks.

To create custom Time Profiles, click the New Entries button and enter a Time Profile code in the Time Profile field and a description in the description field that is to the right of the Customizing ID field (which should almost certainly include a verbal description of the horizon defined, i.e., "Planning period −2 to +4 months"). There are two boxes that must be maintained: "Display Period" for the DS Planning Board and "Planning Period" for the planning run (Exhibit 8.39). In each case setting rules are essentially the same. The time bucket (day, week, etc.) as well as the relative/absolute attribute is controlled through the "Date" field. Absolute dates, if selected, will result in fields defining calendar dates—these will rarely be used. Relative dates are almost always preferable because

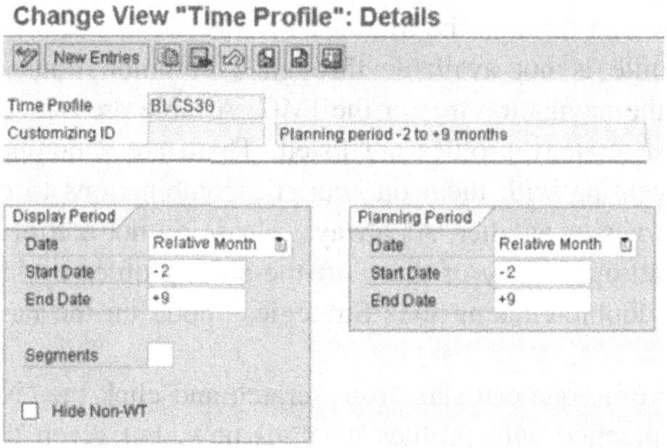

Change View "Time Profile": Details

New Entries

| Time Profile | BLCS36 |
| Customizing ID | | Planning period -2 to +9 months |

Display Period			Planning Period		
Date	Relative Month		Date	Relative Month	
Start Date	-2		Start Date	-2	
End Date	+9		End Date	+9	
Segments					
☐ Hide Non-WT					

EXHIBIT 8.39 TIME PROFILE
Field options vary by choice of relative or absolute. © SAP AG. Used with permission.

they do not require continuous maintenance once set because they move along with the live horizon (i.e., history = today—2 months, future horizon = today + 4 months). Make settings for both Display and Planning, save, and exit.

Strategy Profile

Strategy Profiles are one of the more sophisticated configuration controls available in PP/DS and as such require some more detailed explanation. We must delay for a moment on providing that explanation as it belongs properly in the context of configuring the overall heuristic planning run and will make little sense if addressed separately. Suffice it for now to note that the PP/DS planning run is heuristic based, which means the following: PP/DS plans its tactical horizon (usually from two weeks out to three or four months—generally corresponding to supply lead time) with a *rule-based* solver. SAP provides almost 60 off-the-shelf rules with the SCM package, any of which may be applied in a given planning run configuration (though it is highly unadvisable to use too many; more on that later). Examples of rules might include MRP-based planning (Materials Requirements Planning), called "Product Planning (Comp. acc. LLevl Code)" and "Product Planning (Plan Comp. Immediately)" in APO, which are heuristics "SAP_MRP_001" and "SAP_MRP_002," respectively, as well as "Reschedule Blocks" and "Tolerance Check."

While heuristic rules are the basis of the planning run, they are not the end—Strategy Profiles modify the application of rules in any given planning run. In other words, more than one planning run configuration may be defined using the same heuristics, but *applied in different ways* by way of Strategy Profiles. It may be easiest to think of Strategy Profiles as controlling the range of application of a heuristic. For example, should a heuristic be permitted to choose between separate modes (production path alternatives) available for production on a PPM, or must it retain the same mode from one run to another? If rescheduling an order, should it be rescheduled to the current date, the earliest date available, or a specified date? In which direction should planning be conducted: backward from the finish date (ordinary) or forward from the start date (i.e., when production is already late)? These and many other settings controlling the application of heuristics for planning are all available through the Strategy Profile.

The Strategy Profile is not available through a common transaction and must be accessed via either the navigation tree or the IMG. A table presents on the initial screen where SAP-provided strategy profiles are listed. There are a number of these and we recommend experimenting with them on heuristic combinations to examine the effects of one setting group versus another. As always, please do not edit or delete off-the-shelf profiles. View the settings in any of these off-the-shelf profiles by highlighting an individual profile, then double-clicking the "Strategies" node on the navigation tree in the left-hand panel.

To build a new profile one can start from scratch and click the "New Entries" as has been the preferred practice with profiles up until now, but given the wide number of settings on a Strategy Profile we do not recommend it here. For new Strategy Profiles start by experimenting with the SAP-provided profiles to determine those closest to one's unique needs. Copy this profile to a custom profile by highlighting it and clicking the Copy button. Rename the profile and give it an appropriate description and press the ENTER button on the keyboard or click the green "Continue" check. Choose "Copy all" from the resultant dialog window and save changes.

Modify specific settings of the custom profile by entering the profile in the same way described for viewing settings of off-the-shelf profiles: Highlight the profile and double-click the "Strategies" node on the navigation tree in the left-hand panel. Save any changes made. See the section on configuring the planning run for instructions on how to apply Strategy Profiles to specific heuristics in a planning run.

Configuring Variants for the Heuristic Planning Run

Though the Production Planning heuristic planning run will ordinarily be run in batch, it nonetheless does not have an explicit profile of configuration settings as with other aspects of PP/DS. The planning run is presented as an interactive transaction rather than a set of background settings. We reemphasize that it will normally only be made available for *ad-hoc* use during development when the effects of different settings are being analyzed and tested; it may similarly be available for ad-hoc use during a simulative planning process. The planning run can replan the entire production planning horizon, including procurement and production execution horizons, which makes it exceedingly risky if made available for ad-hoc execution by end-users. In order to configure the planning run for execution in batch, therefore, its settings should be determined and tested during development and saved as a variant that is made accessible to production only through batch.

The planning run settings and execution screen is transaction /SAPAPO/CDPSB0 and is accessed by path *Production Planning → Production Planning Run*. Alternatively, if executed ad hoc from variant settings that have already been saved, it can be executed using transaction /SAPAPO/CDPSB1 or otherwise by the same path but through the transaction Production Planning Run in the Background. Batch programs will normally be configured to execute the latter method with the variant name sent to the program as a parameter, and otherwise if changes to configuration settings are unnecessary, the latter remains the faster way to execute the planning run ad hoc.

The first transaction is required, however, to enter and test configuration settings and to save them as a variant that will be accessible to the alternative background run method. The initial screen of this transaction is really the only screen, with subsequent screens simply being logs or summaries of outcomes of the run. The Planning Version, Time Profile, and Propagation Range must all be specified in the header, delineating respectively (1) the version to execute the run against, (2) the time horizon and boundaries of the run, and (3) the physical scope of the run (i.e., sites, their resources, or sets of parameters). Results logs from a planning run are always generated and can be accessed through either transaction /SAPAPO/RRPEVAL or /SAPAPO/RRPLOG1, both found along path *Production Planning → Reporting → Logs*. The former will display results of the last planning run executed, the latter for a longer running history. If one wishes to view logs at the time of execution, however, one may indicate so by selecting the flag "Display Logs" in the Control Parameters section under the Planning Run header.

From here, "Processing Steps" are necessary to configure the run, which are the specific heuristic processing rules one wishes to be applied. One or more such steps may be applied, though it is unadvisable to apply more than five to eight as this will add processing complexity that is difficult to understand and will not be likely to yield improved planning results. Four settings are necessary for each processing step:

Function/Heuristic	The heuristic rule to be applied at a processing step–these may be any of the 60-some off-the-shelf rules or custom configured rules.
Profile	The strategy profile: This controls the rules for applying a rule. For example, should an MRP scheduling rule be applied using backward or forward scheduling? Should it assume finite or infinite capacity?
Obj. (Processing Object)	Which object should the rule be applied to: resources, orders, operations, and so forth? For example, some rules are applied to products; that is, an MRP rule might mean "plan a product—fulfill unmet supply with demand." Some are applied to operations; that is, a reschedule rule might mean "reschedule existing orders across alternative work centers whenever capacity is exceeded."
Selection Criteria	Few heuristics should be applied globally—when a heuristic is specified to execute on products, orders, or operations, the scope of products (i.e., all products at a site) or of operations (i.e., specific, relevant work center resources) should be specified. When a selection criterion is specified, another settings grouping will appear at screen bottom with filters available to the appropriate object.

Within the planning run transaction, settings for a given heuristic can be viewed by clicking on the applied heuristic and then clicking the Settings for Heuristic button at screen top. Settings for Strategy profiles may similarly be viewed by clicking the concerned profile and then clicking the Strategy button. The Strategy profile is configured according to methods described earlier. Production planning and detailed scheduling planning run heuristic configuration is somewhat more complicated and cannot be done from the user-accessible PP/DS menu, but must be found through the IMG. To do so, using transaction SPRO, click the button SAP Reference IMG, then follow the configuration path *Advanced Planning and Optimization → Supply Chain Planning → Production Planning and Detailed Scheduling → Heuristics*, and then execute transaction "Maintain Heuristics." From here, rules for any off-the-shelf heuristic may be viewed as they were from the button in the planning run screen, but they may be changed and new heuristic profiles may be created. On change and configuration of new heuristics, we offer two cautions: (1) never change an off-the-shelf heuristic and (2) always generate custom profiles by starting with a copy of an off-the-shelf heuristic.

Note that with heuristic configuration there is some difference, however subtle, from other configuration activities. Namely, each off-the-shelf heuristic comes with a definition containing a variety of settings that may be changed; this is in contrast to a "profile" such as with other configuration objects. The "heuristic profile" refers to the list of heuristics available in Detailed Scheduling and is also configured in the IMG. Heuristics, as applied in the PP/DS planning run, are definitions, not profiles.

Between profile settings, heuristics definitions, and combinations of heuristics there are perhaps hundreds of thousands of possible planning run configurations. To derive a planning run that is right for one's own organization, one should familiarize oneself with each of the off-the-shelf heuristics and experiment with a variety of combinations and their effects in a sandbox environment, alternatively changing settings, executing the run, and examining effects in the Product View, for example. Once a configuration is settled upon it may be saved as a variant by clicking the Save button from the SAP button menu at screen top: a disk icon. The variant will require just a name and description. In future planning run executions this variant may be accessed without the need of resetting all the configuration steps, either in the settings version of the transaction by clicking the Get Variant button, which displays as a paper with a stack of files on top, or in the background run transaction where all saved variants will be listed with their descriptions. Planning runs settings that are saved as variants are batch ready.

DETAILED SCHEDULING AND PP/DS USER INTERFACES

The SCC and Alert Monitor are equally available to all modules of APO and are presented as such outside the nodes for any given module. The Planning Book is best applied to Demand Planning and Supply Network Planning and presents in the nodes for both modules, though it may be usefully applied on non-DP and non-SNP applications. The Product View presents in the PP/DS node, though it will be essential to almost all deployments of APO regardless of configuration. Left out of this inventory are two important user interfaces that are primarily for use by the PP and DS aspects of PP/DS, respectively: the Product Planning Table and the Detailed Scheduling Planning Board.

Product Planning Table

The PP aspect of PP/DS encompasses the entirety of the procurement and production execution horizons with the PP aspect addressing the former while including the latter and the DS aspect addressing the latter while assuming the completion of the former. In other words, PP executes procurement and includes production planning while DS assumes procurement completion while scheduling and controlling production execution. With respect to procurement execution during PP/DS, we have considered two tools that will be particularly useful: the Alert Monitor and the Product View. The first is for configuring alert profiles and raising alerts when defined threshold conditions are met, and the second provides a single-product supply/demand order view by which changes can be worked.

Neither of these two data views, however, is likely to fully satisfy the ordinary range of needs that arise during production planning or otherwise during procurement execution and production planning. Sometimes an order-based view is less important than a time-series view, especially when working with long-run procurement schedules. Sometimes a view to supply-versus-demand is less important than a view to production-versus-capacity or delivery-versus-capacity. The PP/DS Product Planning Table addresses these and many other common production planning needs.

Transaction code /SAPAPO/PPT1, the Product Planning Table, is accessed via path *Production Planning → Interactive Production Planning → Product Planning Table*. It may be applied to view a product or a group of products. Regardless of approach (single- or multiple-product), the minimum filter fields necessary for execution are the Planning Version, From and To dates on the Planning Horizon, and a location in the header and a Source or Target designation on the Source/Target tab—the latter indicating whether data is to be viewed for production or receipts. Also regardless of approach, a propagation range must be identified on execution, normally "SAPALL." When searching for a single product, indicate the product on the Product tab. A group of products may be acquired by adding them to the multiple-selection filter or else according to various filter designations. On the Product tab one can filter by group for Product Hierarchy, Planner and/or Procurement Type. On the Line/Resource tab, filters are available for Production Line, Resource, and Planner.

Inside the Product Planning Table the UI contains four major parts: a navigation box, a chart list, a chart board, and a button menu (Exhibit 8.40, steps 1 to 4, respectively). The navigation column itself has two parts: one indicating the products available to view based on filters established in the initial screen, and the other listing "charts" available for display (Exhibit 8.40, step 5). Displayed charts present on the chart board where one or more can be displayed simultaneously (Exhibit 8.40, step 3). The chart navigation menu lists available charts, dividing them between the "Shown," which are visible on the chart board, and the "Hidden," which remain invisible until they are dragged and dropped onto Shown, at which time they display on the chart board. Similarly, charts can be removed from the board by dragging and dropping them to Hidden. No more than three charts may be presented on the chart board simultaneously (or usefully). Order of charts under Shown on the navigation column controls their order of presentation on the chart board, and this order can be rearranged by simple dragging-and-dropping.

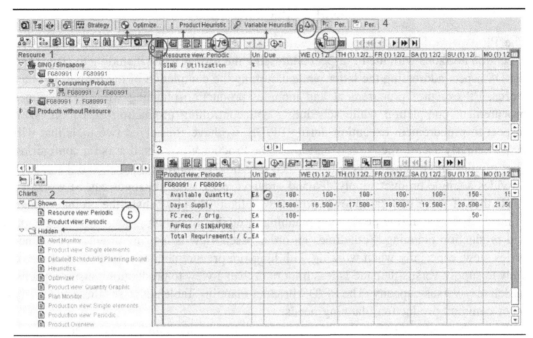

EXHIBIT 8.40 PRODUCT PLANNING TABLE
Move charts back and forth from "Hidden" to "Shown" to display together in the right-hand chart panel. A useful trio of charts is often the Alert Monitor, the Resource View, and the Periodic Product View. © SAP AG. Used with permission.

Any data view available through the Product Planning Table is described within it as a "chart." These charts include, but are not limited to, the Alert Monitor; a Resource (work center) View; the Product View in two forms, Periodic view and Single element; as well as both the PP Planning Run and DS Optimizer. The periodic View of the Product View is the time-phased, period-based rendition of the Product View from the Product View Periods tab and the single-element view is the supply/demand view from the Product View default Elements tab.

A common and useful configuration of charts for the Product Planning Table is the inclusion of the Alert Monitor, Resource View, and Product View. This simultaneous display of data (1) lists alerts according to user specifications, (2) displays a time-phased view of production, and (3) displays a similar time-phased view of productive resource capacity. From this configuration a user may attend to any alerts, plan and work with production, and balance production against work center capacity constraints. The resource view displays each available work center, its percentage utilization by time period, the committed output according to productive demands (per the Product View), and the remaining available productive capacity. Double-clicking an alert in the Alert View will update each of the concurrent charts to the cell where the event of the alert first appears. Generally cells in product or resource views may be double-clicked for detailed under-pinning data.

The chart board may be easily reduced to a full-screen, one-chart view by clicking the Full Screen On/Off button above the top chart but below the button menu (Exhibit 8.40, step 6). From the button menu the DS optimizer may be invoked, as may either the product or variable heuristic (Exhibit 8.40, step 7; see the Product View section for more detail of how these are executed and when they should be used). Use of the DS optimizer here differs very little from its traditional use in the DS Planning Board, except that care should be taken to select the Planning Board as a chart whenever one plans to invoke the optimizer. Similarly, one or both product views should be made available when invoking either heuristic method to properly view their effect in real-time. The Alert Monitor can be invoked as a separate but large pop-up screen from the button menu as well, allowing display of more alerts and larger work charts enabled by quick toggling between screens (Exhibit 8.40, step 8). If displayed periods in time-phased views have subdivisions such as shifts within daily time buckets, then these may be expanded or collapsed from the button menu as well. When necessary, the entire navigation column may also be hidden from view to allow maximal interactive planning using the charts (Exhibit 8.40, step 9).

Detailed Scheduling Planning Board

Ordinarily, procurement execution horizons will yield to a short-range period (i.e., three days to two weeks) that is often described as the "frozen horizon" or the "procurement frozen period," during which changes to procurement orders are disallowed. The reason for freezing procurement in the near term is that at some point little or no utility can be realized by fine-tuning an order, increasing or decreasing quantities, changing orders' parts, or pushing or pulling delivery time. At this point, the cost of change exceeds any potential utility received through change because productive actions are beginning: Materials are being kitted and staged, labor and work stations scheduled, equipment readiness checked, and any final adjustments to last-minute conditions such as nondeliveries, labor absenteeism, or equipment breakdown takes center stage in planning. All of this amounts to quite enough scheduling upheaval without the disruption of late-stage procurement micromanagement. Production at this point is reminiscent of the "point of no return," a term ordinarily applied to planes in the state of takeoff. At some point during takeoff a plane will reach a point where two things become simultaneously true: (1) there is too little runway to stop and (2) the plane is moving to fast to stop anyway. At this point there is no choice; the plane must take off. Manufacturing undergoes its own form of the point of no return, and it will be a certain mix of art and craft by all manufacturers to determine exactly when this point in scheduling-time occurs.

Contained within this very near-term space we have the production execution horizon, which is usually no longer than the time necessary to manufacture either a single major product like an airplane or a complete lot of more minor products like desk lamps. To be clear: The procurement frozen period is *longer* than the manufacturing execution horizon, the latter of which is limited to the approximate time of finished good or lot production. During the manufacturing horizon, often no longer than three to five work days, no new assumptions are made about supply, demand, or capacity: Supply is staged and used as it becomes available, production is fixed to a specific demand target with any new demands pushed out to future production, and capacity is limited to available labor and work center resources.

The objective of planning during this near-term production horizon is to best utilize resources with a target to align demand through supply and capacity bottlenecks in order to minimize labor or work center downtime while maximizing production. What is the least-cost allocation of resources to meet demand when demand is within capacity and supply constraints? What is the most productive allocation of resources to meet demand when it exceeds either capacity or supply constraints, or both?

All of these issues are interacted with through the DS Planning Board, where a PP/DS shop will actually control scheduling of production orders against work centers. Accessed via path *Production Planning* → *Interactive Production Planning* → *Detailed Scheduling Planning Board* → *View 1,* its transaction code is /SAPAPO/CDPS1. The DS Planning Board (1) displays products' production orders against the work centers they have been assigned to, and (2) allows replanning of unreleased production orders manually or (3) via the DS optimizer.

Most PP/DS profiles must be appropriately configured in advance of application of the DS Planning Board, including: the Work Area profile, the Strategy profile, the Planning Board profile, the Heuristic profile, the Time profile, the Optimization profile, and the Propagation Range profile. Of these, three are specific to DS and are applied explicitly in the DS Planning Board: the Planning Board Profile and the Optimization Profile; the Strategy Profile is unique too in that it may be applied separately for the PP and DS horizons, the latter in the context of Planning Board use. To get around the complex use of configuration profiles here we will first address the use of the DS Planning Board and then the specifics of these additional profiles and their interaction with other PP/DS profiles in order to enable the Planning Board.

Using the DS Planning Board

In order to use the DS Planning Board one can either manually input values on all the many profile tabs on the initial screen or else simply specify an "Overall Profile," which contains selections of relevant Planning Board profiles that will automatically update the tabs. As always a planning version is required. Click Execute to enter the board.

The Planning Board is actually subject to a good deal of visual configuration by way of the DS Planning Board profile. For our purposes we will address a fairly standard approach to its use. It consists of five major parts: the resource and product pools, the resource chart, the product chart, and a button menu (Exhibit 8.41, steps 1 to 5, respectively). The pools may be used to navigate and select resources or products available for planning on the board. The product pool displays at screen bottom and can be expanded by simply double-clicking on its top panel and reduced by clicking the Close button. Close both pools by clicking the Resource Pool Close button when the resource pool is in the foreground.

The product and resource charts are intended for collusive use where products are displayed in the product chart and highlighted with Gantt chart bars over a time horizon when there is activity on a resource for the product (Exhibit 8.41, step 6). The resources chart in turn lists available resources, and any resources working a product similarly display as such by way of Gantt chart bars.

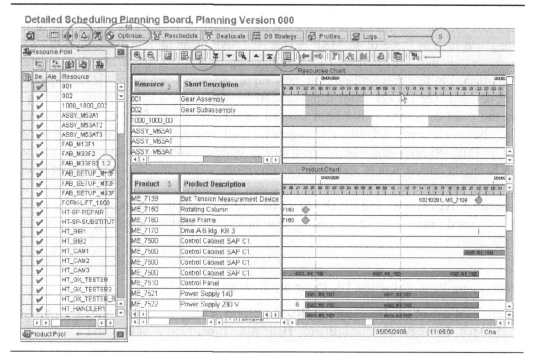

EXHIBIT 8.41   DETAILED SCHEDULING PLANNING BOARD
© SAP AG. Used with permission.

If you are interested in activity on a specific product, find the product by scrolling down the product list on the product chart (or by finding and double-clicking the product in the product pool). In the product chart right-click the product and select "Begin with first graphical object"—the Planning Board will then move to the first occurrence of productive activity on the product. From there, find the resources working the product in the resource view. Note that conversely one can find the first instance of scheduled work on a resource following the same right-click method on the resources chart. Note, too, that resources may at times be multischeduled but that multischeduling does not always display by default. To view multischeduling cases—such as when a single line is overcapacity or else when other lines exist but the planning run and/or optimizer do not solve for alternative lines—right-click the resource and select "Expand Multiple Listing." The first graphical object of the entire board may also be displayed by clicking the first graphical object button from the button menu (Exhibit 8.41, step 7). Order and activity colors on the Planning Board will vary by configuration, but a legend can be displayed (Exhibit 8.41, step 8). As with other screens the Alert Monitor may be invoked where it may be applied here to review alerts relevant to detailed scheduling and manufacturing execution and control (Exhibit 8.41, step 9).

The DS optimizer is run from inside the DS Planning Board by clicking the optimizer button (Exhibit 8.41, step 10). A pop-up window appears requesting specification of dates for the optimization run, defaulting to dates specified on the optimization profile. Press

"Optimize." An optimization window displays with analytical charts. Click Execute to carry out the run. As indicated earlier, the DS optimizer is not a planning run in the pure sense such as those of an MRP engine, the SNP planning runs (including the SNP optimizer), or the heuristic-based PP/DS planning run. All of these planning runs are distinguished in that they will propose new supply sources when supply is inadequate to meet demand. The DS optimizer is not concerned with creating new supplies; it assumes that the point of no return has been crossed and the only way forward is commitment (e.g., shall we take off at 5, 10, or 15 degrees?, shall we pause before starting or get right at it?). This optimizer finds the mathematically optimal schedule for maximum production based on known supply and capacity constraints—including the constraint of orders that have already been committed, are released in production, and which therefore are consuming live capacity and which cannot be further changed. It proposes a schedule for all unplanned orders without suggesting new orders and without changing those already in place.

Configuring Profiles for the DS Planning Board

Unrestricted use of the DS Planning Board requires setting all of the following profiles: Work Area, Strategy, Planning Board, Heuristic, Time, Optimization, and Propagation Range. Moreover, an "Overall Profile" summarizing a collection of the above profiles may be configured and called upon at the time of execution to immediately fill in all the settings necessary to execute and run the Planning Board. The Overall Profile is accessed through the transaction "Maintain Overall Profiles" on path *Production Planning → Environment → Current Settings*, which is where all of these profiles may be maintained except for the Heuristics Profile, which is found in the IMG.

Use the Planning Board Profile to configure display settings of the DS Planning Board (i.e., window size, marking modes and color settings, time-bucket displays, as well as whether multiple loadings should be default displayed). Strategy profiles control planning strategies affecting heuristic planning applications as previously described, though note that profiles are requested both for DS on the "DS Strategy Profile" tab and for PP on the "More Profiles" tab. Planning activities executed via DS functions such as optimization and rescheduling employ the specified DS Strategy Profile. If PP activities like order creation or change are invoked via the DS Planning Board, the specified PP profile is applied. In either case, the same set of profiles are available as maintained in Current Settings under "Maintain Strategy Profile."

The DS optimization run obviously employs the Optimization Profile. Several profiles are provided off the shelf, one applying a genetic algorithm and the other applying a constraint algorithm. As always, custom profiles may be generated and we suggest beginning by copying either of the off-the-shelf profiles and editing them to custom requirements, testing the effects of changes. Very basically the constraint algorithm works by filtering out infeasible solutions while the genetic algorithm propagates continuous new sets of solutions, judges them, and then picks the best from the set, resulting in not just a feasible solution based on constraints, but the best-of-breed solution. The genetic approach would be applied to determine the best scheduling based on setup times, for example. An understanding of the variety of settings in the two optimizer approaches will be best achieved following the same method we suggested for learning macros: experiment. Begin with the two off-the-shelf examples, copy them into new, safe, editable versions, review their settings, run them on test cases, change settings, and compare effects.

NOTE

1. We emphasize point of view because more than one site may be simultaneously planned in sequence and in parallel using the PP aspect of PP/DS, the caveat being that the point of scheduling is site-based management of activities that are about to be or else are in actual execution—not preplanning coordination to keep the network in sync.

9

DEMAND PLANNING MODULE

DP addresses needs for development of an unconstrained demand forecast as well as demand allocation among available global resources.

The Demand Planning (DP) module of SCM APO addresses the business interests of what is broadly described as demand management by both industry and APICS. In the supply chain management (SCM) context there are generally two outcomes sought from the application of DP: (1) analysis and generation of demand forecast, which is more accurately described as a demand signal, and (2) analysis and generation of demand allocations, where unsatisfied demand is delegated or assigned to specific geographies or sites for fulfillment (Exhibit 9.1).

In either case, demand management is not concerned with common supply chain constraints of capacity and supply. An effective demand signal is one that approaches the most accurate, advanced picture of demand possible and neither capacity nor supply amount to very meaningful inputs to such a question. On settlement, however, a demand forecast or signal is provided to supply network planning (SNP) where constraints are introduced to planning. A demand "release" process to seed SNP is described in Chapter 10. Sometimes there will be more than one demand signal fed to SNP, as may be the case with a demand forecast, customer sales orders (i.e., explicit order demand as opposed to forecast), and/or some form of composite forecast of the two (not to be confused with composite forecasting methods!). Multiple demand feeds are often provided to an SNP system on account of the fact that SNP may be empowered to respond to one or more of such signals. For example, in the short run, under constrained capacity conditions, SNP may be configured to respond first to customer order demand, only addressing forecast when all customer orders are shown to be met, whereas in the long run SNP may be configured to respond only to forecast or a composite as the customer orders may be no more valid at future points than the forecast.

Naturally when thinking about demand management most people will think of forecasts. We must nonetheless keep in mind that for organizations a forecast signal is only part of the work. Demand analysis is generally done at an aggregate level, as the larger the demand input pool the more accurate forecasts tend to be. Supplies are met discretely, however, by specific sites. A complete demand management process will consider a rule set (i.e., proximity of supply source to anticipated demand), and delegate demands to locations and resources in the supply chain.

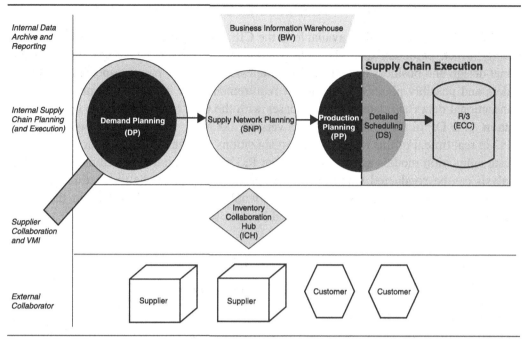

EXHIBIT 9.1   DP in the Supply Chain Context

DP MASTER DATA AND CIF

Master Data

Demand Planning primarily employs both supply chain master data (Chapter 5) and analytical master data (Chapter 6). Familiarity with both data types is essential to understanding the methods, objects, and tools in DP. Minimal supply chain master data for SNP includes locations, calendars, and products.

Core Interface integration models for DP master data will vary between those that can be run once and those running regularly and therefore requiring batch control. Locations probably not do require regular batch reruns as these objects should be fairly stable. Products are more subject to common business change processes and their integration models may require batch management. Daily or several-times-daily batch processes inactivating relevant integration models, creating new ones, and activating them will suffice to keep APO and R/3 in alignment.

While location data is mostly maintained in R/3 and received via one-way master data CIF into APO, there are some APO-specific settings for DP on a DP-specific tab in the APO Location Master, though these settings generally are more concerned with how demand is fulfilled downstream than how it is analyzed in DP. APO calendars must be assigned to the Location Master in addition to the CIF. Demand Planning deployments will require a careful, rigorous, element-by-element review of Product Master settings to derive which ones are necessary, which are not, which are subject to maintenance through CIF, and which must be maintained separately in APO.

Transactional Data

Any kind of transactional data available to the CIF may be relevant for a DP deployment; exactly which particular data elements are relevant is subject to the specific organizational design and business objectives. Nonetheless, demand elements, especially customer orders and possibly planned independent requirements, are some of the most likely DP transactional data candidates. As in all cases with the CIF, changes made to transactional data in APO DP in the active model and version, 000/000, will transfer between R/3 and APO in real time. For this reason many organizations will find it desirable or necessary to create simulation models and versions where R/3 data can be transferred and so that DP analysis can be conducted without affecting production data in the transactional system. Only after commitment decisions are made would such data be returned to the active model and version and subsequently CIF'd back to R/3.

USING DP

Demand Planning Process

Demand Planning requires a number of feeds for the varieties of demand information that are germane to forecasting and allocations. Customer orders—both firm, active orders and long-term reservations—are, of course, one source of such data and are ordinarily acquired from a customer order management system, which for APO adopters will usually be R/3 or CRM (Exhibit 9.2, step 1). In addition, considerable archives can be profitably brought to bear for demand analysis, including historical customer forecasts

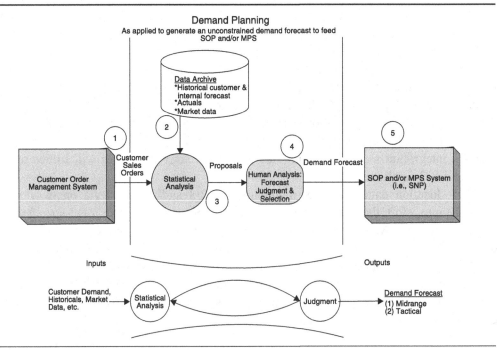

EXHIBIT 9.2   DEMAND PLANNING PROCESS

and reservations versus actual orders, market data as it regards competitor data (Exhibit 9.2, step 2; i.e., the last time(s) a competitor released a competing product and its effect on orders), as well as promotional data (i.e., the time(s) marketing promotions were released and their effects on orders). Similar archival data would also be important for researching and predicting the effects of cannibalization, such as when a new internal product is released, bringing an old product to end-of-life but nonetheless requiring inventory clearing such as through discounts.

All of this data is brought together and made subject to a variety of analyses, statistical and otherwise (Exhibit 9.2, step 3). Promotion analysis simply compares trends from promotions to determine possible effects on current projections. Univariate forecast looks at the effect of a single variable on demand, and multiple linear regression (MLR, or *causal analysis*) looks at a variety of potential factors affecting demand determination.

As with all the varieties of SCM, after these quantitative analyses have had their say, alert monitors are brought to bear to bring in the attention of human analysts who may need to work directly with specific conditions (Exhibit 9.1, step 4). Generally speaking, users will interact with DP through planning books explicitly configured for use with DP, though they may also frequently find recourse in the Product View (see Chapter 8 in both cases as well as for Alert Monitor configuration). Certainly heavy demand spikes or troughs, whether in orders, reservations, or as the result of a statistical run, should be cause for interest, but other possible alerts may be necessary depending on the unique organizational situation. Human inputs may be fed back into a quantitative model or else the proposals from the system may be accepted as-is upon assessment by users. They in turn feed the downstream systems for sales and operations planning (SOP) and master production scheduling (MPS, usually at a network level at this point), which in the case of SCM APO will normally be the SNP module in either case (Exhibit 9.2, step 5). Detailed instructions for the release of DP data to SNP are provided in the Configuring SNP section in Chapter 10. We should note that an acceptable design for APO may include DP and Production Planning and Detailed Scheduling (PP/DS), skipping SNP. This would particularly be the case in smaller organizations strictly concerned with internal site planning, for which cross-site, cross-geography supply networks are not particularly important.

What's the Point? Demand Forecast versus Demand Management

As it is an area prone to widespread misunderstanding, we should reemphasize that there are two broad, achievable ends to the discipline of demand management as practiced with APO DP: (1) generation, via many techniques including but not limited to forecasting, of a demand signal that serves the end of making all subsequent supply-chain planning nonarbitrary, and (2) allocation of judged demand to sources of supply. The second end is fairly straightforward: DP must normally be conducted in aggregate while demand fulfillment is almost always distributed among a variety of sources of supply from distribution centers, factories, suppliers, and subcontractors, which in turn become internally responsible for planning the detailed fulfillment of the demand assignments.

The first point, the demand signal, seems to be an issue of contention for many organizations. To contemplate what makes it problematic for a moment, consider what a demand signal is *not*: (1) It is not exclusively a forecast and (2) insofar as it is a forecast it is not expected to be particularly accurate and becomes less accurate as it forecasts targets that are increasingly remote in time. A demand signal may be said to be a "judged" demand forecast: It is the final product fed to downstream systems for execution. There are many inputs to the demand signal:

- Known promotions
- Known competitive products or competitive product introductions
- Cannibalizing product offers
- Related to the previous: product lifecycle changes
- Customer reservations
- Customer demand

Technically all of these signals, when combined, constitute the discipline of forecasting. Paradoxically we know, however, that the closer we get to actual execution, the less the output of the process is a forecast than it is a straightforward description of actual, working demand. As such, the weight each of these inputs has on the final computation of a demand varies according to the proximity in time at which production must occur and demand expectations must be either met (product sent) or postponed (product stored to inventory). Such a weighted approach to demand inputs will be particularly important in a capacity- or supply-constrained environment where, for example, it is impossible to buy, build, and ship sufficient materials to fulfill all anticipated demand. In such cases, careful discrimination between demand due to live, actionable customer sales orders will likely take precedence over demand "judged" to exist for inventories but that has not yet materialized as an actionable order. Notice that the concern, even at this late stage, is not so much with forecast accuracy as it is with the appropriate *management* of demand: More than one type and quality of demand exists; to which should we plan?

If demand signal or "forecast" accuracy is not particularly important to short-run demand planning, how much less will it be important to long-run planning? The more remote we become from the demand the less relative weight customer orders will carry relative to other forecasting elements. It is not unknown, for example, for customers to open order reservations in advance to reserve capacity, even though customers themselves do not yet have data to substantiate the existence of their own demand. At this more remote stage in the DP process we must become very concerned with factors that place pressure one way or the other on direct customer reports of their own demand. These are such things as known local and global market conditions, marketing activities, competitor activities, and product lifecycle, as well as even customer reliability data where some customers may be data-demonstrated to be better forecasters than others—where better is essentially a function of limited changes to open reservations. The fundamental objective of this process is assuredly not to develop an accurate demand forecast. For most product categories one can no more accurately forecast demand 6 to 12 months out than one can forecast weather. Certainly, we may expect various seasonal patterns, but to expect that we will know how many units of product a specific customer will need for 1 week in 30 weeks is as sensible as expecting to know whether it will be rainy, sunny, hot, or cold on a specific day equally remote.

In contrast to this expectation, the fundamental objective of this activity is twofold: (1) Knowing that we must plan resources, factories, transportation lanes, suppliers, and so on to *some* demand signal, we owe it to ourselves to assure that the demand signal we plan to is not arbitrary but instead is, however flawed, due to best-known demand factors (see above), and (2) with a mind to our earlier remarks that it becomes increasingly proximal, set demand into a sort of sieve so that once demand becomes actionable its patterns, contents, and trends are fully understood. By analogy, if manufacturing and distribution were a race where production planning and execution started when the starting-gun fired, then demand management is everything one does to prepare for the instant of start. Knowing that that moment of start is approaching, one appropriately clothes in racing uniform and shoes up in running shoes. One eats a light but good meal hours earlier but essentially fasts the few hours before, sipping on water. One stretches, studies the course and one's competitors, tries to relax, and focuses the mind. As the last minutes to start lead up, one moves into position near the race start. The activities of DP are in this sense a staging for race start. Of course one is interested in exactly what will happen when the gun fires—who will run first, who last, what competitions will occur for second and third place, and so on, as well as who will fall out of the race and who will win—but ultimately there is no knowing these things. In contrast to forecasting, it is this *staging process* that is incomparably more important than accurate forecasting of events once they start. The difference is between a uniformed, stretched, hydrated, and mentally girded racer with an empty stomach standing at the start line at the moment of race start versus a Levi-clad, tight-necked, thirsty, and distracted racer with a full stomach racing before the race, tearing off his polo shirt mid-run, just to get to the start line in time for the gun.

CONFIGURING DP

The primary interactive user interface (UI) for DP will be the Planning Book, whose configuration is addressed in detail in Chapter 8. A DP Planning Book will require that DP capabilities are configured for a planning book data view at the time of Planning Book configuration (mutually exclusive, for example, to SNP capabilities for a similar planning book data view). Other common user interfaces that find purchase in DP include, of course, the Alert Monitor and the Product View. Model builders, either as developers constructing a supply network model or end-users setting up simulative conditions, will find use for the Supply Chain Cockpit (SCC).

More so than any other module, DP is highly concerned with historical data, which ends up playing a considerable role in forecast analytics and demand judgment. As such, the data storage objects of BW and the APO BW data mart, what we have called "analytical master data," are foundational to any treatment of DP. Prospective DP developers and users should therefore familiarize themselves with the treatment of these objects covered in Chapter 6. Additional instruction on the reporting capabilities of BW using these objects is also available in Chapter 11.

As master data configuration is addressed in Chapters 5 and 6, UI configuration is addressed in Chapter 8, and release of demand data to SNP in Chapter 10, here we will be concerned with configuration of the core capabilities associated with DP. We summarize those capabilities as: (1) proportional factors, (2) forecast profiles, and (3) lifecycle planning. Proportional factors are concerned with disaggregation of aggregated data that is applied in DP to assignment of demand to individual supply chain resources. Forecast profiles control the application of statistical forecasting techniques to analytical datasets. Lifecycle planning informs DP on issues of cannibalization, new product introduction, and product end-of-life, and may even be applied to consider the effects of competition or other market conditions.

Statistical Forecasting Basics

Elsewhere in our treatment we cover the necessary subject of "basics" of this concept or that, and statistical forecasting will be no exception. What is somewhat exceptional will be just how basic our basics treatment here will be. Indeed, use of statistics in forecasting constitutes a highly specialized body of expertise, the rudimentary details of which are far outside the scope of this text. Demand planners and IT specialists in DP systems, if they do not already possess the appropriate expertise, should consider academic coursework in basic statistics, regression models, and categorical data analysis.

Critical to understanding the use of statistical models for forecasting is to understand two different data elements: independent variables and dependent variables. In a statistical context, a dependent variable is the effect for which we are searching for a cause or causes, which are the independent variables. In other words, independent variables are understood to cause dependent variables; hence the *dependency* of the latter. The objective of statistical analysis is to sort out which independent variables are actually not causal at all versus those that are and to filter among those that are causal to determine their relative weight in causation.

For example, a variable we may be interested in for commercial purposes may be sedan sales, and very likely sedan sales during a specific time of the year. This is our "dependent variable," dependent as it is on a variety of causes. Some causes of sedan sales include the price of the sedan, discount campaigns and marketing promotions, as well as seasonal patterns. Note, too, a very statistically nuanced distinction of what we mean here by "sales": We are not referring to the act of sale; instead we are referring to the number of sedans sold. Understood that way, we know there are a number of causes that on first thought may seem *oppositional* to sales, for example, the availability of a competitor's sedan or a sale on a competitor's sedan. In fact, the oppositional nature of such causes is to the act of sale, but these are contributing negative factors to the final quantity of sedans sold, as much so as any positive factor; as such, in trying to determine the most accurate predictive relationship between causes and effects in order to predict a trend, we must take them into account.

Statistical analysis is strictly backward facing, examining as it does events that have already occurred and deriving and quantifying relationships between known factors. When applying statistical analysis to forecast, we seek to take our findings—the relationships between independent and dependent variables—and apply them to current and future conditions to predict trends. Forecasting based on these techniques essentially follows three closely related forms:

1. *Univariate forecast.* Prediction of upward or downward fluctuations in trend based on single-variable analysis. This can be particularly useful when analyzing

considerable but rather instantaneous demand events such as spikes in demand fed by an unexpectedly good economy or troughs in demand brought about by the closure of a geographic market (such as may be due to political instability) or an unexpected and powerfully competing product.

2. *MLR forecast.* Prediction of an overall running trend based on a multiple-variable analysis. This will be more applicable for standard, long-range trend analysis that takes known market forces into account.

3. *Lifecycle planning.* Prediction of an overall demand pattern based on product lifecycle analysis coupled with promotional pattern analysis. This is important for organizing the structure of demand over time. The two strictly statistical techniques provide a view to individual upward or downward pressures on demand at any given point in time, yet we know that products experience a lifecycle drawn out over time that follows a distinct pattern. This pattern, combined with known current and historical quantities, can powerfully illuminate the structure of long-term demand.

In each case the outcome of historical analysis is superimposed over current conditions to derive a predicted demand trend. Univariate and MLR methods are employed to predict the effects of known variables at given points in time, and lifecycle planning to enforce an overall structure to the demand picture. As indicated earlier, the objective with all of this is not so much to derive an *accurate* long-term forecast, especially in the long-run, but instead to assure that the demand signal that feeds planning systems is both nonarbitrary and, once we enter procurement or production execution horizons, well-staged and therefore reasonably stable. In the long-run forecast, accuracy is really unnecessary outside very wide parameters; in the short-run forecast, accuracy is really only an academic question, the more appropriate questions being those concerning which specific demand signals to plan to in an constrained environment and how much inventory accumulation to permit in an unconstrained one.

Proportional Factors

Proportional factors are applied to rationally allocate portions of aggregated data; that is, they are used to disaggregate aggregated data. For example, global forecast data may be stored in an InfoCube but we wish to allocate portions of that forecast to various resources distributed around the world that will be assigned the duty of fulfilling the demands. Our organization may operate in three primary geographies: Asia, Americas, and Europe. Proportional factors may be maintained to allocate forecast to resources in these three geographies either according to a formula for proximity to demand or a formula for availability of supply. The application of a proportional factor to the calculation of a key figure is defined when the key figure is assigned to a planning area. This section is concerned with maintaining the proportional factors that affect dynamic computations on key figures.

Proportional factors are configured in either of two ways: manually or via automatic calculation. Manual configuration will be necessary when historical data is unavailable to feed a formula for factor computation, when for any reason it is necessary to revise automatically computed factors, or else when distributions must be fixed due to a known or otherwise strategic reason. In all other cases, automatic computation is preferable and likely a more dynamic fit to moving-target data.

Factors are changed manually using a DP planning book that was configured for manual proportional factor maintenance at the time of its creation. In the Define Planning Book transaction, Planning Book tab "Maintain proportions maintenance" must be selected. The data view for this planning book should be assigned the key figure APODPDANT, which will display as "Proportional Factors." Key figures affected by the proportional factor must be defined with aggregation types that permit disaggregation, such as "pro rata" or "based on another key figure," and should be defined in their planning area as "fixable key figures." Developers may consider creating a planning book data view with the APODP-DANT key figure alone so as to open access to only specific users responsible for factor maintenance. Using a planning book as thus configured, proportional factors are maintained by loading a detailed characteristic, then choosing the Absolute Percentage button from the data grid toolbar (Exhibit 9.3). This will toggle proportional values from absolute to percentages (and back), and their values as percentages may be adjusted as necessary.

Dynamic, automatic computation of proportional factors is carried out with transaction "Calculate Proportional Factors," code /SAPAPO/MC8V, found on path *Demand Planning → Environment*. In the initial screen identify the planning area source of a proportional factor's computational data, the planning area (or InfoCube) where the results of the proportional factor will be applied, and then execute (Exhibit 9.4, steps 1 to 3, respectively). On the resulting screen, items should be populated to indicate how to compute the proportional factors and to which key figures to apply the computations. The first box, "Basis for proportional calc," asks for specifications on key figures that will be the basis of the proportional allocation. These key figures may, for example, be populated by macros or function modules that continuously update them based on the values of changing, moving-target data. The planning area is inherited from the first screen; its version (i.e., from the active model or some inactive, simulative version), the key figure basis, and a range should be specified (Exhibit 9.4, steps 4 to 7, respectively).

The second box, "Calc proportions for," is applied to distribute calculated proportional factors to stored key figures. Here again the planning area is inherited from the initial screen and the version must be specified along with the specific key figure to which to apply the newly computed proportional factors (Exhibit 9.4, steps 8 to 10, respectively). The third box, "Transfer proportions to horizon," merely specifies the time zone during which to apply the computations (Exhibit 9.4, step 11). Click the Execute button to carry out the computation of proportional factors and their application to key figures (Exhibit 9.4, step 12).

Application of automated proportional factors should be a defined, engineered, deliberate business process. Settings for its application should normally be saved as a variant so as to assure that manual execution follows disciplined application.

EXHIBIT 9.3   ABSOLUTE<=>PROPORTIONAL BUTTON ON THE DATA GRID TOOLBAR IN THE PLANNING BOOK
© SAP AG. Used with permission.

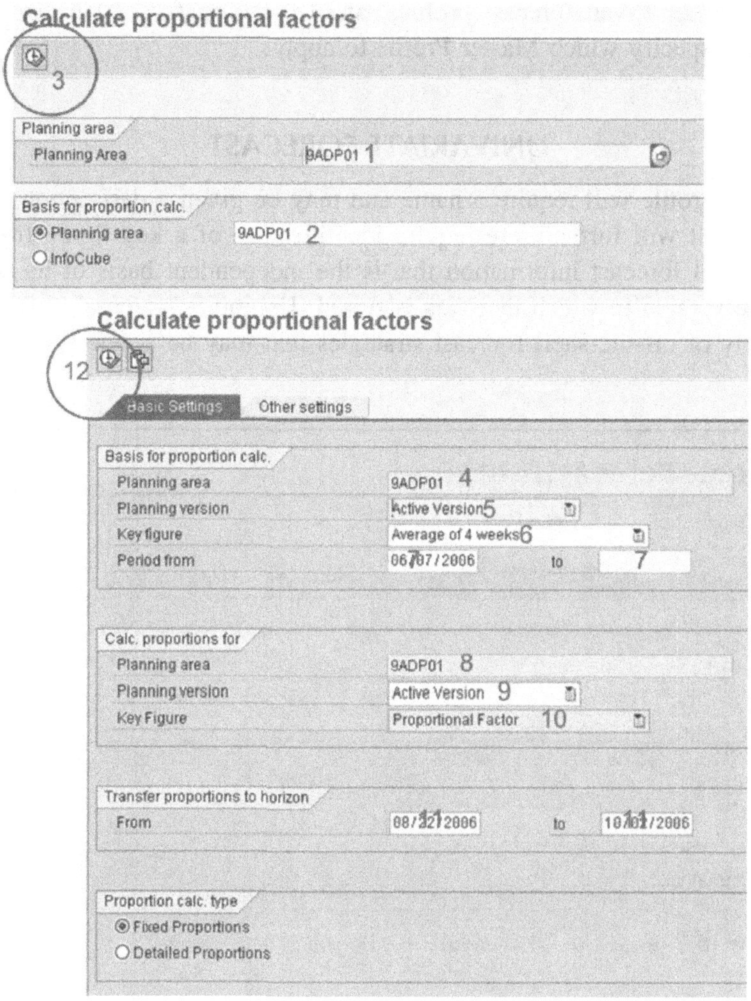

EXHIBIT 9.4 CONFIGURING AUTOMATED COMPUTATION AND APPLICATION OF A PROPORTIONAL FACTOR
© SAP AG. Used with permission.

Forecast Profiles

There are three forecast options available in DP: (1) the univariate forecast, (2) multiple linear regression (MLR or *causal analysis*), and (3) composite forecast. The first is concerned with applying a single input variable to determine its effect on demand. The second considers the effects of a multiplicity of factors on demand and tries to predict a trend. The last combines one or more analysis techniques to yield a demand proposal.

The management of forecast execution in DP is controlled through a "Master" forecast profile, or Master Profile. The Master Profile as well as profiles for each of the three forecast types are all maintained in the transaction, Maintain Forecast Profiles, code /SAPAPO/MC96B, on path *Demand Planning → Environment*. The basic process for profile maintenance and application is to (1) create and save appropriate univariate,

MLR, or composite forecast profiles, (2) create and save a Master Profile that calls on one or more of the saved forecast profiles, and (3) during forecast execution in a DP planning book, specify which Master Profile to apply.

UNIVARIATE FORECAST

The univariate profile will require a name and may be given a description (Exhibit 9.5, steps 1 and 2). It will furthermore require identification of a key figure from which to acquire historical forecast information that is the independent basis of its computation, as well as the version in which that data is stored (Exhibit 9.5, steps 3 and 4). SAP provides a variety of off-the-shelf forecast strategies that may be applied, such as constant

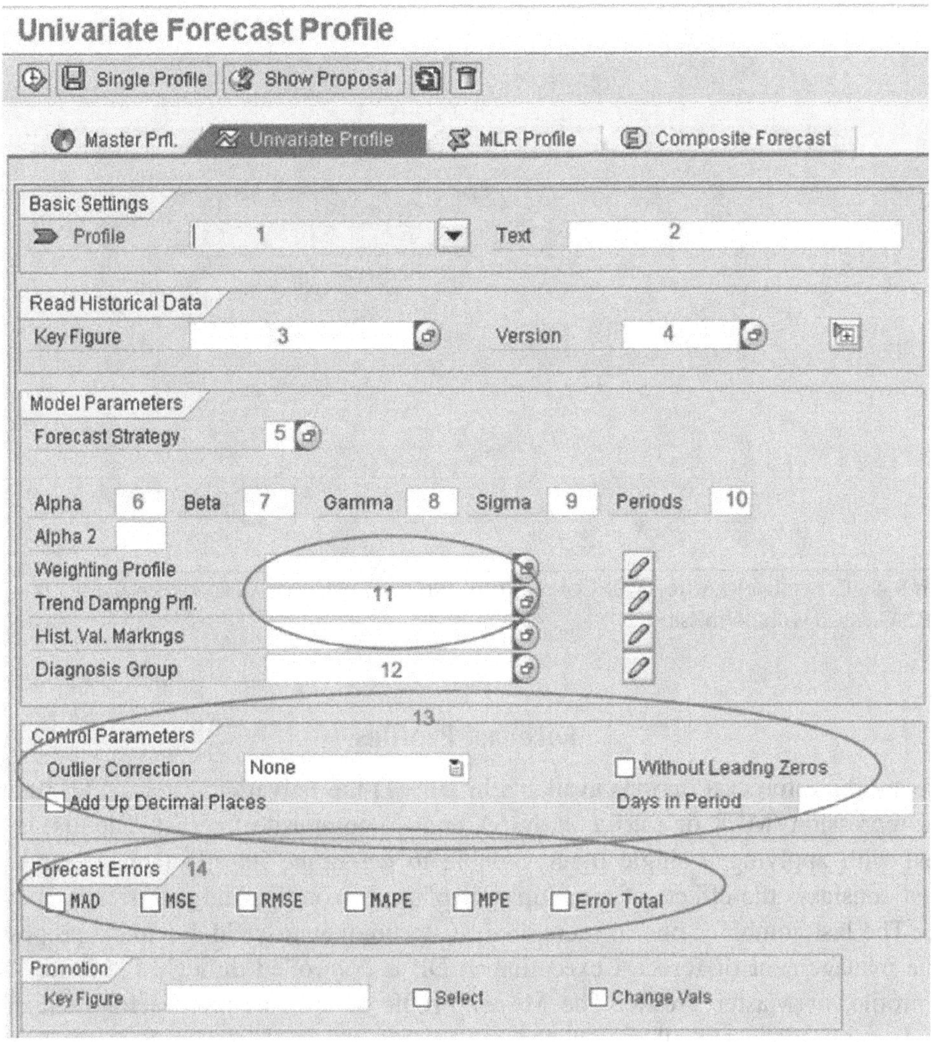

EXHIBIT 9.5 FORECAST PROFILE MAINTENANCE FOR THE UNIVARIATE FORECAST
© SAP AG. Used with permission.

Factor	Use	Instructions
Alpha	Smoothes the basic value in every time series forecast model that exponential smoothing is carried out on.	Make an entry for any alpha factor value other than 0.3.
Beta	Smoothes the trend value in a trend or seasonal trend model.	Make an entry for any beta factor value other than 0.3.
Gamma	Smoothes the seasonal index in a seasonal or seasonal trend model.	Make an entry for any gamma factor value other than 0.3.
Sigma	Correct outliers in the historical data on which the forecast is based. The smaller the sigma factor, the more values are identified as being outliers and are corrected.	SAP recommends a value between 0.6 and 2.0. Otherwise, a sigma factor of 1.25 is used automatically.

EXHIBIT 9.6   UNIVARIATE FACTORS

mode, first-order exponential smoothing, moving average, weighted moving average, and so forth. Use the online help for detailed explanations of the exact effects of each of these, and select one for the univariate profile in the "Forecast Strategy" field (Exhibit 9.5, step 5).

The forecast application requires specification of four *factors* and the number of periods (for seasonal trend models). Exhibit 9.6 addresses population of these factors (Exhibit 9.5, steps 6 to 10). Three fields, Weighting Profile, Trend Damping Profile, and Historical Value Markings, must all be populated if and only if strategy 14, Moving Weighted Average, is used (Exhibit 9.5, step 11). A Diagnosis group is applied for error grouping (Exhibit 9.5, step 12). Control parameters may be defined to manage outlier values—values that set outside expected tolerances (Exhibit 9.5, step 13).

When forecasts are carried out, various "errors" may be computed. Errors here are not so much errors in processing that result from master data setup issues or liveCache (as may be the case in planning runs in SNP and PP/DS) but are statistical values that, under some conditions, may illuminate a quality of the forecast computation. Select which of these errors to display in the Forecast Errors tab on forecast execution (Exhibit 9.5, step 14). When settings are complete, save the profile and assign it to a master profile.

Multiple Linear Regression

As with the univariate forecast profile, the MLR profile also requires a name. It can use a description and specification of a key figure and version from which the historical data values for its independent variables are acquired (Exhibit 9.7, steps 1 to 4). MLR model values of Measured Value Error (more completely: Method for Determining Measured Value Error), Sigma, and Diagnosis group should be maintained (Exhibit 9.7, steps 5 to 7). Measured Value Error concerns one of four possible methods for determining error: (1) normal distribution used with a constant standard deviation, (2) normal distribution used with a variable standard deviation, (3) standard deviation as the square root of the measured (historical) value of the dependent variable, and (4) blank, which causes the standard deviation to be twice the square root of the measured (historical) value of the dependent variable. The Sigma field should ordinarily be left with a value of 1 when a normal distribution is used with constant standard deviation unless there is good,

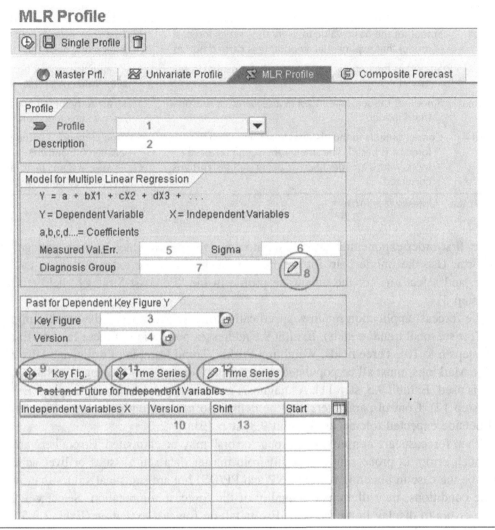

EXHIBIT 9.7   MULTIPLE LINEAR REGRESSION FORECAST PROFILE
© SAP AG. Used with permission.

known reason for it to be any other value. The Diagnosis Group groups measures of fit that are used to assess the quality of the MLR model. Diagnosis Groups can be created or maintained within this transaction by clicking the Change Diagnosis Group button (Exhibit 9.7, step 8). Finally, to apply MLR to generate a forecast one must specify the data elements with historical values whose trend values can be determined and applied to the forecast for the key figure. Select and apply these data elements to your model with the Key Figure button atop the table "Past and Future for Independent Variable" (Exhibit 9.7, step 9). Select a key figure from the resulting table and indicate the version that should be used (Exhibit 9.7, step 10; i.e., active or some other version). Also identify a time series during which data should be selected and/or created for the key figure(s) by clicking the Time Series Select and Create buttons and providing a name for the time series and a starting date, as well as the number of historical periods counting backward from start that may be included in the computation (Exhibit 9.7, steps 11 and 12). Here a time series may need to be defined on the spot to indicate the start date from which data should be collected. A lag time off the time series can be applied with the Shift field (Exhibit 9.7, step 13). Once all settings are applied, save the profile. As with a univariate forecast profile, a completed MLR profile should be assigned to a master profile for execution during interactive planning or combined with one or more other univariate or MLR forecast profiles in a composite profile, and then assigned to the master.

Composite Forecast

Use composite forecasts when it is desirable to incrementally apply the results of different forecast approaches to a demand value in order to derive a final combined outcome that systematically incorporates a multiplicity of weighted factors. Each factor or factor group can be set up as its own individual univariate or MLR forecast profile, then weighted and combined in sequence in the composite profile. Composite profiles require a name and may be given a description (Exhibit 9.8, steps 1 and 2). They also require a profile-specific classification called a *mode* (Exhibit 9.8, step 3). There are two classifications of modes available with a variety of subtypes possible for the nonstandard mode: (1) standard

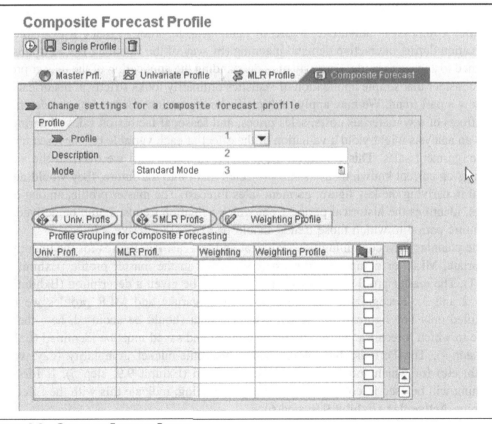

Exhibit 9.8   Composite Forecast Profile
© SAP AG. Used with permission.

and (2) Automatic Selection in Composite Forecasting. The standard mode carries out forecasts with profiles specified in the composite profile and totals the results, taking into account the weighting factors assigned to each listed univariate and MLR profile. With Automatic Selection in Composite Forecasting the composite profile contains several univariate profiles. Specify that, based on one measure of error, the system automatically selects the best profile from among those assigned. Select the measure of error that the system should use to make this determination at the time of mode assignment from among the error-types listed in the mode drop-down list.

Univariate and MLR profiles are assigned to the composite profile in the table "Profile Grouping for Composite Forecasting," which, like the MLR Independent Variables table, is populated using the buttons above it: Univariate Profiles, MLR Profiles, and Weighting Profile (Exhibit 9.8, steps 4 to 6). The buttons for univariate and MLR profiles will list available profiles for each forecast type and post them to the table below. Weighting profiles may be created in this transaction on the fly with the Weighting Profile button and affect the relative value that each listed univariate or MLR forecast will have on the overall forecast derivation. When all settings are made, save the composite forecast profile and assign it to a master profile for retrieval and application during interactive demand planning.

Master Forecast Profile

Whether a forecast is univariate, MLR, or composite, in order to make it available for application during interactive demand planning (by way of the Planning Book) it must be assigned to a master profile. One way of understanding the application of the master profile is to consider that simple application of statistics ordinarily looks strictly at historical data to show a past trend. We may apply multiple linear regression, for example, to determine the effects of raw materials costs, sales prices, and seasonal factors on sales of garments. Such an analysis might yield a valuation of the effect of each variable on our research key figure: garment sales. This would not be a useful forecast; until we overlaid the values findings on current known datasets and projected them into the future, they would not be useful in deriving the key figure: garment sales forecast. The master profile, among other things, identifies the historical period from which valuation trends should be derived and the future period to which those trends should be applied to derive a forecast.

The planning area containing the analytical and forecast key figures for the underlying univariate, MLR, or composite forecast is identified in the master profile (Exhibit 9.9, step 1). The master profile requires a name and may be given a description (Exhibit 9.9, steps 2 and 3). Recognizing that until now, in univariate and MLR profiles we have identified only key figures from which historical data should be acquired, here the key figure to which forecast analyses should be applied and saved must be identified (Exhibit 9.9, step 4). The Periodic Indicator specifies the time-bucket granularity (day, week, month, etc) for which forecasts should be generated (Exhibit 9.9, step 5). If lifecycle planning will be used in collusion with forecast planning, indicate this with the Lifecycle Planning Active flag (Exhibit 9.9, step 6).

Identify a forecast horizon for which a forecast should be generated on the forecast key figure (Exhibit 9.9, step 7) as well as the historical period from which trend data should

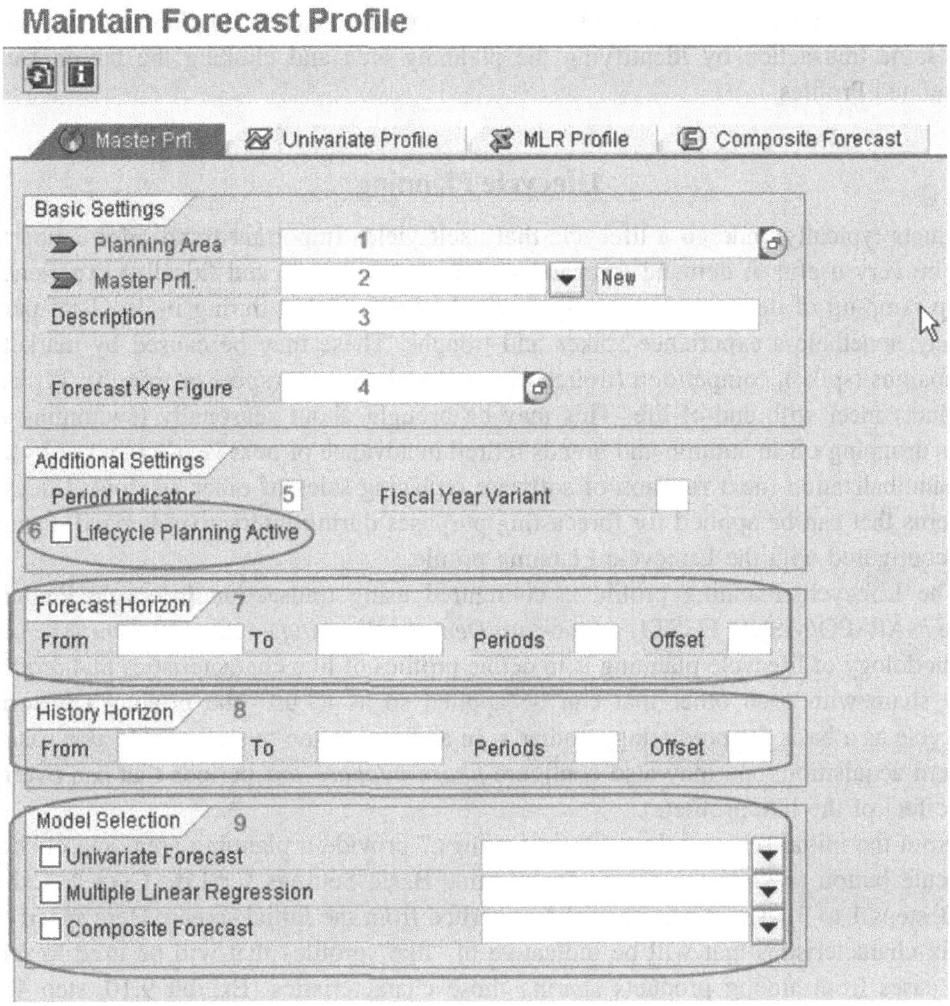

Maintain Forecast Profile

| Master Prfl. | Univariate Profile | MLR Profile | Composite Forecast |

Basic Settings

➡ Planning Area	1
➡ Master Prfl.	2	▼ New
Description	3

| Forecast Key Figure | 4 |

Additional Settings

| Period Indicator | 5 | Fiscal Year Variant |
| 6 ☐ Lifecycle Planning Active |

Forecast Horizon 7

| From | | To | | Periods | | Offset | |

History Horizon 8

| From | | To | | Periods | | Offset | |

Model Selection 9

☐ Univariate Forecast ▼
☐ Multiple Linear Regression ▼
☐ Composite Forecast ▼

EXHIBIT 9.9 MASTER FORECAST PROFILE
© SAP AG. Used with permission.

be analyzed (Exhibit 9.9, step 8). Finally, select which univariate, MLR, and composite forecasts will be available as selections when this master profile is called from a DP planning book (Exhibit 9.9, step 9).

Assigning Forecast Profiles to a Selection

Once defined, forecast profiles must be assigned to a dataset in order to be available for interactive planning. This activity is carried out with the transaction, Assign Forecast Profiles to a Selection using code /SAPAPO/MSDP_FCST2, also on path *Demand Planning → Environment*. Minimal settings are to assign a planning area to which a whole profile may be assigned. Forecasts may be limited in application to specific subsets of the planning area or to a planning area in a nonactive version by assigning a selection. The selections available here will be those saved as selection IDs in the Planning Book following the process for creating selection IDs described in the Planning Book section in Chapter 8. Assignments of obsolete profiles can be deleted from planning areas using this same transaction by identifying the planning area and clicking the button Delete Generated Profiles.

Lifecycle Planning

Products typically undergo a lifecycle that itself yields important trend information that can be very useful to demand forecasting. They are released and (ideally) experience a steep ramp-up of demand. Eventually demand levels off, but during its level-off period it may nonetheless experience spikes and troughs. These may be caused by marketing campaigns (spike), competition (trough), or seasonal patterns (spike or trough). Typically products meet with end-of-life. This may be brought about seasonally (swimming suit sales dropping off in autumn and brands retired in advance of next year's runs) or by way of cannibalization (next revision of software replacing sales of older version). Lifecycle patterns that can be applied for forecasting purposes during interactive demand planning are configured with the Lifecycle Planning profile.

The Lifecycle Planning profile is configured using transaction Lifecycle Planning, code /SAPAPO/MSDP_FCST1, on the path *Demand Planning → Environment*. The basic methodology of lifecycle planning is to define profiles of like characteristics that products may share with each other that can be applied so as to use one product's historical lifecycle as a basis for predicting another's. In addition to the overall profile as a basis of pattern acquisition, one may also configure *phase-in/phase-out* periods that can override the effect of the like profile(s).

From the initial screen select "Basic Settings," provide a planning area, and click the Execute button to view the screen for "Define Basic Settings for Life Cycle" (Exhibit 9.10, steps 1 to 3). The planning area is inherited from the initial screen. Here specify up to six characteristics that will be indicative of "like" profiles that will be used to select like cases from among products sharing those characteristics (Exhibit 9.10, step 4). If lifecycles may be attributed to aggregated groups (i.e., if the lifecycle of a product may be applied to the lifecycle of a product group), then indicate so here by selecting the flag for "Aggregated Lifecycle Planning with Like Profiles" (Exhibit 9.10, step 5). If aggregated planning is available for phase-in/phase-out profiles, that flag must be indicated here separately (Exhibit 9.10, step 6). Click the Execute button to adopt the changes (Exhibit 9.10, step 7).

Once characteristics that select for life profiles are selected, like profiles themselves should be created. On the initial screen for the Lifecycle Planning profile, select "Assignments" and click the Like Profiles button (Exhibit 9.10, steps 8 and 9). As before, the planning area from the initial screen is inherited (Exhibit 9.11, step 1). Use this resulting screen to attach characteristics to profiles and configure them for select behaviors. Select a characteristic using the pull-down and resulting dialog window (Exhibit 9.11, steps 2 and 3). Next select a profile from the pull-down window or else manually key in a value for a new one if none exists (Exhibit 9.11, steps 4 and 5). From here populate reference values to influence the lifecycle trend based on reference cases (Exhibit 9.11, step 6). Either of two "actions" may be assigned to control how the reference value is assigned to

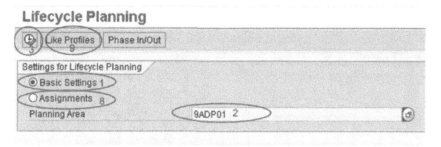

Lifecycle Planning

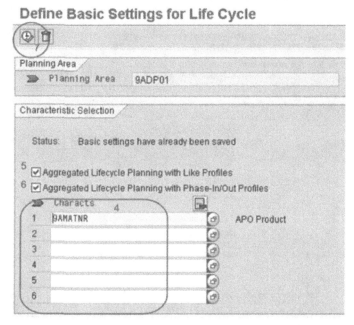

Define Basic Settings for Life Cycle

EXHIBIT 9.10 LIFECYCLE PLANNING: BASIC SETTINGS
© SAP AG. Used with permission.

influence the lifecycle: "A" (average values) and "S" (sum) (Exhibit 9.11, step 7). When A is selected, the historical average value for all reference products with the value of "A" is used to determine the lifecycle trend. When S is selected, the weighted (relative) value of all reference products with a value of "S" is applied where weight scores are acquired through the field for proportional factor (Exhibit 9.11, step 8). Note that these are relative values, so they may add up to more than 100. Time-phase or otherwise restrict the aggregate historical computation of weighted values using the Weighted Profile (Exhibit 9.11, step 9). Time series may be defined for the Weighted Profile field by clicking the Pencil button (Exhibit 9.11, step 10). Click the Execute button when finished making changes (Exhibit 9.11, step 11).

The Like Profiles of lifecycle planning may be overlaid with controlled product phase-in/phase-out ramps. From the initial screen of Lifecycle Planning, select "Assignments" and click the Phase In/Out button, which will open the Time Series Maintenance screen. As with other screens the planning area is inherited from the initial screen (Exhibit 9.12,

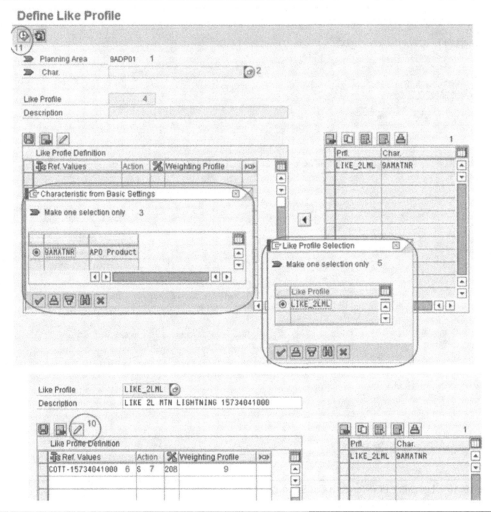

EXHIBIT 9.11 LIFECYCLE PROFILE: "LIKE PROFILES"
© SAP AG. Used with permission.

step 1). Select a time series from the Time Series drop-down or enter the name of one to create a new one (Exhibit 9.12, steps 2 and 3). A time series here will be configured to address specifically the product ramp-up or ramp-down. Enter the start and end dates for the ramp and the time-bucket type for which computations should be conducted (Exhibit 9.12, steps 4 to 6). A constant growth or decay value may be entered as percentages by selecting the appropriate indicator for either "Before start date, apply constant factor" or "After start date, apply constant factor" (Exhibit 9.12, steps 7 to 10). On making this selection and setting a factor, press Enter and the periods identified with the start date, end date, and period fields will populate in the "Maintain Values" table (Exhibit 9.12, step 11). Once the time series starts, the values maintained in the "Vals" column for this table take over for the periods indicated. Assign growth or decay values as appropriate and click the Adopt button to save (Exhibit 9.12, steps 12 and 13).

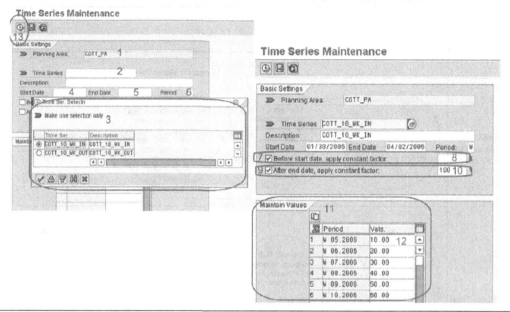

EXHIBIT 9.12   LIFECYCLE PLANNING: PHASE-IN/PHASE-OUT TIME SERIES MAINTENANCE
© SAP AG. Used with permission.

Finally, as with forecast profiles, lifecycle profiles must be assigned to a planning area and more specifically to individual products. This is conducted from the initial screen of the Lifecycle Planning transaction by selecting "Assignment" and clicking the Execute button once Like Profiles have been set and saved. With all profiles in place this is a relatively straightforward task where one assigns the product for which a lifecycle will be applied, the Like Profile containing the lifecycle histories, and phase-in and phase-out profiles with from and to dates for each. Click the Adopt button to apply changes, save, and exit.

DEMAND PLANNING CONFIGURATION RECIPE

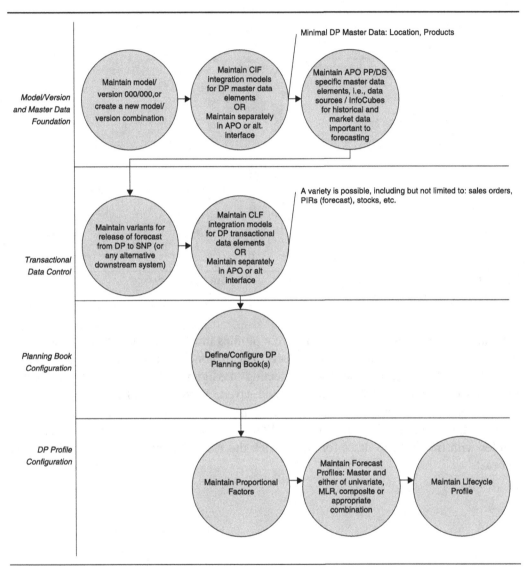

EXHIBIT 9.13   DP CONFIGURATION RECIPE

10

SUPPLY NETWORK PLANNING

The APO SNP module may be employed to meet the needs of either sales and operations planning (SOP) or master scheduling: in the former case for medium-range organizational planning and in the latter for medium-range product-family (or more detailed) planning for sites on the production route for the product family or else for individual productive sites including factories, distribution centers, ports, and so forth. Whichever way it is applied, supply network planning (SNP) is primarily a medium-range planning tool. As APO modules come, it is the most pure planning tool, where detailed planning (DP) may be applied for forecasting and production planning and detailed scheduling (PP/DS) may be applied for some level of execution control; APO lies strictly in the planning space.

The medium-range horizon that is the province of APO is inclusive of the horizons found within it. That is, while subject to organizational requirements, the most common horizons for APO will be 3 to 6, 3 to 9, and 3 to 12 months, with the tactical horizon falling within the first three months in either case but with specific applications (i.e., two to four months) varying normally according to the length of product delivery lead-time (i.e., the amount of time required to acquire inventory for use in production through purchasing). The tactical horizon, whether two, three, four months, or whatever, is visible to SNP. The caveat is that while ordinarily visible, the tactical horizon is normally off-limits to SNP functionality; that is, SNP will apply its tools to plan for the medium-range horizon (e.g., three to nine months) and it will have visibility to the tactical horizon (i.e., the three inside months), but its tools will be configured not to affect scheduling for those tactical months. An exception is that when used together with PP/DS, SNP and PP/DS can be configured to account for a limited overlap period where both systems make schedule proposals and a planner is left to select which one to use.

Supply network planning in many respects represents the culmination of everything that people believe is special about APO in general. Though DP contains all of the most advanced best-known method (BKM) capabilities for demand management and forecast while providing access to the powerful BW data basis, its primary contribution is to be a union of these two overall features together with wider integration with the other APO modules. Forecast BKMs, online analytical processing (OLAP) data warehouses, and integration, individually, in and of themselves do not constitute a perfectly new way of going about demand management. On the other side, PP/DS has use of a heuristic planning run, that is, a planning run that can propose a multisite build/buy schedule based on sophisticated business rules, as well as a limited optimizer that will optimize

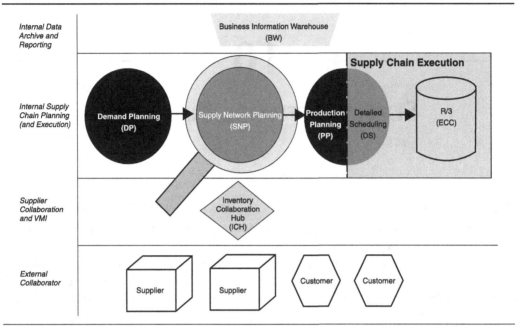

EXHIBIT 10.1   SNP IN THE SUPPLY CHAIN CONTEXT
SNP is the first point in the supply chain where constraints are introduced to the planning process. Having received an unconstrained, resource-allocated demand plan from DP, SNP applies known constraints to build a *network* master schedule that aligns supply network resources in advance of procurement and production execution.

a short-term order-assignment schedule without proposing new orders. Both of these are powerful capabilities and certainly represent something evolutionary in terms of tactical and detailed scheduling applications, but nonetheless fall short of the most powerful combination of features available in APO. That combination comes to the fore in SNP.

Supply network planning brings to bear three planning run engines that may be used individually or in combination: heuristic, capable-to-match (CTM), and the optimizer. As with PP/DS, the heuristic engine applies rules, very similar to standard Materials Requirements Planning (MRP), to plan and propose a schedule. Capable-to-Match takes this a step further and applies priorities and is wise to capacity constraints at resources or work centers. Optimization may similarly apply priorities and recognize capacity constraints, but it uses costs to control priorities and recognizes capacity constraints at storage locations and on transportation lanes, above and beyond work centers. Very often a combination of heuristics with the CTM or heuristics with the optimizer will render the best planning solution.

With these powerful planning engines SNP remakes the planning landscape for SOP and master scheduling. Before SNP this landscape was characterized by organizational goal-setting and coordinated calendaring supported by limited MRP runs. The most important "pre-SNP" characteristic is that without a modeling tool SOP and master scheduling had to be conducted in three separate tasks: (1) supply planning (i.e., procurement planning), (2) capacity planning, and (3) production planning—all combined to make for the discipline of master scheduling, yielding a master production schedule. While these three processes could be done in parallel or sequentially or both, in any case iteratively feeding each other, without the aid of a sophisticated supply chain modeling tool they could not be conducted ideally: simultaneously. Supply network planning changes that. An organization's supply network that is modeled as master and transactional data in APO can be subjected to one or more of SNP's powerful planning run tools to plan supply, capacity, and production all at the same time. A fully powered, fully deployed model and optimizer, therefore, may provide for cross-geography, cross-site planning on a scale of combined breadth and detail that has never previously been known to planning and logistics.

SNP MASTER DATA AND CIF

Model Setup

Several SNP-specific settings are available at the level of model definition. If used these should, of course, minimally be addressed for active model/version 000/000, but may additionally be applied to any inactive model that might be created for simulation.

Master Data

Supply network planning primarily employs supply chain master data (Chapter 5). Though not dependent on analytical master data for its core planning run functions, some familiarity there will prove useful in understanding the planning object structures and planning areas that are at the core of the Planning Book, SNP's favored user interface (UI). Minimal supply chain master data for SNP includes:

- Location(s)
- Calendar
- Products
- Resources
- Production Process Models

Any SNP deployment using more than one site—which ordinarily should be almost all SNP deployments—will additionally require Transportation Lanes and their requisite External Procurement Relationships and Quota Arrangements. In other words, therefore, the full volley of supply chain master data and a dabbling of analytical master data will be necessary for almost every SNP deployment.

Core interface (CIF) integration models for SNP master data will vary between those that can be run once and otherwise ad hoc versus those that may require batch control. Locations, resources, and potentially transportation lanes will probably not require regular batch reruns as these objects should be fairly stable. In fact, the introduction of any new such objects to the supply chain network model should probably be carried out deliberately and not be subject to automatic extension. Conversely products, production process models (PPMs), external procurement relationships (EPRs), and quota arrangements are more subject to common business change processes and their integration models may require batch management. In most organizations, for example, products are regularly added and removed from active production; it will be desirable to have these added and removed from integration models in APO in as close concert with their R/3 changes as possible. Daily or several-times-daily batch processes inactivating relevant integration models, creating new ones, and activating them will suffice to keep APO and R/3 in alignment.

While location data is mostly maintained in R/3 and received via one-way master data CIF into APO, there are some APO-specific settings for SNP on an SNP-specific tab in the APO Location Master, though several of these relate to SNP's role in deployment, which falls outside our immediate scope. APO calendars must be assigned to the Location Master in addition to the CIF. Additionally, a wide variety of SNP-specific settings are available in the Product Master that are not maintainable through the CIF, especially on the SNP 1 and SNP 2 tabs; we address the use of these in Chapter 5. It is not unusual for SNP deployments to find uses for settings in the Demand and Lot Size tabs of the Location Master that also are unavailable for CIF. Generally on SNP deployments it will be necessary to conduct a careful, rigorous, element-by-element review of Product Master settings to derive which is necessary, which is not, which is subject to maintenance through CIF, and which must be maintained separately in APO. Recall, too, that PPMs that are CIF'd from R/3 are received in APO as PP/DS PPMs and must undergo a conversion for use by SNP (for more information see Chapter 7).

Transactional CIFs

Any kind of transactional data available to the CIF may be relevant for an SNP deployment. Exactly which particular data elements are relevant is subject to the specific organizational design and business objectives. Thus any kind of stock information in R/3 may be necessary as supply inputs to SNP as well as any kind of order. In the latter case, orders may include planned independent requirements, planned orders and purchase requisitions, in addition to sales orders, purchase orders, and production orders. Sales orders and planned independent requirements will come over as elements of demand while the other orders will come over as elements of supply. Initial population of these elements into APO from the CIF will be based on their status in R/3; however, transactional data is two-way in the CIF. Hence, changes made to transactional data in APO SNP in the active model and version, 000/000, will return to R/3 in real time. For this reason many organizations will find it desirable or necessary to create simulation models and versions where R/3 data can be transferred and so that SNP analysis can be conducted without affecting production data in the transactional system. Only after commitment decisions are made would such data be returned to the active model and version and subsequently CIF'd back to R/3.

USING SNP

As with DP and PP/DS, as a highly configurable system exact details of SNP designs and deployments will vary from organization to organization. Our intent is to examine the foundational process here and leave guidance for customization. First, SNP must be fed with a demand plan or forecast, which may originate in either APO DP or another legacy planning system (Exhibit 10.2, step 1). This will be an *unconstrained* forecast in that

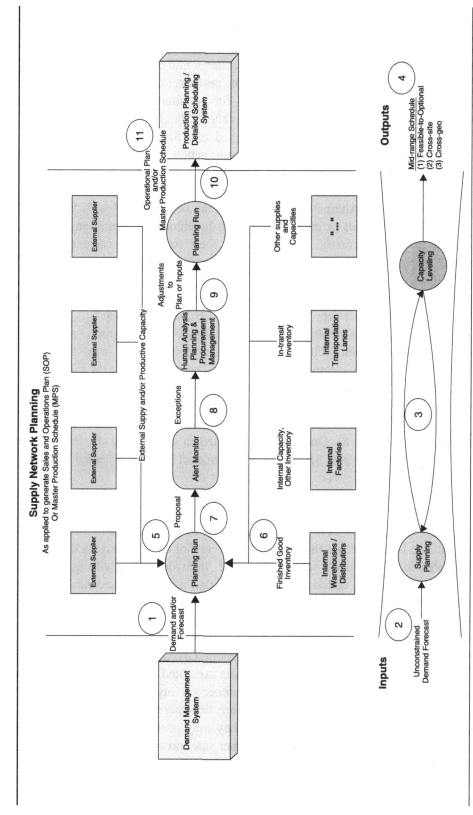

EXHIBIT 10.2 SUPPLY NETWORK PLANNING PROCESS

SNP will ordinarily be the first part of the planning supply chain where constraints such as supply or capacity are applied to level a plan (Exhibit 10.2, step 2). Using a variety of inputs, system-based and human processes that typically will be applied iteratively and reciprocally (Exhibit 10.2, step 3), SNP generates a mid-range schedule with several characteristics (Exhibit 10.2, step 4). If CTM or the optimizer are used it should be at least feasible and potentially optimal. It may be single-site but almost always will be cross-site or cross-geography. In fact, to justify the investment, it should be either or both.

External supply can be modeled and/or received into SNP by a variety of methods. For one, suppliers and subcontractors and their work center capacities and transportation lanes can of course be modeled as master data based on known data. For example, it may be known that a supplier is committed to provide a certain service-level of capacity according to time periods. Alternatively, suppliers may be connected with SNP directly through its collaboration tools or indirectly through Inventory Collaboration Hub (ICH), enabling them to provide current information on their supply and capacity situations (Exhibit 10.2, step 5; more on both of these in Chapter 12). Supply network planning, of course, will require internal supply feeds with respect to any ordinary internal sources of supply, including but not limited to finished goods inventory, raw-materials inventory, productive capacity, in-transit supplies, and so forth (Exhibit 10.2, step 6).

Supply network planning combines its demand signal with its supply and capacity constraints in a planning run, which we have indicated may be by way of heuristics, CTM, the optimizer, or some combination thereof. The planning run in turn generates schedule proposals in the form of planned orders and purchase requisitions (Exhibit 10.2, step 7). Ordinarily the Alert Monitor will then be configured to examine planning run outputs for threshold conditions that require intervention by production or purchasing planners (Exhibit 10.2, step 8). Outputs are examined in detail using the Product View and the Planning Book (Chapter 8); note that the Product View is accessed through the PP/DS navigation path.

Supply network planning, being concerned with medium-range planning, will not ordinarily require analysis of data at a particularly atomic level of detail. The Planning Book is a favored user interface for SNP because it may be used to execute a number of SNP functions, but also because it is a time-series-based view of data, portraying data in quantities aggregated to time buckets spread over time. Individual cells with quantities can be double-clicked to peg to underlying orders, but that is strictly a secondary view. At times, order-based data will nonetheless be important to analysis in SNP, and whenever this is the case, use of the Product View is appropriate.

Presented with exceptions from the planning run, planners have a variety of options all subject to their faculty for qualitative human judgment. Given an order that is unsupported by supplies, they may contact a supplier and request expedited service for the procurement of additional raw materials, which may be negotiated on any basis from price to favor. They may check into storage locations and assure that there is not undisclosed supply that is not visible to the system. Conversely, they may push out the order, contacting customers and engaging in negotiation on the other side: proposing some supply on time and some a little later, or offering substitutions or lower prices, and so on.

Based on these kinds of qualitative, unique, human activities, planners may make adjustments to the planning run output in the Planning Book (Exhibit 10.2, step 9).

They may furthermore engage in simulation—trying out alternative scenarios of pulling in and pushing out production, based for example on varying demand priorities. Upon application of their adjustments ordinarily the planning run will be executed once again to generate a finalized production schedule (Exhibit 10.2, step 10). In its finalized form this schedule is passed on to the tactical planning system, which may be APO PP/DS or a legacy product (Exhibit 10.2, step 11).

Supply network planning orders will ordinarily remain planned orders for the purpose of production, and either purchase requisitions or scheduling agreement schedule lines for the purpose of procurement. Schedule lines execute on their own schedule, as it is, but planned orders and purchase requisitions will not ordinarily graduate to a more firmed status until their delivery dates pass into the tactical horizon. We address firming more with PP/DS, but for SNP, middle-range planning purposes, generally the greatest flexibility is desirable to assure maximum replanning flexibility based on changing network supply chain conditions.

CONFIGURING SNP

Planning Run Overview and Comparisons

The intention of each SNP planning run engine is to apply quantitative analytics against a supply network model to generate a schedule proposal. Recall that SNP's schedule proposals are distinct in that they are mid-range, include production and procurement planning simultaneously, and include supply/demand analysis as well as supply and capacity constraint analysis simultaneously for an entire supply network, which may include several sites, an entire geography, or the global supply chain complex. Demand Planning and SNP alike are intended as "big fish" solutions; though while DP can probably be profitably employed for demand forecasting at lower levels of magnitude, the same cannot be said of SNP. Generally speaking, the smaller the network, the more likely that SNP is a solution overkill.

Supply network planning's three native planning run engines, heuristics, CTM, and the optimizer, can be used individually or in combination and may correspondingly be understood as crawling, walking, and running from the point of view of relative complexity. Moreover, we cannot overemphasize that from the point of view of organizational development with APO and the consequent adoption of advanced planning methods, these should be genuinely embraced as developmental stages, not unlike the image of the growing child that "crawl, walk, run" is supposed to evoke. It is genuinely more difficult to adopt CTM than heuristics, and optimization than CTM. Organizations still making the shift from yesteryear's manual planning methodologies will be well counseled to exercise deliberation and caution and avoid overreaching during initial deployments.

As with PP/DS, the heuristic-based planning run is a *rule-based* engine: It applies business rules to generate a proposed schedule. Readers familiar with materials requirements planning (MRP) engines from traditional enterprise resource planning (ERP) systems would do well to compare MRP closely with heuristics as they follow essentially identical principles of application. The heuristic planning run recognizes supply constraints and responds to them by proposing purchase requisitions for procurement of raw materials to cover materials shortages and planned orders for production of finished goods to cover sales shortages. It does not take priorities or capacity limitations into account. The outcome of a heuristics planning run, therefore, will be a supply-feasible schedule that is not necessarily capacity feasible. When used without the combination of CTM or the optimizer, a capacity analysis effort must be undertaken separately from the heuristic run and the results combined manually to yield a feasible schedule.

This process does not differ considerably from pre-APO SOP and master scheduling procedures except that heuristics takes the planning run a step beyond MRP and proposes schedules for finished goods. Heuristic planning runs are valuable for two reasons: (1) Initially they are necessary as an *organizational* learning step to the adoption and exploitation of advanced planning systems, and (2) in the long run they are extremely powerful when used in tandem with CTM or optimization—filling in an aggregate-analysis space for which neither of the latter two engines is well suited. Hence, while the optimizer is the most powerful planning run in and of itself, the optimizer and heuristics used in tandem will yield the most powerful automated planning solution.

There is a wide variety of off-the-shelf heuristics provided with APO, and custom heuristics can always be configured. In this respect the heuristic engine is a considerably more powerful tool than the MRP engine from which it is descended. Additionally, more than one heuristic can be applied on a given heuristic run. We repeatedly caution, however, that developers should not get carried away with the use of heuristics. Each heuristic added in combination with another during a given heuristic run will substantially increase its analytical complexity. Moreover, eventually a law-of-diminishing-returns is reached where lobbing more and more heuristics into a heuristic run does nothing to meaningfully improve planning, while considerably tying up processing resources. We advise no more than five to eight heuristics on any given heuristic run definition.

WORD TO THE WISE

Do not begrudge "organizational learning" when planning APO adoption (or adoption of any advanced planning system for that matter). It is easy to think of learning in terms of individuals learning, and it may be tempting when thinking of learning exclusively this way to believe that the individuals in one's organization are specially endowed with unusual intelligence and capable of enormous feats when challenged. That may be true, but to focus exclusively on one's smart employees or team members and ignore organizational requirements for learning is to invite peril when adopting APO, especially with SNP. Supply network planning requires new habits of communication and cooperation at a team level and often even a geographical-area level that really must be acquired through practice and time; rote, individual knowledge acquisition will not suffice. Given time to absorb how APO goes about planning differently—simultaneously planning supply and capacity for whole geographies at many hierarchical levels, in contrast to the sequential and iterative methods of the past—employees will begin to appreciate that they have at their fingertips something *new*. Appreciation, acquired through time and practice, will yield to imagination for the expanded world of opportunity provided by APO. This acquired imagination, far more than rote learning or executive command, will foment change and the adoption of twenty-first-century advanced planning methods.

The Capable-to-Match (CTM) engine differs from heuristics in that it takes both priorities and capacities into account when generating a schedule. Note that it does not take costs into account and it settles on the first feasible solution, where *feasible* is understood as a schedule that fulfills demand with available supplies within known capacity constraints. As such, CTM is looking for a *capable* potentiality, taking it a step beyond heuristics, which generates a schedule fulfilling demand but one for which an organization may not be capable. However, unlike the optimizer, CTM stops as soon as it arrives at a supply- and capacity-feasible schedule, so the CTM-proposed schedule, though feasible, is not optimal.

The optimizer goes beyond both heuristics and CTM and applies linear programming based on studiously maintained costs that provide a quantitative model of the supply network that goes considerably beyond the basic qualitative modeling addressed in Chapter 5. There are hundreds of costs one can maintain for the optimizer to consider, ranging from costs associated with transportation lanes to procurement and production to costs of delivery, delivery delays, and nondelivery. As with adding heuristics to the heuristic run, adding excessive cost to an optimization run is an area where developers and APO adopters have been known to go wrong.

Acquiring and Processing Demand

DP Release of Demand to SNP

Before SNP goes to work on data, the process of demand management including demand forecast and planning should be concluded. By design this occurs in APO DP but sources of demand for SNP will often vary according to the state of APO deployment in an organization. When using DP, demand is released to SNP using the transaction /SAPAPO/MC90, Release Demand Planning to Supply Network Planning, found on path *Demand Planning → Planning → Release*. To carry out the release, indicate which demand value to send to SNP by choosing from a planning area, planning version, and the specific demand key figure (Exhibit 10.3, step 1). Also include the planning area for the target of the release; for example, one may initially release demand to an inactive version for simulation and then release to the active version once plan-of-record determinations are made (Exhibit 10.3, step 2). Specify the time horizon for the release and apply filters for the scope of data element objects to be released (i.e., locations and products) (Exhibit 10.3, step 3). Click the Extended button to further specify a Requirements Strategy (Exhibit 10.3, steps 4 and 5). When releases are conducted in batch, their settings must be saved as a variant. See instructions for saving PP/DS planning run settings in Chapter 8 for the detail of saving variants. For cases where multiple demand line key figures are sent to SNP, more than one release variant should be set and saved.

Requirements Strategies

There are two sources of Requirements Strategy for SNP: the setting in the DP release or the Product Master setting for individual products, the latter of which is applied when the DP release is not. Requirements Strategies are configured in the Requirements Strategy Profile on transaction Define SNP Requirements Strategies in path *Supply Network Planning → Environment → Current Settings → Profiles*. These strategies, often called "Planning Strategies" in industry, control the demand fulfillment method that SNP will

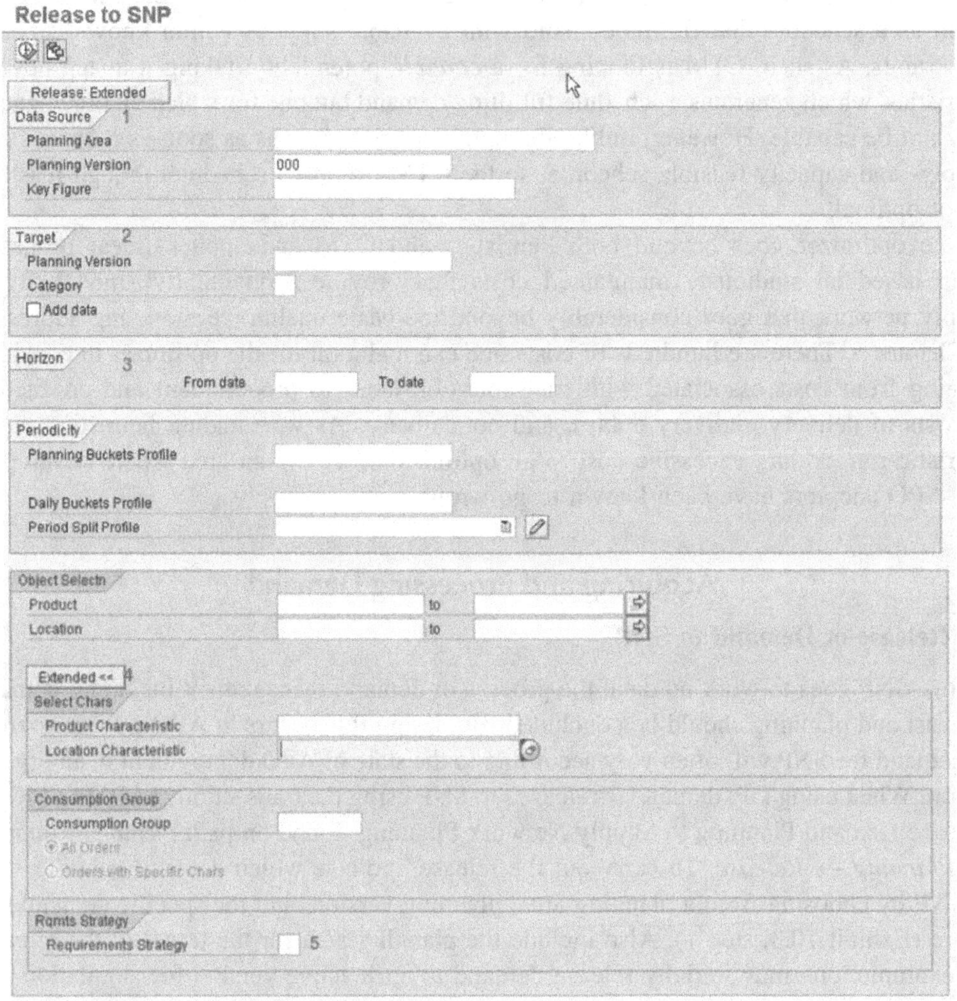

Release to SNP

Release: Extended

Data Source   1
  Planning Area
  Planning Version   000
  Key Figure

Target   2
  Planning Version
  Category
  ☐ Add data

Horizon   3
        From date   To date

Periodicity
  Planning Buckets Profile

  Daily Buckets Profile
  Period Split Profile

Object Selectn
  Product   to
  Location   to

Extended <<   4
Select Chars
  Product Characteristic
  Location Characteristic

Consumption Group
  Consumption Group
  ◉ All Orders
  ○ Orders with Specific Chars

Rqmts Strategy
  Requirements Strategy   5

EXHIBIT 10.3   DP RELEASE OF DEMAND TO SNP
This DP transaction is necessary both to provide demand for SNP and to control the demand fulfillment strategy. © SAP AG. Used with permission.

apply when addressing shortages created by new demand with as-yet unfulfilled demand. They are similar in effect to the Strategy Profiles of PP/DS, yet are more explicitly defined and follow the same patterns as their closely related MRP cousins in R/3.

Off-the-shelf SAP provides four Requirements Strategies, as follows:

- *Strategy 10:* Make-to-Stock
- *Strategy 20:* Planning with Final Assembly
- *Strategy 30:* Planning without Final Assembly
- *Strategy 40:* Planning Product

Additional profiles can be defined for custom use and as always we recommend copying the original off-the-shelf profiles and then working from them as a starting point, while never changing settings in the off-the-shelf versions. Requirements Strategies may essentially be understood as follows. Make-to-Stock can be thought of as the fast-food approach to manufacturing. Fast-food restaurants have a series of pre-made products, each with given specifications. These are made continuously, shelved, and left to the customer to order at which time they are immediately pulled of the shelf and delivered. Make-to-Order (not an explicit off-the-shelf strategy but we'll get to that in a minute) may be thought of as the exact polar opposite of make-to-stock, wherein manufacturing is more like a gourmet restaurant. Here a list of entrées is provided on a menu but a customer may make very specific requests of how to prepare the meal as well as what to include, not include, or add. Between these two extremes is Plan without Final Assembly. This method could be thought of as a standard Chinese restaurant approach. The Chinese restaurant also provides a menu with a variety of entrées that are not prepared until the customer orders. Yet in the back, in the kitchen, vats are boiling and grills simmering with bamboo shoots, scallions, water chestnuts, baby corn, carrots, chicken, beef, pork, and so on. When the customer places an order these precooked ingredients are combined at the last minute to serve to the customer what is an otherwise transparently "custom" request. Strategies 20, 30, and 40 all amount to some variety of make-to-order or plan-without-final-assembly approach, each with mildly different flavors. Exact application will vary generally depending on the nature of demand (i.e., how well or poorly can demand be forecasted?), as well as the nature of the product (i.e., is the product suitable to custom order?).

Configuring for Heuristics

Begin SNP heuristic configuration in the IMG along the path *Advanced Planning and Optimization → Supply Chain Planning → Supply Network Planning → Basic Settings → Maintain Global Settings*. Here in the Profile:Active field indicate whether this profile will be available for all planning run varieties by setting it to "Active," or not, by setting it to "Inactive." If set to Inactive, separate profiles are necessary for each planning run variety applied. The heuristics run will take into account a number of settings on this screen, in particular: (1) SNP: GR for Planned Orders, (2) SNP: Scrap, and (3) all fields prefixed by "HEU."

The default global profile is "SAP." When only this profile exists, the transaction immediately steps to the maintenance window. View the "Change" window where new profiles may be defined by clicking Cancel from the maintenance window. There, click New Entries to define new global profiles that may be applied separately by different instances of the SNP planning run. Achieve a similar effect by simply clicking the New Entries button, which will open a nameless profile window with original settings defaulted to the "SAP" case.

An SNP heuristic planning run may be carried out from within the Planning Book or else in a transaction that runs in the background that may be executed either ad hoc or in batch, though of course in ordinary production environments the background method will probably be disallowed for end-users. At the time of Planning Book configuration developers must specify whether the Planning Book will be for SNP or DP. SNP Planning Books display Location and Network buttons, which will apply the heuristic either to the specific location or to the entire planning network defined in the open model and planning version.

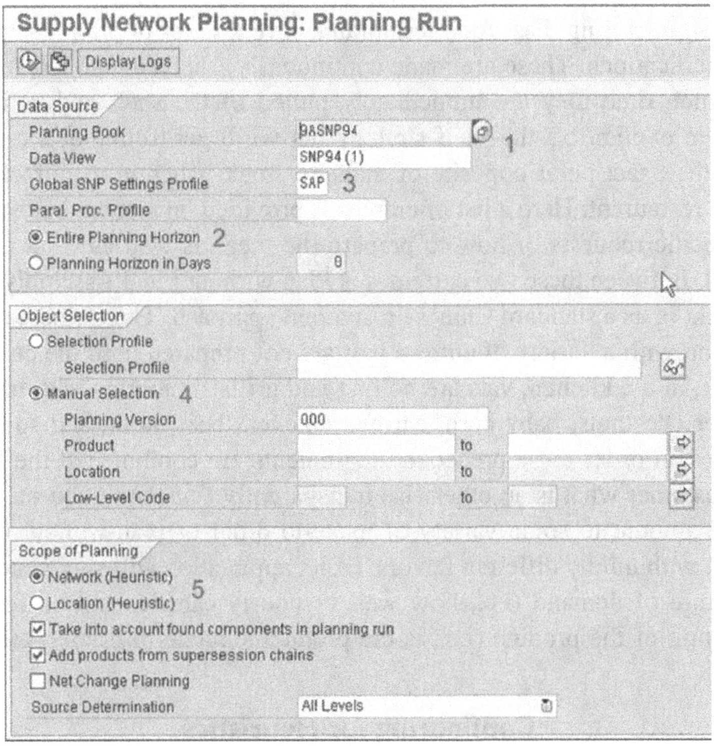

EXHIBIT 10.4 HEURISTIC PLANNING RUN IN THE BACKGROUND
© SAP AG. Used with permission.

For a background heuristic planning run use the transaction /SAPAPO/SNP01, Supply Network Planning in the Background, found on path *Supply Network Planning → Planning → Supply Network Planning in the Background*. Specify a Planning Book and Data View to account for the scope of planning as it includes fields to consider for supply and demand as well as effective time horizon, which may be either the entire horizon of the Planning Book or one that is specified in the run itself (Exhibit 10.4, steps 1 and 2). The Global Settings Profile addressed earlier must also be specified (Exhibit 10.4, step 3). Objects to apply the run to (i.e., which locations to include) are specified in the Object Selection box (Exhibit 10.4, step 4). An object selection profile may be defined and referenced here, but it is unnecessary to do so as long as the planning run settings are saved as a variant. One must also indicate whether the run should be location or network based (Exhibit 10.4, step 5). A location-based run will be limited exclusively to locations specified in the object box while a network run will expand out to plan supply to meet demand for every node found along the PPM or PDS models found in the executing model and version.

Settings for the background heuristic planning run are not saved as a profile but instead should be saved as a variant. As with the release variant, see the planning run configuration section for PP/DS in Chapter 8 for instructions. Settings should be saved as variants whether they will be used ad hoc or in batch. In ad hoc cases one will of course want to rely on tested and proven settings and will not wish to be exposed to the human data-entry error that may occur when resetting fields. Additionally, it is always important simply to remember past lessons. Batch execution requires that settings be saved in variant.

Configuring for Capable-to-Match (CTM)

As with so much other configuration, CTM settings begin in master data on the Product Master. In a CTM box in the SNP2 tab of the Product Master there are three potential CTM configuration fields: Demand Selection Horizon, Order Creation Frame, and Time-based Priority. Use the first two fields if time horizons for demand selection or order creation are to be any different from the CTM horizon defined later in the CTM profile. Select Time-based Priority to deactivate the default product-based priority that CTM will apply and replace it with a time-based approach that is explicitly concerned with timely delivery rather than product priority rank. This setting can be used only if a CTM definition has already been established that specifies in the Demands tab the use of the MPRIO criterion for demand rather than MRANK. If Time-based Priority is not selected and product-based defaults are preserved, set the product rank in the Priority field.

Capable-to-Match can run on all master data in a model or on a specified subset. Use the transaction /SAPAPO/CTMMSEL, Master Data Selection, on the path *Multilevel Supply & Demand Matching → Environment* to create and save master data filters that can be called upon later by CTM runs to limit their application. A similar selection filter profile may be defined on the same node, the Order Selection filter. This profile may be used for supply or demand selections with separate filters defined and saved for later application for either.

The CTM transaction as well as much documentation refers to a "CTM Profile," and technically this may not be entirely inaccurate in that CTM definitions may be saved similar to profiles, without recourse to variants, on which one must rely for the production planning (PP) run or the SNP heuristics planning run. Nevertheless, in effect CTM definitions behave more like the latter than they are like profiles and the transaction is found in a run node, not a profile node. This discrepancy is unimportant except for the minor deviation from an otherwise consistent application across planning run designs and is probably due simply to different development teams working on different aspects of the product.

Find the CTM definition and foreground run transaction /SAPAPO/CTM, Capable-to-Match (CTM) Planning, on path *Multilevel Supply & Demand Matching → Planning*. To call a preexisting profile, select one from the match-codes for the CTM Profile field and then click the Refresh/Update button (Exhibit 10.5, step 1). Alternatively, create a new profile from scratch by pressing the Create New Profile button or by selecting a preexisting one as described above, then switching to change mode and clicking the Copy Profile button (Exhibit 10.5, step 2). In the Planning Scope tab indicate the planning version to run on as well as any filters for master data, demand, and supply as well as the general time-horizon application (Exhibit 10.5, steps 3 to 5). Use the Strategies tab to add specific CTM nuances on the Requirements Strategy for the run, including when to replan, when to delete planned orders, as well as application of backward or forward scheduling. For more detail on use of planning strategies, see earlier relevant sections for PP/DS and the SNP heuristic planning run.

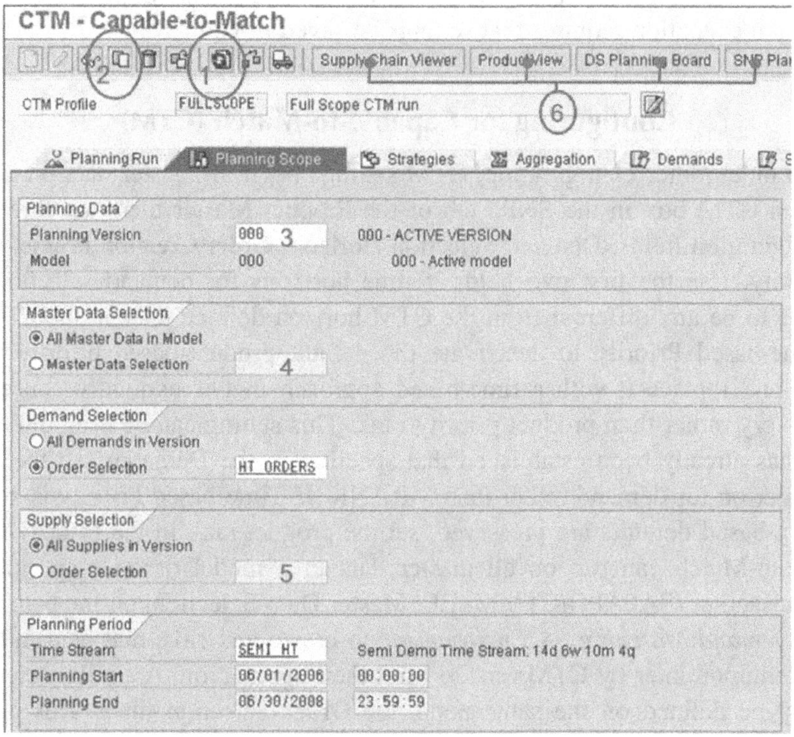

EXHIBIT 10.5 CTM "PROFILE"
© SAP AG. Used with permission.

If time-based prioritization is used in lieu of product rank–based prioritization, then define this in the Demand tab. Use (or nonuse) and requisite planning of safety stock is defined in the Supplies tab (Exhibit 10.6, step 1). The Settings tab has additional fields to control whether SNP or PP/DS resources will be applied for capacity determination and how supply generation will be generated out of them (Exhibit 10.7, steps 1 to 3). It is additionally used to define whether planning results of this particular run should be shared with R/3 (Exhibit 10.7, step 4). There are powerful subtabs under settings for Master Data and Technical Settings. The former can be used to configure whether to ignore or otherwise qualify specific items of master data in conducting a solve, such as planned delivery time or goods receipt processing time as well as method for determining available external supply sources. The latter may be applied for a variety of purposes, ranging from business solve issues such as rounding of planned quantities and minimum planned quantities to technical run issues like maximum scheduling time allowed per demand element and methods for managing the resulting CTM log from a run.

From the CTM Profile definition view, CTM can be run only when it is in change mode. In this mode Demand and Supply simulations may be executed from their respective tabs without carrying out planning runs to evaluate CTM's resultant prioritization and generations based on settings (i.e., Exhibit 10.6, step 2). Actual execution is carried out by clicking the Start Planning button on the Planning Run tab. Specific results may be viewed by clicking buttons respective of any of the UIs at the top of the screen (Exhibit 10.5,

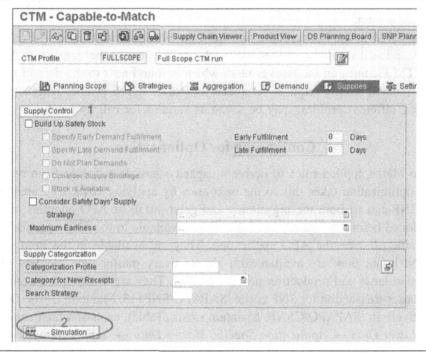

EXHIBIT 10.6 CTM PROFILE, SUPPLIES TAB

Note that the Demands and Supplies tabs allow simulation in change mode to determine the effects of their settings. © SAP AG. Used with permission.

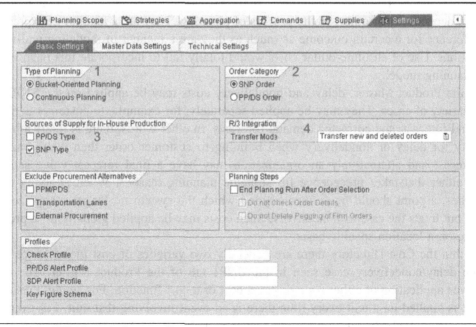

EXHIBIT 10.7 CTM PROFILE, SETTINGS TAB

Of primary concern here is which resources to use and how to use them, but also configured is whether to send results to R/3. © SAP AG. Used with permission.

step 6, i.e., Product View, Product Planning Table, etc.) or by opening a planning book in a separate session.

Running CTM in the background, as would be the common method of execution for production and as it would be applied via batch, requires use of the transaction /SAPAPO/ CTMB, CTM Planning in the Background, which is found next to the definition transaction. This method simply requires reference to a saved CTM profile. Alternative forms of it, calling different profiles, may be saved as variants for call by batch.

Configuring for Optimization

Capable-to-Match applied rules to derive a capacity-feasible schedule from its planning run. SNP optimization takes this to the next level by applying costs. The arena of cost-usage in SNP can be both the big-money and great-pitfall of APO adopters, and as we have cautioned before, so we remind here. Costs available to the SNP optimizer are, for one, available *all over* the APO application. They are available in the Product Master on the SNP1 tab; they are available on almost every master data element including transportation lanes and production process models. They are furthermore available in a specific master-transaction for SNP costs: /SAPAPO/SNP113, Maintain Costs (Directory), or alternatively in /SAPAPO/CSNP, Maintain Costs (Table), each of which can be found on path *Master Data → Application-Specific Master Data → Supply Network Planning*. There are six broad categories of costs: production, handling, storage, transportation, procurement, and delay/nondelivery.

We must emphasize that costs in SNP should be treated as relative costs, not absolute dollar-value costs. Remember, we are on the weather-simulator model, not the artificial-intelligence model. Costs are applied by the optimizer in order to run simulations and determine the best possible solutions. The costs, as such, nudge the system to favor certain decisions over others in the process of planning. They are a manner of expressing a preference for a certain outcome as much as they are a manner of modeling real-world conditions. Use of absolute-dollar costs would totally fail to incorporate this nuance into the planning model.

In the Product Master, delay and nondelivery costs may be applied on the SNP1 tab to a variety of cases. They may be applied separately, for example, to customer demand, demand forecast, and corrected demand forecasts. In other words, there is likely a higher penalty for delay or nondelivery when building to customer order than when building to forecast and alternatively an organization may have a final forecast value separate from either that takes precedence for strategic planning reasons. When applying delay penalties, a point should be defined beyond which the system no longer recognizes the delay but treats the case as nondelivery. Such costs may be applied globally for a product or else on a location-specific basis.

Within the Cost Directory there are generally two varieties of cost maintenance. One is the delay/nondelivery case seen in the SNP1 tab of the Product Master. The other involves application of either a single-level cost or a cost function. For single-level costs a cost is applied on a unit every time there is an event involving that unit. For example, every time a product is built on a given resource, a cost of 200 may be assigned, or every

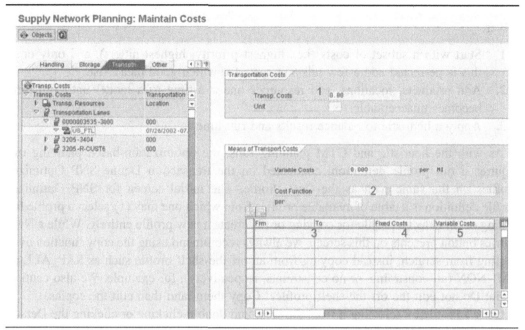

EXHIBIT 10.8 SNP COST DIRECTORY
Cost application for cases of either single-level costs or cost functions. © SAP AG. Used with permission.

time a specific transportation lane is employed a cost of 150 is added (Exhibit 10.8, step 1). Alternatively a cost function may be used (Exhibit 10.8, step 2). Cost functions allow specification of applicability by time (i.e., it may differ from one week, month, or year to another), and they allow application of both fixed and variable costs (Exhibit 10, steps 3 to 5). The fixed cost applies in all cases regardless of quantity while the variable cost is applied as a multiplicative of the number of units involved in the activity. Use of a transportation lane, for example, may carry a fixed cost of 100 plus a variable cost of 10 per unit on the lane during October, with all values doubling during the November and December holiday seasons.

In addition to these costs SNP also has a transaction Maintain Cost Profile, found on path *Supply Network Planning → Environment → Current → Settings → Profiles*. The profile actually contains no additional costs from those available in the directory or in master data, but instead contains multipliers of costs. One application of the cost profile is to replace the cost of nondelay with profit, moving other costs to the other side of the equation. The effect here is to shift from a simple cost-minimization approach to optimization to a profit-maximization approach. We should hasten to note, however, that the difference is really one of angle and serves only to punctuate the almost qualitative (some have even said *artistic*) nature of what appears to be a highly scientific, quantitative exercise, as either method, cost minimization or profit maximization, should result in the same quantitative outcome.

Earlier we mentioned an unofficial street rule of keeping costs in solves to less than 12. Of course no absolute, hard rule of this kind could really be feasible, but three guidepost rules are recommended from SAP for organizations building a cost-based solver:

1. Start with a subset of costs (i.e., highest priority, highest hitters), and only once this is perfected add a few relevant costs for which good data exist.
2. Add products, locations, and resources one-at-a-time to a model until run time becomes unacceptable.
3. Apply a heuristic to balance results and run time.

As with the heuristic and CTM planning runs, the optimization-based planning run requires a run profile definition, conducted on the transaction Define SNP Optimizer Profiles on the same path as the Cost Profile. The initial screen for SNP Optimizer Profile definition is a table of available profiles from which one may (1) select a profile for editing or (2) select a profile for copying or (3) create a new profile entirely. While a New Entries button presents on this screen, we always recommend using the copy function over starting from scratch, instead copying from an off-the-shelf profile such as SAP_ALL or SAP_NON (all constraints or no constraints, respectively), for example. We also caution again: Do not edit the off-the-shelf profiles! Copy them, and then edit the copies.

Copy a profile by selecting it from the table and double-clicking or clicking the Details button. In the resulting screen simply click the Copy As button. The immediate outcome of pressing this button may seem a bit counterintuitive and one should be prepared for it. The new screen will appear almost exactly as the last, even retaining the name and description of a profile. One must change these, and then click Maintain Profile to continue. Otherwise, when simply maintaining, reviewing, or changing a profile, just click the Maintain Profile button from this second screen.

The Optimization Profile consists of a header and six tabs. The header requires that the developer decide whether to use linear or discrete optimization (Exhibit 10.9, step 1). Linear optimization will apply constraints from the General Constraints tab, whereas discrete applies those from the tab of the same name (Exhibit 10.9, steps 2 and 3). The choice of linear optimization requires selecting a "LP Solution Procedure" on the Solutions Tab page (Exhibit 10.9, step 4).

There are a number of factors that go into the choice of which optimization approach to apply. General constraints considers a variety of capacity constraints, maximum lot sizes, can include or exclude safety stock from consideration, and may consider or ignore product shelf life. Discrete constraints go further to include PPM/PDS lot sizes and transportation lots sizes, material and resource consumptions, and cross-period lot sizes. Additionally, if one wishes to couple a heuristic planning run with an optimization run, one must use discrete optimization and apply the heuristic as a "First Solution" on the Solution Methods tab (Exhibit 10.9, step 5). Earlier we alluded to the fact that one does not so much "optimize a supply chain" as one aims the optimizer at specific, tricky but high-return problems. This method of combining the heuristic with the optimizer may considerably reduce solve time by yielding an initial, feasible solution, and then addressing the sticky problems that only a sophisticated cost model can resolve.

An optimization planning run can be carried out in one of two or three ways. First, it may be conducted from inside an SNP planning book where buttons display, allowing selection of the optimizer. Often this requires clicking the toggle-right button from the

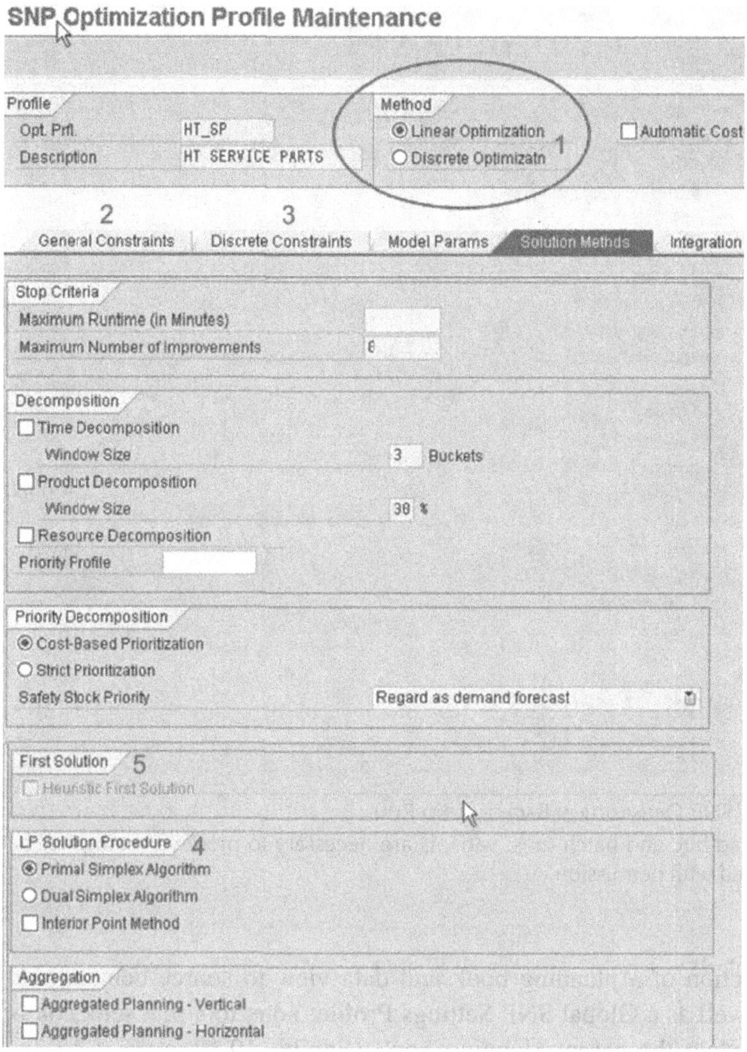

SNP Optimization Profile Maintenance

Profile
Opt. Prfl.   HT_SP
Description   HT SERVICE PARTS

Method
◉ Linear Optimization   1
○ Discrete Optimizatn

☐ Automatic Cost

2   3
General Constraints | Discrete Constraints | Model Params | Solution Methds | Integration

Stop Criteria
Maximum Runtime (in Minutes)
Maximum Number of Improvements   6

Decomposition
☐ Time Decomposition
  Window Size   3   Buckets
☐ Product Decomposition
  Window Size   30 %
☐ Resource Decomposition
Priority Frofile

Priority Decomposition
◉ Cost-Based Prioritization
○ Strict Prioritization
Safety Stock Priority   Regard as demand forecast

First Solution   5
☐ Heuristic First Solution

LP Solution Procedure   4
◉ Primal Simplex Algorithm
○ Dual Simplex Algorithm
☐ Interior Point Method

Aggregation
☐ Aggregated Planning - Vertical
☐ Aggregated Planning - Horizontal

EXHIBIT 10.9   SNP OPTIMIZATION PROFILE
© SAP AG. Used with permission.

Planning Book data-grid's button menu. When selected, an execution window displays, allowing additional selection of an optimization profile and optionally of a cost profile (a default cost profile with global multipliers of "1" is available when the cost profile is not important to the model). From here optimization may be carried out and logs will immediately display. Users may immediately return to the Planning Book view to examine outcomes. Alternatively, as with other planning runs, the optimization run can be executed in the background, which itself may be conducted ad hoc or in batch. Developers will probably seek the ad-hoc method while it is similarly likely to be disallowed during production. The background transaction /SAPAPO/SNPOP, Supply Network Optimization, is found on path *Supply Network Planning → Planning → Supply Network Planning in the Background*. It is very similar in use to the Heuristics planning run transaction and

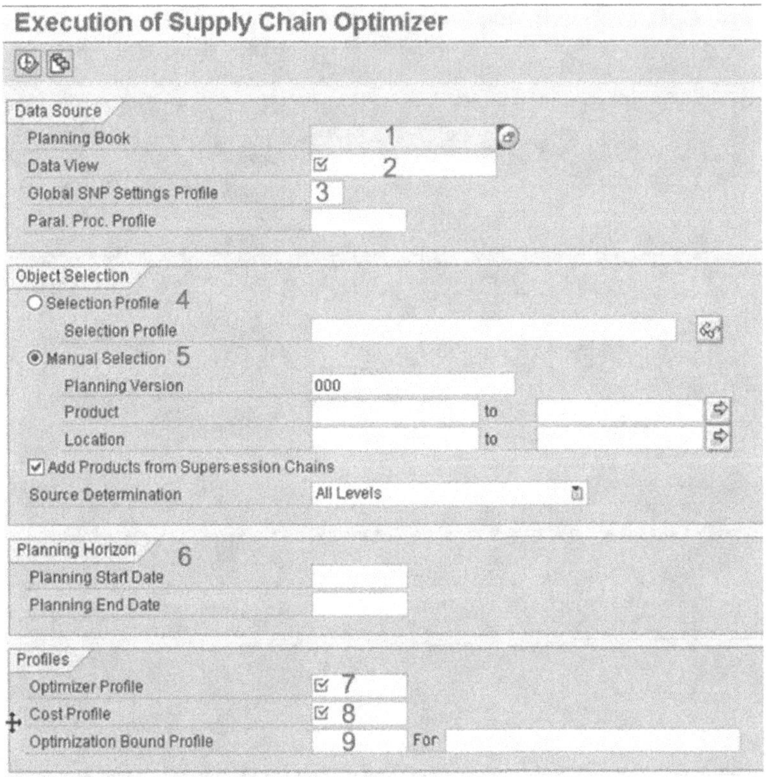

Execution of Supply Chain Optimizer

Data Source
- Planning Book — 1
- Data View — 2
- Global SNP Settings Profile — 3
- Paral. Proc. Profile

Object Selection
- ○ Selection Profile — 4
  - Selection Profile
- ● Manual Selection — 5
  - Planning Version — 000
  - Product — to
  - Location — to
  - ☑ Add Products from Supersession Chains
  - Source Determination — All Levels

Planning Horizon — 6
- Planning Start Date
- Planning End Date

Profiles
- Optimizer Profile — 7
- Cost Profile — 8
- Optimization Bound Profile — 9   For

EXHIBIT 10.10   SNP OPTIMIZATION BACKGROUND RUN
Used for both ad-hoc and batch runs, variants are necessary to preserve settings for batch execution.
© SAP AG. Used with permission.

requires selection of a planning book and data view to source demand and supply data elements as well as a Global SNP Settings Profile; note, too, that selection of a data view will autopopulate the parent planning book (Exhibit 10.10, steps 1 to 3). As with the heuristics method, data elements may be filtered directly or by using a Selection Profile, and the start and end date of the run may be constrained; in that case filter selections saved as a variant are an adequate stand-in for defining a Selection Profile (Exhibit 10.10, steps 4 to 6). Optimizer and cost profiles are required (Exhibit 10.10, steps 7 and 8). Profiles are not used to save background optimization run settings, so settings should be saved as a variant, as with the PP/DS planning run described in Chapter 8, whenever the background run is configured for batch.

Bound Profiles and Multiple Planning Runs

Finally, for cases where the optimization run precedes another planning run, a Bound Profile may be applied (Exhibit 10.10, step 9). This would be the opposite of the earlier case where a "First Method" preceded the optimization run; in this case optimization precedes an alternative method. Bound profiles create stability across runs by limiting allowed deviations from one run to another. Allowed deviations may vary, for example, by time-proximity, where little deviation is allowed in the near term while greater deviation is allowed further out in time. Bound profiles together with multiple, unlike planning-run bundling, may be applied to aim the optimizer at specific products, locations, or groups of products, for example, which require substantial cost-optimization consideration, while applying a more general heuristic or CTM run to the remainder of the model to solve for lesser constrained parts. Bound profiles are created and maintained in the transaction Define SNP Optimization Bound Profiles, off path *Supply Network Planning → Environment → Current Settings → Profiles.*

SNP CONFIGURATION RECIPE

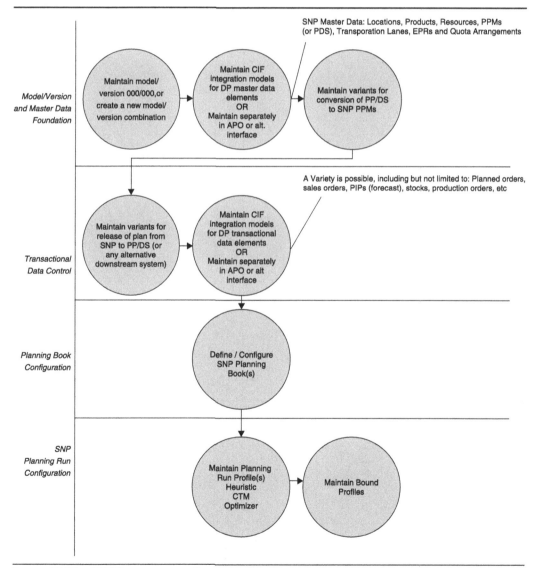

EXHIBIT 10.11   SNP CONFIGURATION RECIPE

4

BEYOND PLANNING: ANALYTICS, COLLABORATION, AND KEYS FOR SUCCESS

11

BW PRIMER PART II

NOT JUST A DATA WAREHOUSE: REENGINEERING ERP

We began our discussion of BW and its place in SAP SCM and APO in Chapter 6 with an examination of it as the master data analytical object foundation of the APO tool. This is one manifestation of BW and an important one, but BW is much more than that. BW is SAP's wider data warehouse and reporting/analytics solution. We have seen that it comes off the shelf in a *data mart* form with SAP SCM as well as in an individual *enterprise* data warehouse package, separate from any other tool. In fact, BW is also available as a data mart in two other SAP products: Customer Relationship Management (CRM) and Strategic Enterprise Management (SEM). As of 2003, BW was reported to be in 6,500

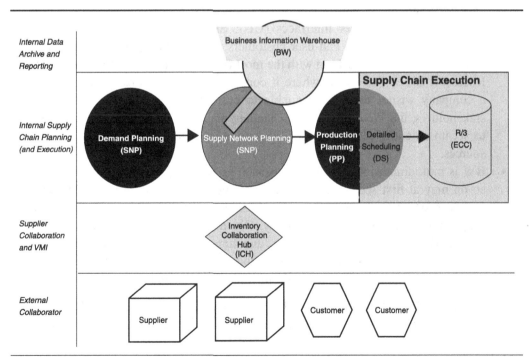

Exhibit 11.1   BW in the Supply Chain Context

BW is applied to support all SCM planning functions of APO with a data warehouse archive and advanced analytics and reporting tools that incorporate Microsoft Excel.

deployments worldwide, positioning it as a leading data warehouse and analytical solution product.

As a data warehouse, BW has a number of benefits for organizations with other SAP products in use for either transactional management, such as R/3, or decision support, such as APO. SAP-provided data extractors are widely available to port data into BW without cumbersome, custom interface development. Furthermore, as a combined data warehouse and reporting solution, BW encourages sound information architectures. Too often, data warehousing is a second thought on IT projects and must take a back seat to more urgent business objectives. Reporting, however, is typically well aligned with the strategic goals of IT projects. By piggy-backing off of the reporting function and coming hand-in-hand with the reporting tool, BW makes the transition to warehousing fairly seamless and relatively painless.

As an analytical tool BW is particularly useful for a number of reasons, among them:

- In its data mart form it can be exploited to provide analytical and reporting functionality to any of the three product packages it comes delivered with without the necessity of executing a full-blown enterprise deployment.
- BW provides object-based reporting, removing the need for much coding that is often associated with report building. That said, some caution should be noted here: Once BW is fully in place, with data extractors working to move all the appropriate data from source systems to the BW basis, object-based report development is well enabled. Often enough, however, many organizations will find it necessary to employ a degree of coding when laying the original groundwork to assure all the data transports are in place.
- BW has two report user interfaces (UIs): Excel and the Web. This should be particularly gratifying to end-user customers who habitually will gravitate toward use of a UI that provides them with the most freedom, which so often turns out to be Microsoft Excel. Moreover, where it concerns external reporting, such as reports a company wishes to make available to customers, suppliers, or other external stakeholders, the Web provides an excellent platform without making it necessary to set up an entire physical architecture to grant externals access to internal data sources.
- BW is multidimensional; while terms such as "InfoObjects," "InfoPackages," and so on may at first seem a bit arcane, the data modeling structure of BW does in fact correspond to the way that most business users think about the information they analyze and use from day to day. Given any report, structural, foundational characteristics like product, location, and time are laid out as columns and key figures; the numerical data of business like forecasts, orders, and production and delivery plans and the like are laid out in the body of the report in rows.

The utility of Microsoft Excel as a UI really cannot be understated. Many an IT professional has run into this seeming roadblock in the deployment of comprehensive enterprise solutions: Business end-users love using Microsoft Excel. The user love affair with Excel, if not consciously addressed as part of project planning and solution design, will very often mean the death-knell for even the best laid out software engineering efforts.

A common pattern as it relates to Excel is that a business problem will be identified that is significant enough that solving it will deliver a notable return on investment. Teams of management, developers, and end-users are formed to address the problem and out of their collusion a software-based solution emerges and is eventually deployed. In that process, users are trained on the new software and dutifully work with developers to put the software to work during deployment stages. Once stabilized, success is declared, the project is disbanded, and the developers move on. The project's product, as stabilized, is then expected to produce a margin as a result of its solution that delivers continuously over time, justifying the project's cost.

At this stage, without developers watching closely over the maturation of their product in production, Excel-related problems begin to take shape. During the course of business a number of things tend to happen. Unexpected events occur in production that have no perfect analog in the processes or analytics delivered by the project. These often require immediate analytical attention, and the best-available way to deliver that attention is to export data from the system into Excel and work there. Just as often, the system, having had its desired effect, generates its own level of margin and allows business users to focus their attention on previously unattended niche issues that may not have been addressed. Here they will often leverage off the foundation provided by the new system, export its data to Excel, and work from there. Sometimes bugs are found in the course of production and we have known of cases where instead of reporting the bug, business users simply compensate by working around it offline, again, in Excel. There may also be problems that the IT project deliberately decided to ignore, often for budgetary reasons (i.e., "it fell below ZBB"). We must not forget that problems that may fall out of scope for a project—as budget must often dictate—continue to be problems in the business. Again, enter Excel. Finally, end-users experience attrition. Unless excellent training regimens are in place to ensure new users fully understand and exploit enterprise systems, the constant rollover of business often tends toward a loss of institutional knowledge for enterprise system functionality—yet the problems the functionality was developed for go on being problems for the new users, who almost inevitably come from off-the-street knowing one tool, and knowing it well: Microsoft Excel.

By employing Microsoft Excel as the analytical user-interface, BW finally provides developers and management with a nearly locked-tight tool to address the seemingly inevitable Excel attrition that bedevils enterprise efforts of all sorts. Excel, in effect, "renders unto Microsoft what is Microsoft's" and gives it up to Microsoft that they have developed and proliferated a multidimensional, feature-packed spreadsheet application of unparalleled flexibility and near-universal access. That given to Microsoft, there is just so much that Excel does not, cannot, and will not ever do. Excel cannot produce a demand forecast employing the best tools of multiple-linear regression acting on a database containing perhaps three years of forecast relevant data; that is, unless it is linked to BW. Excel cannot apply heuristic and linear optimization across all the plants, customers, suppliers, transportation lanes, and resources of a supply network, unless it is linked to BW. Excel knows nothing of an ATP check, unless it is linked to BW. Excel cannot conduct detailed resource capacity scheduling and optimization, unless it is linked to BW. In fact, to be quite precise, even when linked to BW Excel still cannot do any of these things: SAP APO does these things, but Excel can be used as a primary user interface to, at a minimum, a plurality of the data that is interacted with during the course of supply chain planning.

By integrating APO with Excel, BW provides management and developers with the opportunity to both trump Excel attrition while simultaneously exploiting the best of both worlds: the data processing and storage abilities of SAP APO and BW (and any other such product) linked with Excel's unparalleled flexibility and availability for the niches and hiccups that inevitably arise during the course of business.

We believe that there is a message to BW: Enterprise projects must change. We cannot continue to think of projects as delivering a single packaged "solution" fixed at a point in time. Instead, IT projects must deliver business-enabling platforms. APO without doubt is one of the most powerful supply-chain enabling platforms available on the market today, but no project configuring and deploying APO can anticipate all the business needs that will arise and distract the business community in the three, six, and nine months following deployment. Developers who comprehend this and who integrate Excel into their solution as a fundamental UI—wherever possible in the system-business process—will alter enterprise resource planning (ERP) solutions as we know them.

Developers must move beyond this-or-that system-based UI or transaction. Every transaction and UI will by necessity be somewhat inflexible and occasionally found wanting during business, with Excel always ready to step in—disrupting an otherwise powerful comprehensive solution. Whenever an Excel report, enabled through BW, is employed in lieu of a transaction or other UI, this inflexibility is avoided and the temptations that get users off of otherwise well-engineered solutions are removed. Users are free—in fact encouraged—to work in Excel, directly, easily, and seamlessly extracting data from BW, and then do anything they find fitting with it above and beyond the prescribed business process solution. BW, in effect, balances the needs of the many, as represented by an "enterprise" solution, and the one, as represented by the lone end-user, on the ground, facing the day-to-day ruckus and chaos that is twenty-first-century commerce.

USING BEx

The tool provided in BW for setting up BW-based reports in Microsoft Excel is "BEx," the "Business Explorer." This text is primarily interested in use of APO, and while a powerful adjunct, BW is an adjunct in that context. As such we will not be exploring the use and capabilities of BW at the same level of depth that we have thus far examined aspects of APO. We do wish, nonetheless, to lay the basic groundwork for applying BW on APO projects. To do so, we will first note that the master data object fundamentals have already been covered in Chapter 6. Master data setup for Detailed Planning and analysis is identical to setup for use of BW reports. Before addressing use of BW reports, therefore, readers should be fully versed in the lessons of Chapter 6.

Note, too, that for our purposes it will suffice to explore use of BEx to generate Excel reports. We are not looking at BW's capabilities for Web integration.[1] BEx can be accessed either of two ways, from the Windows Start button or from a transaction executed in SCM. For the former path, from Start, follow *All Programs → SAP Front End → Business Explorer → Analyzer*; for the latter, execute transaction RRMX from

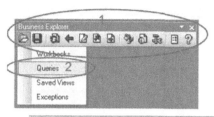

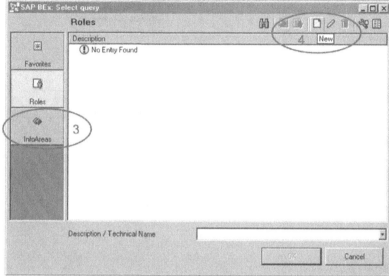

Exhibit 11.2   BEx: The Business Explorer Menu in Microsoft Excel
© SAP AG. Used with permission. Microsoft product screen shot(s) reprinted with permission from Microsoft Corporation.

the transaction window in SCM. Execution of either path will launch Microsoft Excel, but with a "Business Explorer" dialog window in display (Exhibit 11.2, step 1). Queries may be generated in Excel using BEx by way of this dialog window, which is a gateway to the data objects stored in BW using the techniques explained in Chapter 6.

To create a new query, click the "Open" icon on the Business Explorer dialog window and select the "Queries" option (Exhibit 11.2, step 2). A new dialog window will open indicating that there are no queries (assuming no previous use). Click the InfoAreas button from the left-side panel (Exhibit 11.2, step 3) and choose an InfoCube, then click the "New" icon (Exhibit 11.2, step 4).

The BW Query Designer Dialog will open (Exhibit 11.3). Take a moment to examine the structure of this window. The key figures and characteristics available for querying are displayed in a navigation tree in the left-side column titled by the name of the InfoCube selected in the earlier step (Exhibit 11.3, step 1). The right side of the dialog has panels for filter selections, which include rows (Exhibit 11.2, step 2, normally to correspond to key figures), columns (Exhibit 11.3, step 3, normally to correspond to characteristics), and user-defined characteristics. The bottom-right panel contains a preview window illustrating the resulting query/report output on Excel based on selections as they have been set up in the Query Designer Dialog thus far (Exhibit 11.3, step 4).

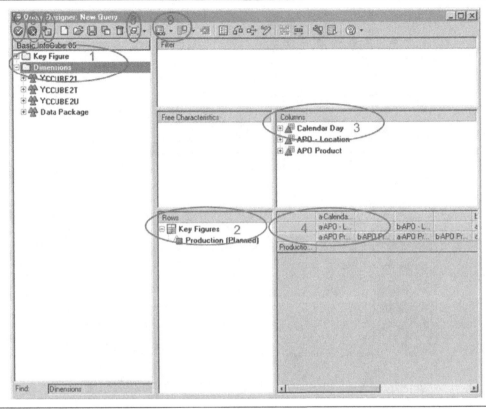

EXHIBIT 11.3   BW QUERY DESIGNER

Accessed through the BEx menu in Microsoft Excel (launched by transaction RRMX), this dialog may be used to build queries and reports for use in Excel and publication to the Web based on data extracted from BW. © SAP AG. Used with permission. Microsoft product screen shot(s) reprinted with permission from Microsoft Corporation.

To build a simple query, expand the key figures node on the left-side panel and select a key figure as a row, and drag-and-drop the key figure on the Rows panel. Minimize key figures and expand the nodes for Dimensions, or characteristics, to select columns for the report. A natural first choice might be a time dimension, such as month, week, or day, to populate the top-row of the report, then rudimentary leftmost structural columns such as location and product. As with key figures and rows, drag-and-drop the selected characteristic/dimension from the navigation tree over to the Columns panel.

The Query Designer Dialog has its own menu, many of whose selections are fairly standard and require no elucidation, but several of which will point the reader in the direction of exploiting powerful features of the tool. The common SAP green circle with white check will exit the Query Designer Dialog, execute the query, and display it in Excel (Exhibit 11.3, step 5). The red circle with white "X" exits the Query Designer Dialog and returns to the BEx menu (Exhibit 11.3, step 6). The box/circle to the right of the red circle exits the Query Designer Dialog, executes the query, and displays it on a web browser (Exhibit 11.3, step 7). Several other icons are entirely common, such as save, save-as, and delete. Another important icon has two small overlapping boxes with arrows coming out all four corners: Publish. This makes the query available for web users (Exhibit 11.3, step 8). The two icon-buttons to the right of Publish allow creation of exceptions and conditions for queries, enabling creation of dynamic queries where users provide conditions or limits on query output (Exhibit 11.3, step 9).

BW ENTERPRISE AND BW DATA MART

BW in SAP Solutions

Except for organizations that have worked out formal policies as regards use of BW, the question will inevitably arise about whether and how to use BW. We have already stated that we believe the question of *whether* is clearly a *yes*. If APO itself is the dimension of length and APO's macros and function modules are the dimension of height, then the employment of BW by any APO project may be thought of as depth in terms of the gravity of power, flexibility, and sophistication that it will add to any final, delivered solution. The difference is not $10 + 10 + 10$; it is $10 \times 10 \times 10$. As to how, organizations will require some understanding of the BW as enterprise versus BW as data mart divide. For some organizations that have deployed BW as a data warehouse, data marts may be eschewed on the basis of keeping all analytics closely tied to the data warehouse. Other organizations may find that splitting functionality across similarly capable systems may go a long way to balance data-processing demands that might otherwise hinder performance, thereby best balancing available system capacity. For those looking to lay this groundwork, however, we can offer a little advice.

Enterprise or Data Mart?

Facing the question of using BW enterprise or the BW data mart in SCM as part of one's APO solution, we may begin with some relatively simple rules and work from there to caveats. First, the BW data mart should not be employed as a data warehouse. This is absolutely not the reason for including BW with SCM. Remember that in deploying SCM our primary objective is to effect an enterprise planning solution. We want our SCM box, therefore, reserved primarily for SCM-related processing. For data warehousing solutions, use BW enterprise on a BW box; do not use a data mart.

In principle, if it is only reporting that is germane, the BW data mart on supply chain management (SCM) (or customer relationship management (CRM) or SEM as the case might be) will suffice, but here many organizations may find themselves running into the "caveats." First, if it is only SCM master and transactional data that is necessary for BW analytics and reporting, then there probably will not be issues with using the data mart so long as a great deal of forecast history (or any significant historical data segment) is not necessary—as might be the case on a DP deployment (more on that shortly). If data from R/3 is necessary for reporting, however, use of the BW data mart will turn out to be problematic. One may at first think that the CIF can be employed to migrate R/3 data to SCM, then data sources created to extract that data to BW structures where it can be used for reporting, but this will not always work. The core interface (CIF) transports data into order-based liveCache, while BW operates on time-series-based liveCache. Organizations that choose to go this way will face one of two choices: (1) Write macros that convert the order-based liveCache data to time-series based, requiring that users enter and exit the Planning Book to execute those macros and effect the data transformation, or (2) employ an ABAP developer to write function modules that can do the same in batch, requiring custom coding. Neither solution is particularly appealing. For cases where R/3 data is required, therefore, it is most often advisable to use an enterprise BW client separate from the data mart and apply SAP-provided extractors to retrieve data from R/3 and SCM.

What then of DP? Detailed Planning provides a particularly ironic case as it is the module of APO most fully integrated with the BW data mart. Detailed Planning, as it turns out, is a demand forecasting tool and forecasting, in contrast to planning, must often make use of voluminous historical information. Planning, whether mid-range with SNP or tactical with PP/DS, is concerned with getting supply to match demand in the present. Forecasting must determine what demand will be, and minimally a plurality of organizations will find quantitative historical data to be a highly germane and useful input to excellent forecasting. As we have already noted, the BW data mart is simply not suited for this. The more historical data is populated in large data-cubes, the more a system intended for supply-chain management will be weighed down under the yoke of archiving. Detailed Planning solutions, therefore, will often require BW enterprise counterparts.

PROFILE OF A FULL-POWERED APO DEPLOYMENT

In Chapter 4 we profiled a successful APO project. There we were interested in strategic, management decisions that when well made lead to successful deployments and that when poorly made lead to often insurmountable hindrance. Here we are interested in what APO looks like when an APO solution is well designed. As with management decisions, it is too often easy to go wrong and the decisions that lead down the path to dead-ends are typically made early at the level of project planning and conceptual design. We find that full-powered APO deployments have these characteristics: (1) phased solutions, (2) focused deployments, (3) realistic expectations, and (4) expansive use of "flexibility features." Let us consider each of these.

Perhaps one of the biggest problems with APO is that it tempts. By offering a wall-to-wall supply chain planning solution, rather than the until-now more common single-problem solution, APO tempts managers to overreach with project proposals that address all aspects of organizations' supply chain planning issues, rather than focus attention on the most important problems and pick them off one-at-time. And it tempts developers, who, perhaps too accustomed to the tool and excited by "world-hunger" project possibilities, may overrepresent its ease-of-configuration in support of a manager's grand vision rather than providing the studied, judicious, and rationally cautious feedback that we must often rely on them for.

In the medium to long run we want APO to be a wall-to-wall solution, but in order to get there it is essential that we understand that each of the areas APO addresses—demand, supply networks, PP/DS—is an entire supply chain discipline constituting its own veritable plethora of unique specializations, processes, and zones of expertise. Any company or organization sophisticated enough to need a tool like APO will have one of the more sophisticated manifestations of these supply chain disciplines at work, on the ground, actively working the operations of business. Such organizations cannot change overnight, not even from quarter to quarter.

All of this leads directly to the second characteristic of full-powered APO deployments: focus. APO solutions will work for organizations when they are phased (i.e., broken out from one area to another), allowing teams to focus on the detailed specialized business problems that each module is used to address, exactly because they allow developers and end-users alike the time to focus acutely on the specialized needs of each business area and therefore apply all the most powerful tools of APO to those areas in the most customized manner possible. Regardless of how tempting it may be to wow the corporate universe with a wall-to-wall supply chain management solution, such as APO can ultimately enable, managers must take to heart that APO is too plainly powerful for any organization that is simple enough and therefore capable of adopting all of its modules in one sweep. Developers must be given time to absorb the complexities of each business unit and supply chain specialization in order to fully apply the wide range of APO solutions (data processing, UIs, macros, BW, its reports and analytics); end-users must be given time to absorb all of these technologies as well as the deep connection that APO provides them with the wider supply chain.

Full-powered APO deployments studiously avoid unrealistic expectations. APO is not artificial intelligence. It maximally enhances the qualitative reasoning and negotiating capacities of human users; it does not replace them. APO will not "optimize the supply chain." It does provide optimization engines to apply to specific supply chain problems. Moreover, APO provides a wide array of technologies, all of which are not suitable to every business problem. Developers must take heed to intelligently apply APO's technologies; that often means that the sexiest technologies are not necessarily the best fit for specific problems.

Management and developers should train and lead end-users to think of APO as a powerful tool for "exception-based planning." In APO solutions, costs, priorities, and rules are sought to configure APO to solve for 80 to 90% of business planning, and explicit thresholds are defined to identify when conditions fall outside the limits of quantitative analytics. Alert profiles notify customers when those thresholds are crossed and user interaction is required to apply the unique abilities of humans to resolve business problems. These are things that no computer can do: Call in favors, request expedites, hire temps, negotiate trade-offs, schedule factory overtime, schedule a mandatory factory vacation day (i.e., for demand troughs to avoid excess inventory), or look for supplies hidden away under desks or in drawers or lost in factory bins. Armed with new information, such users may then input new details to APO to inform better and up-to-date planning run solves.

When designing APO solutions, managers and developers would do well to take a lesson from science and recall the notion of "Ockham's Razor." A principle attributed to fourteenth-century English logician and Franciscan friar William of Ockham, Ockham's Razor is a maxim that informs the valuation of scientific theories and hypotheses. The explicit principle is expressed: "Entities should not be multiplied beyond necessity." It is generally applied in science when considering two or more hypotheses that each successfully and adequately account for observed behavior or events during experimentation. Provided with such a conundrum, scientists favor from these hypotheses the one that is most simple. In other words, if there is more than one way to explain something or do something and each way results in the same outcome, favor the simplest.

Consider Ockham's Razor when choosing, for example, between using heuristics, capable-to-match (CTM), the optimizer, or some combination thereof in SNP. Heuristics, being rule-based planning, may be thought of as "top-down" solutions, whereas the optimizer, using math based on costs, is "bottom-up." If there are many objects in a system and each must operate differently, optimization will often be called for. If business rules dictate, however, that the many objects should generally behave the same, then heuristics will be more suitable. For example, soldiers in the thick of battle are not trained to think for themselves, all acting as independent agents; they are taught to rigorously follow orders, following their leader. Birds flying in a flock likewise do not all simultaneously compute speed and direction, but follow the leader of the flock, simply taking turns as leader.

Generally any problem that can be solved with heuristics can also be solved with linear programming, costs, and the optimizer. This is often, however, not wise. Wherever possible in APO, do not be tempted to use the sexiest technology merely because it is the sexiest. This may serve to enhance the perception of the developer or manager initially—because what a smart person it is who can understand the complex math necessary to apply linear programming to solve this or that business problem! But the glow will quickly fade when projects proceed and colleagues come to realize the complexity of applying optimization while they simultaneously realize how much more simple it would have been to apply heuristics.

The final characteristic of full-powered APO deployments is the employment of APO's flexibility features. We have taken great pains in this text to emphasize what we describe here as APO's flexibility features, and those are: macros and BW integration. Developers and end-users who simply attend APO-module classes for DP, SNP, Global Available to Promise (GATP), and PP/DS will too often be biased by what we might call a *transaction-centric* perspective of APO. This view of APO, which considers its technologies in a manner prescribed by given APO transactions, processes, and screens, is not altogether inaccurate so much as it is needlessly limiting. Again, if we compare APO to spatial dimensions, if APO and all its transactions, UIs, and data processing tools constitute width alone, then macros constitute height and BW integration provides depth: Use of each additional tool provides an entire dimension's worth of power over the exclusive use of the previous. Anyone can imagine how much more useful a three-dimensional image is than a single straight line. So much more powerful, then, is an APO deployment empowered by highly customized macros and BW reports available in Excel or on the Web—both of which are available for further *ad-hoc* customization, directly by end-users, without the necessity of programmers or developers, immediately, as needs arise during the course of business, when the IT projects that came and deployed APO have come and gone.

NOTE

1. For a complete treatment of enterprise BW, see *Mastering the SAP Business Information Warehouse* by Kevin McDonald, Andreas Wilmsmeier, David C. Dixon, and W.H. Inmon (Hoboken, NJ: Wiley, 2006).

12

INVENTORY COLLABORATION HUB AND APO COLLABORATION

B2B CONTEXT OF ICH AND COLLABORATION

VMI, B2C, and B2B

The dot-com bomb of 2000 did much to take the wind out of the sails of B2C (*business-to-customer* e-commerce). While the web-driven retail e-commerce storm of the 1990s rapidly proceeded to undergo consolidation, a much more stable form of e-commerce was in equally rapid gestation: B2B (*business-to-business* e-commerce). B2B e-commerce held and holds several qualities that positively distinguish it from B2C. For one, B2B arose at the same time as the vendor-managed-inventory (VMI) concept was gaining traction. That is, historically vendor interest in sold inventory ended somewhere between shipment and receipt, with the periodic exception of returns or lost shipments. A commercial outlet shelving the vendor's products for sale traditionally took on inventory management responsibility, including replenishment. When stock on the shelf fell below an adequate level, for example, a new order was procured to the vendor. This model was applicable both for finished goods, such as product sold at a retail outlet, or for raw materials and semifinished goods, such as materials stocked for use in the production of a finished good by a manufacturer.

Enabled by better transactional inventory tracking through UPC codes and radio frequency identification (RFID), modern VMI evolves this arrangement by extending vendor planning of inventory beyond delivery. In a VMI arrangement the vendor tracks its product not just through delivery but all the way through sale in the case of retail, and consumption in the case of manufacture. The business customer, which in a VMI case will then be a retailer, manufacturer, hospital—or any organization stocking and consuming or selling goods—need not continuously track every item of inventory. Instead the business customer outsources this inventory management responsibility to the vendor that provided said inventory, who automatically restocks it when supplies reach agreed-upon lows.

Vendor-managed inventory (VMI) for B2B, coupled with the more stable contractual relationships of businesses with vendors, as opposed to customers with retailers, makes for a more secure e-commerce foundation that is in many respects better suited to automation than its B2C cousin. B2C can hardly be said to be dead, but at issue for us as regards value from SAP SCM is that B2C has probably exhausted its growth-based return-on-investment

ICH in an Integrated SAP SCM Solution

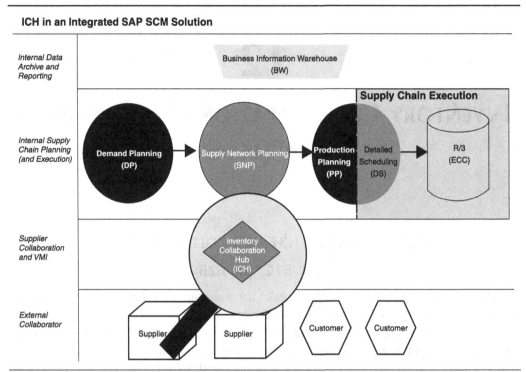

EXHIBIT 12.1   ICH IN THE SUPPLY CHAIN CONTEXT

ICH provides collaboration capabilities with external partners in the supply chain, including customers, suppliers, and subcontractors. It allows for transmission of demand and inventory data that will empower planning as well as actual vendor/supplier-managed inventory abilities to improve supply replenishment.

in the e-commerce economy. In other words, to the extent that B2C e-commerce is used—has been mastered and commoditized—no further supply-efficiency gains are likely through technology application. This cannot be said of B2B and VMI, where improved business-to-business supply management exposes vast pools of opportunity for efficiency gains through effective full- and semiautomation.

ICH and APO in SCM

With the necessary exception of BW, which forms the data basis of APO at the same time as it presents itself as a separate tool from the APO application, we have until now limited ourselves to APO, ignoring the wider SAP SCM package. APO was originally marketed as a standalone application that integrated with R/3 by way of the core interface (CIF). Starting with the 4.0 revision, however, APO was sold in a larger SCM package that includes SAP's most comprehensive VMI solution: the Inventory Collaboration Hub (ICH) (Exhibit 12.2). As it happens, SAP prefers to refer to the capability of ICH as Supplier Managed Inventory (SMI), and as we are concerned here with an SAP product we will henceforth follow that convention. This packaging of APO with ICH is noteworthy because it provides a direct link between global and site-level product forecast and planning and a *hub* for B2B collaboration of inventory management. It is furthermore

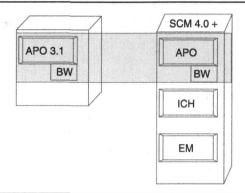

EXHIBIT 12.2   APO AND ICH IN THE SCM PACKAGE
Beginning with version 4.0, APO was released as part of a wider package of integrated applications called Supply Chain Management, including the Inventory Collaboration Hub.

noteworthy that the SMI features of ICH are in addition to the VMI capabilities packaged in APO collaboration. We will look at detailed differences later, but suffice it to say for now a larger SMI B2B solution is available in SCM ICH, while a distinctive VMI B2B *collaborative planning* solution is available in SCM APO SNP.

ICH Capabilities and B2B

Capabilities

The SCM 5.0 release of ICH contains an expansive set of major capabilities over its 4.1 predecessor: an Alert Monitor, SMI, a release process for scheduling agreements, dynamic replenishment, a purchase order process, Kanban process, Delivery Control Monitor (DCM), contract manufacturing purchasing, supply network inventory, a demand monitor, and ASN (Automated Shipping Notices) transmissions. Supplier-managed inventory continues to be the hallmark feature of ICH and it will be our focus in this treatment. There are a number of enhancements to ICH in SCM 5.0 over 4.1, including specialized capabilities for subcontracting manufacturers. In general, SMI enables a minimum/maximum-based replenishment and inventory monitoring process owned by the supplier. Closely related to SMI is the release process enabling customer-driven replenishment via Scheduling Agreements driven by the customer enterprise resource planning (ERP) system. Dynamic replenishment goes beyond strict stock resupply and combines customer and supplier replenishment for collaborative planning based on comparison of sales plans with orders. The purchase order process enables customer-driven replenishment using the purchase orders in cooperation with customer Materials Requirements Planning (MRP) runs.

With the Kanban process, businesses can extend Kanban requirements to external suppliers, enabling suppliers to monitor and refill them using a web-based interface. Using the DCM suppliers can monitor deliveries and create shipments or ASNs as necessary based on replenishment agreements. The contract manufacturing process addresses specialized needs of subcontractors, enabling both transmission of subcontracting purchase orders and subcontractor reporting of production status to the contracting customer business. Supply network inventory enables collaboration by way of inventory tracking, stock projection, minimum/maximum limits, and alerts at both supplier and customer locations.

ICH in B2B E-Commerce

In the context of B2B it should be understood that the *off-the-shelf* ICH *application* is a semiautomated solution that both lays and constitutes the groundwork of a fully automated solution, but some technical development will be required in any case to secure a 100% automated B2B solution. ICH, in effect, takes one several steps toward 100% automation, especially for organizations using R/3, while filling several business gaps in the process. Integrated so closely with APO, BW, and R/3 as it is, ICH could not be better suited to be the cornerstone of a fully automated B2B architecture. A fully automated B2B solution will generally be characterized by three major capability structures: (1) an alert system to notify a supplier of action conditions such as inventory falling below certain targets, (2) a web-based user interface where inventory or demand data may be published to a supplier, allowing manual and ad-hoc monitoring by the supplier, and (3) a middleware solution connecting the business customer's inventory management or planning systems to the supplier's ERP system.

Common technologies for middleware include Tibco for cross-organization data payload management and RosettaNet (RN) data template medium to map interorganizational data elements to their appropriate other-side counterparts. The XML layer between R/3 and SCM that enables ICH may work for some organizations as a stand-in for other middleware options. In its off-the-shelf application form, without middleware development, ICH provides the first two capabilities but not the third. These two structures are visually contrasted in Exhibits 12.3 and 12.4. Even when a fully automated B2B solution is employed, the semiautomated solution should almost always be deployed as a backup. Catastrophic failure of a middleware structure or even persistent data glitches have the potential to carry onerous cost, especially in just-in-time environments; so a web backup will ordinarily prove its worth. Moreover, during what are often highly sensitive and always technically complex interbusiness testing phases of B2B projects wherein two or more companies' ERP systems are linked for the first time, a stable web-based user interface will prove invaluable to data validation.

A fully automated B2B architecture is, of course, advisable for any two organizations that can realize mutual benefit from the arrangement. That ICH does not go the full distance in this measure is in no sense a reason not to build one's B2B solution on the basis of ICH. As discussed, ICH minimally provides the first two major components of the fully automated solution. Moreover, it cannot be overemphasized that for organizations already using APO for supply chain planning and R/3 for supply chain execution (to say nothing of BW, too, for data warehousing and analytics), ICH comes off the shelf, plugged into these tools. Thus, in addition to starting two steps ahead with alerts and web publication, the ICH adopter avoids all manner of internal development, linking each ERP or data management tool to external data communications systems. Note, too, that B2B solutions, especially automated B2B solutions, are simply not suitable for one-size-fits-all strategies. Often a fully automated SMI solution will be altogether ill-advised, such as may be the case when supplied parts are both high volume and high value, and particularly

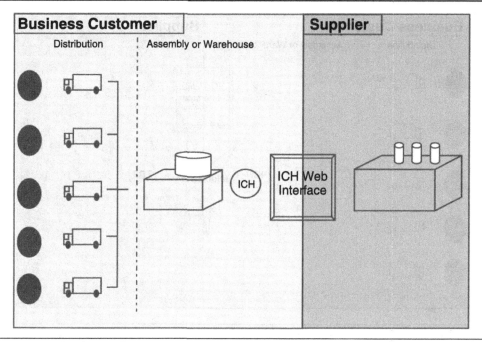

Exhibit 12.3 ICH OFF THE SHELF

Semiautomated B2B: ICH enables alerts, supplier web monitoring of inventory and plan, and supplier response to plan or provision of inventory. ICH does not enable a direct interface to the supplier's ERP system.

if they are high value and subject to frequent demand changes. Low-value goods in high or low volumes are generally well suited to fully automated B2B. High-value goods are more sensitive for obvious reasons and present for cases where a semiautomated solution will provide the best return-on-investment.

ICH MASTER DATA

ICH master data includes data in common with a supply-chain model but some additional elements specific to the ICH applications, all of which include locations, products, "product determination," transportation lanes, packaging, partner data, number ranges, users, and tools. Old R/3 hats will recognize that user definitions have not historically been considered an aspect of master data maintenance, but they are treated as such in ICH 5.0. Master data elements of ICH originate from R/3 as they do with APO and are likewise shared in supply chain management (SCM) with APO. They may be viewed and even modified in SCM from windows accessible through the ICH web front-end, allowing master data maintenance for ICH users without use of the APO navigation node in SCM. These transactions are nevertheless also available off the ICH node in SCM under Master Data. As most data originates in R/3, however, most such work will be adding individual SCM/ICH-specific settings.

A particular exception to be expected is the creation of a business partner. Inventory Collaboration Hub (ICH) must recognize outside-facing entities to respond to its

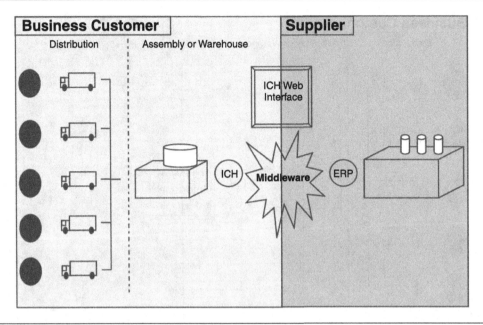

EXHIBIT 12.4   ICH AS PART OF A FULLY AUTOMATED B2B SOLUTION

ICH continues to provide alerts and a web basis for communication that will be employed during times of middleware breakdown, but an additional middleware layer connects to the supplier's ERP system allowing the supplier to plan and manage the business customer's inventory from inside its own planning systems.

transmissions, which are set up as external ICH users. Such users may be people, organizations, groups, or "business partners." Internal individuals (employees) who need access to the web front-end, for example, are set up as persons. A supplier or customer employing the front-end may be set up as a business partner, a testing body might be a group, and a department would be an organization. Business partners are established with transaction BP, Create Business Partner, off path *Inventory Collaboration Hub → Master Data.*

USING ICH AND APO COLLABORATION

Common Processes for SMI

When thinking about ICH solutions, some care should be given to the difference between strict inventory management and the planning discipline. Throughout this text so far we have been deeply interested in the art and science of product planning, that is, anticipating demand, controlling for capacity and supply constraints, and navigating the best proactive plan among these three factors to construct build-and-buy schedules for products and their parts. Simple inventory replenishment, in contrast, typically refers to a reactive reorder-point strategy for maintaining stocks—nothing more complicated than opening a new order whenever stocks fall below specific targets. Companies employing B2B broadly and ICH specifically must concern themselves with whether their suppliers will simply manage stock replenishment or else participate in the more complicated practice of product planning. Moreover, for companies that are uncomfortable shifting purchasing capabilities to a vendor, some integration of the inventory replenishment process with the procurement planning process may nonetheless be called for.

Consider three business cases. In the first case, a business customer and supplier employ strict inventory replenishment. In the second case, a business customer enables supplier response to inventory, integrating the response into the procurement planning process, but retains final control of procurement internally. In the third, a business customer enables supplier planning of inventory, including purchasing.

For strict inventory replenishment, ICH will be configured to notify the supplier with alerts when stocks fall below a target. The notification will trigger the supplier to check with the monitor and determine actual statuses, and there may, of course, be more than one possible response. A supplier may contact the business customer for more information (recall here our admonition earlier about fully automating high-value goods), schedule a new delivery, or simply note data and return later. In any case, however, the supplier is able to increase inventory deliveries and does so generally based on an agreed-upon replenishment framework.

In the second case we can apply a similar process whether the supplier is working with actual inventory data or simply with plan or forecast. In this case the supplier is not asked to provide new deliveries of inventory under a framework, but instead is included in the procurement planning process. Alerts may be applied as in the first case to notify a supplier of conditions that require analysis and/or a response, but the response does not immediately elicit a new order. The response, for example, is not always going to be the same as the need. A supplier may be able to provide only a fraction of the goods necessary to fulfill either plan or inventory targets; or in other cases the supplier may be able to meet targets and may, when able, volunteer additional buffer stocks according to an agreed-upon framework. This response is then treated internally by the business customer as a supply or capacity constraint to wider production planning as well as a feed to the procurement process that results in the generation of purchase orders to the vendor. In other words, using the vendor response as a constraint, planning is scheduled around limited vendor supply and orders are cut to fulfill supply based on the vendor response.

In the final scenario the vendor actually participates in or leads product planning. This will normally be applicable for subcontractor-like cases where the vendor is producing the finished good or something very close to it (as might be the case when either finished-good production is outsourced or else for subcontracting combined with a planning strategy of "build without final assembly", e.g. subcontractor completing all but a final step such as test out or custom coloring based on customer specifications). For this scenario, customer demand or a master production schedule is sent to the vendor, which determines plan feasibility and uses its own ERP system to construct a build-and-ship schedule and then responds with the schedule to the business customer.

Supplier User Interface

Throughout this text, whenever referring to the navigation paths off the SCM navigation tree, we've assumed that the user is working from inside the Advanced Planner and

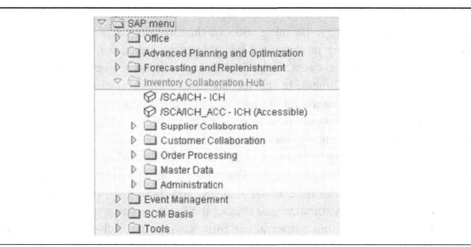

EXHIBIT 12.5   ICH IN THE SCM NAVIGATION TREE
ICH's location on the SCM navigation tree reflects its status as an application independent of, but closely tied to, APO. © SAP AG. Used with permission.

Optimizer node, and this has been appropriate even when discussing BW, whose connections to SCM are all found within that node. Inventory Collaboration Hub, however, being an entirely separate application from APO, packaged together in SCM, has its own master node at the same level as APO (Exhibit 12.5).

The ICH transaction, code/SCA/ICH, directly off the ICH node, will open a web-logon for the external-facing tool. This approach is fine for internal users of ICH, though the URL of the tool-logon window will have to be provided to external users.

The external-facing UI consists of four major parts: (1) a header, (2) a navigation panel, (3) a selection panel, and (4) data views (Exhibit 12.6, steps 1 to 4). The header has an important Back button allowing users to move backward through screens that have been visited (Exhibit 12.6, step 5). This may be a wiser avenue than the standard browser Back button, which may not have the same application intelligence. It also contains a "Personalize" hypertext, which opens a window to configure which fields to display, on what screen, and in what order (Exhibit 12.6, step 6).

Selections are made in the user interface (UI) by entering filter data in the selection panel such as a location or product value, and then clicking the Go button (Exhibit 12.6, step 7). Data view panels vary widely according to business function (i.e., Alert Monitor versus SMI versus release process, etc.).

As an example, the Alert Monitor view, accessed by selecting Alert Monitor from the navigation panel, will display an upper panel listing alert groupings found for the selection criteria under each alert (Exhibit 12.7, step 1). A lower panel displays a list of tabs for each alert category (Exhibit 12.7, step 2) and tables of rows in each tab where detailed alerts display when selected from the upper listing panel. To carry out an alert population a user can select alert grouping types for the listing panel and then select a hypertext from the enumerated groups (Exhibit 12.7, step 3). The alerts in turn display in the lower panel with details (Exhibit 12.7, step 4).

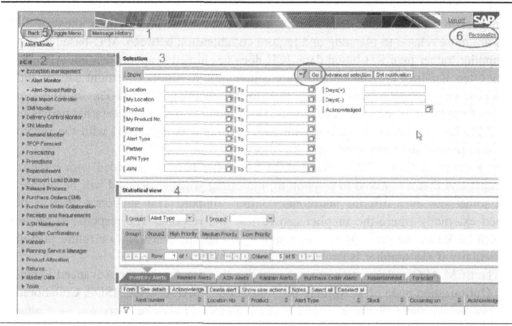

EXHIBIT 12.6   ICH EXTERNAL-FACING USER INTERFACE
Web based, this may be accessed either via URL or from the ICH transaction in SCM. © SAP AG. Used with permission. Microsoft product screen shot(s) reprinted with permission from Microsoft Corporation.

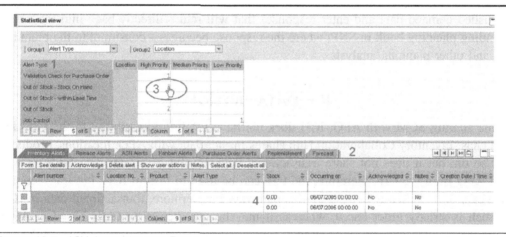

EXHIBIT 12.7   ICH ALERT MONITOR DETAIL
© SAP AG. Used with permission. Microsoft product screen shot(s) reprinted with permission from Microsoft Corporation.

APO SNP Collaboration

SNP Collaboration

Inventory Collaboration Hub collaboration (1) connects external parties (customers or suppliers) with R/3, normally R/3 inventory data, and generally will allow parties as much control as to initiate purchase orders in R/3, and (2) is concerned with the inventory management process. Other collaborative interests come into play in the context of SCM that are more related to planning and require collaboration between APO-based data and a supplier, rather than R/3-based data. ICH does not directly support this but APO does. Very often suppliers or subcontractors are called upon to supply constraint data on either materials or production capacity as a feed to the planning process. This business case differs from the ICH model on two counts: (1) It requires connecting external parties with the APO application of SCM, not with R/3, and (2) it is concerned with the planning process, several steps removed from inventory management.

In a common form of this arrangement a supplier may be provided with a demand forecast line that it is asked to respond to, indicating whether demand will be supported and sometimes even offering additional "buffer" support. This support request is published externally where the supplier can review and respond. The response is received in turn back into the planning tool as a supply or capacity constraint on future planning, particularly if the supplier is unable to support demand.

The SCM APO collaboration process supports this use case. In the Advanced Planning and Optimization node of SCM there is a transaction, /SAPAPO/CLPISDP, Collaborative Supply and Demand Planning, found on path *Supply Chain Collaboration → Collaborative Supply and Demand Planning → Time Series Based Collaborative Planning.* As with the ICH transaction accessed from SCM, this transaction will open a window to a web-based logon, the URL of which would be provided to an external supplier. On login, rather than an external ICH UI, the user is presented with options for displaying SCM APO *planning books.* Here an external supplier or subcontractor can view and analyze published demand data and enter responses that will return directly back into the corresponding planning book in SNP, where the response becomes a constraint to the planning run and other planning analysis.

ICH DATA PIPELINES

While sharing SCM with APO, ICH does not have the full accessibility to the CIF that APO has. Inventory Collaboration Hub shares master data with APO: locations, products, and so on, but it does not share transactional data. Insofar as master data finds its way into APO from the CIF, therefore, the CIF can be used to inform ICH, but transactional data cannot find its way to ICH by this pathway. Furthermore, transactional data in ICH as such is strictly order based, whereas it may be time series *or* order based in APO. Moreover and quite naturally given their separate pipelines, transactional data in APO and ICH will often vary. We noted earlier that fully automated SMI is generally best suited to low-value parts, but APO's planning power should generally be reserved for high-value parts. Inclusion of transactional data in the CIF, therefore, may unnecessarily clog data pipelines because usage strategies oppose their mutual overlap. Instead of the CIF, ICH uses XML to acquire transactional data from R/3 (Exhibit 12.8). While appropriate to data pipelines, this will create some level of data transport complexity for developers and system administrators who are involved in both the APO and ICH applications.

The XML communications layer from R/3 through ICH and out to a web engine simultaneously forms the basis for any further going automated ICH solution. Developers

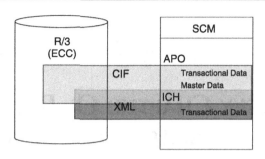

EXHIBIT 12.8   ICH DATA PIPELINES
Master data is shared with APO inside SCM and may be acquired by CIF; transactional data requires XML transfer.

looking to create fully automated B2B solutions may begin from this basis and redirect or parallel-direct data pipes out through an alternative communications medium to connect directly with outside customer or supplier ERP systems. In this model two data flows originating from the same XML pool can flow outward and back in: (1) one to the web engine as a backup and (2) one directly to the external ERP system.

13

THE LUCKY CHAPTER: OF BOATS AND SOFTWARE—FOUR KEYS TO UNLOCKING SCM

Call this the "lucky" chapter. The act of writing a book, like the similar act of teaching a class, inevitably has the effect of teaching the author much that he or she either did not or could not know before engaging in the writing enterprise. I came about my knowledge of SAP SCM (supply chain management) the hard way: I took lots of classes, several of them twice, and I worked on a variety of projects, solidifying my learnings and putting them to good use on development and deployment projects. Though this is the way that most people acquire expertise in SCM, it remains a "high road," expensive in both dollars and time, that is not sufficiently open to the many who need to acquire expertise in the tool in order for their organizations to best exploit it.

In writing this text I have noticed that as vast as SCM is, it has patterns: There are certain critical details that repeat themselves everywhere across the product. Opinions of purists and elitists notwithstanding, if you can drive a Dodge Neon, you can drive a BMW. I believe that if the student is primed to know the right key patterns, patterns that became evident to me only as I carried out the process of distilling my own knowledge to the written word, then he or she should be able to step into one or another module or tool of SCM and learn the way around quickly, like an old driver on a new car. Can we cut the learning curve in half? That would be really lucky! That is our objective here and that is what makes this the lucky chapter.

The exploration of SAP SCM and especially APO finds us beset by a problem of multitude: There are more than 4,300 transactions in SCM that combine to yield tens of thousands of data elements; when one considers all the possible combinations and permutations of settings available to us when configuring those data elements, we feel safe speculating that there are probably millions of alternatives. It has been regrettably necessary to pick and choose from among the cornucopia of capabilities to provide the reader with a working knowledge of both the landscape of the tool and the nimble footing that will enable him to systematically configure and interact with it while possessing the wherewithal to fill in gaps using online documentation whenever those gaps arise.

To achieve these ends we should look at what we have *excluded* in order to expeditiously achieve this basic core of understanding and competence. An incomplete list of capabilities excluded from this text includes: interchangeability, Materials Requirements Planning (MRP) areas, rules configuration, capacity leveling, any detailed coverage of promotion or capacity variants, as well as product and location splits, safety stock planning, use of the Supply Chain Engineer, detailed use of the Production Data Structure (PDS), and detail on conversion of Supply Network Planning (SNP) Production Process Models to their Production Planning/Detailed Scheduling (PP/DS) form; we have completely excluded both the Global Available to Promise (GATP) and Transportation Planning/Vehicle Scheduling (TP/VS) modules and both the Transport Load Builder (TLB) and deployment submodules. Excluding all of this and more, we have still found over 100,000 words to say about what remains of SAP SCM.

With a concrete appreciation of the sheer size and complexity of SCM, one can begin to address the fact that it is this very complexity that may stand as an obstacle to effective adoption and successful deployment and use of the product. Too often, end-users simply cannot fully appreciate the tool they are asked to work with. Often enough, nontechnical project leaders responsible for SCM development and deployment themselves possess only the most rudimentary sense of the nature of the tool they are charged to champion and deliver. If end-users are accustomed to working with a speed boat and we either cannot explain to them or do not ourselves understand that we are teaching them to work with a twenty-first-century state-of-the-art luxury yacht, we will all go on doing business as if we had just the speed boat. Critical to our exercise, therefore, is cutting APO down to size.

"KEYS": TO NEUTER A CLICHÉ

We are taught in high school English to avoid using clichés. Clichés are in many respects undeserving victims of their own linguistic ignominy because they start out, after all, as creative word formations whose unusually high capacity for the containment of meaning is exactly what made them so popular and catchy to start with. Alas, use, reuse, and endless popular repetition take their toll on poor clichés and in time their meaning gets overused, recycled, abused, tossed, and discarded until these phrases are thrown around with such careless disregard that they almost carry "anti-meaning," that is, the creation of a sense of mutual understanding between communicators when very little real communication has actually taken place. Users and hearers of clichés, so jaded by familiarity, believe themselves to know a cliché's meaning without really thinking about it, considering it, or unpacking it. We state, we acknowledge, we believe we have experienced communication and we move on, but the rich content of what was once a smart phrase actually plays us for fools.

This is all a very distressing state of affairs for us now as it is a particularly cliché-like word that is so especially important to the message and mission of this text: *keys*. "The *key* solution," "the *key* to finding the restaurant when going downtown," "the *key* to resolving the diplomatic impasse with the Kremlin," "the *key* to winning the election," and so on and so on! But what makes something a "key" and why are they so important? Let us take a moment to "unlock" the problem of the keys.

Dune author Frank Herbert wrote once in a novel of the old concept of a *key log*. About key logs he wrote that in times past trees were cut down, stripped, and dumped in a river to move the logs downstream. There would from time to time be a blockage and all the logs would get stopped up as the river water flowed underneath them. At times such as these an expert was called in who would examine the log blockage and determine the key log, which was the one log from among hundreds or thousands that, when moved, would unlock the entire blockage and allow all the other logs to continue their way down the river.

As regards what has been included in this text versus what has not, we have taken pains to sort out those ideas, concepts, tools, techniques, and processes that are primarily instrumental to achieving a working knowledge of SCM from those that may still be useful tools but are nonetheless rather "niche" in nature. We have avoided topics that may be a detour from our primary objectives of creating users and developers who are comprehensively familiar with the breadth of the tool and sufficiently nimble with primary techniques such that they are positioned to fend for themselves when faced with the remains. But that still is not enough. From among the ideas, concepts, tools, and so forth that form SCM, we must ask ourselves whether we can further sort through the noise and clamor and separate the gold-dust from the sand to identify the essential keys of SCM, the *key log* concepts that will unblock the river and allow all the thousands of other details to flow down to us. Fortunately, the answer is yes: There are in fact just a few key concepts that unlock the mighty fortress of SCM for all its customers, from end-users to developers to executives. There are four keys to be exact, but to be able to use them there is just one more thing to know.

IT'S ONLY A KEY IF YOU *KNOW* IT'S A KEY

Imagine you were given a key to a section of a building, but that the person giving you the key did not tell you what the key locked and unlocked or else did not even tell you that what he was giving you was a key at all (such as might be the case with an inconspicuous magnetic card, key fob, or PIN). You might stand at the building, magnetic device, card, or code in hand, not even knowing what lies in the building to be opened and unpackaged; you do not even know you are holding a key! Throughout industry, wherever we champion the adoption of SCM, this is the fundamental problem that must be overcome both in training and more generally in our representation of SCM to business sponsors, stakeholders, and executives. Not only must we provide the keys clearly; we must let our audience know that we are giving them no less than the keys to the building.

How to sort the keys from the "not-keys"? For one thing, we do not mean by this to disparage aspects of the tool that are not-keys. Not-keys are often great things, negative-sounding prefix notwithstanding. After all, the whole value of a key is the access it provides to the goodies in the building, the not-keys. A *not-key* is any idea, concept, tool, and so forth that, however useful in its application to resolve a particular business problem, nonetheless contributes little or nothing to understanding other ideas, concepts, tools, and so forth and that similarly adds little or nothing to an overall understanding of the product. A not-key is the expertise necessary to tie a particular knot that we might use to raise a sail or drop an anchor, for example, but it is not a list of all the knots we need to know how to tie to be a sailor, nor is it a map to the interior of the ship.

Keys are the opposite. Keys are those very special kinds of information that, when they become understood by the learner, not only suffice as a single point of internal mastery but unlock and unpack whole regions of other ideas, concepts, tools, and so on within and throughout the entire body of SCM. One other thing about keys: There are not many and there should not be. A house, like SCM, is jammed full of stuff, but typically has one and no more than three or four keys (such as a door key, a garage key, and a pool or basement key). *Too often, in the process of training users to work with SAP SCM, we address "keys," yet we fail to point out their nature as keys, presenting them in the same way we do every other piece of information.* We must be mindful of the fact that as it is with training sailors—being novices to sailing, students might not recognize a ship's map unless one takes pains to point out that it *is* a map—so it is with SCM.

THE KEYS

If APO and SCM adopters can be made to understand that keys describe the product's boundaries and patterns all throughout the application, no matter which module or tool is in use, then the rest will unravel for them, letting loose with its habits, patterns, strengths, weaknesses, opportunities, niches, and secrets. Point out APO's "keys" and watch learning curves evaporate and proceed to unload the massive toolbox that is SCM.

What are these keys? There are four:

1. Planning time horizons
2. Order-versus-time series structures
3. SCM business process
4. APO configuration process

Knowing these, project managers, stakeholders, and executives alike will make vast strides toward effective strategic decisions that properly exploit the tool while avoiding wasted efforts. Knowing these, developers can rapidly speed their own acquisition of competence in the configuration and delivery of the product. Knowing these, often-siloed end-users whose expertise is limited to areas like demand or planning or purchasing or shop floor control may broaden and reform their entire understanding of the supply chain management discipline. Knowing the keys, one will know SCM and APO.

As they say, all the rest is detail.

Planning Time Horizons

All the planning modules of APO are designed around the notion of planning time horizons. Too often, with enterprise resource planning (ERP)-type planning tools we instruct students on time horizons, time fences, and so on, assuming their familiarity and comfort with the terms, but assuming so in error. Individual businesspeople, both in the trenches and at headquarters, tend to have experience with one or sometimes just two areas of the supply chain. From their perspective, that experience anchors their understanding of the supply chain in such a way as to diminish other links in the chain. Demand specialists tend to know very little about procurement; planners tend to know relatively little about ground control; buyers tend to know very little about production scheduling. Those who have started out successfully in any of these roles and rise through the ranks to positions of executive decision making—the level where an integrated business-user vision is critical to the success and nature of an SCM deployment—often retain much of their silo-specific perspectives and biases on SCM. Beyond all of this, many people, even supply chain specialists, take planning horizons for granted so much that they virtually see right through them when presented with this foundational, critical piece of information. Planning horizons in that respect become something like our abused clichés.

This is too bad, because APO is explicitly organized around planning time horizons—so much so that if they sufficiently grasp the horizons independent of the tool, users will immediately appreciate much of how the modules are designed to work with one another. Order of operations here is critical. Before learning about sedans versus trucks versus SUVs, before learning about Saturn versus Honda versus BMW, one should learn about steering wheels, transmissions, accelerators, brakes, rear-view mirrors, and emergency brakes. Knowing these things first, the driver may set foot in any car, knowing much about the car without ever having to learn anything about it. Learn the planning time horizons first, before studying anything about the various modules of APO, and one will know much of the most important aspects of those modules without having learned a thing about them.

There are five planning time horizons:

1. Strategic planning horizon
2. Demand planning horizon
3. Operational planning horizon
4. Procurement execution horizon
5. Manufacturing execution horizon

Five Horizons

The *strategic horizon* encompasses planning space that exists largely *outside* the range of the SCM tool. In strategic supply chain planning we ask such questions as whether, when, and where to open new sites or close old ones or otherwise enter or exit entire market geographies. These are capital decisions that are executive in nature and that involve forces and resources that generally fall entirely outside the scope of SCM. Exceptions occur when there is an entrance to a new market in 12 months that may change the outer edges of a demand picture or else an opening or closing of a site that might have an effect on a supply network planning solve by increasing build opportunities or decreasing available supply or production capacity.

The strategic planning horizon is the longest horizon and sits outside the range of APO, but all four remaining horizons belong inside APO's scope. We may begin our review at the opposite end from the strategic horizon, at the most tactical of the bunch. The shortest time horizon for any organization is typically the *manufacturing execution horizon,* which is also called the *production execution horizon,* the latter of which is a more inclusive description. A port, for example, does not manufacture anything but nonetheless may find it necessary to conduct detailed lot scheduling in much the same way as a manufacturing enterprise and may as such have a similar "docking horizon," which is effectively the "production period" during which port activities are controlled and carried out. Similar analogous horizons will occur for any complex operation requiring detailed scheduling but that does not conduct manufacturing, such as a distribution center.

If we are dealing with large products, the production execution horizon is normally established according to the amount of time it takes to make or otherwise process a product; alternatively, it might be the amount of time it takes to complete a given lot of products when dealing with smaller units, though these are not rigid rules. An airplane manufacturer, for example, might define the production execution horizon as the time required to build just one plane. An automobile manufacturer may define the horizon as the length of time necessary to compile and package a single lot of sedans. A produce distributor, capable of processing and packaging hundreds of lots a day, may semi-arbitrarily define this period as a week or half a week. Generically, we can define the production execution horizon as the amount of time necessary to (1) provide immediate scheduling flexibility for lots that are being released into production while (2) also providing assembly stability for those that have already been released. For most organizations with human-scale product lines, as with the produce distributor, this may be three to five days and is usually no more than a week.

Outside of and feeding into the production execution horizon is the *procurement execution horizon.* This horizon aligns to the outer limits of time necessary to procure raw materials, semifinished goods, subcontracted products, and any other services necessary to stage for final, production execution. The procurement horizon will naturally vary somewhat from one product to another, but the extent of the entire horizon is defined by that of the longest lead-time part. As lead-times for purchased parts vary so widely, we see horizons of four weeks, eight weeks, three months, and sometimes longer. The procurement execution horizon is one and the same with the "production planning" horizon, a fact that leads to some confusion. To plan production, such as one does during the production planning horizon, is to schedule, control, and execute all the activities of procurement such that raw materials, semifinished goods, labor, and equipment are all appropriately staged to enter into the production execution horizon. That much is typically well enough understood; but lost on many erstwhile developers is the fact that while all of these activities (materials, goods, labor, and equipment staging) are part and parcel of "production planning," it is the procurement execution horizon that concretely defines when network-level operational planning must give way to detailed, localized, procurement execution and management.

The *operational planning horizon* is the entire horizon beyond the procurement execution horizon during which operations are planned, including planning of supply, capacity, transportation, and any sort of resources present in the supply network that might incur constraints. This horizon is often mistitled the "strategic" horizon by organizations; it is more commonly and more accurately described as the "midrange horizon," "midrange planning horizon," "supply network horizon," or simply the "planning horizon." Regardless of its title, the defining characteristics of this horizon are that on one side it abuts with the procurement execution horizon, and more important, with execution activities, while on the other side it ends at the point at which it is no longer profitable for an organization to be concerned with the planning of constrained resources. In its best-known methods (BKMs), the Association for Operations Management (APICS) applies this horizon to the business of sales and operations planning (SOP). Still in APICS parlance we may also say that the needs of *network-level* master production scheduling (MPS) are addressed in this horizon.

The *demand planning horizon* is, simply, the length of time we wish to forecast, plan, and manage demand. The longest horizon in SCM, it may at times slip into events that are strategic in nature. We should note that sometimes the operational planning horizon stretches to the whole length of the demand planning horizon, and other times it is contained within it; but it is never longer, as it simply makes no sense to plan operationally for resource constraints when we have no visibility to demand.

Organizations will differ widely in their use of demand planning horizons. Companies producing very large products such as airplanes or ships will often find it necessary to conduct demand planning for two to five years out. Most organizations, however, will find a demand planning horizon of within 12 months to be perfectly sufficient.

Other Horizons Used in Supply Chain Planning

In industry we often hear of two additional horizon types that manage to claw into the space of the procurement and production execution horizons: (1) the "tactical horizon" and (2) the "frozen horizon," which is often called the "frozen period." The tactical horizon is normally understood to be synonymous with the procurement execution horizon and as such is inclusive of both the procurement and production execution horizons. As before, the trick is to be clear on the concrete point of the horizon's definition: *the commencement of procurement execution activity, regardless of applied title.*

A frozen horizon or frozen period is commonly applied to a time fence that approaches but does not quite start with that of the procurement or production execution horizons. At issue is the fact that throughout the leading horizons up to either procurement or production execution, changes in demand often result in changes in procurement patterns in order to maximize early production while minimizing inventories. Yet there comes a point of diminishing returns wherein the cost or risk associated with such changes exceeds any benefit. For example, changing the details of a purchase order may delay receipt of critical parts that are about to be staged for production. If that delay occurs within a week of the requirements date to begin production, then the failure of availability of the parts will result in production-lines down, which is typically the worst possible condition for any outfit. To avoid this, many organizations apply frozen horizons during which procurement changes are forbidden shortly in advance of the start of the procurement or production horizons, in order to assure the stability of supplies.

Consider two examples. Outside the procurement execution horizon sits the operational planning horizon, during which supply network operations are planned and scheduled. During a crossover period, perhaps eight to nine weeks out, where the operational planning horizon yields to the procurement execution horizon, one may disallow changes to the operational plan for procurement while continuing to allow for changes to production so long as the production changes continue to be supported by purchased materials. Closer in, when the procurement execution horizon yields to the production execution horizon, one may disallow certain changes to the production schedule a short time in advance of actual start of production. The exact configuration of finished goods scheduled to be built, for example, may change, though the specific scheduling of when production is allowed to start may remain the same. Each of these represents the application of a frozen period to account for changes that occur when one time horizon yields to another.

We point out tactical and frozen horizons primarily to prepare the reader for the question, not necessarily to suggest that these horizons should be addressed proactively when explaining the relationship of horizons to the organization of APO. Inevitably some users will be so accustomed to the notion of a tactical horizon, for example, that they may have lost conscious sense of the fact that tactical horizons originate from procurement execution horizons and are merely a convenient way of grouping the procurement and production execution horizons together in speech. Also likely is that some buyers, being siloed as end-users often are, will have a stronger sense of the frozen horizon than the production horizon because it is the frozen horizon that effects a change in their day-to-day buying behaviors while production activities remain largely transparent to them.

Time Horizons and APO's Modules

Users who are introduced to APO's modules as distinct modules outside the context of their programmatically organized role in addressing specific, time-based problems of the supply chain must learn these lessons from the inside out. Their plight is like being dropped into the middle of a maze and asked to find their way back to the entrance. They may, of course, succeed and learn their way around the maze, but their task would be much easier if they were first given an aerial picture of the maze that led them to the entrance. However, without knowing a thing about APO, supply chain specialists and most commercial practitioners will easily acquire, understand, and appreciate the particularities of planning time horizons and their effects on business activities. By *starting* with the horizons and imparting sufficient, immediate aptitude to learners, we may achieve in an hour what often takes users months, years, and/or many classes to come to appreciate—and which many never do. Having considered the planning horizons of the supply chain, let us address how APO and its modules apply specialized competencies to address the requirements of each such horizon (Exhibit 13.1).

The Detailed Scheduling (DS) tool of the APO PP/DS module is explicitly designed to serve the needs of the production execution horizon. The larger PP/DS module in which DS is presented is used to create the orders that feed DS while staging supplies, labor, and equipment so that everything is prepared when DS is ready to take over. Once the manufacturing execution horizon is entered, DS effectively takes control of operations from PP and all other modules and applications.

The PP tool of PP/DS is designed to address the business needs of the procurement execution horizon, specialized as it is in receiving a network-blessed plan from SNP

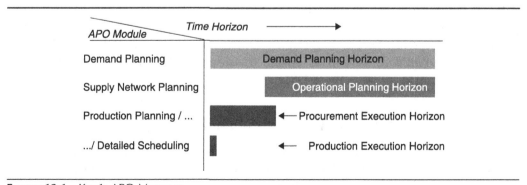

EXHIBIT 13.1 KEY 1: APO MODULES
APO modules are built around the requirements of supply chain planning time horizons.

and applying that plan at a site level to (1) schedule, manage, and execute procurement and (2) stage all necessary components (materials, goods, labor, and equipment) for final production.

The SNP module of APO is designed for the activities of what APICS calls sales and operations planning (SOP) and what we prefer to describe as network master production scheduling (nMPS). As a point of fact SNP constitutes the most pure "planning" module of the entire APO application, concerned neither with the analytics and determination of demand nor with execution in any form. One of the most powerful and complicated tools of APO, successful employment of SNP demands that project planners and developers be sensitive to its boundaries and competencies.

We use SNP as the first point at which constraints are introduced to planning. On the outside of the timeline, SNP should not be applied to conduct network resource planning when it is so far out in time as to yield little profitable value. Beyond this point it may or may not be necessary to be concerned with forecasting demand, for example; but there is certainly a point beyond which it is no longer useful to plan supply. On the inside of the timeline, SNP is not competent for procurement execution. SNP is a *pure* planning tool. Certainly some features of APO commonly associated with SNP may be useful for procurement execution. The Planning Book user interface may be useful to almost any horizon and by extension any module, for example. Complex *network* solvers that employ linear programming, however, are probably severe overkill once one moves into the execution space and are even dangerous insofar as their value is predicated on the ability to constantly replan to changing demand signals and constraint situations, whereas short-term planning and procurement interests typically rely on a higher degree of planning stability.

Finally, the APO DP tool is organized around the standard supply chain business requirements of the demand planning horizon. In the demand planning space we are interested in development of an *unconstrained* forecast and/or demand plan, that is, a forecast of demand that is disinterested in any constraints that would restrict it, because here, where accuracy of forecast is most difficult to achieve, near-exclusive focus on the problem of accuracy is necessary. Besides demand forecasting, however, DP is designed to address the broader aegis of demand planning, where we not only predict demand via forecast, but we disaggregate demand, assigning bits and pieces of it to various geographies or producers in the supply network.

When customizing and designing APO modules to operate with one another it is important to consider frozen periods. Frozen periods will normally be applied in the transition from operational planning to procurement execution and production planning, or from SNP to PP/DS, as well as on the transition from procurement execution to production execution, or from PP to DS.

Order and Time-Series-Based Structures

Planning time horizons address what APO is in aggregate. "Order" and "time" come at it from another direction and are concerned how it goes about its functions in the atomic, discrete details. We take pains in the Component: liveCache section in Chapter 2 to explain the use and contrasts of these two methods of storing and displaying data and their potential mixing as it relates to display of order-based data as time series, for example, and we will not repeat that. It is nonetheless necessary here to point out that this distinction—time versus order—is one of the "keys" to the tool. Every module is concerned with the method of storage and method of display of data, which becomes a particular kind of business/technical question where very often for technical purposes it may be necessary to store data one way whereas for business purposes it is necessary to display it the other way.

Without giving a thought to APO, let us first imagine three problems and consider what kind of graphical user interface might be most useful to meet the needs of end-users who employ computers and software to address those problems. What if our concern was traffic, any kind of traffic: air, ship, automobile, train? For users of such software, a user interface with a *geographical view* of the data may be most useful (Exhibit 13.2, step A). Such a user interface would display the flight paths of planes between cities, all of which would be superimposed over a map, for example.

However, what if our concern was with direct management of execution of production? Here we would be interested in discrete, detailed units of demand that drive production, like forecast or customer sales orders, as well as corresponding units of supply that fulfill the demand, like purchase orders or production orders. For this level of detail an *order-based view* that depicts *each-and-every* individual order in tabular or spreadsheet form with loads of detail on the orders would most likely serve our needs (Exhibit 13.2, step B).

Finally, what if our concern was with scheduling? Here, too, we may be interested in demand, supply, or both. We may be interested in additional constraints like labor

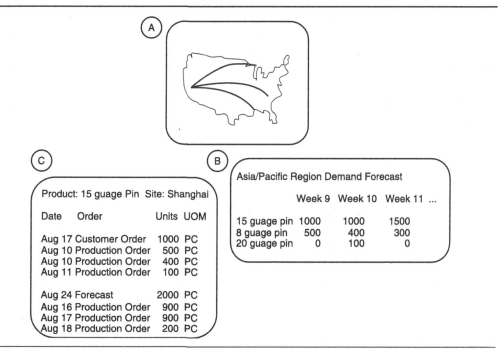

EXHIBIT 13.2   KEY 2: THREE USER INTERFACE STYLES
Three user interface styles; B and C reflect the order/time-series dichotomy.

or physical resource capacity. At this level, order-level details are not so important. For scheduling, as opposed to execution, one usually needs the long view, a *longitudinal, time-series view of activities that aggregates order information according to units of time* (Exhibit 13.2, step C). At high levels of scheduling it usually does not matter if it is one, two, or ten individual orders that are driving demand ten weeks from now. All that matters is the total demand in week 10. Similarly it does not matter how many orders of production will be divided to meet that demand, so long as they are set up in such a way as to be within capacity limitations. If one order, at one location, is sufficient to cover demand, fine; but maybe there will be four or five orders split between work centers or sites. All that matters for scheduling, however, is the aggregate plan for the time bucket: How much will we produce in total in that week or in that week at that site?

Of these three views, we bring up the first, the geographical view, as a sort of honorable mention that is necessary because, while it is relatively minor among the features and capabilities of APO, there is in fact a geographic view as well as a related *logical view* of the supply chain model as it is modeled by users by way of the supply chain cockpit (SCC). The other two views, order based and time series, however, are virtually universal in their application throughout APO. We must emphasize that the order/time dichotomy is not just descriptive of data-display: It is directly related to the strategy of data storage that underlies almost every feature of APO. So universal are these two concepts that students would do well to consider the question of order based or time-series based with the introduction of almost every user interface, data store, or transport technique (such as livecache and the core interface).

In other words, when presented with the four nongeographical user interfaces that we address in this text (the Product View, the Planning Book, the Product Planning Table, and the Detailed Scheduling Planning Board), the very first question that should be considered is whether the problem that any of these user interfaces address is suited to an order-based or time-series-based analysis. When presented with the liveCache memory bank that controls data between APO and R/3, users should ask if data is being stored as order-only or both order and time series. When presented with the core interface (CIF) that moves data between APO and R/3, recall that CIF always deposits data in APO first as order based, and if a time-series view of data is needed, such as with the Planning Book, translation to time-series objects will be necessary.

SCM Business Process

The process of training both end-users and developers of SCM typically entails addressing the overall objectives of one or another SCM application or module, and then spending the balance of the course addressing the massive variety of features, capabilities, processes, bells, whistles, and so on that make up the aspect of SCM in question. Students typically graduate from classes filled to the spilling point with details of dials, switches, and components, but not with a sense of how the tool is actually used to go about solving business problems. This is unfortunate and unnecessary because one of the most delightful things about SCM is that despite its complexity, regardless of tool or module, it almost always follows exactly the same process for carrying out business problems; what is more, the process itself, while rich in details, is relatively simple.

The vanilla SCM business process is:

1. *Computational Process.* An advanced best-known-method (BKM) computational process is brought to bear to use the quantitative powers of the software to analyze a problem and produce a result that is effectively a suggestion. As we can see, as just one-third or one-fourth of the overall process of SCM, the computational processes do tend to be the advertised features of the product: statistical analyses for demand planning, heuristics and optimization for supply network and production planning, and so on (Exhibit 13.3, step A).

2. *Alert Monitor.* Computational techniques, especially techniques of the advanced sort provided by SCM, will get you somewhere, but at the end of the day they can get you only so far. Good old human, qualitative reasoning and subjective awareness skills remain essential to what is both the art and science of supply chain planning. Alert Monitors in SCM employ customized "alert profiles" that scan the results of computational processes looking for specific conditions or thresholds that should alert a human buyer, planner, or controller to further analysis or action (Exhibit 13.3, step B).

3. *Human Intervention via User Interface.* Once alerted to specific conditions (i.e., purchase order is late, demand has spiked, etc.), buyers, planners, and controllers may go to work doing things that only humans can do that may make a material difference to planning (i.e., calling a supplier and bargaining for a pull-in, calling a customer and bargaining for a product swap, calling the shop floor and asking if there is unreported raw materials inventory hiding behind the bin in the back corner, etc.). Having made or discovered changes in facts on the ground, or having reexecuted more detailed analyses such as by using reports generated by SAP's

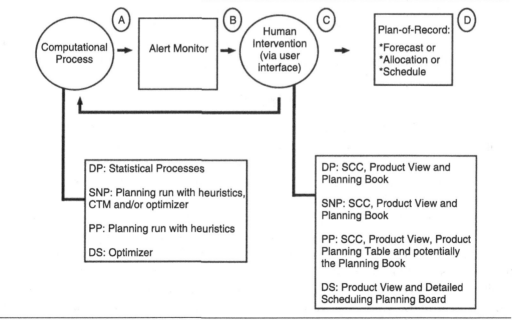

EXHIBIT 13.3 KEY 3: SCM PROCESS

Business Information Warehouse (BW), the users may input changes via user interfaces to refeed the inputs through the computational processes, yielding a new proposal, which users in turn will either accept and pass to production or analyze and change further (Exhibit 13.3, step C).

4. *Plan-of-Record (POR)*. This is the output. The output of Demand Planning is a demand plan that is fed to SNP. The output of SNP is a network production schedule that is fed to PP/DS. The output of Production Planning is a feed of raw materials to production and a final staging of resources necessary to production for Detailed Scheduling and control. The output of Detailed Scheduling is actual productive work on the ground. The output of Inventory Collaboration Hub (ICH) depends on specific application, but may be a forecast of demand sent to a supplier or similarly a forecast of demand received from a customer. For vendor-managed inventory (VMI) applications of ICH, the output will be actual inventory levels that will trigger alerts by suppliers to carry out automatic replenishment of stocks (Exhibit 13.3, step D).

Armed with a knowledge of this core, vanilla business process of SCM, project teams are well empowered to "divide and conquer." Business analysts and consultants charged with collecting business requirements for SCM customization may explicitly organize and divide their task into four parts: computational requirements, alert profiles for the Alert Monitor, user-interface requirements, and output plans of record. We acknowledge, of course, that in the wider business landscape some additional areas may be required, such as data interfaces to external systems, but the value of this key is that regardless of such additional cases, we can be sure of the original four. We can further be sure that more detail-oriented versions of this business process will expand on this template. In earlier chapters that addressed configuration and use of specific APO modules as well as ICH (Chapters 8, 9, 10, and 12), we introduced a more detailed data and business process decomposition at the beginning of each section. Examine how these more expanded versions are built on the basic template by comparing them with Exhibit 13.3. Finally, besides as a guide to project organization, these four steps may further be utilized as an organizing principle for the development of any internal training materials targeting end-users.

APO Configuration Process

This is of particular interest to developers: As much as the business process for employment of SCM tools and modules is similar from application to application, so, too, is the basic configuration process. As configuration is without doubt the most complicated aspect of APO, we should not go into any substantial detail here; nonetheless developers and consultants should be primed to look for specific patterns that are particularly likely to emerge in the "cookbook recipes" found in Parts Two, Three, and Four of this text. Configuration of APO, regardless of module, follows a pattern. As developers work out the settings necessary to meet the unique business needs of end-users, we advise that they compose "build books" that carefully delineate the process of rolling out configuration, setting-by-setting, in such a way as to build complete supply network models quickly, expeditiously, without mistake, and without losing learnings from one project phase or deployment to the next. Such build books would include all of the settings appropriate to each configuration area (i.e., CIF model variant configuration, module profile configuration, etc.) but will follow the APO configuration sequence depicted in Exhibit 13.4.

The APO configuration process aligns with six general steps and one or more substeps:

1. *Master data setup.* This includes configuration of CIF integration profiles and variants for profiles, activation/deactivation transactions, and deletion and change pointer transactions. Separately it also includes setup and configuration of master data elements that can only be maintained in APO apart from R/3.

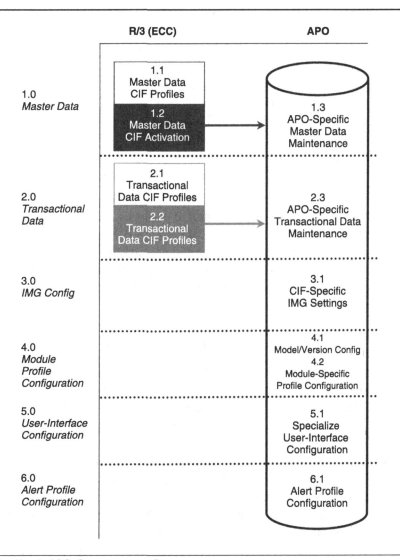

EXHIBIT 13.4 KEY 4: APO CONFIGURATION PROCESS
Note that depending on whether configuration is conducted during development or deployment, the order of Master Data configuration (step 1) and IMG Configuration (step 3) may be reversed—additional steps may also be required such as extension of function modules as well as external interfaces and/or extractors.

2. *Transactional data setup.* Similar to master data setup, this also includes configuration of CIF integration profiles—in this case for transactional data—as well as their variants and any associated CIF maintenance transactions.

3. *IMG (Implementation Guide) configuration.* There are some settings in the IMG that may be necessary for proper CIF function, for example, the Distribution Definition.

4. *Model/module profile configuration.* This has two parts. First it is necessary to configure the model(s) and version(s) that will be employed in APO. For example, model 000, version 000 will always need to be configured for active production use with any special module-specific settings, but another model/version (i.e., model 000, version SIM) may be configured for inactive, simulation use. Once this is complete, configuration profiles specific to the module in use (i.e., DP, SNP, PP/DS, etc.) are configured according to the business process requirements defined for the module by earlier business/gap analysis.

5. *User interface configuration.* Many user interfaces are configured as a consequence of module-specific configuration done in step 4, but others, such as the Planning Book, require their own unique configuration.

6. *Alert profile configuration.* Alert profiles, customized to individual job roles or users, will be configured to notify end-users when important conditions arise as a result of computational processes, interfaces, or other user data entries.

Apart from these six steps, which will be close to universal to all APO projects, some other cases are likely to arise. Configuration of BW objects, for example, including data extractors, will be necessary for any project that employs BW for data archiving, retrieval, or reports. Obviously, additional maintenance and construction activities will be required of any project that employs code changes or additional function modules. Nonetheless, these six steps will form a secure basis that any project should be able to add to as necessary to meet its overall development requirements.

WHAT WOULD YOU PAY FOR WAL-MART's OR UPS's SUPPLY CHAIN?

Love them or hate them, Wal-Mart and UPS both command a measure of respect in the universe of SCM, and in each case a good deal of what has made them successful is directly attributable to their successful exploitation of the supply chain. Let us consider just what it is about Wal-Mart's and UPS's supply chain exploits that has made these companies so admired and successful.

When it comes to supply chain, there are two critical *signals*: (1) the demand signal and (2) the inventory signal. Almost always, so long as one has reasonably good planning tools in place, one can realize value by improving either of these two signals. In the latter case, for example, by increasing the speed with which changes in the demand signal get transmitted across the supply chain, such as by reducing orders to suppliers in response to a reduction in orders from customers, and in the former case, by having advanced knowledge of inventory opportunities (new supplies made available or supplies delivered early, etc.) as well as advanced knowledge of inventory issues (supply source late or canceled), one can most rapidly make changes to plan-of-record to best account for the changed conditions.

Wal-Mart pioneered several regions of supply chain excellence by building systems that married customer demand information as closely to suppliers as possible. By deploying radio frequency identification (RFID) on retail floors, stores' stocks can be transmitted directly to suppliers, who can respond to alerts when stocks fall below predefined threshold conditions, automatically triggering the supplier to replenish the stores.[1] Using similar RFID technology, UPS rigorously tracks its constantly moving post throughout its distribution network, making detailed reporting of inventory status available both internally and to customers.[2] In both cases, at the core of these advanced supply chain deployments are advanced planning systems that forecast demand, plan and coordinate entire networks of supply resources, and carry out detailed execution at points of delivery.

Wal-Mart and UPS got ahead of the supply chain curve by employing their considerable internal financial muscle to construct advanced SCM systems. Few companies, indeed few organizations of any kind, have sufficient financial clout, to say nothing of the specialized intellectual capital, to pull off audacious supply chain gains of this kind. Many organizations, however, can afford to purchase off-the-shelf software that provides many of these same features that can be configured to closely match organizations' unique situational requirements.

It is time to stop thinking of SCM as "what we have been doing" and start thinking about SCM as "what we are indeed capable of doing now but have not yet adopted." SAP SCM's newest application, Event Management (EM), though not covered in this text, makes exploitation of the RFID technology that has been so successful for Wal-Mart and UPS available to any SCM customer. SCM's ICH empowers organizations to set up advanced collaborative networks with external customers, suppliers, and subcontractors. SCM APO provides planning and execution management tools as well as data analytics that remain at the beating heart of SCM. The combined power of these products provides exciting opportunities to organizations for which advanced technological products of this sort have been financially and practically out of reach while they remained limited to those who could afford to build them in-house. Focused first on APO and supply chain planning, this text should help unlock the SCM product to get organizations started on firm footing on the road to integrated twenty-first-century SCM.

NOTES

1. Laurie Sullivan, "Wal-Mart's Way: Heavyweight Retailer Looks Inward to Stay Innovative in Business Technology," *InformationWeek*, Sept. 27, 2004;
    http://www.informationweek.com/story/showArticle.jhtml?articleID=47902662.

2. Elena Malykhina, "UPS Stepping Up RFID Efforts," *InformationWeek*, Sept. 27, 2004; http://www. informationweek.com/story/showArticle.jhtml?articleID=48800112.

    Michael Sullivan, and Susan Happek, "Demystifying RFID in the Supply Chain: An Overview of the Promise and the Pitfalls," UPS Supply Chain Solutions, 2005; http://www.ups-scs.com/solutions/white_papers/wp_RFID.pdf.

INDEX